THE PRIVILEGED PARTNERSHIP

THE PRIVILEGED
PARTNERSHIP

FRANCO-GERMAN RELATIONS
IN THE EUROPEAN COMMUNITY
1969–1984

HAIG SIMONIAN

CLARENDON PRESS · OXFORD

1985

Oxford University Press, Walton Street, Oxford OX2 6DP

London New York Toronto
Delhi Bombay Calcutta Madras Karachi
Kuala Lumpur Singapore Hong Kong Tokyo
Nairobi Dar es Salaam Cape Town
Melbourne Auckland

and associated companies in
Beirut Berlin Ibadan Mexico City Nicosia

Oxford is a trade mark of Oxford University Press

Published in the United States
by Oxford University Press, New York

British Library Cataloguing in Publication Data
Simonian, A.H.
The privileged partnership : Franco-German
relations in the European Community 1969–1984.
1. Germany (West)—Foreign relations—France
2. France—Foreign relations—Germany (West)
I. Title
327.43044   DD258.85.F8
ISBN 0–19–821959–8

Library of Congress Cataloging in Publication Data
Simonian, A. H. (A. Haig)
The privileged partnership.
Bibliography: p.
Includes index.
1. France—Relations—Germany (West)
2. Germany (West)—Relations—France.
3. European Economic Community—France.
4. European Economic Community—Germany (West)
I. Title
DC59.8.G3S56 1985   327.44043   84–27364
ISBN 0–19–821959–8

Set by Burgess & Son (Abingdon) Ltd
Printed in Great Britain
at the Oxford University Press
by David Stanford
Printer to the University

To my Mother

Acknowledgements

I SHOULD particularly like to thank my former supervisor at Oxford, Dr Loukas Tsoukalis, for his constant encouragement and advice during the time I spent researching and writing the doctoral thesis on which much of this book is based. My thanks are also due to Dr Roger Morgan for his helpful comments on this book and on an earlier article.

I am indebted to the German Academic Exchange Service and to the French Government for assistance which helped me to conduct much of my research in Bonn and Paris during the late 1970s. In particular, special thanks are due to the Director and staff of the Research Institute of the Deutsche Gesellschaft für Auswärtige Politik in Bonn, where I was able to gain a better understanding of the subject from the German point of view. I am also grateful to the Institut d'Études Politiques in Paris, where I spent a pleasant interval studying, and enjoying some of the more interesting aspects of Parisian life.

With foreign policy affairs generally clouded by a veil of secrecy, this book owes much to the many academics, politicians, civil servants, and journalists who gave up their time to discuss it with me. A list of their names is included at the end of the bibliography.

Finally, the project was considerably assisted by the helpful staff and comprehensive facilities at the excellent press library at Chatham House.

London,   A. H. S.
November, 1984

Contents

Abbreviations

BDI	Bundesverband der Deutschen Industrie
CAP	Common Agricultural Policy
CDU	Christlich-Demokratische Union
CGT	Confédération Générale du Travail
COREPER	Committee of Permanent Representatives
CSCE	Conference on Security and Co-operation in Europe
CSU	Christlich-Soziale Union
DBV	Deutscher Bauernverband
DDR	Deutsche Demokratische Republik
DFJW	Deutsch-Französisches Jugendwerk
EAEC	European Atomic Energy Commission
ECSC	European Coal and Steel Community
EDC	European Defence Community
EEC	European Economic Community
EMF	European Monetary Fund
EMS	European Monetary System
EMU	Economic and Monetary Union
EURATOM	European Atomic Energy Community
FDP	Freie Demokratische Partei
FNSEA	Fédération Nationale des Syndicats d'Exploitants Agricoles
GATT	General Agreement on Tariffs and Trade
GDR	German Democratic Republic
IMF	International Monetary Fund
MBFR	Mutually Balanced Force Reductions
MCA	Monetary Compensatory Amount
MLF	Multilateral Force
NATO	North Atlantic Treaty Organization
OECD	Organization for European Co-operation and Development

OEEC	Organization for European Economic Co-operation
OFAJ	Office Franco-Allemand pour la Jeunesse
OPEC	Organization of Petroleum Exporting Countries
ORTF	Office de Radiodiffusion-Télévision Française
PLO	Palestine Liberation Organization
RDF	Regional Development Fund
SALT	Strategic Arms Limitation Talks
SGCI	Secrétariat Général du Comité Interministériel
SITC	Standard International Trade Classification
SPD	Sozialdemokratische Partei Deutschlands
u.a.	unit of account
WEU	Western European Union

1

Introduction

THE Franco-German *entente* at the heart of the European Community is a topic which has attracted attention in international relations circles since the early days of integration. In the later 1970s, the particularly close bond between Chancellor Schmidt of West Germany and President Giscard d'Estaing of France, a key element in a renewed phase of integration, increased this interest and sparked off a lively debate in the literature.[1] Curiously, though, while such bilateral collaboration had long been a precondition for progress in the Community, it was largely the influence of the Schmidt–Giscard era which triggered a revival of popular interest.

By contrast, the preceding period, that of Brandt and Pompidou, was surprisingly neglected by the academic community. While many pundits commented on Brandt's Eastern policy, his approach to Western Europe received scant attention. Even more striking was the dearth of literature on Pompidou's foreign policy. The handicap of following a towering figure like de Gaulle, his natural reticence, and the fact that he had been prematurely afflicted by a terrible illness were all factors which contributed to the general classification of the Pompidolian era as a mere 'interlude' sandwiched between the reigns of more charismatic figures.[2]

It is a primary aim of the present book to redress the imbalance and refocus attention on the early 1970s. In this sense, the work is intended to form a worthy successor to that earlier admirable study on Franco-German relations and European

[1] See e.g. Jonathan Story, 'The Franco-German Alliance within the Community', *The World Today* (June 1980); James O. Goldsborough, 'The Franco-German Entente', *Foreign Affairs* (April 1976); Paul Friedrich, 'The SPD and the Politics of Europe: From Willy Brandt to Helmut Schmidt', *Journal of Common Market Studies* (hereafter *JCMS*) 4 (1974–5); Haig Simonian, 'France, Germany and Europe', *JCMS* 3 (1980–1); Wolfgang F. Hanrieder, 'Germany as Number Two?', *International Studies Quarterly* (March 1982).

[2] In 1984, ten years after his death, the former President has finally been made the subject of a worthwhile biography. See Eric Roussel, *Georges Pompidou* (Paris, Lattès, 1984).

integration by F. Roy Willis.[3] Accordingly, on one level at least, what follows is a broad historical account of European developments since 1969, with the accent firmly on the central role of France and Germany. As a rule, attention will be focused on the topmost tier of decision-making, with a concentration on events at Head of Government rather than bureaucratic or administrative levels.

The 1970s were undoubtedly the most testing period for the Community since its origins some twenty years earlier. Politically, the EEC's first enlargement imposed new strains on a group which had hitherto been composed of relatively homogeneous members. More important, on the economic side, the gradual collapse of the Bretton Woods system of fixed exchange rates and, above all, the two oil crises of the decade, almost paralysed a Community which had until then enjoyed reasonable monetary stability and steady economic growth. The quadrupling of oil prices, especially, and the major inflation and recession set off in its wake, provided a jolt from which the member states have not yet fully recovered.

Despite such novel difficulties, the continuing importance of Franco-German accord for wider progress in the Community was a theme constantly in evidence. Both the first and second enlargements of the Community depended on a similarity of French and German views. In the economic and monetary fields, the EEC's original and ill-fated steps towards a full Economic and Monetary Union (and its later creation of the successful European Monetary System) were firmly based on a convergence of French and German interests. A similar, though less obvious, process also took place on the political and institutional fronts. Thus the rise of political co-operation as a means of making heard Europe's voice in the world and the eventual arrival of direct elections both benefited from Franco-German co-operation. Not even the United Kingdom's accession to the EEC altered this picture—contrary to many people's original expectations—a failure that later chapters of this book will seek to clarify.

While a new general history of the European Community in a

---

[3] F. Roy Willis, *France, Germany and the New Europe* (London, Stanford University Press/OUP, 1968).

crucial phase of its development is a valuable addition to the literature on integration, this book will seek to go further, and focus more specifically on the evolution of French and German foreign policy in the 1970s and 1980s. Examining the two countries' Community policies is a major element in this process; assessing their responses to certain wider changes—notably relations with the United States and the Soviet Union—marks the essential corollary.

The early 1970s in particular represented a decisive period of transition for both France and Germany. It is this reason more than any other that calls for concentration on the Brandt–Pompidou era. In fact, many fundamentals of the close bilateral collaboration subsequently established under Schmidt and Giscard—a period notable for its more confident German external stance and more pragmatic and interdependent French attitude—can be traced back to transitionary forces exhibited earlier. This book will seek to shed light on these continuities (as well as certain divergences), aspects of a bilateral relationship which have not always been given due weight by those focusing on the post-1974 period.

In the Federal Republic, for instance, the advent of Brandt's Socialist-led Government represented not just a decisive political break with the former domination of the Christian Democrats, but also a major psychological shift. That West Germany, twenty-five years after the Second World War, was now being led by a figure untainted by Nazism and highly respected abroad was itself a boost to the country's external standing. More important, Brandt's *Ostpolitik* was the prime factor in bringing about the transition of Germany's accumulated economic strength into a more forceful political stance, dispelling a plethora of constraints and vastly increasing the room for manœuvre in Bonn's foreign policy. Moreover, the simultaneous elevation of international monetary affairs—once regarded as a topic of 'low' politics—into a major preoccupation of Atlantic relations, confirmed the Federal Republic's economic prowess while endowing its voice with a new political weight. Finally, West Germany's considerable economic success—establishing the image of 'Modell Deutschland'—brought about the trend of identifying the West German economy as one to be imitated, additionally boosting Bonn's prestige and authority.

The transitionary nature of the period 1969–74 was almost as marked in France. Pompidou's presidency heralded a turning-point, representing the post-de Gaulle adjustment of French foreign policy towards its partners. The period was one of undoubted evolution towards the developments that took place under Giscard d'Estaing. Paris finally sanctioned enlargement and also instigated new Community initiatives. Above all, the opening phase of Pompidou's term of office suggested a new realism in French relations with the United States. That this development could be so swiftly reversed in the turmoil of 1973–4 casts doubt on the extent of the change in French policy under Pompidou. The question remains controversial, but this book will seek to provide its own explanation for the shift that took place.

The third, and final, level on which it is intended to consider Franco-German relations is on a purely bilateral basis. Seldom have two countries so consciously set out to improve their mutual relations, establishing a large number of institutions and procedures to further this aim. The role of bodies such as the Franco-German Youth Office, and the efforts made to foster closer political, economic, and cultural ties are all important elements in Franco-German relations. Their function will be illustrated in Chapter 2.

Most important among these procedures were the semi-annual Franco-German summit meetings. Yet it is here that the difficulty of distinguishing between the purely bilateral and the wider Community and world aspects of Franco-German relations is seen at its sharpest. It is this interaction which in fact forms one of the most absorbing features of any study of the Franco-German bond in Europe. On the Community side, the association was most striking during the Schmidt–Giscard era, when talk of a Franco-German 'axis' in Europe was at its height. Certainly, the apparent exclusivity of the bilateral bond was, to some outsiders at least, a cause of considerable resentment. Hence contemporary objections that the normal—and generally accepted—pattern of Franco-German pre-eminence in Community affairs had gone too far, with the initiative for decision-making and forward-planning having been usurped from the other member states by a duopoly. Though exaggerated, such fears were very real in certain quarters, notably in the Benelux countries, and they illustrated the narrow divide that has always existed between the obviously central role of Bonn and Paris in Community initiatives and the danger of creating the impression of too pronounced a bilateral dominance.

At the same time, however, it should be recognized that the model has not always operated in this manner. In the mid- and later 1960s especially, the gradual accretion of German economic and political strength had a profound effect on French Community policy. Most notably, Paris grew much more sympathetic to the idea of British membership of the EEC, a trend hesitantly initiated by de Gaulle and carried through by Pompidou.

As will be seen, this association between wider developments in French and German foreign policy and in the two countries' international standing, and their bilateral relations, would become even more apparent in the 1970s. In the early part of the decade especially, it was Brandt's *Ostpolitik* which exerted a major dynamic influence on relations between Bonn and Paris. The Federal Republic's greatly enhanced political status as a result of Brandt's Eastern policy sharply tilted the balance between France and Germany, bringing about an equilibrium more in Bonn's favour. No longer was West Germany politically handicapped in its dealings with the Eastern bloc, but a much more independent actor. As a result, strong fears were kindled in France regarding the possibility of an accommodation between the Federal Republic and its Eastern neighbours. In conjunction with the international climate of superpower negotiations (at times bearing hostile comparison in France with Yalta),[4] there followed a period of considerable strain in Franco-German contacts. It is worth bearing in mind that although matters improved greatly under Giscard, beneath the relaxed exterior of bilateral co-operation, there still lurked deep-seated French anxieties regarding the future of its neighbour across the Rhine. As the penultimate chapter of this book shows, the SPD's internal difficulties over the deployment of new Theatre Nuclear Forces at the close of the Schmidt Chancellorship meant that there were those in France who once again found some justification in their earlier misgivings. Such fears have not been

---

[4] On the fascinating Yalta theme, see Alfred Grosser, *Les Occidentaux* (Paris, Fayard, 1978), 59.

wholly put aside despite the election in March 1983 of a stable
CDU–CSU–FDP coalition and the subsequent deployment of
Cruise and Pershing missiles.

Yet in spite of the uncertainties and frictions that have at
times arisen in Franco-German relations in the 1970s and 1980s,
taken over a longer span, it is hoped here to demonstrate the
value of European integration as an important contributor to
post-war Franco-German reconciliation. Though integration at
the outset partly represented an expedient for governments in
both countries to overcome immediate political problems, co-
operation between Bonn and Paris within the framework of the
European Communities has played a vital part in cementing,
and even accelerating, the restoration of good bilateral relations.
Although doubts and misgivings persist, the economic and
political importance of France and Germany within Europe, in
conjunction with the institutionalization of their bilateral co-
operation, has served to establish a firm and lasting rapport.
Whether this Franco-German model is one that can be copied
elsewhere is a question which warrants closer attention.

As to methodology, the analysis here will be primarily
historical, beginning with the Hague summit of 1969 and
running to 1984. Chapters will be divided by significant turning-
points—with two exceptions. Chapters 2 and 3 will examine, in
analytical style, some of the decisive influences on French and
German foreign policy in the post-war period. Chapter 2 will
consider the role of geographical, economic, historical, and
psychological influences; Chapter 3 will look at the political and
institutional sides.

The bulk of the book, Chapters 4–8, embracing the years
1969–74, takes the form of a narrative account. Although a case-
studies approach might have brought the analysis into sharper
relief, the very marked interconnection between issues, particularly in the years 1973 and 1974, convincingly worked against
such a formula. The book's specific intention to focus on the
underlying causes for change in French and German foreign
policy—which requires the broadest approach—added powerfully to this argument, as did the desire to highlight the frequent
interlinkages between superficially unrelated items.

By contrast, Chapters 9–11 adopt the case-studies method.
The rationale for the change is simple. In the period after May

1974, it is more the repercussions of earlier events rather than independent developments which are to be highlighted. This is not, of course, to say that newer factors in Franco-German relations during these years were unimportant, nor by any means to suggest that they will not be given due weight. It is understood that the period was notable above all for the rise of a more distanced German approach towards the United States and a more pragmatic French attitude to the international political and economic environment. Rather, the case-studies method will, it is hoped, offer the best of both worlds, particularly considering that the narrative, still lacking an ideal historical perspective and the fullest benefit of hindsight, will of necessity be less detailed than that on the early 1970s.

The penultimate chapter of the book covers the short-lived Schmidt–Mitterrand period and goes on to look at bilateral relations under Chancellor Kohl. These years are worth considering in view of the arrival of a new French President, due to serve until 1988, and the change of power in Germany after thirteen years of Socialist-led rule. The period is instructive as an object lesson in the speed with which good working relationships were established between the French President and the two German Chancellors. Neither the Mitterrand–Schmidt nor the Mitterrand–Kohl partnership would at first glance appear tailor-made. Yet the relationship that was quickly formed between Mitterrand and Schmidt in particular was striking in view of what appeared to be the highly unpropitious omens at the outset. The fact that the bilateral Franco-German role in Europe has been highly resilient to these leadership changes in the early 1980s provides an indication both of the likely permanency of the bond between the two countries and of the subordination of personalities to broader convergences of national interest in bilateral relations. This question of personalities is one of the topics that will be addressed at greater length in the Conclusion.

Finally, a note about sources. As with any study in contemporary history, considerable use has been made of newspapers. In addition, a number of valuable published memoirs have been consulted, notably that of Brandt. Pompidou's own recollections have also appeared. Though not directly related to the period in question, they do offer a penetrating insight into the mind of what remains a somewhat elusive figure. Furthermore, the subject of Franco-German relations is unusual in the large number of specialized journals devoted to it, all of which have proved useful. The important American angle is also well documented, with Kissinger's first, and his rather less satisfactory second, volume of memoirs standing out. Finally, the present book has greatly benefited from a large number of private interviews. The vast majority of these (even allowing for failings of memory and an occasional trace of personal bias) have been extremely helpful. While unfortunate, the fact that officials of the French Foreign Ministry proved consistently more elusive than their German counterparts underlines the comments made in Chapter 3 regarding the relative openness of the foreign policy process in France and Germany.

2

The Shaping of French and German Foreign Policy

Introduction

THERE is little doubt that certain objective factors play a central role in shaping the priorities and opportunities facing a state in its external relations. Of these, geographical factors, resource allocations and economic influences, historical and psychological considerations, and political and institutional factors are pre-eminent. At their simplest, geographical considerations are likely to have a bearing on a state's traditional policy towards its neighbours; resource allocations and economic influences largely shape external economic policy preferences; historical and psychological considerations significantly mould national attitudes and foreign perceptions; and political and institutional factors can potentially aid or constrain governmental policy and freedom of action. In this and the following chapter, these influences will be examined in turn in order to provide some insight into the formation of policy in France and Germany and to offer some clearer understanding of the reasons behind particular policy preferences in the two countries.

Precise demarcation will not, however, always be possible between different areas. This applies particularly to the present chapter, where the influences to be tackled are often interlinked. For example, both differing resource allocations and divergent historical backgrounds have played a part in moulding French and German external trading patterns. Similarly, geographical factors have to be considered with historical events and contemporary circumstances firmly in mind: the special restrictions created by West Germany's geographical position follow on directly from the post-war division of Europe. Nor is it always possible to maintain a strict balance between the two countries. The particular constraints imposed on West German foreign policy by the Second World War demand special attention to be given to that country when dealing with historical and psychological factors.

Despite these limitations, the method of analysis chosen provides a very effective means of highlighting formative influences in French and German foreign policy. These forces in turn are often critical when the analysis is broadened, as is done in later chapters, to embrace the development of the European Community as a whole. Thus in the case of Germany, for example, the importance of controlling inflation, guaranteeing liberal international trade, and seeking stable East–West relations, emerge as primary and abiding policy aims. Similarly, in the case of France, the need to maintain the concept—not always precisely defined—of national sovereignty and the necessity of emphasizing an independent defence capability are seen to be equally constant motives. Such tenets have outlived the lifetimes of individual governments, irrespective of political complexion, and have come to be engraved into the 'rules of the game', boundaries which are very seldom transgressed in the conduct of the two countries' external relations. The reasons underlying these national choices will become clearer in the pages that follow, their repercussions for the Community as a whole more apparent thereafter.

Geographical considerations

Alfred Grosser has rightly described the Federal Republic as 'a twin sister of the Atlantic Pact and a daughter of the Cold War'.[1] With its long, exposed border to the East, and the isolated position and political and emotional significance of West Berlin, its most populous city, within the German Democratic Republic, West Germany has been particularly susceptible to tension in East–West relations—often focusing on Berlin —and preoccupied throughout its history with security. For the latter it has had to rely on others, principally the United States.

While these factors have placed severe constraints on Bonn's foreign policy, the greater immunity afforded to France by its less vulnerable position has undoubtedly assisted in the pursuit

[1] Alfred Grosser, *Die Bundesrepublik Deutschland. Bilanz einer Entwicklung* (Tübingen, 1967), 12.

of a more autonomous external line.[2] Though sharing in the
Western Alliance's concern with security issues in general,
France's location to one side of any likely East-West military
confrontation in Europe has tended to leave Paris less acutely
concerned about security than Bonn. Over the years, this has
allowed successive French leaders a much greater freedom of
action in their external relations compared to their German
counterparts, a distinction which found clearest expression in the
independent line pursued by de Gaulle.

The Federal Republic's difficulties have been exacerbated by
partition and the reunification issue. Prior to the *Ostpolitik*, the
rigid and legalistic Hallstein doctrine of non-recognition of states
establishing diplomatic links with the GDR greatly circum-
scribed Bonn's freedom of manœuvre and often left it open to
leverage from third parties. Considerable efforts were made to
avoid the arousal of interest in the GDR in international bodies,
while Bonn also strove to counter its neighbour's influence in
other countries. Within West Germany itself, reunification was
often a source of bitter political debate. There is little doubt that
in the 1950s the country's external posture was weakened by the
conflicting views of the two major parties regarding foreign
policy priorities. That concern with all-German issues—particularly the desire to avoid any impression of a *de jure* separation—
was a significant constraint on the Federal Government's West
European policy was seen in its efforts to secure equal trading
rights for the GDR in the negotiations for the creation of the
EEC. These talks to some extent put Bonn in the position of
demandeur.[3] France, by contrast, faced no such geographical
preoccupations on its negotiating stance. In demanding wide-
ranging economic concessions from the Germans, Paris was,

[2] For an introduction to the effects of West Germany's position and its dependence on
the Alliance, see Eberhard Schulz, 'Die Weiterentwicklung der deutschen Frage',
Forschungsinstitut der Deutschen Gesellschaft für Auswärtige Politik (hereafter DGAP),
Aussenpolitische Perspektiven des westdeutschen Staates, i (Munich Oldenbourg, 1971), 160;
Helga Haftendorn, 'Verflechtung und Interdependenz als Strukturbedingungen west-
deutscher Aussenpolitik', in Haftendorn *et al.* (edd.), *Verwaltete Aussenpolitik — Sicherheits-
und entspannungspolitische Entscheidungsprozesse in Bonn* (Cologne, Verlag Wissenschaft und
Politik/Nottbeck, 1978); Alfred Grosser, *Wann wird die Bundesrepublik ein normaler Staat?*
(Bergsdorfer Gesprächskreis Pamphlet); Jean-Paul Picaper, 'Les Constantes de la
politique extérieure de la République Fédérale', *Politique Étrangère* 1 (1975).

[3] For the influence of partition on German foreign policy, see Waldemar Besson,
'Prinzipienfragen der westdeutschen Aussenpolitik', *Politische Vierteljahresschrift* 9 (1968),

rather, to some extent able to exploit the Federal Republic's relative disadvantage.

The effect, principally of geographical, though also of historical and economic factors, on French and German foreign policy has been most visible in the two countries' differing attitudes towards the United States. The contrast was particularly salient in the 1960s, when the Federal Republic's position and its inflexible stance *vis-à-vis* the Communist bloc placed it firmly under American military tutelage. This required in turn a political and economic pay-off, which was most obviously demonstrated in continued support for the dollar. The situation was exemplified in the March 1967 Blessing letter, written in response to the pressures of the Mansfield lobby, and in Bonn's actions in many of the monetary crises of the period. Shonfield observes that Germany's need for American nuclear and conventional military support, 'Produced a docility and compliance with American wishes which was the more remarkable as German economic strength continued to grow and to be acknowledged ... The basis of the alliance obviously was primarily military, but the pay-off was primarily monetary.'[4] German concern not to antagonize the United States extended to the trading sector, where Bonn sought to steer Community policy away from confrontation with the Americans and prevent European measures endangering its close relationship with Washington. In addition, American policy preferences and hostility to restrictive Community trading structures intensified Bonn's own desire for greater liberalization, leading in turn to friction with Paris.

By contrast, France's less constrained position and particularly its less obvious dependence on the United States greatly helped

31-3; Ulrich Everling, 'Die Europapolitischen Strategien der Bundesregierung in den siebziger Jahren', (unpublished paper), 4; Grosser, *Wann wird die Bundesrepublik ein normaler Staat?* For the effect in terms of relations with the EEC, see Hans B. Krämer, 'OECD Länder', in DGAP, *Aussenpolitische Perspiktiven*, iii. 178.

[4] Andrew Shonfield (ed.) *International Economic Relations of the Western World 1959-71*, ii. 46-7. It is interesting to note that Britain also tried to use its military influence, although much less successfully. See John Mackintosh, 'Britain in Europe. Historical Perspective and contemporary reality', *International Affairs* (Apr. 1969), 257, and Hans-Thomas Panek, *Die Währungskrisen von November 1969 bis Mai 1971 im politischen Prozess der Bundesrepublik Deutschland* (Institut für Wirtschaftspolitik an der Universität zu Köln, Untersuchungen No. 41, Cologne, 1977), 103.

de Gaulle in his external policy aims. The benefit of the continuing American nuclear guarantee over Europe, in conjunction with a much less pressing need for the deployment of American troops on French soil (and careful management of the balance of payments) allowed the General a far greater scope and flexibility in his foreign policy than that enjoyed by German leaders. It is not mistakenly that France in this period has been described as a 'free rider' on the international system, secure to act independently under the protection of the American nuclear umbrella.[5] Hence de Gaulle was able to pursue his vision of a multipolar world. On the one hand the General sought improved relations with the Communist and non-aligned countries, while on the other he used French monetary policy as a major weapon in his foreign policy arsenal during his campaign to demonstrate American fallibility. Only at times of internal or external crises, such as the 'events' of May 1968 or the Russian invasion of Czechoslovakia in August that year, did the situation oblige France to fall back into line with the rest of the Alliance.

It was in the defence sector above all that geographic factors accentuated differences between Paris and Bonn. In particular, their divergent attitudes to the proposed Multilateral Force in the early 1950s and to NATO in the 1960s testified to the asymmetric constraints facing the two capitals. The contrast was seen most sharply in de Gaulle's decision to remove France from the military wing of the Alliance, a dissimilarity in the two countries' foreign policies that has remained to the present day (though there have been steps towards closer co-ordination under Mitterrand). De Gaulle's step highlighted the distinctive French and German outlooks towards the United States. This discrepancy had already been heralded in the Bundestag's Preamble to the 1963 Franco–German Treaty, which, in a clear attempt to avoid a choice between Paris and Washington, asserted that the new arrangement should not conflict with existing treaty commitments and emphasized established links with the United States and NATO.

---

[5] On this theme, see Shonfield, i. 104; Grosser, *Les Occidentaux*, 240. On Gaullist policy in the 1960s, see also Edward J. Kolodziej, *French International Policy under de Gaulle and Pompidou. The Politics of Grandeur* (Ithaca, Cornell University Press, 1974); Edward L. Morse, *Foreign Policy and Interdependence in Gaullist France* (Princeton, Princeton University Press, 1978); Edward L. Morse, 'France', in Wilfrid L. Kohl (ed.), *Economic Foreign Policies of Industrial States* (Lexington, Lexington Books, 1977), 82.

Only in the 1970s did an evolution take place in French defence policy, with a shift under Giscard towards a more integrated Western approach. The change of strategy from the concept of *sanctuarisation*—by which it was understood that France's line of defence rested on its national frontiers—to *sanctuarisation élargie*—envisaging the possible necessity to fight somewhere beyond national borders (for instance, in West Germany)—represented an important, and public, redefinition of defence policy. Simultaneously, there developed increasing informal co-operation between the French military and its NATO counterparts, a trend continued under Mitterrand.

Though there were in the 1960s isolated episodes of forcefulness in German policy towards its allies, notably in the economic sector, as at the November 1968 Group of Ten meeting in Bonn, Kissinger's description of the Federal Republic in 1969 as 'an economy in search of political purpose'[6] remained apt. It was only in the early 1970s, largely on account of the *Ostpolitik*, that matters began to change. Brandt's *rapprochement* with the East, bringing about *détente* and the assurance of safe frontiers, permitted the transition of the Federal Republic's steadily accruing economic strength into a more forceful political stance, and vastly increased the room for manœuvre in Bonn's foreign policy.[7] The simultaneous elevation of international monetary affairs—once regarded as a topic of 'low' politics—into a major preoccupation of the Western world, confirmed West Germany's prowess while endowing its voice with a new political weight.

Yet it would be wrong to overestimate the Federal Republic's strength as a result of the *Ostpolitik*. There are definitely two sides to the coin. Brandt's initiative required acceptance of the post-war territorial status quo, renunciation of sovereign rights over West Berlin, and recognition, *de facto* if not yet *de jure*, of the country's partition. Though border tension has been greatly eased,

[6] Henry Kissinger, *The White House Years* (London, Weidenfeld and Nicholson/Michael Joseph, 1979), 97.

[7] As an introduction to the value of the *Ostpolitik*, see Roger Tilford (ed.), *The Ostpolitik and Political Change in Germany* (Farnborough and Lexington, Saxon House/Lexington Books, 1975); Michael Kreile, 'Ostpolitik Reconsidered', in Ekkehart Krippendorff and Volker Rittberger (edd.) *The Foreign Policy of West Germany. Formation and Contents* (London, Sage Publications, 1980), 123–46; Lawrence L. Whetten, *Germany's Ostpolitik* (London, RIIA/OUP, 1971).

West Germany remains the most vulnerable member of the Alliance, and retains the greatest interest in the preservation of *détente*. This situation led, in the later 1970s, to difficulties with President Carter on account of different priorities. It saw its most forceful expression in early 1982, when the originally muted German reaction to the military take-over in Poland contrasted with the noisy response which the move received in Washington and Paris, provoking attacks on German 'appeasement'. Similarly, under the Kohl Government, it is worth noting that as East–West relations have declined, Bonn has striven to maintain good relations with the GDR. This has required policy shifts by the CDU–CSU, as, for example, over the question of making large loans to East Germany.

The *Ostpolitik* also had marked internal repercussions. During the Brandt Chancellorship, bitter arguments, offering a mirror image of those of the 1950s, raged over claims that excessive attention was being paid to Eastern policy to the detriment of relations with West European partners. Even in 1984, fourteen years after the signing of the Federal Republic's first Eastern treaties, there remains an underlying dichotomy in—stated— long-run German foreign policy aims between the continuing goal of reunification on the one hand and that of European federation on the other. Under Schmidt, it can well be argued, however, that both these considerations were so overshadowed by a sense of pragmatism that neither was any longer viewed as more than an appealing, but unattainable, ambition by German politicians and public alike.

For some statesmen, however—notably Pompidou—the threat of reunification, or at least of German neutrality, was sufficiently strong to impose a significant constraint on bilateral relations. Even today, the vaguest hints by German politicians of unorthodox options, such as neutrality, in the country's long-run foreign policy raise the alarm in other Western capitals, and require a swift diplomatic response by Bonn. Again, the reaction in some foreign quarters to the early German attitude to the Polish military take-over was telling. Despite its economic success and the freedom of action permitted by *détente* with the East, the Federal Republic, in contrast to France, remains a country whose geographical position leaves it unusually constrained in its external relations and more open than most to suspicion.

Economic factors

Differences in resource allocations, contributing to contrasting economic structures and philosophies, have played a major part in shaping French and German foreign economic policies over the years. Historically, relative French self-sufficiency in food and certain raw materials stood out against West Germany's greater dependence on external trade. This fostered protectionist tendencies in France and more liberal-minded policies in the Federal Republic. The German Reich's later, but far more intensive, industrialization and its concentration on 'modern' industrial sectors such as electrical engineering and chemicals heightened this firm interest in world markets. Furthermore, Germany's relatively late start in the colonial race of the nineteenth century and its territorial penalties following the Treaty of Versailles contrasted with France's possession of an overseas empire, which provided a cheap and dependable source of raw materials and a tied export market.[8] The partition of Germany after the Second World War, involving the loss of the chiefly agricultural regions to the east, further weakened the position of the new Federal Republic, reinforcing its more outward-looking commercial attitude. Thus, by 1956, pending negotiations for the creation of the EEC, France and Germany had developed highly distinct trading patterns While 31.3 per cent of French exports were directed to its overseas territories, 25.3 per cent to its five European partners, and 17.4 per cent to other OEEC states, a mere 0.7 per cent of German exports was sold to the French colonies, 29.5 per cent to the Five, and 30.8 per cent to other OEEC members.[9]

Commodity statistics for the period highlighted the disparity in French and German resource allocations, illustrating the

[8] For a concise look at the historical differences in French and German economic and social structures, see Dieter Menyesch and Henrik Uterwedde, 'Wirtschaftliche und Soziale Strukturen in der Bundesrepublik und in Frankreich', in Robert Picht (ed.) *Deutschland—Frankreich—Europa* (Munich, Piper, 1978), 47–50. For contemporary analysis, see Guy de Carmoy, 'Industrie française et industrie allemande: Performances et stratégies', *Politique Internationale* 6 (Winter 1979–80); Christian Deubner, Udo Rehfeldt, and Frieder Schlupp, 'Die Internationalisierung der westdeutschen Wirtschaft: Das "Modell Deutschland" in der Weltmarktkonkurrenz', in René Lasserre, Wolfgang Neumann, Robert Picht (edd.), *Deutschland—Frankreich: Bausteine zum Systemvergleich*, ii (Gerlingen, Bleicher, 1981), 17–80.

[9] Figures from Mario Levi, 'Réflexions sur l'avenir de la co-opération européenne', *Politique Étrangère* 5 (1959).

Federal Republic's greater dependence on trade. In 1958, food (SITC 0), represented 24.27 per cent of Germany's total imports, while for France, the corresponding figure was 17.13 per cent.[10] France has by far the larger agricultural sector, a factor which has contributed to its constant stress on farm policy both nationally and at Community level. In 1958, food constituted 9.39 per cent of French total exports, compared with 1.76 per cent for Germany.[11] In terms of employment by sector, 24.6 per cent of the French working population was involved in agriculture in 1957, as against 16.3 per cent in the Federal Republic.[12] Even by 1981, 8.6 per cent of the French work-force was still involved in agriculture, forestry, or fishing, compared with 5.5 per cent in West Germany.[13] This relative German deficiency in food and raw materials has, however, been compensated by a specialization in the industrial sector. In 1958 machinery and transport equipment (SITC 7), the best individual indicator of the two countries' heavy industrial sectors, comprised 44.9 per cent of total German exports, as against only 22.7 per cent for France.[14] This dissimilarity formed a key element underlining the two countries' contrasting policy preferences.

The Federal Republic's more international commercial orientation, which contributed to its interest in low tariffs, is corroborated by trade statistics for the late 1950s. At the birth of the EEC, exports of goods and services represented 24.0 per cent and imports 20.0 per cent of German GDP (average 1955–9 = 100). In comparison, the corresponding figures for France were 14 per cent and 13 per cent respectively (average 1957–9 = 100, including franc zone).[15] This commercial disparity has continued, in slightly attenuated form, to the present day. In 1982, exports formed 26.6 per cent of German GDP, as against only 17.1 per cent in the case of France.[16]

Resource factors have not been alone in shaping French and

---

[10] Calculated from OEEC Series IV, Jan.–Dec. 1958.

[11] Ibid.

[12] Source: *France* (Paris, OECD, Feb. 1973), 40.

[13] Source: *France* (Paris, OECD, July 1984), Basic Statistics; International Comparisons.

[14] Calculated from OEEC Series IV, Jan.–Dec. 1958.

[15] Source: *Germany* (Paris, OECD, 1960), Basic Statistics; *France* (Paris, OECD, 1960), Basic Statistics.

[16] Source: *France* (Paris, OECD, July 1984), Basic Statistics, International Comparisons.

German post-war economic policy preferences. Certain special considerations apply to the Federal Republic. American influences during the occupation played a part in forming the country's liberal post-war industrial policies, which were a reaction too against the controls of the Nazi era. Liberalizing industrial trade, thereby exposing German industry to international competition, was also viewed as a catalyst to economic recovery. Hager goes so far as to identify an 'existential' significance in free trade for post-war Germany, linked closely with the preservation of democratic values.[17] Yet it must be noted that while the Federal Republic has sought freer international trade in industrial goods, it has maintained a protectionist approach to agriculture.

French and German attitudes to investment by foreign firms have in some ways mirrored their policies towards international trade. The highly restrictive line pursued by the French, particularly for political reasons under de Gaulle,[18] contrasted sharply with the relative openness of the German economy. Yet there has undoubtedly been an evolution in French thinking since 1969. Pompidou's greater willingness to put doctrinaire considerations aside in his desire to accelerate French industrialization can be seen not just as a shift in policy emphasis, but also as indicating a recognition of the gradual transformation of France's trading patterns, in which commerce with European partners has steadily gained ground.[19] Thus it is interesting to note that although Germany remains the larger trading nation, by 1983, commerce with the EEC accounted for 49.2 per cent of

[17] Wolfgang Hager, 'Germany as an Extra-ordinary Trader', in Wilfrid L. Kohl and Giorgio Bassevi (edd.), *West Germany. A European Global Power* (Lexington, Lexington Books, 1980). On background factors, see also Michael Kreile, 'West Germany: the dynamics of expansion', in Peter J. Katzenstein (ed.), *Between Power and Plenty—Foreign Economic Policies of Advanced Industrial States* (*International Organization*, Special Number, Autumn 1977), 782.

[18] In this context see Peter J. Katzenstein, 'International relations and domestic structures: Foreign Economic Policies of Advanced Industrial States', *International Organization* (Winter 1976), 29. For figures on foreign investment in France and Germany, see Gilbert Ziebura, 'Strukturprobleme der deutsch-französischen Wirtschaftsbeziehungen', in Schriftenreihe der Deutsch-Französischen Instituts (hereafter DFI) Ludwigsburg, No. 3, *Strukturprobleme der deutsch-französischen Wirtschaftsbeziehungen* (Ludwigsburg, DFI, 1976), 6–7.

[19] For Pompidou's views on industrialization and foreign investment, see Stéphane Rials, *Les Idées politiques du Président Georges Pompidou* (Paris, Presses Universitaires de France, 1977), 78.

total French exports and 49.8 per cent of total imports, compared with 48.1 per cent and 49.3 per cent respectively for West Germany.[20]

This emphasis on developing France's industrial position and concentrating on new growth industries, such as information technology, electronics, and nuclear energy, was a hallmark of Giscard's presidency and a pillar to the Eighth Five Year Plan. Similarly, there was a further liberalization towards foreign investment. The position has been more complex under Mitterrand. While the President can be likened to Pompidou in his preoccupation with the development of French industry, particularly in the newest technologies, his choice of methods is more akin to de Gaulle. In seeking to make France 'the Japan of Europe', the Socialist Government has clearly been attracted to the path of protectionism in areas such as high technology. Hence, for instance, the strong desire to foster new pan-European industrial co-operative ventures in key industries such as electronics and telecommunications in order to ensure France's—and Europe's—'rightful' position at the forefront of these new technologies (though one should be aware of the signs of much greater pragmatism towards foreign investment in France by 1984).

Though equally concerned about the threat of foreign competition, especially from Japan, the Kohl Government has tended towards a different approach. Rather than thinking in terms of long-range strategies, Bonn has preferred a more pragmatic, case by case policy. No harm is seen in co-operating with Japanese or American rivals, even to the extent of utilizing their innovations. This contrasts with the French philosophy of wishing to foster purely European alternatives which would be protected by external trade barriers. Though the description over-simplifies the two countries' positions (and there are already exceptions to both rules), the future development of policy in Paris and Bonn is one of the more interesting areas for academic observers. The situation could become particularly complicated on the French side should internal political developments strengthen the position of more radical, protectionist-minded, members of the Socialist Party.

[20] Source: OECD Monthly Statistics of Foreign Trade, June 1984.

In both France and Germany, special emphasis has long been placed on the export sector—though until the early 1970s this was for somewhat different reasons. In the Federal Republic, the importance of trade has largely been responsible for the export sector's primary role in the country's industrial structure. Its function in furthering growth has in turn intensified German interest in lowering industrial tariff barriers. In the 1950s and 1960s, deliberate undervaluation of the Deutschemark and resistance to parity changes actively promoted this process, enhancing the country's export orientation. Broad similarities between the views of trade unions and management regarding external aims also assisted. Thus, by 1982, exports accounted for 65.8 per cent of total sales for Daimler–Benz, 74 per cent for Hoechst, 58 per cent for Mannesmann, and 46 per cent for Thyssen. On a sectoral basis, in the car and commercial vehicle industry alone, exports in 1983 equalled some 56.9 per cent of total production.[21]

This German reliance on external markets has had a number of side-effects. Principally, assisted by the close links between business interests and the Ministries of Finance and Economics, the export sector has gained a considerable say over the formation of foreign economic policy. Secondly, Germany's dependence on a fair-weather world economy has left it particularly vulnerable to international economic upsets and accentuated its interdependence with other industrialized states, thereby imposing an indirect constraint on its foreign policy. Hence, for instance, the alarm in Bonn caused by the temporary French imposition of export subsidies and selective import quotas in 1968. Similarly, in 1981, the French Prime Minister's call for the 'reconquest of the domestic market' caused considerable anxiety in the German capital. Notwithstanding the protectionist instincts of some Socialists, it should be noted, however, that the growing 'internationalization' of the French economy, and especially its very high level of dependence on external energy sources, have increasingly made it, too, more vulnerable to wider world economic currents.

As with the Federal Republic, post-war French foreign

---

[21] Figures from 1982 Annual Reports of Daimler–Benz, Hoechst, and Mannesmann; Thyssen's Annual Report. 1981–2; *Financial Times*, 25 Jan. 1984.

economic policy also sought to boost the country's export sector, though under de Gaulle this was almost invariably for more overtly political reasons.[22] Likewise with the Germans, undervaluation of the currency was the prime instrument. Yet, while the methods used by both countries bore similarities, their goals were highly disparate. A healthy balance of payments, underlying a strong currency, large reserves, and, in the longer term a vigorous industrial structure, formed the solid bases on which de Gaulle was able to construct his more flamboyant foreign policies. Similarly, careful economic management had the effect of leaving France relatively secure against any exploitation of economic or (as practised by de Gaulle himself against the dollar) monetary disruption. This latter area provides the best illustration of the close link for de Gaulle between economic policies and wider political aims. Thus France's anti-American stance and emphasis on a gold-based reform of the international monetary system was intimately associated with the General's political goal of demonstrating the vulnerability of America's leading world role.

Domestic economic considerations were often subsumed into external requirements in this quest for autonomy on the world stage. By contrast, de Gaulle's successors have shown a greater appreciation of western economic interdependence, resulting in a shift away from principally external policy motives towards domestic economic considerations. However, the stimulation of exports has remained a key element of government strategy. It is interesting to note, by way of contrast, the evolution in the Federal Republic in the later 1970s towards a pattern closer to that associated with France. Bonn has come to place greater weight on more exclusively political ends in its foreign economic policy. This development was seen very clearly in the financial aid given in the 1970s to fledgling democracies such as Spain, Portugal, and, until the military take-over, Turkey.

Two other influences underscore differences in French and German external economic policies. History and tradition have

[22] On French foreign economic policy, see Morse, 'France', and *Foreign Policy and Interdependence in Gaullist France*; Kolodziej, *French International Policy*; John Zysman, 'The French State in the International Economy', in Katzenstein, *Between Power and Plenty*; Henrik and Michèle Schmiegelow, 'The New Mercantilism in International Relations. The Case of France's External Monetary Policy', *International Organization* (Spring 1975).

resulted in divergent attitudes towards *dirigisme*, an accepted facet of economic life in France, exemplified by the Commissariat du Plan, and, superficially at least, a *bête noire* of the free market system enshrined in the Federal Republic. In the 1950s, the distinction was clearly demonstrated in the two countries' stands in the negotiations prior to the creation of the European Coal and Steel Community and the Common Market.[23] German hostility to excessive external control has continued almost unabated to the present day. This has been seen, for instance, in Bonn's opposition to any commodity price stabilization schemes or to centrally ordained Community steel production quotas (which were only accepted after lengthy wrangling). It should be noted, however, that there is more to the German picture than meets the eye. While successive Federal Governments have ostensibly remained hostile to the concept of a centrally guided industrial policy, one should not forget the existence in Bonn of a large and powerful Research Ministry, which has an important role, nor of the operation of a variety of subsidies and methods of assistance at state government level.

By contrast, there were signs of some change from previous priorities in France under Giscard. Barre's removal of price controls and his efforts to reduce the Government's role in industry represented an attempt to liberalize and, in part, to emulate the German model. In May 1981, however, the pattern shifted back towards its original form. The Socialists' wide-ranging nationalization programme was intended to give the Government a say over key investment and production decisions, as well as guaranteeing it further control over the financial sector. French and German attitudes, particularly after the election of the CDU–CSU–FDP coalition, appeared to be diverging once again. But there has since been some movement back towards the centre in France, particularly following the government reshuffle of summer 1984.

Inflation is the second area in which policy in the two countries has differed—largely as a result of historic factors. Again, though, the French model has shifted, first one way, then the other, and now once again. For the Germans, the hyper-

---

[23] The article by Christian Deubner, 'The Expansion of West German Capital and the Founding of Euratom', *International Organization* (Spring 1979), is especially interesting in illustrating the effect of hostility to *dirigisme*.

inflation of 1923–4, which contributed to popular disaffection with the Weimar Republic and assisted in the rise of Hitler, has caused inflation to be regarded not only as the gravest of economic ills, but also as a potentially politically destabilizing force. The Reichmark's loss of value following the Second World War was an added factor in creating such feelings. This pernicious character of inflation has been recognized in the constitutional function assigned to the Bundesbank as a protector of monetary stability. To the mind of one of its ex-Presidents, in no other country are anti-inflationary measures so strongly supported by public opinion.[24] Maintaining low inflation rates has also been an important component of the Federal Republic's export-orien-tated commercial strategy, assisting the undervaluation of the currency and enhancing competitiveness. Certainly, helped by structural factors, West German inflation rates have been consistently lower than those of France, as well as most other European partners.[25] Though outsiders voiced irritation with the tendency of many German leaders to preach about economic policy and to praise their country's example as one to be universally followed, there is no denying the Federal Republic's considerable achievements in keeping down inflation. It is no less hard to ignore the widespread adoption—notably in Britain and the United States—of tough monetarist tactics *à l'allemande*.

In France, by comparison, greater emphasis has often been placed on stimulating industrial growth and limiting unem-ployment (a shared characteristic with Britain at one time, in contrast to the somewhat lower priority given to full employ-ment in West Germany). As shall be seen, these divergent French and German policy interests have at times given rise to considerable friction at Community level. Matters have also been complicated by the shifts in French policy between

[24] Otmar Emminger, 'Die Stellung der Deutschen Mark in der Welt', in Schriftenreihe des Forschungsinstituts der Deutschen Gesellschaft für Auswärtige Politik, *Aussenpolitik nach der Wahl des 6. Bundestages* (Opladen, Leske, 1969), 75.

[25] For comparison of German against international price and cost trends, see Otmar Emminger, *The D-Mark in the Conflict between Internal and External Equilibrium 1948–75*, Essays in International Finance No. 122 (International Finance Section, Department of Economics, Princeton University, June 1977), 19. For German monetary policy, see also Alphonse Losser, 'Bilan économique de la R.F.A. 1948–1968', *La Revue d'Allemagne* (Jan.–Mar. 1969), and 'La Politique monétaire de la R.F.A.', *Documents* (Sept.–Oct. 1973).

different Presidents. While the Federal Republic has sought throughout its membership of the Community to encourage economic and cyclical stability among the member states, only under Giscard did this become a major French preoccupation. The fight against inflation formed a prime objective of Barre's economic policies and a decisive influence in French participation in the EMS. Under Mitterrand, priorities have shifted widely. Until the Government's austerity measures of 1982, and especially March 1983, the emphasis was firmly placed on generous social welfare benefits. As has been seen, however, such *largesse* took its toll in terms of increasing domestic cost trends, and French inflation rates moved considerably out of line with the generally downward pattern elsewhere in Europe. Such differing economic trends have hardly gone unnoticed in the foreign exchange markets, and the upshot has been a series of forced devaluations of the franc in order to maintain competitiveness. Naturally, this has not been without consequences for the EMS. The devaluations of October 1981, June 1982, and March 1983 bring to mind certain (perhaps increasing) similarities with the experience of Britain in the mid- and later 1970s, when a depreciating currency and ineffective government attempts to restrain incomes became depressingly commonplace.

The historical differences between French and German economic policies cited above account for many of the discrepancies in the two countries' approaches to Community trade. In the late 1950s, during negotiations for the establishment of the EEC, the Germans opposed high common industrial tariff levels, which were viewed as a threat to their world-orientated trading interests. Rather, Bonn sought to insure against EEC isolationism, which might result in trade diversion rather than creation. Yet high tariff barriers and Community preference were an essential pre-condition for Paris, preventing the premature exposure of French industry to the fullest international competition and allowing the expansion of French agriculture into neighbouring markets unchallenged by cheaper non-Community imports. Not surprisingly, while the 1958 British Free Trade Area proposals, which offered the Federal Republic many of the economic benefits of the EEC with few of the drawbacks, were welcomed in certain German quarters, they were anathema in France (although for political as well as economic reasons). The

German position was, however, more complicated in the agricultural sector, where the interests of the nation's powerful farm lobby conflicted with, and eventually outweighed, wishes elsewhere in the economy for cheap food purchases on the world market. Such a model would have been more akin to that of Britain. This possibility of converging Anglo–German interests regarding food policy goes much of the way to explain the recurrent French fears of a bilateral alignment against the CAP. However, the French have tended to underestimate the complexities of the German position: though politicians in Bonn have since the early 1970s fiercely criticized the cost and wastefulness of the CAP, the Federal Republic has seen a substantial increase in the size of its agricultural output in recent years on account of the distortions caused by the divergences in value between Community currencies and their 'green' counterparts.[26] The German position as regards agriculture therefore is a great deal more complex than some politicians' statements might suggest.

Structural economic differences have not obstructed bilateral Franco-German trade. This has, in fact, benefited from the element of complementarity between the two economies, especially in earlier years, with cross shipments of French agricultural products and German industrial goods. This pattern has not, however, remained static. The ratio, in value terms, of food and live animals (SITC 0) to machinery and transport equipment (SITC 7) in French total exports to the Federal Republic has altered from 9.8 per cent : 13.4 per cent in 1958, to 12.5 per cent : 27.0 per cent in 1982. By contrast, however, in 1982 by value, machinery and transport equipment accounted for no less than 50.1 per cent of German exports to France.[27] The common frontier, making for low transport and communication costs, shared languages in the Alsace-Lorraine region, and a psychological aspect, with Germans often prizing French luxury goods and the French valuing German technical quality, have also played a part in stimulating bilateral trade, which tripled in value between 1958 and 1962.[28]

[26] On this theme, see Yao-Su Hu, 'German agricultural power: the impact on France and Britain', *The World Today* (Nov. 1979).

[27] Figures calculated from OEEC, Series IV, Jan.–Dec. 1958, and OECD, Series C, Commodity Trade: Exports, Jan.–Dec. 1982.

[28] European Commission, Statistical Office, *General Statistical Bulletin*, No. 3 (Mar. 1973), 29, 68.

The effects of integration are clearly illustrated in the changes in shares of bilateral trade since the late 1950s. France, however, remains relatively more dependent on trade with the Federal Republic than vice versa. The German share of total French imports has climbed from 11.64 per cent in 1958 to 16.94 per cent in 1983, while the French stake in total German imports has risen from 7.64 per cent in 1958 to 11.50 per cent in 1983. Export figures bear out this evolution, while again illustrating France's greater dependence and the Federal Republic's wider-ranging trading interests. In 1983, in value terms, sales to West Germany accounted for 15.55 per cent of total French exports compared to 10.46 per cent in 1958, while German sales to France rose from 7.75 per cent of total exports in 1958 to 12.94 per cent in 1983.[29] Successive revaluations of the Deutschemark and the decreasing value of the franc have failed to shift the balance of payments out of Germany's favour in recent years, a discrepancy accentuated by the greater proportion of finished products, notably machinery and capital goods, in German exports to France than vice versa. Though by 1968 France had managed to dislodge the United States as the Federal Republic's principal supplier, by 1973 it, in turn, had been replaced by the Netherlands, which has since not only maintained, but increased its lead.[30]

It should be noted in this context that the question of trade imbalances between the French and German economies at one time became a major issue under the Socialists. At least 40 per cent (representing some 38 billion francs) of France's 1982 balance of trade deficit was attributable to German imports, sucked into an expanding French economy at a time of marked domestic recession across the Rhine. Hence the rather sour note injected into the May 1983 Franco-German summit in Paris, when Mme Cresson, the French Industry Minister, broadcast a clear threat to impose indirect curbs on German imports. Since then, economic recovery in the United States has proved a counter-attraction for German goods, reducing the level of sales to France and diffusing some of the tension. Moreover, the French Government's own austerity programmes have

[29] Figures calculated from OEEC, Series IV, Jan.–Dec. 1958, and OECD Monthly Statistics of Foreign Trade, June 1984.

[30] Source: OECD Series C, Commodity Trade: Imports, Jan.–Dec. 1973.

themselves played some part in stemming the tide of German imports.

Although trade has flourished over the years, dissimilarities in French and German economic structures and priorities, occasionally combined with nationalistic considerations, usually on the French side, have often impeded bilateral economic cooperation, belying the aspirations of the 1963 treaty between the two countries.[31] Joint aid policies towards developing states have been complicated by French emphasis on the francophone region. In the industrial sphere, commercial and technological considerations have often dictated joint ventures in the past with the United States or other European partners. Nuclear cooperation, although a long-standing topic of bilateral talks, has also had only limited results, while the two countries have participated in rival uranium enrichment schemes—a source of some bitterness to President Pompidou. Private French and German companies have also been reluctant to work together in this field, witnessed in their vigorous competition to secure nuclear sales abroad. The closer contacts predicted by some observers have yet to materialize.[32]

Certainly, in the later 1970s and early 1980s, the effects of

[31] On Franco-German bilateral trade, economic co-operation, and mutual investment, see Gilbert Ziebura, *Die deutsch-französischen Beziehungen seit 1945. Mythen und Realitäten* (Pfullingen, Neske, 1970), 141–55. The author's critical assessment contrasts with the understandably more favourable picture presented by two statesmen in charge of bilateral co-operation, Pierre-Olivier Lapie and Carlo Schmid, *La Coopération franco-allemande* (Paris, La Documentation Française, 1977), 14–16, 33–53. François Bilger makes a very detailed appraisal in 'Les Relations économiques franco-allemandes de 1945 à 1971. Bilan et perspectives', *La Revue d'Allemagne* (July–Sept. 1972); see also DFI, *Strukturprobleme der deutsch-französischen Wirtschaftsbeziehungen*; Klaus-Peter Schmid, 'Komplementarität und Konkurrenz in den deutsch-französischen Wirtschaftsbeziehungen', in Schriftenreihe des deutsch-französischen Instituts Ludwigsburg No. 2, *Deutschland, Frankreich und die europäische Krise* (Ludwigsburg, DFI, 1978), 51–62; John E. Farquharson and Stephen C. Holt, *Europe from Below. An Assessment of Franco–German Popular Contacts* (London, George Allen and Unwin, 1975), 89–107; Raymond Poidevin and Jacques Bariéty, *Les Relations franco-allemandes 1815–1975* (Paris, Colin, 1977), 344–8; Christian Deubner, Udo Rehfeldt, and Frieder Schlupp, 'Deutsch-französische Wirtschaftsbeziehungen im Rahmen der weltwirtschaftlichen Arbeitsteilung: Interdependenz, Divergenz, oder strukturelle Dominanz?' in Picht (ed.) *Deutschland—Frankreich—Europa*. Finally, Willy Brandt's comments on the problem of co-operation in the economic field are instructive, in *People and Politics* (London, Collins, 1978), 268.

[32] See e.g. Peter Scholz and Reinhart Kraus, 'Aspekte der bilateralen Zusammenarbeit auf der Grundlage des deutsch-französischen Vertrages', in Picht. Picht himself makes some very realistic observations on the nuclear question, in 'Deutschland—Frankreich—Europa: Der Zwang zur Partnerschaft', in Lasserre, Neumann, and Picht (edd.), i. 42.

worldwide economic recession have not been mirrored in any great tightening of Franco-German industrial and economic bonds. In fact, the opposite is often true. The duration of the economic downturn has exacerbated existing problems. Competitive pressures between private industry in the two countries have increased in the battle for shrinking and increasingly crowded world markets. Apart from certain recent ventures in the telecommunications field, the situation has not always been helped by government policy in Bonn or Paris, with the accession to power of new and inexperienced teams who have often given more attention to the independent solution of national economic problems than to joint remedies.

To take the experience of one industry—computers—as an example, hopes under de Gaulle in the 1960s to establish a dominant French, and perhaps European, manufacturer—the 'Plan Calcul', a venture nurtured by subsidies and guaranteed government orders—were dashed in May 1975. For Giscard opted to merge CII, the amalgam created in 1966 by de Gaulle, with the American firm Honeywell–Bull. Giscard's decision was deeply criticized by the Gaullists, who saw it as a betrayal of the General's policy of independent national development. The decision also drew fire in certain European circles, where it was censured as another lost opportunity in establishing a pan-European computer conglomerate. Grosser goes so far as to suggest that reluctance to enter into too close links with the Germans may have been a motive for the French decision.[33] Nationalist and European-minded critics alike should not forget, however, that Giscard's move did not set a precedent. Already in 1970, Pompidou, no doubt feeling, like his successor, that the best future for the French computer industry lay in collaboration with American interests, had sanctioned the transfer of Bull, a French electronics firm, from General Electric to Honeywell. This move was greeted no less critically by advocates of a wider European grouping. It is worth noting, however, that the product of Pompidou's and Giscard's labours—the eventual amalgam CII/Honeywell–Bull—has not turned out to be the

---

[33] In this context, see the comments and detailed references in Grosser, *Les Occidentaux*, 381–2, and Pierre Maillet, 'Les Effets des politiques communes sur l'industrie française', in Joël Rideau *et al.* (edd.), *La France et les Communautés Européennes* (Paris, LGDJ, 1975), 1009–10.

success story intended. Although progress has been made, the company's financial performance has hardly been outstanding. On the other hand, it should be borne in mind that the firm's nationalization under Mitterrand and the consequent reduction in Honeywell's stake from 47 per cent to a little under 20 per cent has marked a step back in the direction of de Gaulle's original autarchic policy.[34] Although the Socialists have become the butt of Gaullist criticism, in certain areas of economic and industrial policy, there are evidently some similarities.

Successful bilateral Franco-German economic co-operation has, until recently, largely been limited to aerospace and military ventures. In space technology, Bonn's withdrawal from an earlier European rocket scheme and the latter's termination in 1973 created friction with Paris. However, in aviation, the European Airbus has been an outstanding success, though it should be recalled that this is a multilateral entreprise.[35] In the military sphere, the C160 'Transall' transport plane and the Bréguet Atlantic reconnaissance aircraft have been produced jointly or with German minority participation. The 'Alpha Jet' military trainer is a more recent project. Yet even in this apparently successful area, it is worth noting Schwarz's observation that joint ventures with the Federal Republic have proved attractive to France for the financial rather than the technical contribution of the German aerospace industry.[36] One should also recall that France has co-operated with the United Kingdom on high technology projects such as Concorde and the Jaguar fighter. Nor have all bilateral Franco-German ventures borne fruit: plans for a joint battle tank, vertical take-off aircraft, and helicopter all proved stillborn in the 1960s.

The tank project indeed provides an object lesson in the susceptibility of co-operative ventures to political vicissitudes, both internal and external. Resurrected enthusiastically in February 1980 in the wake of the Soviet invasion of Afghanistan,

---

[34] Figures from the *Financial Times*, 6 Feb. 1982. On recent profitability, see the *Financial Times*, 11 Aug. and 13 Sept. 1984.

[35] On the Airbus, see Hanns H. Schumacher, 'Europe's Airbus Programme and the Impact of British Participation', *The World Today* (Aug. 1979).

[36] Jürgen Schwarz, *Die Europapolitik Frankreichs unter Georges Pompidou als Problem der westeuropäischen Gemeinschaftsbildung* (Ebenhausen/Isar, Stiftung Wissenschaft und Politik, 1973), 119.

the project turned into a political yo-yo. Misgivings on the German side had already become evident by July 1980, and by March 1981 the scheme appeared likely to fall victim to German budget cuts, an impression confirmed at the May 1982 Schmidt–Mitterrand summit. The German change of Government of 1983 appeared to offer the venture a new lease of life, with the CDU-led coalition setting great store by the prospect of increased bilateral co-operation with France in the military field. But the fundamental problem that military leaders in the two countries still had rather different conceptions of the tank's operational role remained unresolved. Finally, by early 1984 the tank scheme had been shelved. With an irony that befits some aspects of military planning, it is now an anti-tank helicopter, which is shaping up to be the major Franco-German collaborative venture of the 1980s.

Finally, it is worth taking note of the former imbalance in bilateral military co-operation. This is illustrated by the Federal Republic's heavy investment in French military equipment, amounting to some six billion Deutschemarks by 1973.[37] It should be recalled, however, that this figure is inflated by the constraints on indigenous German military production in the immediate post-war period.

The generally disappointing nature of bilateral economic co-operation at government level has often been mirrored in the private sector, despite government attempts to improve contacts between firms and stimulate mutual investment. Capital movements and investment between the two countries have not matched the intensity of their bilateral trade. At the end of 1977, France ranked fifth in terms of the size of its investment in the Federal Republic, while the latter in 1975 came first in France. Two years later, France was accounting for 9.8 per cent of total German foreign investment.[38] As to where these funds have been directed, both countries have tended to concentrate their investments in chemicals, pharmaceuticals, and heavy industry, as well as other major industrial sectors such as electronics and machine tools.

A number of factors have contributed to the relatively low

[37] Lapie and Schmid, 10.
[38] Data from Deubner *et al.* 'Deutsch-französische Wirtschaftsbeziehungen', 94, and Deubner *et al.* 'Die Internationalisierung der westdeutschen Wirtschaft', 48.

levels of Franco-German bilateral investment. Amongst these must be included capital shortages in France and French industry's historically lower export orientation. The French Government's more restrictive policy towards foreign investment has probably also been a disincentive. Yet this has not been an exclusively French phenomenon. In an uncharacteristic display of chauvinism, Bonn in late 1968 blocked the sale of Gelsenkirchener Bergwerks—the country's largest mineral oil refining concern—to the Compagnie Française des Pétroles. The decision aroused considerable hostility in France. In the 1980's, it has been interesting to follow the Federal Cartel Office's treatment of a variety of acquisition proposals in the domestic electronics field. A scheme by Philips to purchase Grundig was rejected, the proposal by France's Thomson-Brandt to take on the loss-making domestic appliance division of AEG-Telefunken approved, and a second Philips offer for Grundig also sanctioned. These differing reactions say much for the changing views of Germany's anti-trust authorities towards rationalizations and the creation of larger European combines in the face of intensive, often non-EEC, competition and technological challenge.

There has also developed a troubling demographic aspect to bilateral Franco-German investment, in the form of the concentration of German firms in Alsace-Lorraine. While describing the level of German investment in France as low, Pompidou on his visit to Bonn in September 1969 expressed the clear desire that it should not in future be so regionally focused.[39] In the late 1960s and early 1970s, German firms in fact accounted for almost one third of new jobs created in the *départements* on France's eastern border.[40] Yet although the issue has caused some concern in Paris it is hardly surprising that local authorities in these depressed regions should have sought to encourage new investment, irrespective of origin. This approach bears comparison with the action of certain British authorities, notably in Wales, where Japanese investment has been energetically attracted. The establishment of German concerns in Alsace-Lorraine has also

[39] In Ziebura, *Die deutsch-französischen Beziehungen*, 149.
[40] Lapie and Schmid, 37. See also the article by Susan J. Koch, 'The Local Impact of the European Economic Community: The Economic and Social Ties of Alsace with West Germany', *International Organization* (Spring 1974).

been presented as preferable to further increases in the very large number of French workers crossing the border every day, drawn by the higher wages and often better working conditions found in German factories.[41] On a different note, the effect on land and property values of purchases by wealthy Germans seeking holiday homes has also caused local resentment.

Historical and psychological influences

In terms of political structure and international standing, the end of the Second World War left France and Germany on very different footings. While one nation was aligned with the victors, the other lay occupied and discredited. Whereas France retained the trappings of a traditional nation state, the Federal Republic, gaining its sovereignty only in 1949, represented (theoretically, at least) a break with the past. This difference in the two countries' backgrounds often resulted in dissimilar attitudes towards European integration—generally viewed more sympathetically in Germany than France. In addition, the war also imposed a considerable and continuing constraint on German foreign policy, which is still capable of arousing suspicion among its partners.

The assurance of external security and the restoration of international respectability formed twin aims of Adenauer's immediate post-war foreign policy.[42] To a large extent the two objectives overlapped, as in membership of NATO and, to a lesser degree, integrative schemes like the ECSC and EEC, which in themselves greatly assisted the country's rehabilitation. From the outset, European integration had a predominantly political significance for the Federal Republic, representing a guarantee of peace, freedom, and security, and ensuring a free and equitable internal social and political system. Interestingly, this latter political aspect has been re-echoed in some of the arguments in recent years for the accession of new democracies like Greece, Spain, and Portugal into the Community. Not least, integration would accelerate the Federal Republic's rehabilita-

[41] On this theme see Farquharson and Holt, *Europe from Below*, 95–7.
[42] On Adenauer's twin aims, see Konrad Adenauer, 'Germany and Europe', *Foreign Affairs* (Apr. 1953), and 'The German Problem—a world problem', *Foreign Affairs* (Oct.–1962).

tion and provide an alternative identity to its discredited nationalism. To quote Besson: 'In the post-war period, the very word Europe had a fascination like no other because it seemed to hold all hope for the future.'[43] Hence the appeal of European integration for many German politicians, especially a Catholic Rhinelander like Adenauer. This allure, combined with the removal of any nationalist options in the country's foreign policy, was reflected (as in the case of Italy and the IVth French Republic, but certainly not the Vth) in the inclusion of the principle of a transfer of sovereignty to a future supranational body in the national Constitution. As Dahrendorf has written: 'For our divided country, Europe has always been a substitute for lost national identity.'[44]

As suggested above, disillusionment with nationalism and the nation state in the aftermath of the war was not an exclusively German phenomenon, but widespread throughout Europe (though bypassing most Britons). It found expression in the upsurge of federalism, which aimed to create, by way of the 'political will' of the people, a pan-European institutional structure intended to prevent a recurrence of the mistakes of the past. Nor was France, despite its long tradition of nationalism, isolated from such sentiment. The work of Jean Monnet and his collaborators in fact provided the impetus for post-war integration.[45] Yet from the outset the French position was less clear-cut than that of the other Europeans. Furthermore, while German support for a measure of supranationality continued largely undimmed into the 1970s, only more recently coming to be underplayed, feeling in France waned considerably earlier, in a complicated jumble of causes in which latent nationalism and traditional suspicion of Germany played a notable part.

For the Germans, political considerations remained pre-eminent throughout the 1950s, witnessed vividly in Adenauer's

[43] Waldemar Besson, *Die Aussenpolitik der Bundesrepublik. Erfahrungen und Massstäbe* (Munich, Piper, 1970), 89.

[44] Ralf Dahrendorf, quoted in Wolfgang J. Mommsen, 'Nationalbewusstsein und Staatsverständnis der Deutschen', in Picht, *Deutschland–Frankreich—Europa*, 41.

[45] For comparison of French and German attitudes to nationalism, see Mommsen, op. cit.; René Rémond, 'Staat und Nation in Frankreich'; and Jürgen Schwarz, 'National-staat versus internationale Föderation; Divergenzen und Konvergenzen in der französischen und deutschen Europapolitik', all in Picht, *Deutschland—Frankreich—Europa*; also, Klaus Otto Nass, *Gefährdete Freundschaft* (Bonn, Europa Union, 1971).

support for the EEC rather than the rival British Free Trade Area proposals. Unlike the latter, the Community would provide the Federal Republic with a political cloak—and later a springboard—for its foreign policy, permitting a role in international affairs otherwise unattainable so soon after the war. Yet neither were considerations of economic self-interest absent from the Federal Republic's calculations.

In the 1960s, the effect of dissimilar historical backgrounds and post-war positions on French and German foreign policy was arguably even more salient than in the previous decade. This was a result principally of de Gaulle's accession to the presidency. For the General, France was a country whose history and tradition placed it at the forefront of Europe, and whose entire self-presentation, therefore, should reflect that world power status. If anything, the slights France had suffered at the hands of Germany and (to de Gaulle's mind) the Allies during the war, the shame of defeat in Indo–China, and especially the trauma of the Algerian crisis, had increased the importance of these considerations. Hence the constant stress in French external policy under de Gaulle on prestige and autonomy. This was manifested most assertively in the creation of an independent nuclear deterrent—an option wholly precluded to countries like Germany (and Japan, no less strong economically) by their past. This image of France has proved surprizingly durable, despite setbacks both at home and abroad, notably in 1968, its continuing credibility owing much to a governmental system concentrating power in the presidency, making for clear and decisive articulation of policy. These characteristics were highly evident throughout French European policy under de Gaulle, and were seen in his emphasis on the nation state and consequent hostility to supranationality. Not for him the *apatrides* of Brussels. Inter-governmentalism, rather, was the watchword.

For the Federal Republic, historical and psychological factors extended the value of integration well into the 1960s.[46] Hence German reluctance, in conjunction with other constraints, to oppose French European policy preferences, such as the 1963

---

[46] See, for instance, Ulrich Scheuner, 'Die aussenpolitischen Probleme der neuen Bundesregierung', in DGAP, *Aussenpolitik nach der Wahl des 6. Bundestages*, 21.

and 1967 vetoes on Britain, and Bonn's desire generally to avoid friction in Community relations. Only in cases of major conflicts of interest, such as between relations with France and the United States over the Multilateral Force and GATT in the early 1960s the domestic farm vote and Paris during the formation of the CAP at a similar period, and internal economic stability and external relations during the 1968 monetary crisis, was Bonn obliged to adopt a more forceful strategy. The instances testify to some of the key criteria which govern German policy: namely maintaining good relations with the United States, preserving the agricultural vote, and combating inflation. All of these, as will be seen, have remained highly active since 1969. Only in the later 1970s have the farm vote and, to a very much lesser degree, relations with Washington, decreased in importance.

Pompidou's arrival at the Élysée heralded a greater pragmatism in French European policy.[47] Yet there was no change in presidential antipathy towards supranationality.[48] This was witnessed in the minimalist institutional approach adopted towards EMU, and the similar attitude displayed towards the proposed political co-ordination secretariat. Paris continued to stress a strict demarcation between inter-governmentalism and supranationality, sometimes taken to extremes, as in July 1973.

Such doctrinaire differentiations were only eased after May 1974. Under Giscard French European policy was placed on a more practical footing, marking at least as wide a shift from Pompidou as the latter had from de Gaulle. Although Giscard by no means shared the enthusiasm for federalism to be found in certain German circles, he none the less came to put less stress on national independence and moved away from the legalistic formulas and strict lines of demarcation between supranationality and inter-governmentalism observed in the past. Most significantly, he accepted the creation of a directly elected

[47] For an introduction to Pompidou's European policy, see Vincent Berger, 'Monsieur Pompidou et la construction de l'Europe', Mémoire pour le Diplôme d'Études Supérieures de Science Politique (Paris, Université de Droit, d'Économie et de Sciences sociales, 1973), unpublished typescript; Rials, *Les Idées politiques du Président*; Schwarz, *Die Europapolitik Frankreichs*.

[48] Jean-Pierre Teyssier, 'L'Année 1973 dans la politique étrangère du Président Pompidou', *Politique Étrangère* 4–5 (1974) 492–3, gives a good indication of the President's outlook.

European Parliament, though in the teeth of opposition objections. These, it should be noted, were partly based on the underlying thought that France could come under German domination in a more politically integrated Europe.

As to prestige, Pompidou retained his predecessor's emphasis on France's international role and standing. This was seen in the continued commitment of sizeable funds to the nuclear deterrent, despite doubts about its cost-effectiveness, and to projects such as Concorde. The tendency was no less marked in relations with other European partners—notably the Federal Republic. In this context, it is worth drawing attention to Pompidou's efforts to ensure that France should appear to speak for Europe and jointly to take credit with the United States for resolving the 1971 international monetary crisis. There undoubtedly existed an implicit sense of competition with the Germans—a consequence of traditional rivalry—which was expressed through an intensified French emphasis on prestige.[49] Hence also the weight placed on occupation rights in Germany and on France's status as one of the Four Berlin Powers.

Despite the differences in policy towards the European Community between Pompidou and Giscard, considerations of national prestige and French status in the world did not noticeably diminish after 1974. But internal political divisions may have played a role. The lack of respect shown to Giscard by the frequently uncooperative tactics of Chirac and the Gaullists after 1976 did have some limited side-effects in international terms in dulling the lustre of the President and, as a consequence, France itself. Chirac's announcement, for instance, of his candidacy for the mayorship of Paris in opposition to d'Ornano, the President's chosen representative, was made on the eve of Giscard's state visit to Saudi Arabia. Internal political differences aside, Giscard's presidency undoubtedly made for a relaxation in the often stifling atmosphere of state ceremonial, although this change of style was not intended to detract from the importance of the occasions themselves.

Internationally, Giscard continued to emphasize France's major role in world affairs. This was illustrated most conspicu-

---

[49] On this question of prestige, especially in comparison with the Federal Republic, see Alfred Frisch, 'Les Relations franco-allemandes, une amitié solide et fragile à la fois', *Documents* (Sept. 1976), 6–7.

ously in his African policy, where French military intervention exemplified the country's ability and determination, not only to intervene abroad in order to protect its own citizens and the territorial integrity of a friendly state, but also to act, like the United States, as a policeman in world affairs when necessary. Only after increased Libyan activity in Chad in the late 1970s and France's inability to provide an adequate response was this image tarnished. As to the picture after May 1981, first impressions might have suggested that foreign interventions on a Giscardian scale would be less likely under Mitterrand. However, the prolonged deployment of 2,000 French troops in Lebanon as part of the international peace-keeping force and the sanctioning of direct air strikes against 'terrorist' targets, implied that the new President was likely to pursue a course as active as his predecessor. Mitterrand clearly has a highly Gaullist conception of the international role of France—and its leader— and there are no grounds to suppose that the traditional emphasis on French prestige and *rayonnement* in the world will in any way abate under the Élysée's new tenant. Certainly, the President himself—urbane, highly literate, widely travelled, and a little Olympian—aptly fits in with the image of previous incumbents in the Vth Republic.

Defence policy is a particularly interesting field for comparing French and German attitudes. Pompidou's decision to station France's short-range Pluton missiles on its eastern border, thereby restricting their capability to within the bounds of the Federal Republic, rather than positioning them in West Germany itself, provided a vivid example both of France's continuing emphasis on strategic independence and the some-what equivocal nature of its relations with its neighbour.[50] This is made abundantly clear in comments reportedly made by Messmer, a former defence minister under de Gaulle and Prime Minister under Pompidou, who implied that France's defence policy, based on the sanctity of its national frontiers, was designed to provide an inbuilt element of delay before the decision to use nuclear weapons would have to be taken. Only when a Soviet aggressor had broken into West Germany and was

[50] On the missile issue, see Poidevin and Bariéty, 339. For the position under Giscard, see Otto Pick, 'Theme and Variations: the foreign policy of France', *The World Today* (Oct. 1980).

threatening France itself would the weapons be fired. Under these circumstances, it was reasoned, the Russians would not themselves respond with a nuclear strike on France as their troops would have been attacked on West German soil and Soviet territory itself would not have been harmed. If accurate, this is a remarkably cynical and short-sighted assessment.[51]

However, it was in the economic sector that a sense of competition with West Germany was most evident under Pompidou. The President's interest—exceeding even that shown by de Gaulle—in building up French industry represented an ambition aimed at least partly (for outward electoral purposes, if not more) at equalling and outstripping the Federal Republic.[52] This emphasis on French industrialization and, what is more, the use of Germany and Japan as economic models, have been equally characteristic of the Giscard and Mitterrand presidencies. In fact, it has been plausibly argued that Giscard's repeated invocations of France's need to compete with such countries and his honest expositions of the difficulties and sacrifices required in order to succeed were amongst the factors which cost him the presidency.[53] Certainly, the rosier economic options offered by Mitterrand during the election campaign were more effective in vote-catching terms.

What can be said of the role of historical and psychological forces in West Germany in the early 1970s? Although Brandt, unlike his predecessor Kiesinger, could not be identified with the Third Reich, and the occasional outbursts of German politicians such as Schmidt or Apel belied the impression, historical factors remained an important constraint on external policy. Outside the economic sector, the Federal Republic's willingness to take on greater responsibilities appeared inconsistent, if not erratic. The 1973 Middle East war and the oil crisis provided an object lesson in the country's continuing dependence on the European Community. With the whole question of relations with Israel and the Arabs coloured by the genocide, the underlying value for the Germans of joint Community statements on the Middle East

---

[51] The information derives from Françoise Giroud, *La Comédie du pouvoir* (Paris, Le Livre de Poche, 1979), 184.

[52] On Pompidou's attitude to German industrial competition and on French industrialization see Rials, 65–78; Roussel, *Pompidou*, 438–44; Berger, 30; Frisch, 7–8.

[53] See Alain Duhamel, *La République de M. Mitterrand* (Paris, Grasset, 1982), 31–6.

and energy was brought into the sharpest relief.[54] Some seven and a half years later, in early 1981, both Premier Begin's bitter attacks on the Federal Republic and Chancellor Schmidt personally, and the German Government's dilemma regarding the question of arms sales to Saudi Arabia illustrated the continued currency of the problem. Further confirmation, if any were required, came in the renewed Israeli castigations of February 1982 and in Germany's uneasy position in the Community's decisions on the Middle East, both at Venice in summer 1980 and, in the wake of the Israeli invasion of Lebanon of June 1982, at the European Council meeting in Brussels later that month. Most recently, Chancellor Kohl's visit to Israel in January 1984 proved only a little more successful than that undertaken by his predecessor, the question of arms sales to the Saudis still being a major bone of contention.

There were, however, signs of changing German attitudes to the principle of federalism in the European Community during Brandt's term of office. The shift indicated the development of West Germany's own position since the 1950s, and also a pragmatic assessment in Bonn that a reduced emphasis on supranationality was a perhaps unavoidable price to pay for minimizing friction in relations with Paris. Certainly, in the later 1970s, Schmidt's less sympathetic attitude towards federalist aims indirectly helped to promote the *rapprochement* with Giscard and thus progress in the Community.

Despite these developments, the force of historical and psychological factors remains such that it will be many years before Germany's self-presentation and its foreign policy match those of France. Post-1974 Giscardian liberalism and realistic awareness of interdependence notwithstanding, the nation state remains supreme, even under Mitterrand. For the Germans, there persist significant constraints. Politicians in Bonn sense the danger of isolation arising out of a possible defensive reaction from their partners when faced with the country's overwhelming economic strength. For example, there were clear signs of such a response by the Gaullists and Communists in France in the face

---

[54] For the German position in the oil crisis, see Henri Ménudier, 'L'Allemagne Fédérale. Puissance et dépendance', in Alfred Grosser (ed.), *Les Politiques extérieures européennes dans la crise*, Fondation Nationale des Sciences Politiques, Travaux et Recherches de Science Politique No. 43 (Paris, Presses de la FNSP, 1976).

of Giscard's European policies and tight links with Schmidt. Similarly, one German policy-maker suggested to the author that the decision to site the Joint European Torus project at Culham in Britain rather than Garching in Bavaria implied the influence of considerations other than those strictly relevant to the venture's scientific and economic success. Such comments may be passed off as sour grapes, but the upshot has been a reluctance in Bonn to press its weight, both out of self-interest—to maximize gains from the Community—and to advance integration. Memories of the war, combined with the Federal Republic's geopolitical significance as a fulcrum between East and West, place German actions under close international scrutiny. This was tellingly illustrated in President Carter's letter of warning to Chancellor Schmidt in summer 1980, prior to his visit to Moscow, and, in early 1982, in the similar suspicions that were aroused in Washington and some European capitals regarding Bonn's response to the declaration of martial law in Poland. Thus, in order to avoid friction, German leaders are conscious of a greater obligation to consult with their allies and explain their actions than colleagues abroad. This situation was regularly visible during the *Ostpolitik*, when the Brandt Government sought to keep its partners informed of developments, though often failing to allay suspicions about its actions, notably in France. The other side of the coin is a possible tendency in Bonn to overcompensate at times in its dealings with its allies.

Despite the lowered constraints on German foreign policy since the *Ostpolitik*, the European Community remains more important for the Federal Republic than for its partners. The Community continues to provide a convenient political cloak and to represent a workable substitute to forgotten or repressed nationalism. Any attempt by German leaders to recreate an overtly nationalist approach to European policy would be both artificial and regarded as highly suspect by Germans and foreigners alike. Instead, national identity has grown synonymous with the survival of the Community, which has become second nature to the Germans. This approach contrasts markedly with attitudes in France (and Britain) and is more akin to feelings in the Benelux countries.

As in the 1960s, it is in the military sphere that the contrast between the external opportunities facing France and Germany has in recent years been most obviously exposed. Above all, Giscard's interventionist policies in Africa highlighted this distinction. It would be out of the question for Bonn to undertake similar measures outside the NATO framework in emulation of Paris.[55] Giscard's military involvement in Mauritania, Chad, the Central African Empire, and Zaïre, entailing logistical support, supplies of equipment, and direct participation by French war planes or troops, forcefully illustrated the President's determination to ensure the continued availability of imported sources of raw materials and to protect French economic interests and citizens abroad.[56] A similar readiness to lend assistance has already been demonstrated by Mitterrand in Lebanon and Chad.

Though criticized in some quarters, at a time of American inaction Giscard's bold strokes, calling to mind de Gaulle's own interventionist measures, demonstrated France's determination and power. In terms of relations with Germany, they illustrated the distance between the two countries as far as the military sector was concerned. It should be recalled that even the (perhaps ill-considered) venture by an independent German consortium to develop a satellite rocket launcher in Zaïre came to nothing, partly as a result of the international controversy and suggestions of potential military spin-offs aroused.[57]

Perhaps most interesting from a British point of view were the signally different reactions from Paris and Bonn to the Falklands war of 1982. These gave a further indication of the disparity between the two countries' attitudes towards military options. Mitterrand's firm support for Britain's deployment of a naval task force contrasted with Schmidt's less convinced appraisal. Such divergent reactions, not only reflected differing policy interests (and not least, trading priorities) between France and Germany. More deeply, they also brought to light substantially different conceptions of the use of military force as an instrument in foreign policy. There appeared to be a sharp cleft between the

[55] Note Schmidt's comments along these lines in *The Economist*, 26 May 1979.
[56] On Giscard's African policy, see especially Julian Crandall Hollick, 'French intervention in Africa in 1978', *The World Today* Feb. (1979); J. R. Frears, *France in the Giscard Presidency* (London, George Allen and Unwin, 1981), 112–17.
[57] On this topic and the venture's troubles, see e.g. *The Economist*, 19 May 1979.

broad acceptance of this principle within the French Government, and the much more measured consideration of the pros and cons on the German side. Such differences lay rooted in the two countries' dissimilar historical backgrounds and the continuing after-effects of the Second World War on German policy. On nuclear disarmament too, the substantially different levels of support given to anti-nuclear movements in the two countries provides another indication of the same phenomenon. Though naturally the subject arouses greater passions in Germany because of that country's exposed position, deeper reasons are also involved, resting on dissimilar views among significant blocks of the French and German people, notably the young, concerning the role of military power in foreign policy.

The influence of historical and psychological factors on France and Germany has been reflected most clearly in their bilateral relations. Great emphasis was placed after 1945 on fostering popular links between the two countries, seen as an essential element in the reconciliation process. The humanitarian side featured widely in the 1963 Franco-German Treaty, which in itself formalized and extended a number of earlier schemes. Particular attention has been paid to the young, the enlightened views of a new generation seen as holding out the best prospect for preventing future conflict. Youth exchanges, town-twinnings, and cultural events have all been organized on an unprecedented scale. Since 1963, this has largely been under the auspices of the Franco-German Youth Office.[58] The results have been in many ways impressive; though, partly on account of what has been achieved and also, perhaps, under pressure from competing

---

[58] On these activities and the role of cultural co-operation, see Office Franco-Allemand pour la Jeunesse (OFAJ)—Deutsch-französische Jugendwerk (DFJW), *Rapport d'activité- —Tätigkeitsbericht 1963-73* (Bad Honnef, OFAJ/DFJW, 1973) OFAJ/DFJW, *15 Ans Office Franco-Allemand pour la Jeunesse 1963-78* (Bad Honnef, OFAJ/DFJW, 1978). Empirical evidence on the results of youth exchanges can be seen in OFAJ/DFJW, 'Les 15-24 ans et les échanges franco-allemands', OFAJ/DFJW, *Rapports et Documents* 9 and 10 (1976); B. M. Boyer, *L'Étude Scientifique des stéréotypes nationaux dans les rapports franco-allemands* (Paris, Université de Paris 1, Département de Science Politique, 1972). For critical appraisal of the Franco-German Youth Office, see: Farquharson and Holt, *Europe from Below*; Ziebura, *Die deutsch-französischen Beziehungen*, 155-7; Robert Picht, 'Kulturelle Beziehungen als Voraussetzung deutsch-französischer Kommunikation'; and Rüdiger Stephan, 'Die akademische Beziehungen—Für eine transnationale Konzeption internationaler Zusammenarbeit', both in Picht, *Deutschland—Frankreich—Europa*, 243-306; Lapie and Schmid, 17-31; Poidevin and Bariéty, 352-3.

Anglo–Saxon, especially American, influences, there appears to have been a loss of momentum in recent years, accompanied by a rethinking of ideas and reduced funding. However, certain continuing problems should be pointed out. First of all, although the evidence of opinion polls confirms that a warm bond has been established on both sides of the Rhine, other data strongly suggests an asymmetry in Franco-German mutual attitudes.[59] Figures demonstrate that Germans have generally been more responsive to bilateral projects and the activities of the Youth Office than their French partners. Furthermore, one must also bear in mind Ziebura's view (although it is over-critical) that, despite the enormous efforts made, none but the grossest misunderstandings have in fact been eradicated.[60]

The lesson for the 1980s must be to direct the resources of the Youth Office further towards applied or functional projects in order to overcome the danger of the institution degenerating into little more than a large-scale travel agency. In particular, attention should be given to contemporary social questions such as unemployment, the role of new technology, and the effect of the shorter working week, subjects which would all benefit from discussion and treatment at bilateral level. Many of the original functions of the Youth Office as first conceived have already been fulfilled. There are now strong arguments in favour of new projects, like improving communication between groups such as trade unions and ordinary businessmen in the two countries. Efforts should also be directed towards those whose knowledge of the partner country's language is weak or lacking—formerly a neglected sector. Co-operation between economic research bodies in France and Germany is another area that might be suitable for action.

In education, considerable attention has been placed in both countries on stimulating the learning of one another's language. The experiment has not, however, entirely lived up to expectations. In fact, the language issue provides an interesting

[59] For opinion poll data, see, in addition to the Franco-German Youth Office material cited above Jacques-René Rabier, 'Préjugés français et préjugés allemands', *Documents* (Jan.–Feb. 1969); Henri Isaïa, 'L'Opinion publique française et les Communautés Européennes', in Rideau *et al.*, 342–3; Robert James Shepherd, *Public Opinion and European Integration* (Farnborough, Saxon House, 1975); Ziebura, *Die deutsch-französischen Beziehungen*, 82–84, 130–1.

[60] Ziebura, 155.

illustration of the role of culture and prestige in French foreign policy.[61] President Pompidou, in particular, held the place of his mother tongue extremely dear—a reflection, no doubt, of his early pedagogical career. Certainly, the subjugation of French to English on the school curriculum in many of the *Länder* was a frequent topic of complaint at the bilateral Franco-German summits.[62] Despite changes made by the Germans to put French on an equal footing, it is instructive to note that English remains by far the most popular choice of second language in both France and the Federal Republic. That German is learned much more widely in France than vice versa is a possible illustration of the Federal Republic's impact on French schoolchildren as the dominant economic power.

It is in the field of information and mutual knowledge that the effect of psychological factors on bilateral Franco-German relations has been most evident and the asymmetry most marked, though matters have improved since the mid-1970s.[63] Obstacles remain, however, and there continues a disquieting tendency in the press, particularly on the French side, to revert to clichés during periods of friction. Study of the media in the two countries reveals a distinct imbalance, good relations with France meaning more for the Germans than vice versa. This factor is attributable to a variety of causes. There persists in the Federal Republic a tendency to view friendship with other countries as a means of enhancing national

[61] On this theme, see Nass, *Gefährdete Freundschaft*, 78.

[62] On the language question, see Rials, 133; Dieter Menyesch and Henrik Uterwedde, 'Der deutsch-französische Vertrag und seine Verwirklichung', in *Dokumente*, Special number, 'Die deutsch-französischen Beziehungen seit 1963' (Dec. 1978); Poidevin and Bariéty, 351; Lapie and Schmid, 14.

[63] A great deal has come to be written on the subject of information in Franco-German relations and the influence of the media on mutual attitudes. See especially OFAJ/DFJW, *Bulletin de Liaison*, June 1974, 'Les Problèmes d'information dans les relations franco-allemandes'; Henri Ménudier, 'Die Rolle der Information in den deutsch-französischen Beziehungen', in Picht, *Deutschland — Frankreich — Europa*, and 'Die Information — Quelle für Konflikte oder Kooperation?', in *Dokumente*, 'Die deutsch-französischen Beziehungen'; Christoph Steinbrink, 'Bilan critique des relations franco-allemandes dix ans après le traité entre la France et la RFA', *L'Allemagne d'aujourd'hui* (Sept.–Oct. 1973); Robert Picht, 'La Réception de l'information par l'opinion publique', and Henri Ménudier, 'L'Information en France sur la RFA', both in *Documents* (Jan.–Feb. 1974); Alfred Frisch, 'Une symphonie inachevée', *Documents* (Mar.–Apr. 1974), and 'Les Relations franco-allemandes'; Henri Ménudier, 'L'Image de l'Allemagne à la télévision française — ou le bastion du passéisme', *Études* (Apr. 1975). Finally, see *Documents*, Special number, 'Information et communication. Les media et les relations franco-allemandes' (Dec. 1979).

respectability. France, in particular, retains a mystique for many Germans, its culture and lifestyle somewhat reverently respected in a country that, despite a material success envied elsewhere, often appears to search for some undefined quality felt lacking in itself.

On the French side, although the situation improved under Giscard, a number of important groups and élites still retain an unfavourable image of the Federal Republic. Opinion on the left, in particular, has in the past been generally hostile and suspicious of the neighbour across the Rhine. Whether the Socialists' accession to power is bringing about any permanent change of attitudes is a pertinent question. The evidence is as yet insufficient. However, although Jean Genet's apology in *Le Monde* for the activities of the Baader-Meinhof group and castigation of a West German Government within a country which is 'eternal, terrifying, and monstrous' represented an extreme example, the psychological effect of the war has only served in some quarters to intensify more recent impressions of Teutonic ruthlessness and disregard for human rights.[64] Archaic and authoritarian structures such as the *Berufsverbot*; unduly frequent examples of police heavy-handedness; and occasional scandals following revelations about the Nazi backgrounds of prominent politicians; all heighten international scrutiny of the Federal Republic's democratic credentials and prolong the adverse image caused by the war.

Conclusion

The preceding analysis has highlighted various disparities in a number of key areas affecting French and German foreign policy. That such differences have often underscored the dissimilar positions adopted by successive French and German governments will be more fully illustrated later in this book. It has already emerged, however, that the constraints faced by the two countries have by no means remained static. In fact, French and German requirements and responses have in many ways moved closer together, especially since the mid-1970s.

[64] Jean Genet, 'Violence et brutalité', *Le Monde*, 2 Sept. 1977. Henri Ménudier considers the article in the wider context of information and the media in 'De quelle Allemagne parlez-vous?' *Documents* (Dec. 1977). Klaus-Peter Schmidt looks at the question of *Le Monde*'s editorial policy, in 'Le Monde und die Bundesrepublik Deutschland', *Aus Politik und Zeitgeschichte*, No. 12/79. Finally, note Giscard's own comments on the subject in *Le Monde*, 15 Sept. 1977.

Until May 1981, this had been most evident in the economic sphere. Community membership resulted in a gradual evolution in French trading patterns away from former colonies towards European partners in a model closer to that of the Federal Republic. Similarly, between 1969 and 1981, French economic thinking grew more akin to that of West Germany. Greater emphasis came to be placed on combating inflation and a more critical appraisal was made of the state's role in industry. These developments were witnessed most clearly in the economic policies pursued by Barre in the later 1970s.

With the Socialists' accession to power, however, a new divergence appeared to be in the offing. The policy of widespread nationalization and the large increases in social security benefits and the minimum wage energetically carried out by the new government in its first year of office all suggested a novel set of priorities substantially different from those of West Germany. That there has been a signal reversal of course more recently owes as much to the force of circumstances as to growing experience and pragmatism. Certainly, for the time being at least, the control of inflation and management of the balance of payments, even at the expense of economic growth, are imperatives as characteristic of France as the Federal Republic. Whether paths will once again diverge in a period of restored economic recovery or in the wake of a shift to the left in the French Socialist Party remains an open question.

Elsewhere, the *détente* in East–West relations of the early 1970s meant that the influence of geographical factors—above all the Federal Republic's proximity to the Eastern bloc—eased considerably. As has been seen, this allowed Bonn a far wider room for manœuvre in its foreign policy and put it on a more equal footing with Paris in terms of its external opportunities. Yet geographical considerations still impose a special handicap on German foreign policy. This makes Bonn far more conscious of security needs and, above all, puts a special premium on the preservation of good relations with the United States.

However, with East–West relations having entered a new period of tension in the 1980s, the Federal Republic's position has grown more complicated. A return to the restricted scope of the 1950s and 1960s is hardly likely. But Bonn will have to proceed carefully, balancing solidarity with Washington against the need to maintain a line of contact, however weak, with Moscow. In this already complex network of relationships, matters are further confused by the prospect of friction between the United States and West Germany over trade, not only with the Eastern bloc, but also across the Atlantic.

As for France, its Alliance policy since 1969 (and especially 1974) was marked by a greater sense of interdependence and a more collaborative approach in the military sphere. However, its less exposed geographical position has throughout meant that external security, though undoubtedly treated as a priority, does not provoke the same singular anxiety or necessitate the same degree of external dependence as is the case in the Federal Republic. This has remained no less true since May 1981. Yet Mitterrand's accession to power and his emphasis on Western security, and, ironically, the very existence of Communist ministers in the Government, until summer 1984, have resulted in an intensification of French support for the Alliance. The reintegration of French forces into the military wing of NATO is not on the cards, but the West has gained a forceful advocate of collective security and firm tactics towards Moscow.

In terms of psychological influences, the differences between France and West Germany remain considerable. Though the constraints imposed by the Second World War on German foreign policy will continue to abate gradually, one can only speculate as to when this process will reach an end. In certain areas—most obviously German relations with Israel—this hypothetical point in time seems extremely distant. On the other hand, it is worth bearing in mind the contemporary observations made by one German newspaper regarding certain of Schmidt's followers that: 'Today they are suffering in Bonn from the complex of no longer wanting to have any complexes.'[65] While there is some truth in this statement, it is undeniable that psychological constraints leave German policy-makers with more restricted options than their colleagues in other Community capitals. In the only slightly exaggerated words of one official, 'Europeans would not want to be led by Germany even towards paradise.'[66] The psychological

---

[65] *Deutsche Allgemeine Sonntagsblatt*, quoted in Alfred Grosser, 'Portée et limites du bilatéralisme franco-allemand', in DFI, *Deutschland, Frankreich und die europäische Krise*, 21.

[66] Geoffrey Edwards and Helen Wallace, 'Germany in the Chair', *The World Today* (Jan. 1979), 5.

constraints on independent German action are most evident in the military sphere, and it is here that the contrast with France has consistently been at its most marked.

As to French attitudes, national prestige and identity, and France's role as a world power, remain key elements. Thus Giscard's African interventions represented not just attempts to secure specific external objectives, but were also statements affirming a particular place for France in the world. French views towards West Germany are considerably more complex. Despite the post-war reconciliation between the two countries, there persists a degree of uncertainty on the French side regarding its partner. In the 1980s, the widespread and very vocal activities of anti-nuclear and peace groups have heightened French anxieties. However, as will become evident in later chapters, concern about German policy and intentions was to be especially characteristic of the Pompidou presidency, at a time when Germany's external standing was undergoing a substantial revision.

3

Politics and Institutions

The institutional framework

The historical differences between France and Germany outlined in the previous chapter have been reflected in dissimilarities between their political institutions. These differences have in turn played an important part in both the formation and presentation of the two countries' foreign policies. Dissimilar constitutional arrangements, making for greater or lesser degrees of executive authority, parliamentary control, and interest group penetration, have established the framework for different sets of constraints and opportunities for governmental policy-makers. Such institutional and political factors have consequently had an influence on the broad lines of foreign policy—assertive or conciliatory, strident or lower-key—that have become characteristic of Paris and Bonn. Added to the effect of these institutional forces has been the influence of dissimilar policy co-ordination systems in the two countries. Co-ordination mechanisms have become particularly important as a result of the increasing complexities of European policy-making, and efficient policy co-ordination has consequently become a *sine qua non* for a coherent external stance. As will become clear, French and German policy co-ordination methods have not always been equally effective.

It is in the national Constitutions, and the bodies established thereunder, that historical differences between France and Germany have been most strikingly illustrated.[1] The Constitution of the Vth French Republic was a clear attempt to break

---

[1] As an introduction to the effect of different political structures on French and German foreign policies, see Schwarz, 'Nationalstaat versus internationale Föderation', 158–61. On the IVth Republic's Constitution, see David Thomson, *Democracy in France since 1870*, 5th edn., (London, OUP/RIIA, 1969), 237–44. Also, on the Vth Republic's Constitution, see Thomson, 265–74; H. Ehrmann, *Politics in France*, 3rd edn. (Boston, Little Brown, 1976). On the Constitution of the Federal Republic of Germany, see Thomas Ellwein, *Das Regierungssystem der Bundesrepublik Deutschland*, 4th edn. (Opladen, Westdeutscher Verlag, 1972); L. J. Edinger, *Politics in West Germany* (Boston, Little Brown, 1977).

away from the serious instability of its predecessor. Hence the stress on a strong executive and weak legislature in a Constitution which, as Thomson notes, 'was privately tailor-made to fit General de Gaulle by a government that he had handpicked'.[2] The result was a structure of executive authority which has to this day greatly assisted the exercise of an assertive foreign policy.

The German *Grundgesetz* of 1949 was an even more radical departure, representing a reaction against both the weaknesses of the Weimar Republic and, more important, the abuses of power of the Third Reich. This last concern underscored the devolution of many responsibilities to the separate *Länder* in the country's federal structure, a sharp contrast with the legalistic and highly centralized formula traditional in France. In its deliberate system of checks and balances, recalling the American model, the German Constitution further stood out against the deliberate imbalance of power enshrined in the Vth Republic. While the latter's Constitution had the effect of weakening the legislature, the *Grundgesetz* was drafted with the express purpose of fostering large and responsible political parties. In addition, whereas the French system has tended to minimize public debate on foreign policy by concentrating power in the presidency, assisting decisive executive action, the German model, again like that of the United States, has permitted more open discussion. This has indirectly militated against an assertive external stance, and complicated policy co-ordination.

Such constraints on the German side have been intensified by the relatively weak position of the executive. The President of France enjoys considerably greater powers than the German Chancellor, who depends on majority support in the Bundestag, and cannot claim direct election by universal suffrage as in France. This crucial development came about as a result of a constitutional amendment introduced by de Gaulle in 1962, reflecting the General's distaste for party politics, and his desire, rather, to speak directly to the French people. Nor was de Gaulle unaware of the enormous advantage direct election would grant the President over other political forces.[3]

---

[2] Thomson, 265.

[3] Note here Pompidou's comments in his memoirs, *Pour rétablir une vérité* (Paris, Flammarion, 1982), 71, 127.

This concentration of power in the French presidency has eased the formation of a decisive and coherent stance in foreign affairs—its presentation enhanced by executive control over the broadcasting media. In this area, it has been interesting to follow the Socialist Government's progress in its election pledges to place French radio and television under independent control. As regards television at least the situation is little changed from that under Giscard. Although the latter introduced an act in 1974 to reorganize the state broadcasting media, the Élysée retained a powerful informal influence through the appointment of trusted supporters to key posts.[4] Elsewhere, the Socialists' record has been mixed. Radio broadcasting has been liberalized, but controversial legislation has been passed to break up large press monopolies. Though ostensibly put forward in the name of greater press freedom, weakening the opposition Hersant newspaper group is probably the Government's main spur.

French foreign policy formulation is centred on the Élysée, under the President's direct authority. As is observed 'the French President is fully in charge of the conduct of foreign policy and, in that field, enjoys an independence far greater than the American President, who is constantly having to keep a wary eye on the reactions of Congress.'[5] Presidential authority over foreign policy has been accentuated by the tendency of incumbents to appoint close advisers to the post of Foreign Minister. This occurred with de Gaulle and Couve de Murville, Pompidou and Jobert—formerly his Secretary-General at the Élysée—and Giscard and François-Poncet.[6] This trend has been continued under Mitterrand, whose Minister for External Relations, Cheysson, was previously a close personal adviser. In this context it is interesting to note the comments to the author of one highly placed former French diplomat, who recalled Couve de Murville's care not to let himself be caught in agreement with a

---

[4] On this theme, see Duhamel, *La République de M. Mitterrand*, 118–19; Giroud, 173–4. On Mitterrand's policy, see *The Economist*, 27 Feb. 1982, and *The Times*, 1 Apr. 1982.

[5] Vincent Wright, *The Government and Politics of France* (London, Hutchinson, 1978), 33.

[6] On the position of the President in the foreign policy-making process, see, in addition to the works cited above, Pierre Gerbet, 'L'Élaboration des politiques communautaires au niveau national français', in Rideau *et al.*, 393–4; Christoph Sasse *et al.*, *Decision-making in the European Community* (New York, Praeger, 1977), 69; William Wallace, 'Old States and New Circumstances', in William E. Paterson and William Wallace (edd.), *Foreign policy-making in Western Europe* (Farnborough, Hants., Saxon House, 1978), 45–6.

ministerial proposal which might be unacceptable to the Élysée. The same source described Pompidou's first Foreign Minister, Maurice Schumann, as little more than a 'mouthpiece'. In more measured terms, Wright notes of Couve de Murville and of Giscard's first two Foreign Ministers, Sauvagnargues and de Guiringaud, that 'Each was noticeable by making himself unnoticeable, carrying diplomatic discretion to the lengths of total self-effacement.'[7] Such is the traditional role of the French Foreign Minister.

Matters are very different in Bonn, where the Chancellor is obliged to work far more closely within the confines of his party. Nor is he, like the French President, isolated from everyday political life by the presence of a Prime Minister. Within the Cabinet, the Chancellor does, however, have the *Richtlinienkompetenz*, the constitutional right to push through his views. Yet use of this power largely depends on the attitude and personality of the incumbent. As shall be seen, Chancellor Brandt was often reluctant to assert his views. By contrast, his successor proved consistently less self-denying.[8] Chancellor Kohl for his part appears to have reverted to a more collegial style.

The Chancellor's position has also been restricted by the frequency of coalition governments. Especially given political parties which are in themselves coalitions of different interests, this has complicated decision-making and increased the need for consensus. The result has generally been policies of centrism and continuity. Another effect of coalitions has been to give the Free Democrats a say over policy incommensurate with their size, a state of affairs which has often aroused or exacerbated factional conflict between the coalition partners. This occurred notably during Brandt's second term of office, and it sharply recurred

[7] Wright, 77.

[8] On the position of the Chancellor in German foreign policy-making, see, in addition to the works already cited, Hans-Peter Schwarz, 'Die Bundesregierung und die auswärtigen Beziehungen', in Hans-Peter Schwarz (ed.), *Handbuch der deutschen Aussenpolitik* (hereafter *Handbuch*) (Munich, Piper, 1976), 60–70; Nevil Johnson, *Government in the Federal Republic of Germany—the Executive at Work* (Oxford, Pergamon Press, 1973), 49–60. The best case study of the Chancellor's role is the very detailed account by Arnulf Baring, *Aussenpolitik in Adenauers Kanzlerdemokratie* (Munich, Oldenbourg, 1969). On Brandt's attitude to Cabinet government, see Brandt, 229; Terence Prittie, *Willy Brandt. Portrait of a Statesman* (London, Weidenfeld and Nicholson, 1974), 233–4; most recently, see Arnulf Baring, *Machtwechsel. Die Ära Brandt–Schmidt* (Stuttgart, Deutsche Verlags-Anstalt, 1982), 633, 657–8.

during the wranglings over the fate of the Schmidt–Genscher Government in autumn 1982. The position has not altered markedly since the March 1983 elections, although the FDP was obliged to surrender one Cabinet post. While Chancellor Kohl and other CDU leaders appear content with the present division of responsibilities, there are many, notably Strauss, who are deeply discontented with the hold that the Free Democrats have still managed to retain.

The contrast with France is particularly marked in the field of foreign affairs, where the leader of the junior German coalition partner has generally taken the post of Foreign Minister, granting him a much greater degree of independence than his French counterpart and complicating policy co-ordination. Though Brandt and Scheel shared a similar outlook on international affairs and had a good working relationship, once over a difficult initiation period, Scheel did on occasion use the influence of his party position within the coalition to secure specific foreign policy goals.[9] Similarly, during his coalition with Schmidt, Genscher was not averse to exercising occasional leverage, notably over internal policy. The intra-Coalition disputes over extending the principle of worker participation and, in 1982, on the size of the Federal budget, provided the foremost examples. It should also be recalled that, once resolved to make the break with the Social Democrats, Genscher pursued his course single-mindedly. It will be interesting to see how relations between the parties—particularly the FDP and CSU—develop in the Kohl Government.

Under Brandt, it was the FDP Minister of Agriculture, Josef Ertl, who was best able to exploit both his party and ministerial position in order to further sectional policy interests. Farm ministers in all the member states are in a relatively strong position compared to their Cabinet colleagues. Their post enjoys powerful pressure group backing and often requires specialized knowledge or expertise lacking elsewhere in the Government,

[9] On the effect of coalition Governments in German policy-making, see Udo Bermbach, 'Koalition', in Kurt Sontheimer and Hans H. Röhring, *Handbuch des politischen Systems der Bundesrepublik Deutschland* (Munich, Piper, 1978), 319–24. On relations between Brandt and Scheel and their like-minded views on foreign policy, see Karl Moersch, *Kurs-Revision. Deutsche Politik nach Adenauer* (Frankfurt, Societäts-Verlag, 1978), 168–71; Baring, *Machtwechsel*, 303.

thereby increasing their independence. The frequent necessity for compromise and package deals at Community level has reinforced this relative freedom of action. In the mid-1970s, Britain's Mr Silkin was something of an exception in his reluctance to err from his Westminster mandate—though his behaviour should be seen in the context of the Labour Party's overall attitude to the Community and the special place of farm interests in the United Kingdom. Ertl's own ability to exert pressure on government policy emanated chiefly from his position as an influential member of the FDP, and his role in keeping the party alive in Bavaria. The consequences of his behaviour were, however, seen in frequent friction in the Cabinet. This was often in turn transferred to Community level, where it on occasion restricted Bonn's bargaining power and complicated agreement among the Nine.

In all the member states certain general restrictions limit the national leglislatures' supervisory capacity over European policy.[10] Foreign policy-making is an executive task, with members of national Parliaments as a rule more concerned with domestic affairs and constituency interests. The ever-increasing volume and technicality of Community business hinders scrutiny, as does the pressure of time. In addition, particularly since direct elections, the dual mandate of some parliamentarians to both national and European assemblies can potentially result in the occasional absence from the home Parliament of those members most interested or best informed about Community affairs.

Among Community legislatures, the Bundestag enjoys rights over European policy-making second only to the Danish Folketing. The latter keeps an extremely tight rein over its Government in EEC affairs. The French National Assembly, by contrast, is in a very weak position. Thus, while there is very open debate in Bonn, bearing comparison with that in Washington, the formation of foreign policy in Paris is a much more

---

[10] On the role of the legislature in Community policy-making, see Michael Niblock, *The EEC: National Parliaments in Community Decision-making* (London, Chatham House/PEP, 1973); Helen Wallace, 'National Bulls in the Community China Shop: the role of National Governments in Community Policy-making', in Helen Wallace, William Wallace, and Carole Webb (edd.), *Policy-making in the European Communities* (London, Wiley, 1977), 47–8; Sasse, 43–73.

secretive affair. Though Community issues have become more politicized in recent years, the French National Assembly remains narrowly confined by the Vth Republic's Constitution,[11] with the governmental majority—at least under de Gaulle and Pompidou—largely an instrument of the President's will. Under Giscard the increasingly bitter in-fighting between the Gaullists and Independent Republicans altered this picture somewhat. Most recently of all, however, the traditional pattern has been reasserted. Thanks to the 1981 legislative elections, Mauroy commanded a large Socialist majority in the National Assembly, as now does Fabius. Where the cracks have emerged, however, is on the unpalatable economic policy choices being forced on the Government. These have strained—and eventually broken—the coalition with the Communists and have also caused friction within the Socialist Party itself.

The National Assembly has no procedure for obtaining prior information about decisions to be made by Community bodies, nor any opportunity to convey policy guidelines to the Government. Its Foreign Affairs Committee has little influence, the Chamber as a whole even less. As a result of the Vth Republic's Constitution, no minister can remain a member of the National Assembly; in fact, the Foreign Minister has seldom been a practising politician, thereby contributing to the Government's freedom of action. Questions relating to European integration are seldom discussed in the French Parliament, and what debate there is in France on Community affairs has not generally been conducted within its walls. The relative secrecy of the French foreign policy process has undoubtedly assisted co-ordination, particularly as the initiative has almost invariably come from the Élysée. As Gerbet notes:

On account of the executive's primacy, Parliament can hardly interfere. Under these conditions, French Community policy has been characterised by a coherence and a continuity which explain its effectiveness in defending national positions.[12]

---

[11] On the position of the National Assembly in French European policy-making, see Gerbet, 395–8; J. R. Frears, 'The French Parliament and the European Community', *JCMS* 2 (1975–6); Marie-Claude Smouts, 'French Foreign Policy: The Domestic Debate', *International Affairs* (Jan. 1977), 36–50.

[12] Gerbet, 379.

The Bundestag, by contrast, is the only chamber of the original Six to have secured safeguards for its position in the EEC legislative process.[13] The German Parliament largely exercises its statutory rights over foreign policy through a system of specialized committees, in particular that on Foreign Economic Affairs, which have the power to inspect Commission proposals, question ministers, and recommend changes in draft legislation. The committees have access to Commission documentation, and make full use of their rights to summon ministers. The Bundestag as a whole is kept fully abreast of deliberations from within the Government, with a minister or state secretary reporting to it on what has been discussed at the end of the weekly Cabinet meeting. This is a far cry from the situation in France. The German Government also keeps the legislature informed on the course of European affairs by giving it a progress report on integration every six months and details, at least annually, of its integration policy.

However, one must distinguish between theoretical rights and actual power over foreign policy-making. Though the Government pays some attention to Committee reports, especially to avoid friction if legislation is to be enacted, neither the committee system nor the amount of time spent on Community affairs have granted the Bundestag a preponderant influence on the foreign policy process. It has even been suggested that the very comprehensiveness of the German consultative procedure tends to impair its efficiency.[14] More important, there normally exists a constructive dialogue between government and legislature on European policy based on the broad bipartisan support that European integration commands in the Federal Republic.

This relative homogeneity of aims contrasts markedly with the political situation in France, where deep ideological cleavages separate the parties, in spite of occasional attempts at coalition-building amongst the rival blocks. Many Communists retain

---

[13] On the Bundestag's role in German European policy-making, see Ernst Majonica, 'Bundestag und Aussenpolitik', in Schwarz, *Handbuch*, 112–23; Juliet Lodge, 'The Organization and Control of European Integration in the Federal Republic of Germany', *Parliamentary Affairs* 4 (1974–5), 426–9; Renate Mayntz and Fritz W. Scharpf, *Policy-making in the German Federal Republic* (Amsterdam, Elsevier, 1975), 31–6; Wolf-Dieter Karl and Joachim Krause, 'Aussenpolitischer Strukturwandel und parlementarischer Entscheidungsprozess', in Haftendorn *et al.*, 55–82.

[14] Niblock, 41.

a hostile view of integration (the official acceptance of recent years still appears rather grudging). The Gaullists, for their part, certainly no longer bear the outright hostility to the EEC that they did at the outset. Yet they continue to place great weight on the protection of national rights. This situation has at times made the Communists and Gaullists unlikely bedfellows. This occurred, for instance, on the issue of defending national sovereignty in the lengthy prelude to the 1979 European elections, when the Communist Party made distinct overtures towards the Gaullists.[15] It is worth adding that before May 1981 contacts between the French Socialists and German Social Democrats were not notably successful.[16] However, in the brief Schmidt–Mitterrand period the responsibilities of office on the one hand, and the greater appreciation of the need for close Franco-German co-operation on the other, brought about a more cordial approach towards German counterparts in high Socialist circles.

The Federal Republic also stands out from France and its other European partners in being the only member state with a system of regional representation—though there was in fact a (not always successful) trend towards greater regional devolution elsewhere in Europe in the later 1970s. Though this division of responsibility in Germany principally affects domestic policy-making, as Community issues have come to cut across traditional boundaries between internal and external affairs—and hence constitutional demarcation lines between the Federal and *Land* Governments—the Bundesrat has paid closer attention to European topics.[17] The *Länder* have placed particular emphasis on ensuring that the European Communities do not exceed their role. In 1957, the Bundesrat established a Committee to co-ordinate its activities on European matters and keep it fully

[15] See Dorothy Pickles, *Problems of Contemporary French Politics* (London, Methuen, 1982), 41; Frears, *France in the Giscard Presidency*, 78.

[16] On this topic, see Poidevin and Bariéty, 353, and Brandt's remarks in Henri Ménudier, *L'Allemagne selon Willy Brandt* (Paris, Stock, 1976), 28–9.

[17] On the Bundesrat's role in foreign policy-making, see Thomas Oppermann, 'Bundesrat und auswärtige Gewalt', and Christoph Sasse, 'Bundesrat und europäische Gemeinschaft', in Bundesrat Verfassungsorgen, *Der Bundesrat als Verfassungs-und politische Kraft–Beiträge zum 25jährigen Bestehen des Bundesrates der Bundesrepublik Deutschland* (Bad Honnef, Darmstadt, Neue Darmstädter Verlagsamt, 1974), 301–31, 333–63; Werner Billing, 'Der Einfluss des Bundesrats auf die Aussenpolitik', in Schwarz, *Handbuch*, 123–32.

informed of events in Brussels, where the *Länder* also maintain an office. In addition, an observer from the German states sits with his country's delegation to the Council of Ministers. Like the German lower house, the Bundesrat is well placed as regards information and consultative rights, in contrast to the much less favoured position of the French Senate. To a limited extent, it can also impede the Government's foreign policy. This was seen most clearly in the Opposition's attempts to use its Bundesrat majority to block controversial legislation during the *Ostpolitik* —another parallel with American political practice where the opposition party has often made use of its Senate majority to obstruct and delay presidential policy. Finally, the frequency of *Land* elections can also weaken the Government, diverting its attention and, in the event of bad results, sapping its morale.[18]

It can be argued that this last influence also grew more significant in France in the 1970s. With a close finish in the 1974 presidential election and an additional element of uncertainty created as a result of the fissures within the governmental majority later in the decade, elections at communal, departmental, national, and European levels, attracted ever increasing attention, and sapped the Government's reserves. Pickles rightly notes the 'problem of electoralism' that developed during the period and aptly quotes Giscard's June 1978 description of his country as having been involved in 'a more or less permanent electoral campaign ever since 1973'.[19] In this regard, the constraints on governmental action in France and Germany have grown more akin.

Though part of the executive branch, the Bundesbank stands out from its European counterparts and even the American Federal Reserve System in its autonomy and influence over policy-making.[20] This unusually elevated position requires some special attention. The Bundesbank's power stems principally

---

[18] On the influence of *Land* elections, see Geoffrey Pridham, 'A "Nationalization" Process? Federal Politics and State Elections in West Germany', *Government and Opposition* 8 (1973), 455–72. For the situation in 1974, see Brandt, 230.

[19] Pickles, 14.

[20] Emminger gives some idea of the strength and importance of the Bundesbank in 'The D-Mark in the Conflict between Internal and External Equilibrium'. See also Panek, 46–7; Johnson, 198–9; Kreile, 'West Germany: the dynamics of expansion', 792–800; William P. Wadbrook, *West German Balance of Payments Policy* (New York, Praeger, 1972).

from its clearly defined constitutional function. As Klasen observes, 'No other EEC bank of issue has so legally guaranteed an independence'.[21] The Bank can control the money supply independently of the Government, though it cannot make parity changes or set the exchange rate. Yet its monetary policy obviously has an effect on the parity level. In fact, with the collapse of the Bretton Woods system, the balance of power swung sharply in its favour. The Bundesbank's position has been reinforced by its constitutional role as a guardian against inflation and by the recognized authority of its President. As Wadbrook states:

Powerfully influenced in its institutional shape and through its personnel by memories of Germany's two great inflations, the Bundesbank has consistently seen defence of the DM's domestic value and international parity as the primary goal, not only of its own, but of all economic policy.[22]

Although this special stress on price stability has occasionally brought the Bank into conflict with the Government, as will be seen, for politicians in Bonn as much as for Bank officials in Frankfurt, the control of inflation has long been one of the prime determinants of economic policy.

The Bundesbank's power and influence can complicate German policy co-ordination. Those in power have been reluctant to embark on new ventures without its backing. Opposition from the Bank played a major part in the Brandt Government's cautious approach to Economic and Monetary Union at the outset. More recently, the Bundesbank was strongly opposed to the initiative for an EMS. However, on this occasion Schmidt's determination to push ahead provided a telling example not just of a greater German willingness to take a bold political step, but also of a readiness to act in the face of acknowledged Bundesbank hostility. Yet despite such upsets, the bank's overall importance has not declined. Its influence over the economy as a whole is illustrated, not least, by its close links with the business community, particularly in the *Aufsichtsräte*—the supervisory councils of major companies in which bankers are strongly represented.

[21] Karl Klasen, 'Die Verwirklichung der Wirtschafts-und Währungsunion in der EWG aus der Sicht der Deutschen Bundesbank', *Europa-Archiv* 13 (1970), 451.

[22] Wadbrook, 90.

By contrast to the Bundesbank, the Banque de France plays a highly subservient role to the Government. Its relationship with the executive is well illustrated by the remarks of one highly placed former official who spoke of a tendency in the Ministry of Finance to view the Bank as one of its departments. As with other French institutions, this relative weakness has assisted the Government in conducting its policy free from opposition.

Opinion differs as to the role of interest groups in foreign policy-making.[23] Certainly, as the distinction between domestic and foreign affairs has been increasingly blurred by integration, groups in all the member states have come to pay greater attention to Community matters. Yet similar sectoral lobbies in different Community countries do not necessarily carry the same weight, their influence a function of their nation's history, economic and political structure, and popular attitudes. As a preliminary observation, it is likely that a more open governmental system, such as in Germany or the United States, will be more susceptible to lobbying than one more concentrated and secretive, as in France. Policy co-ordination will also tend to be more complex in the more permeable system. Unfortunately there is relatively little literature on the French side, especially regarding business groups. However, what evidence there is strongly suggests that interest groups play a greater role in Bonn, where they are granted a clear consultative function under the Constitution and are actively engaged in lobbying, than in Paris, where their influence is limited by the weakness of the National Assembly and the *domaine réservé* of foreign policy for the President. French farm groups have, however, been both vocal and highly influential.

Business groups in both countries, the Federal Republic in particular, have had some effect on foreign economic policy. This has stemmed not least from the stress placed in both Paris and Bonn on the export sector. The most notable result has been the creation of strong links between industrial and trading

[23] On the general role of interest groups in foreign policy-making, see Jean Meynaud and Dusan Sidjanski, *Les Groupes de pression dans la Communauté Européenne 1958–1968* (Brussels, Institut d'Études Européennes, 1971). For observations on the role of interest groups in French and German foreign policy-making, see Dusan Sidjanski and T. H. Ballmer-Cao, 'Les Syndicats et les groupes de pression français face à l'intégration européenne', in Rideau *et al.*, 204–31; Gerbet, 396–8; Johnson, 88–91.

bodies and sectoral ministries.[24] In a powerful exposition Deubner has revealed the dominant, self-interested role of industry in shaping German policy towards Euratom in the 1950s. In fact, the Bundesverband der Deutschen Industrie—the German Employers' Federation—has consistently sought to exploit all the avenues at its disposal. This has applied particularly to the numerous Ministerial Advisory Councils— especially that on foreign trade in the Ministry of Economics—where its influence has been most sharply felt.

The effect of business opinion on German foreign economic policy was highly evident in the Government's desire in the 1950s and 1960s to maintain an undervalued currency. Furthermore, the wish of the Minister of Finance, Karl Schiller, to revalue in 1969 was overruled by the CDU, responding to business anxiety. The October 1969 revaluation marked a turning-point, though once in power neither the SPD, nor especially the FDP, were at all indifferent to the claims of industry or by any means unaware of the continuing importance of the export sector.

The situation regarding business group power in France is less easy to judge. This is partly on account of the lack of recent material, and also because of the closely interwoven relationship between many sections of industry and the central bureaucracy.[25] As in the Federal Republic, there exist a large number of consultative bodies between the two sides. Furthermore, the French system is such that a high-flying *cadre* can and often does easily alternate between business and the bureaucracy in the course of a professional career, making for an osmosis of interests and granting industry privileged access into officialdom. Wright well describes the process of *pantouflage* that takes place in the upper echelons of the bureaucracy, where the appointment of top civil servants to well-paid posts in the public and private sectors of industry is commonplace. However, there is a two-way process here and it may well be argued that it is the Government

[24] On the role of business groups in Germany, see Gerard Braunthal, *The Federation of German Industry in Politics* (New York, Cornell University Press, 1965); Dieter Piel, 'Die Aussenpolitische Rolle der Wirtschaftsverbände', in Schwarz, *Handbuch*, 207–15; Deubner, 'The Expansion of West German Capital'.

[25] On business groups in France, see H. W. Ehrmann, *Organized Business in France* (Princeton, Princeton University Press, 1957); J. Szokoloczy-Syllara, *Les Organisations professionelles françaises et le Marché Commun* (Paris, Colin, 1965).

which comes off best. Hence 'The result of *pantouflage* is to
establish a widespread network of personal relations which
enables the state to transmit, on a purely informal basis, its
wishes.'[26] Matters do not appear to have changed greatly under
the Socialists. Thus although France, like the Federal Republic,
has placed great emphasis on the export sector, this has not
shifted the lead in foreign economic policy-making away from
the executive, which has pursued a highly interventionist
industrial strategy, in contrast with the very different philosophy
in the Federal Republic. The heterogeneity of the Conseil
National du Patronat Français—the French Employers' Federation—has been an additional debilitating factor. For instance, in
the late 1950s when business opinion was deeply split over the
EEC, small firms were very hostile while larger and more
modern industries were more sanguine about the idea of
membership.[27] Hence articulation of clear preferences has at
times been complicated.

Trade unions in France and Germany, like those in most other
European countries, play only a very minor part in foreign
policy-making. Not surprisingly, they have concentrated on
internal economic and political issues. Foremost amongst these
was *Mitbestimmung*—co-determination in industry—in the Federal Republic, and job security in France.[28] However, deepening
European recession in the later 1970s brought about some
change, and the question of unemployment has shifted to the top
of the agenda. This development has forced unions to become
more conscious of foreign political and economic developments
and made them more vocal accordingly. There have been two
main aspects involved; increasing pressures for protectionism,
notably in France (though also on the left in Britain), and the
issue of job security. On protectionism, the French Socialists'
victory offered unions the prospect of translating their wishes

---

[26] Wright, 90.
[27] For the views of the Patronat towards the EEC, see Nicole Céline Braun, 'Le Patronat français et l'intégration européenne', *Revue du Marché Commun* (Mar. 1969).
[28] On the role of trade unions in Europe, see Emil J. Kirchner, *Trade Unions as a Pressure Group in the European Community* (Farnborough, Hants., Saxon House, 1977); *West European Politics* (Jan. 1980), Special issue on 'Trade Unions and Politics in Western Europe'; Peter Lieser, 'Gewerkschaften und Aussenpolitik', in Schwarz, *Handbuch*, 215–19. For compari-son of French and German trade union groups, see Deubner *et al.*, 'Deutsch-französische Wirtschaftsbeziehungen', 76–81.

into action. It is worth noting, however, that the Government has not gone beyond verbal threats—at least towards other European partners. Hence, for example, Mauroy's calls to 'recapture the domestic market.' Matters may yet change should the balance of power within the Socialist Party shift back towards the left, or should there be a loss of confidence in the Government's existing measures.

Though protectionist influences are much stronger in France than in Germany, the rise of unemployment has provoked very similar reactions on both sides of the Rhine, with a strong shared emphasis among unions on preserving jobs. The most important consequence in foreign economic policy terms has been a greater hostility to those foreign workers already in the two countries and much tighter restrictions on immigration. Although the legal rights of those immigrants already in France have been strengthened, some at least of the liberal immigration measures which formed part of the Socialists' election manifesto have been put aside. 'Retraining' or even generous repatriation grants have been suggested as a means of helping to deal with overmanning in many traditional industries like car building.

Matters are somewhat different in Germany. But what has developed, arguably to a greater degree than in France, is a marked hostility in many quarters to those *Gastarbeiter* already present.[29] Feelings have been intensified as unemployment has risen, and reactions have focused on groups, notably the Turks, whose origins and customs appear most egregious. Government policy towards future projected Turkish membership of the Community has cooled appreciably. Although political developments in that country—notably the military take-over—supplied the pretext, financial and employment considerations lurked not far behind. The problem may well recur following the restoration of democracy in Ankara, and Bonn may be obliged to reassess its position. However, the new Turkish administration itself appears less concerned to press its membership claims than earlier counterparts.

It should be borne in mind that despite the increasing reservations in both France and Germany towards foreign

[29] On this theme, see articles in *The Times*, 2 Apr. and 16 Aug. 1982; *The Economist*, 15 May 1982. For the situation in France, see *The Times*, 19 Aug. 1982.

workers, these groups form an important part of the domestic
economy. Mediterranean labourers comprise ten per cent of the
work-force in Germany and seven per cent in France. As might
be expected, they are concentrated in unattractive sectors such as
coal-mining, construction, catering, and sanitary services.[30] In
the car industry, even in the recession year of 1975, the Ford
motor works in Cologne had to fill seventy-five per cent of its
additional vacancies from the immigrant community.[31] With
continuing recession and rising unemployment, the issue of
foreign workers and, in the future, of second generation
immigrants, raises important problems for policy-makers in
Bonn and Paris alike.

Recent economic difficulties aside, the relative homogeneity in
external aims between German workers and management, based
on their shared belief in the country's 'export mystique' and the
solid consensus between the two sides on the industrial relations
front, contributed to the unions' limited influence over the years
on foreign economic policy. This relatively harmonious picture
contrasts markedly with the position in France where, as with
the political parties, deep ideological cleavages divide the rival
Communist, Socialist, and independent trade union groups.
Furthermore, whereas in Germany the unions swung round
sharply in favour of integration after doubts in the 1950s, in
France the Communist CGT still appears unsympathetic towards the European Community. Certainly, as with French and
German political parties, so with trade unions; attempts to
establish links between certain affiliates of the Deutsche Gewerk-
schaftsbund and French union groups have not been at all
fruitful.[32] In sum, until the 1981 elections at least, doctrinal
differences, and the fact that France is the least unionized of the
original Six, merely intensified constitutional factors in excluding union influence over foreign policy-making. Under the
Socialists, though the unions' say on domestic matters has
grown, it is hard to isolate any specific role on the foreign
economic side. Mitterrand's concern to establish an 'espace social
européen' and later an 'espace industriel européen', embracing a

[30] Information from G. N. Yannopoulos, 'Mediterranean labour in an era of slow
Community growth', *The World Today* (Dec. 1979).
[31] Ibid. 493.
[32] See Poidevin and Bariéty, 353–4.

bevy of social welfare and industrial reforms, can be seen as concerns which stem as much from the President's own long-standing social convictions as from any outside union influence.

As in all the member states, farmers' groups in France and Germany have been very vocal regarding national positions in Community farm policy.[33] The influence of these groups is attributable to the strategic and environmental value of farmers and, in many Community countries, their electoral significance as a large, homogeneous, and often geographically crucial interest group. Both the Fédération Nationale des Syndicats d'Exploitants Agricoles and the Deutsche Bauernverband have had an influence over government policy highly disproportionate to their economic size in terms of GNP contribution. Successive governments in both Paris and Bonn have placed great weight on placating and fostering the farm constituency. The relatively large number of small and inefficient full- or part-time farmers in both countries has also been a significant factor in aligning government policy in defence of the CAP and stalling reappraisals.[34] However, with spending cuts and budgetary constraints very much the order of the day in the 1980s, there are at long last better prospects of more positive action from Paris and Bonn.

To what extent such moves will presage a lasting decline in the power of national farm lobbies remains to be seen. In 1983, for instance, pressure for greater Community spending on social and industrial policy was still being met, not by any reduction in the agricultural budget, but rather thanks to an easing on farm spending brought about by the rise in some world food prices in 1981–2. The agreement reached in March 1984 on reducing milk production might indicate the beginning of a change. Yet French and German farmers still retain formidable influence. This clout was seen most noticeably in France, where pressure from the agricultural lobby had much to do with Giscard's change of heart on Spanish membership of the Community.

[33] On agricultural groups in the European Community, see William F. Averyt, Jr., *Agropolitics in the European Community. Interest Groups and the Common Agricultural Policy* (New York, Praeger, 1977); Yves Tavernier, 'Le syndicalisme paysan et la Vᵉ République (1962–5)', *Revue française de Science Politique* (hereafter *RfSP*) (Oct. 1966).

[34] For data on relative farm size in the Community, see John S. Marsh and Pamela J. Swanney, *Agriculture and the European Community* (London, George Allen and Unwin/UACES, 1980), Tables 4 (*a*) and 4 (*b*).

Admittedly, much greater progress has been made under Mitterrand.

One rather unusual and ofter forgotten interest group worth mentioning, whose influence on integration appears to have been substantial though difficult to gauge, is Jean Monnet's Action Committee for the United States of Europe.[35] This body of Community notables has consistently pressed for greater integration and vigorously lobbied anti-European groups. Interestingly, Brandt was a member of the Monnet Committee in the late 1960s and while Chancellor. Though no firm evidence exists, the experience and Monnet's influence appear to have had an effect on his European policy.[36] Giscard too was a participant in Monnet's group, though one cannot measure what—if any— part this played.

Public opinion is not generally recognized as a significant factor in foreign policy-making, though it can, on occasion, have a strong negative effect—as, for instance, in the case of relations between the United States and Iran after the overthrow of the Shah. Usually, the public is more interested in domestic affairs.[37] Public opinion does, however, appear to play a greater part in shaping foreign policy in West Germany than in France. The Federal Republic's post-war history, its location, and its partition have all contributed to an atypically high level of popular interest in international affairs. This is reflected in the media. In France, by contrast, though the very impotence of the National Assembly and secrecy of the foreign policy process has sometimes had the effect of drawing debate out into the open, these same institutional factors have minimized the influence of public opinion on external policy-making.

Two other points are worth mentioning in this context. First of

---

[35] See W. Yondorf, 'Monnet and the Action Committee: The formative period of the European Communities', *International Organization* (Autumn 1965). Two recent books give some additional insight into Monnet and the Committee's influence: Henry Kissinger, *Years of Upheaval* (London, Weidenfeld and Nicholson/Michael Joseph, 1982), 137–9; Peter Ludlow, *The Making of the European Monetary System* (London, Butterworths, 1982), 20, 63. For the French side, see Pascal Fontaine, 'V. Giscard d'Estaing et la construction de l'Europe', *Projet* (Jan. 1980).

[36] See Brandt, 247, 249.

[37] On the role of German public opinion in foreign policy-making, see Paul Noack, 'Öffentliche Meinung und Aussenpolitik', in Schwarz, *Handbuch*, 195–207. On the French public's attitude to the European Community, see Henri Isaïa, 'L'Opinion publique française et les Communautés Européennes', in Rideau *et al.*

all, in both France and Germany, as might be expected, the level of public debate has varied in relation to the contentiousness and gravity of the issue at stake. Thus, while in West Germany public opinion was a major factor in the *Ostpolitik*, the Community's second enlargement and direct elections received relatively little attention, reflecting the high degree of consensus on both topics. In France, by contrast, both issues—southern enlargement in particular—have been very controversial, sparking off wide discussion. Secondly, while the German public has grown accustomed, and seems genuinely to desire, a restrained external policy from its government, there is strong reason to believe that in France de Gaulle's legacy has resulted in a large body of opinion coming not just to expect, but actively to desire, a strong and decisive presidential line towards international affairs. The shift to a Socialist Head of State does not appear to have changed this rule. This situation has been demonstrated, for example, by the widespread public support for the President's decisive action in Lebanon.

Policy co-ordination

In any forum where a government has to negotiate with others, it must, in order to maintain a strong bargaining position, both press its views coherently and prevent others from exploiting its divisions. These two demands necessitate an effective system of policy co-ordination. The government able to define its position and goals coherently and consistently is more likely to win concessions than a divided and less certain counterpart. In a multilateral organization like the EEC, in particular, where the distinction between foreign and domestic policy has become increasingly blurred, the need for effective co-ordination is all the greater. Community issues often cut across traditional demarcation lines between ministries, and home departments become involved in negotiations with foreign governments. Problems of control have been accentuated as EEC policy has with time moved beyond more easily definable areas such as agriculture and trade policy into wider matters like the environment, often involving more than one ministry. Thus, there arise dangers, on the one hand, of inter-bureaucratic conflicts, each ministry pressing the priorities and interests of the groups that it sponsors; and, on the other, increased problems of overall control given the plethora of technical councils meeting in Brussels. The peril is that any question which cuts across established lines of responsibility, or which raises the issue of overall priorities, may remain unresolved at the national level and hence lead to a negative or passive position in Community negotiations. Government policy co-ordination procedures must be designed, therefore, so as to minimize such outcomes.

The methods that have been chosen by the member states are by no means identical. In the Federal Republic and Holland, responsibility for each policy sector has been allocated to the appropriate ministry, with a network of interdepartmental co-ordination committees at various levels to sort out demarcation problems, resolve disagreements, and determine priorities. In France, a small body, the Secrétariat Général du Comité Interministériel, has been specifically established for the task of co-ordinating all aspects of European policy. This approach has to some extent been mirrored in Britain, where both interdepartmental committees and, increasingly, the Cabinet Office, have been engaged in co-ordinating Community policy.[38]

Co-ordination problems are not limited to the national level. Domestic interest groups have developed their lobbying activities in Brussels, either individually or in conjunction with European counterparts. More important, members of the European Parliament, enjoying greater independence than domestic colleagues, can, and often do, take a line on specific issues contradicting that of their governments, irrespective of their party affiliations.[39] Thus, SPD members of the European Assembly in the past occasionally opposed Bonn's policy and, up

[38] On French and German policy co-ordination, see Gerbet, 380–94; Yann de l'Écotais, 'Les Ministres et les représentants permanents français', in Rideau *et al.*, 400–12; Schwarz, 'Die Bundesregierung und die auswärtigen Beziehungen', 43–112; Joachim Krause and Lothar Wilker, 'Bureaucracy and Foreign Policy in the Federal Republic of Germany', in Krippendorff and Rittberger, 147–70. Gunther Schmid, *Entscheidung in Bonn. Die Entstehung der Ost- und Deutschlandpolitik 1969/70* (Cologne, Verlag Wissenschaft und Politik, 1979), looks at policy formation in the specific context of the *Ostpolitik*. Both Lodge, op. cit., and Pierre Koenig, 'La Réforme de la chancellerie fédérale et du travail gouvernemental en Allemagne de l'ouest', *La Revue d'Allemagne* (Oct.–Dec. 1971), look at changes in the German Chancellery in the early 1970s. Lodge's conclusions about developments under Ehmke have been disproved by events; for an inside view as to why, see Baring, *Machtwechsel*, 520–4.

[39] On this theme, see Robert Kovar and François Wendling, 'Les Parlementaires français au Parlement Européen', in Rideau *et al.*

to May 1981 at least, French Socialist Euro-MPs in particular contested that of Paris. Their party's former exclusion from power undoubtedly increased their independence from government control and hence complicated national policy co-ordination in Paris.

Policy co-ordination problems, on a scale not found in any other international organization, also exist within the EEC itself. This is hardly surprising in view of the Community's complexity and supranational structure. Difficulties have emerged especially regarding questions of planning, control, and accountability. The latter applies particularly to the activities of the civil servants in the Committee of Permanent Representatives—the group comprising the member states' special delegates to the Communities—who have become increasingly active in decision-making.[40] Various ideas have been mooted as to where overall responsibility for formulating Community policy should rest. These have ranged from a restoration of power to the Foreign Ministers to upgrading and institutionalizing summits. Less fruitful has been the notion of creating special Ministers for Europe, a scheme put forward by Pompidou amongst others.[41] Experiments made in this direction have not been at all successful. The Belgians had a Minister of State for European Affairs in one of their governments in the mid-1960s, while the Danes began their membership with two Foreign Ministers, one of whom was expressly responsible for foreign economic affairs. In both cases, however, the initiative proved short-lived, largely on account of demarcation problems between the special EEC minister and his colleagues, and the attempt has not been repeated. While it is now the regular European Councils which are responsible for setting out the broad lines of Community policy, opinion continues to differ as to whether the authority for

[40] On co-ordination problems at European level, see William Wallace, 'Walking Backwards Towards Unity', in Wallace *et al.*, 311–21; Lawrence Scheinman, 'Some preliminary notes on bureaucratic relations in the EEC', *International Organization* (Autumn 1966); David Marquand, 'Parliamentary accountability and the European Community', *JCMS* (Mar. 1981). On the role of Coreper, see Émile Nöel and Henri Étienne, 'The Permanent Representatives Committee and the "Deepening" of the Communities', in Ghita Ionescu (ed.), *The New Politics of European Integration* (London, Macmillan, 1972), 112.

[41] See Pompidou's press conference of 21 Jan. 1971 (French Embassy, London, Press and Information Service).

planning future Community action should rest with the Commission or the national governments.[42]

Considerable differences exist not just in the specific policy coordination procedures developed in France and Germany, but also in their Foreign Ministries. Morale at the Quai d'Orsay is generally high, and the ministry has a clear conception of its role in the policy process. Despite rivalry with technical ministries, especially that of finance, foreign policy-making is recognized as a distinct activity, providing, as Wallace states, the 'political' input into a dialogue with 'technical' departments.[43] According to Gerbet, this major role of the French Foreign Office compared to its German and Dutch counterparts 'contributed to accentuating the "diplomatic" character of French participation in the Communities and the intergovernmental aspect of the Community's activities'.[44] Shared appreciation in other areas of the bureaucracy of the Quai d'Orsay's position has also assisted coordination by reducing ministerial rivalries. This has been aided by the relative homogeneity of the French civil service (though there are undoubtedly complexities beneath the surface)[45] and the common approach to policy problems in its various branches. This situation contrasts with that in Bonn, where morale and status vary considerably between ministries. Thus it has been easier to achieve integrated policy co-ordination on the range of issues in France, while in the Federal Republic the tradition of ministerial independence and the less developed channels of interdepartmental co-operation have, at least until recent years, impeded smooth co-operation.

The German Foreign Ministry started off at a disadvantage compared to other departments on account of the Federal Republic's immediate post-war loss of sovereignty. The Auswärtiges Amt was only gradually re-established after the war and thus faced problems of morale and recruitment. The ministry was, furthermore, confronted by considerable competition from other departments, notably a strong Kanzleramt—the Federal

---

[42] On the development of the European Council, see Annette Morgan, *From Summit to Council: Evolution in the EEC* (London, Chatham House/PEP, 1976).

[43] Wallace, 'Old States and New Circumstances', 43.

[44] Gerbet, 383.

[45] Note, for instance, the comments in Alain Peyrefitte, *Le Mal français* (Paris, Plon, 1976), 316.

Chancellery—which had been taking responsibility for foreign relations, and, above all, a dominant Ministry of Economics, which was pre-eminent in foreign trade policy. In 1957, the Ministry of Economic Affairs was formally invested with jurisdiction over EEC policy, having already established a specialized department to handle and co-ordinate ECSC matters. As might be expected, friction soon developed between the Ministry of Economics and the Auswärtiges Amt.

Matters were eventually resolved by way of an informal demarcation agreement between the two ministries in 1958. Political problems associated with integration were allocated to the Foreign Ministry while 'technical' questions were to be tackled by the Economics Ministry. Not surprisingly, this vague distinction was not always easy to observe. However, following the allocation of the post of Foreign Minister to the leader of the junior coalition partner in 1966, the Auswärtiges Amt has tended to dominate (though in one official's view a 'precarious' balance still existed between the two in the late 1970s). The Economics Directorate of the Auswärtiges Amt has been steadily expanded, and the chair of the European State Secretaries Committee, which used to rotate between departments, has since the start of 1973 been reserved for one of the Foreign Ministry's Parliamentary State Secretaries. This post has, furthermore, been elevated to Cabinet rank. After 1969, an attempt was made by Ehmke to raise the status of the Chancellery and turn it into a centralized co-ordinating body, in emulation of the Presidential Staff at the White House. Yet although its importance increased under Brandt, not least because of its major role in the *Ostpolitik*, the tradition of departmental independence, safeguarded under the Constitution, and the extremely stiff resistance to Ehmke's plans resulted in their eventual abandonment.

In France, the SGCI was given responsibility for co-ordinating policy towards the ECSC in 1952 and the EEC in 1958. It remained until 1981 a small and specialized body of very high calibre, whose function is to receive and distribute documentation from the Commission and Council secretariats, call for position papers from the various French ministries, hold meetings to discuss them, and transmit instructions on technical matters to the permanent representatives once a policy line has been laid down. The SGCI also attempts to control all national officials going to Brussels to ensure that they follow the government line. These tasks are performed through a series of formal and informal interdepartmental co-ordination meetings.

A large measure of the SGCI's success has sprung from the fact that as a small, non-executive group, it has represented neutral territory, not posing a threat or encroaching on other departments, and hence minimizing interdepartmental rivalries of the type more common in Bonn. As Gerbet notes, the SGCI 'brings about têtes-à-têtes and succeeds in reconciling ministries which would not manage it through bilateral channels'.[46] More important, perhaps, in establishing the SGCI's former authority, have been its close links with the Élysée. Jean Dromer was both the SGCI's Secretary-General and de Gaulle's Economic and Financial Counsellor in the Élysée. A similar dual function was performed for President Pompidou by Jean-René Bernard, who also advised on technical matters. As one Quai d'Orsay official has stated, under Pompidou 'all European matters were judged at the Élysée'.[47]

Friction between the SGCI and the Quai d'Orsay has been kept to a minimum thanks to the close contacts between them and the SGCI's recognition of the latter's role in implementing foreign policy. An informal demarcation line exists between the two bodies. While the SGCI has concentrated on handling medium level, routine matters, the Quai d'Orsay has dealt with major or more contentious issues. Until May 1981, the success of the French co-ordination system was reflected in its consistently effective performance in Brussels, where differences of opinion within the French Government were only rarely apparent. The change of heart over EMU following publication of the Werner Report and, in 1977, signs of division under Giscard on the question of southern enlargement formed the only major examples in this period.

However, since May 1981, there have been changes to the SGCI, of both personnel and emphasis, which have adversely affected its efficacy. On the staffing side, Socialist hostility to the Inspectorat des Finances has meant that the SGCI's head no longer comes from that élite corps, but from a less prestigious

---

[46] Gerbet, 392.

[47] Jean-Louis Gergorin, quoted in DFI, *Deutschland, Frankreich und die europäische Krise*, 95–6.

group, thereby damaging the unit's standing and authority. More important, the direct link with the Élysée has also been broken. No longer is the head of the SGCI an independent adviser to the President. Moreover, the SGCI's own reporting responsibilities have also been downgraded, and the group is now responsible to the junior minister at the Quai d'Orsay rather than to the Prime Minister.

The result of these modifications has been seen in some unusual upsets in French European policy co-ordination under the Socialists. An early discussion document on reforming the European budget was only finalized after much argument in Paris, while in late 1983, the budget and the linked issue of Britain's EEC contribution gave rise to some surprisingly inconsistent French statements at Community level. Conciliatory remarks by Delors, the French Finance Minister, at a preparatory meeting implied greater flexibility in Paris. But Mitterrand's mere repetition at the December Athens summit of the former limited French position in favour of just another temporary British rebate caused great disappointment on the British side. It should be recognized, though, that the President's reticence was also influenced by his hostile response to Mrs Thatcher's insistent tactics in the Greek capital.

Policy co-ordination mechanisms in the Federal Republic are a good deal more complex than in France. The Europaabteilung of the Ministry of Economics is responsible for the first stage of co-ordination, handling some ninety per cent of business. At its weekly meetings, it discusses routine matters, sends instructions to the permanent representatives, and convenes inter-ministerial meetings to prepare the German position in forthcoming sessions of the Council of Ministers. No higher level of co-ordination machinery existed until the formation in 1963 of the Committee of State Secretaries for European Affairs. The latter's membership comprises the State Secretaries in the Auswärtiges Amt and the Ministries of Economics, Finance, Agriculture, and the Chancellery, as well as others, invited as necessary. The group meets every three to four weeks to settle questions passed up by the Europaabteilung—usually matters with political implications. This committee plays the crucial role in German policy co-ordination, especially at times when, as under Brandt, relatively little co-ordination was done within the Cabinet. In 1971, a further bureaucratic layer was established, in the form of the Working Group of Under-Secretaries with European Responsibilities. This body was designed to slot in between the two existing levels. Finally, in 1973, a Cabinet Committee for European Policy was also created, made up of the Chancellor and prominent ministers, with a seat also open for the President of the Bundesbank—another indication of the latter's importance.

Unlike the position in France, certain institutional problems dogged German European policy co-ordination and often damaged its effectiveness until the later 1970s. Under Brandt, there were numerous cases of open division between ministers regarding certain aspects of Community affairs. Notably, there were differences between Schiller and Scheel over German monetary policy and relations with France in 1971, and a conflict of interests between Ertl and Schmidt over farm price policy the following year. The Chancellor himself was responsible for additional problems stemming from his relative disinterest and lack of knowledge about detailed economic issues, qualities particularly desirable at a time when such matters were very much to the fore in both European and Atlantic relations.[48] It is well worth bearing in mind the improvement that came about under Schmidt. This was a consequence both of the Chancellor's dominant personality and more self-assertive attitude to Cabinet government and his much firmer grasp of economic and monetary issues. Most recently, under Kohl, the evidence suggests a shift back towards earlier practices.

The major shortcomings that emerged in German co-ordination under Brandt, notably in 1972–3 over the EEC regional fund and the question of the British sterling balances, bore witness to a wider problem facing all the member states. This concerns the difficulty of reconciling the desire of national leaders for grand gestures of 'high' politics, which can arise not only from sincere convictions, but also for public relations reasons or even through inadequate detailed information, with the responsibilities of technical ministries at the 'low' politics level, confronted with the task of elaborating the necessary plans.

---

[48] Interview material suggests that Brandt showed a much greater interest in detailed and technical matters when Foreign Minister.

This situation had led on occasion to serious and embarrassing obstacles. In the later 1970s, French reticence over Spanish (and, by implication, Portuguese) membership of the EEC provided an example of a measure desirable in principle, which became much less attractive after detailed consideration and better appreciation of the repercussions. This instance apart, policy co-ordination in both France and Germany under Schmidt and Giscard, both like-minded technocrats with similar economic and financial expertise, and both well aware of technical constraints, was generally highly efficient.

One reason for the improvement on the German side was the acute consciousness of former shortcomings. Thus, considerable attention was paid to overcoming former failings during the Schmidt Chancellorship. This was seen most clearly in the creation of new co-ordinating strata. Under Brandt, too, numerous attempts had been made to make the system more effective. Yet neither the initiative to strengthen the Chancellery, nor that to increase discussion of Community issues in the Cabinet had proved successful. While the former plan had foundered largely on the back of ministerial resistance and lack of active support from the Chancellor, the latter had to some extent proved intractable in the face of Brandt's own belief in a collegial system of government and his consequent reluctance to use the *Richtlinienkompetenz*. The assertive personalities and entrenched positions of some of his ministers had undoubtedly played an additional part.

Matters changed markedly under Schmidt. Not only was the Chancellor a tough manager of government by no means unwilling to press his views, he also possessed a clear understanding of the complex economic and financial issues often heading the contemporary agenda. Consequently, co-ordination of European policy at Cabinet level became routine. Community matters were regularly discussed at the weekly Cabinet meetings as a permanent agenda item. Changes also took place in the bureaucratic machinery: the European State Secretaries Committee, ever decisive, grew stronger still, while contacts between top officials, notably in the Economics and Foreign Ministries, also improved. All these developments contributed to the much more coherent and confident German stance in international, and especially Community, affairs that was evident in the later

1970s. Though it is too early to make a definitive judgement about policy co-ordination under Kohl, there are signs of a move back at least some way towards the problems characteristic of the Brandt era. Inexperience among a largely untried governing team has played a part, but Kohl's own, more relaxed, style of management has also been responsible, with less co-ordination now taking place out of the Chancellery than under Schmidt.

The effect of the differences in French and German institutions and political practices that have been described above have long been evident in the two countries' foreign policies. The following chapters will illustrate the value of the benefits derived. These have stemmed, for example, from the concentration of power in the French presidency, which has contributed to an assertive foreign policy. Similarly, in the Federal Republic, constitutional devices designed to prevent the abuse of power, and also the influence of coalition governments, have complicated decision-making and tended to establish policies of centrism and continuity.

However, matters have not remained static. Already there has been substantial change in France as a result of the Socialist victory. Steps have been taken towards decentralization, with the revision of the prefectoral system, and there has been much talk, though little action as yet, about reform of the television service. In foreign policy-making, the Vth Republic's Constitution continues to grant the President a crucial role and the Government a dominant position over opposing political forces. Consequently, the advent of a new team, albeit untried and reforming, has brought no obvious change in the type of wide-ranging foreign policy initiatives closely associated with the Republic's first three Presidents.

As to policy co-ordination in France and Germany, the Federal Republic's constitutional arrangements and bureaucratic practices have in the past given rise to difficulties and misunderstandings in the formation and expression of policy. Bonn consequently often found its position weakened at Community level. Yet here too matters changed. Between 1974 and 1982, at least, marked improvements took place. In France, by contrast, the much more centralized system allowed, with only very rare exceptions, for the coherent and effective articulation of policy. Again, though, there have been transitional problems since May 1981.

However, as shall be seen in the chapters that follow, as far as the vital early 1970s were concerned, the result of the dissimilarities in French and German policy co-ordination methods was often to increase the constraints facing German foreign policy-makers, while at times granting Paris a privileged hearing.

4

The Relaunching of Europe?
1969-1971

The Hague summit

The changes of government that took place in Paris and Bonn in 1969 held out the prospect of revitalizing the European Community. Principally, Georges Pompidou's election as President of France, replacing General de Gaulle by whom he had been removed from office as Prime Minister only the previous year, cleared the air among the member states of the EEC and dispelled the former prevailing atmosphere of mistrust.[1] In his election campaign the new President had already voiced his interest in developing the Community's activities.[2] With Willy Brandt now holding the reins across the Rhine any new initiative from Paris was sure to be reciprocated in Bonn. This desire to move forward was echoed in the other Community capitals. Hence the decision, at French behest, to hold a summit conference of the Six in The Hague on 1-2 December 1969.

Attention focused on three issue areas prior to the summit: the finalization of the financial regulation for the CAP and the Community's funding by *resources propres*, the issue that had indirectly led to the French boycott of the Community's institutions in 1965; the creation of new monetary policies; and the opening of the EEC to new members. These aims were succinctly covered by Pompidou's triptych of 'completion', 'deepening', and 'enlargement'. In his election campaign the President had shown himself ready to consider enlargement, provided completion took pride of place. This was a lesson learned from 1963, when the British entry negotiations had become perilously intertwined with the Community's own talks

---

[1] For Pompidou's recently revealed feelings on his dismissal, see *Pour Rétablir une vérité*, 200-8.

[2] See, for instance, Pompidou's speech at Orléans on 20 May, in *Le Monde*, 22 May 1969. On the campaign note also Roussel, *Pompidou*, 309-20.

on the formation of the CAP. France was eager to avoid making the same mistake twice. Less explicit was the bond between completion and the need for the co-ordination of the monetary policies of the Six, a consequence of the monetary instability of 1968–9. The new measure was intended to protect the agricultural sector, dependent on uniform Community pricing, from parity changes. In negotiations among the Council of Ministers prior to the summit, an informal link had already emerged between this French stress on agriculture and the wish of the Five, led by the Germans, for enlargement. Given the importance of German economic backing for any new monetary measures there was clearly scope for a package deal built around interlocking French and German interests.

Numerous reasons underscored Pompidou's willingness to contemplate British membership.[3] The President was well aware that de Gaulle himself had been moving in this direction.[4] In February 1969, the British Ambassador to Paris, Sir Christopher Soames, had been summoned to a meeting at the Élysée where the French leader had painted, in very broad brush, a possible future for Europe guided by France, Britain, Germany, and Italy.[5] Though the initiative had come to nothing, it had clearly illustrated the prevailing train of de Gaulle's thought.

Pompidou himself was by no means hostile to the idea of enlargement. He cast himself as a 'European' President, sincerely desiring the regeneration of the Community, not least in so far as this would benefit France's industrial progress, by which he set

[3] For a very detailed examination of Pompidou's motives towards enlargement, deepening, and the summit, see Berger, *M. Pompidou et la construction de l'Europe*; Roussel, op. cit. 370–5. Also worthwhile are Theo M. Loch, 'Ausgangspositionen für die europäische Gipfelkonferenz in Den Haag', *Europa-Archiv* 20 (1969), 707–16; Uwe Kitzinger, *Diplomacy and Persuasion* (London, Thames and Hudson, 1973), 68–72.

[4] See Michel Jobert, *Mémoires d'avenir* (Paris, Collection Livre de Poche, 1976), 204 and *L'Autre Regard* (Paris, Grasset, 1976), 92.

[5] On de Gaulle's plans, and the role of Germany in them, see especially André Fontaine, 'Comment avorta le dialogue franco-britannique', *Le Monde*, 11 Mar. 1969. In addition, there is C. L. Sulzberger's interview with de Gaulle, published only at the General's death, in *International Herald Tribune*, 11 Nov 1970. See also the revelations in Kissinger, *White House Years*, 87, 110, 384; Philippe de Saint Robert, *Les Septennats interrompus* (Paris, Laffont, 1977), is an interesting source, though to be treated with caution. Finally, see the very full account given by Alan Campbell, 'Anglo-French Relations a Decade Ago: A New Assessment (1)', *International Affairs* (Spring 1982), 239–48.

great store.[6] Certainly, he wanted to avoid a third veto, which could cause a Community crisis and spill over into domestic politics. Feeling at home had also grown more favourable to new developments in the Six. This mood had been cautiously exploited by Pompidou in the presidential campaign, both from personal conviction, and also from fear of losing votes to Alain Poher, his more 'European' rival. Once in power, a sympathetic attitude in EEC affairs and enlargement would also please the Centrists and Independent Republicans, the Gaullists' more Community-minded coalition partners.

However, there was undoubtedly another aspect to Pompidou's strategy, forged by his feelings towards West Germany, whose rising economic strength he, like de Gaulle and Debré, viewed with some disquiet. British membership would counterbalance the Germans, and the timing of the new initiative was also influenced by the fact that the French still felt sufficiently strong *vis-à-vis* Bonn to achieve enlargement broadly on their own terms. This impression is confirmed by Jobert and Seydoux, while Kissinger's record of a meeting is emphatic: 'It was fear of a resurgent Germany, Pompidou averred, that had caused him to reverse de Gaulle's opposition to Britain's entry into Europe ...'[7] As will be seen, this concern of the President's with West Germany was to develop into a major theme in his thinking in the course of the next four years.

Unease regarding German economic strength also formed a minor component in Pompidou's desire for greater monetary coordination in the Six, though apprehension about the effects of fluctuating exchange rates was the predominant influence.[8] The monetary crises of 1968 and spring 1969 had demonstrated the agricultural policy's susceptibility to parity changes. Moreover, the brief floating of the Deutschemark prior to its revaluation in September 1969, which had involved the introduction of German border levies negating the fundamental concepts of the CAP of common prices and free trade, had elicited severe

---

[6] See especially Pompidou's press conference of 22 Sept., in *Le Monde*, 24 Sept. 1969.

[7] Seydoux, *Dans l'intimité franco-allemande*, 181. See also Michel Jobert, 'De l'Allemagne', *Politique Étrangère* New Series, 1 (1979), 14, and Kissinger, *White House Years*, 422.

[8] For Community monetary policy at this time, see Loukas Tsoukalis, *The Politics and Economics of European Monetary Integration* (London, George Allen and Unwin, 1977), and 'Is the Relaunching of Economic and Monetary Union a Feasible Proposal?', *JCMS* (June 1977), 231–47.

criticism in Paris. Hence French pressure for guaranteed exchange rates to safeguard the agricultural policy.

Such monetary considerations would also have political spin-offs and accord with traditional French policy interests. The creation of a European 'monetary personality' would leave the Community less open to American pressure. This had been keenly felt by the French following their isolation at the 1968 Stockholm IMF conference where Bonn had emerged as the arbiter between Paris and Washington. A new monetary system would also strengthen the Six prior to British entry and diminish the risk of any loosening of ties after enlargement. Furthermore, it would represent a *force motrice* for the EEC. Negative integration (the elimination of intra-Community tariffs and trading barriers) had proved inadequate to cement the Community's existence, while the sole measure of positive integration (the creation of a new joint policy) of the CAP, had been threatened by monetary unrest.

In Germany, Social Democratic enthusiam for enlargement, already strong, was undoubtedly increased by the existence of a Labour Government at Westminster. (It is worth bearing in mind just how much German attitudes were to shift on this score by the later 1970s.) Thus it was judged in Bonn that British entry would not only benefit the Community (and not least, German trade), but also serve the wider cause of Socialism and the Socialist International, in which Brandt took an active interest.[9] As to whether enlargement might be used as a weapon against the Federal Republic, the Chancellor appeared unworried. In words seemingly directed towards Pompidou, Brandt remarked at The Hague that 'anyone who fears that the economic weight of the German Federal Republic may upset the Community's internal balance should favour enlargement for that reason too.'[10]

The German stand on new monetary policies was more complex. Though in the early 1960s it had been judged best to concentrate on economic and monetary co-operation at Atlantic level, developments in trading patterns, and especially the

---

[9] For Brandt's feelings on British membership, see his first Government Declaration, in *Deutsche Bundestag, Stenographische Berichte*, 71 (Bonn 1969–70), 32. Though see also Brandt, 'Aktuelle Fragen der deutschen Aussenpolitik', *Europa-Archiv* 13 (1971), 438.

[10] Brandt, *People and Politics*, 246.

monetary crises of the late 1960s (which had demonstrated the vulnerability of inter-Community free trade despite the customs union), had brought about a change of attitude. In particular, the temporary French imposition of export subsidies and selective import quotas in 1968 had caused concern in Bonn. Closer co-ordination of economic and monetary policies would benefit German trading interests by guaranteeing free trade among the Six, while eliminating embarrassing pressures for revaluation. There were drawbacks, however. Principally, the introduction of new monetary policies would involve a net transfer of credit or resources to other member states and might stimulate inflation. (It is worth noting the continuing currency of this concern at the inauguration of the EMS.) For the Germans, therefore, greater co-ordination of economic policies was the essential corollary for any new measures on the monetary front. Once again, there seemed to be scope for a combination of different, but potentially interlocking, French and German interests.

One crucial reason behind Bonn's enthusiasm for a *relance* of the Six at this particular time was the need for a strong Community and active German policy towards Western Europe to balance and enhance the Government's impending initiative in the East. It has been argued that this motive applied especially to the German position on economic and monetary co-operation, where political concerns overrode economic factors.[11] There is an interesting parallel here with Adenauer's motives towards the creation of the EEC in the 1950s, when, once again, political motives had been uppermost, though economic influences followed closely behind. Not least, one must recall the overall climate in which German thinking was being shaped in the late 1960s. America's concentration on Vietnam and the threat of troop reductions in Europe were causing grave doubts in Bonn about the reliability of future American political and military support. A more vital and unified Western Europe had to compensate for this lack of American political backing for the *Ostpolitik*. Thus, the success of the Hague summit is widely judged as a prerequisite for Brandt's Eastern policy. This was

---

[11] See Tsoukalis, *European Monetary Integration*, 85, and 'Economic and Monetary Union', 239.

presaged by Scheel in a speech on 6 January 1969 in Stuttgart and in remarks to Gromyko in Moscow before the 1969 elections, where the FDP leader stressed that enlargement was a *sine qua non* for the *Ostpolitik*.[12] It is worth noting, too, that the new Government's first contacts with the East took place a few days after the Hague summit.

There is very strong evidence to suggest that active preparatory steps for an exchange of French and German interests at The Hague had already begun at the bilateral level some time before the summit. The very question of holding a conference and the prospects for enlargement were raised during Brandt's visit to Paris in early July 1969 and amplified in Pompidou's talks with Kiesinger in Bonn in September. The following month, Carlo Schmid, the newly appointed Co-ordinator for Franco-German Co-operation, was sent to Paris to gauge French feeling. This mission represented an unorthodox use of the theoretically apolitical Co-ordinator for apparently political ends, though unfortunately there is insufficient evidence to assess the value of Schmid's visit in political terms. Finally, Schumann and Scheel also met for talks on the summit's agenda, and there was a clear awareness of mutual interests in completion and enlargement. There was, according to the German Foreign Minister, 'very broad agreement on almost all problems'.[13] On 27 November, Brandt highlighted the Franco-German role, remarking that, 'Western Europe needs a success at The Hague ... and it depends on Paris and Bonn that that result is obtained.[14] There was also a considerable flow of secret diplomacy between the two leaders, with Pompidou's representatives talking in Bonn about the summit up to one week before it opened. These bilateral contacts increased mutal understanding, and convinced the Germans that Pompidou was in earnest about enlargement, with only the details remaining to be settled at The Hague.

The summit was notable for the authority of Brandt's opening speech. This contrasted markedly with Pompidou's much vaguer address, and was taken by many as a harbinger of a new, more self-assured German stance in international affairs and an indication of a shift in the balance with France. Traditional

---

[12] Interview material.
[13] Quoted in *The Times*, 10 Nov. 1969.
[14] Quoted in *International Herald Tribune*, 29–30 Nov. 1969.

themes were evident in both leaders' attitudes. However, it is worth highlighting Brandt's call for institutional changes, particularly a stronger, directly elected European Parliament. Although support for institutional progress has remained an important part of German European policy to the present day, even by 1972 Brandt's position on the question of direct elections was to shift somewhat from his earlier position. At the Paris summit in October 1972, the Chancellor was careful to put greater emphasis on developments such as an improvement in the Council's decision-making capacity and an increased role for the Parliament than on direct elections. The change can largely be attributed to Brandt's experience of office and greater appreciation of the obstacles involved, particularly on the French side.

The success of the Hague summit and its dependence primarily on bilateral Franco-German agreement was underlined by the private meeting between Brandt and Pompidou on the first night. Despite the preliminary contacts between the two governments Brandt makes clear the continuing uncertainty:

The formula for British entry—and this was the focus of interest—remained open ... Pompidou and I did not agree upon it until the evening of the first day ... The President wanted to satisfy himself that Franco-German co-operation would not in my view suffer from the Community's enlargement. More particularly, he wanted safeguards in respect of agricultural finance—a subject of great political importance to himself.[15]

This concern of Pompidou with the agricultural sector would emerge as a major theme in his European policy. Persuaded by the atmosphere of trust and the reassurance Brandt had given, and doubtless also reacting to the challenge of the Chancellor's speech, Pompidou, in his remarks on the second day, was far more positive and encouraging. The change appeared to confirm the view that the President's non-committal opening address had been partly framed in the light of domestic political considerations, demonstrating to hardline Gaullist opinion that French interests were not going to be undersold. This domestic influence was to remain a factor in Pompidou's European strategy and increase markedly following the 1972 referendum.

---

[15] Brandt, 245, 246. See also Jobert, *L'Autre Regard*, 117.

The summit's final communiqué reflected the underlying exchange of French and German interests that had taken place. France won acceptance for the adoption of a definitive financial regulation for the CAP before the end of the year and for financing by *resources propres*. Furthermore, the Council of Ministers was instructed to draw up a plan for the phased introduction of new economic and monetary policies. German agreement to the latter was secured by the explicit understanding that steps for harmonization of economic policies would be co-ordinated with monetary measures. Various other proposals would ensure further deepening of the Community. Pre-eminent here was the breakthrough on political co-operation, a topic which the foreign ministers were instructed to study further. This was the first time that political co-operation had been tackled by the Six since the collapse of the Fouchet talks in 1963. Most important, the member states agreed on the principle of enlargement, on which talks would commence by 1 July 1970. Negotiations were in fact to open one day before this deadline, and last until the end of 1972.

As for the individual member states, the summit represented an important step for Germany, and for Brandt himself in particular. In the wider context of German foreign policy, it marked a further move in the transition of economic strength into a more forceful political stance. Bonn was now adopting a position of equality towards its main European partner. In contrast to former reticence, the Germans had taken the initiative at The Hague with Brandt himself coming across as a self-confident and knowledgeable statesman. One must, however, guard against exaggerating the Chancellor's performance, as was done in much of the media, where he was lionized. This is an interesting theme, and it has been noted that the performances of both Brandt and Pompidou were judged in gamesmanship terms.[16] One adverse consequence of the popular attention focused on Brandt was the birth of a well-documented resentment on Pompidou's part. While Brandt won his confidence at The Hague, the impression of competition widely canvassed in public was undoubtedly also keenly felt in private. Both leaders, new to office, were seeking the limelight. Though not the

---

[16] Morgan, *From Summit to Council*, 56.

most impartial of observers, Jobert, a source very close to the French President, writes: 'Already, the President of the Republic, although charmed by the chancellor's good nature and joviality, was growing angry at the chorus of praises being sung to Brandt in the foreign and domestic press.'[17] In the course of the next four and a half years, Pompidou's sense of resentment would increase in line with Brandt's repute, undoubtedly coming to colour his attitude to the German leader and impair his judgement of the Federal Republic.

Deepening the Community

The sixteen months following the summit were largely taken up in organizing the various activities it had heralded. Negotiations among the Six preparatory to enlargement, notably concerning the completion of the CAP and the associated topic of *resources propres*, dominated the first half of the period, and discussions on deepening the Community largely characterized the second. The Hague summit had given the go-ahead to two new integrative schemes; political co-operation and Economic and Monetary Union. While achieving the latter turned out to be a protracted and contentious affair, revolving round discordant French and German approaches stemming from their divergent economic interests, the path towards political co-operation was considerably smoother.

It was perhaps hardly surprising that the first report of the Davignon Committee, set up by the foreign ministers to discuss political co-operation, should so clearly have reflected traditional differences of perception between the member states.[18] Certainly, these early divisions offered more than an occasional echo of the disputes that had emerged in the deliberations of the Fouchet Committee some eight years before. While most member states stressed the importance of British participation and took a maximalist view of political co-operation, envisaging ambitious schemes such as the creation of new institutions, the French adopted a far more cautious approach. Paris continually played

---

[17] Jobert, *Mémoires*, 185.

[18] On political co-operation, see William Wallace and David Allen, 'Political Cooperation: Procedure as Substitute for Policy', in Wallace *et al.*, *Policy-Making in the European Communities*, 227–47.

down the role of political co-operation and drew a sharp distinction between inter-governmental meetings of the foreign ministers for political co-operation and gatherings of the same group of men sitting as the Council of Ministers of the European Communities. The attitude was clearly in line with the long-standing French opposition to any increase in supranationalism. Later events would show just how sharply this distinction would be drawn. Under the present circumstances it was no surprise that a compromise could only be struck at the level of lowest common denominator, allowing the submission of the Davignon Report at the end of May 1970 and its formal acceptance in October.

That such an outcome was reached with considerably less friction than in the 1960s was a reflection firstly of the fact that France's strategy (for the time being at least) no longer gave such cause for suspicion, and secondly of the relatively unambitious nature of the proposals themselves. As mentioned earlier, there were marked similarities with some of the suggestions that had been made in the Fouchet discussions. In both cases, the co-ordination of foreign policy as identified as the most suitable area for the début of political co-operation, the aim being not simply an exchange of views, but the more overtly political target of reaching joint Community positions on topics of external policy, 'in order to show the whole world that Europe has a political mission'.[19] This statement was redolent of Gaullist diplomacy of the 1960s. As it happened, events in 1973 were to demonstrate how easily this nascent European cohesion could be harnessed behind a Gaullist-style strategy, notably regarding relations with the United States. It should be borne in mind that this question of how to deal with the Americans has remained contentious to the present day.

Organizationally, the Davignon Report recommended twice-yearly meetings between the foreign ministers and the creation of a Committee of Political Directors from the member states to prepare the ministerial meetings and carry out any other duties delegated to them. Though criticized in some quarters as being too timid, the Report reflected the prevalence of French views, as

[19] First Report of the Foreign Ministers to the Heads of State or Government of the European Community's Member States of 27 October 1970, Part 2: 1.

well as the feeling in some capitals that it would be best to await British membership before pushing ahead too ambitiously. Certainly, though cautious, the Report's restricted, but widely acceptable, findings contrasted sharply with the much more venturesome, but also far more contentious proposals of its contemporary, the Werner Report on Economic and Monetary Union.

A convergence of French and German views played a large part in the creation and shaping of political co-operation. The French position was the more complex, involving as it did a conflict of interest. For Paris, the policy was desirable in so far as it accorded with the long-standing aim of establishing a European stance on matters of external policy and thereby encouraging the development of a distinct European identity. This would assert Europe's independence from the existing power bloc structure and give France, through Europe, a greater weight in world affairs. Yet more pressing policy interests demanded that political co-operation should not be permitted any supranational trappings. Hence the stress on inter-governmentalism and caution that typified the French approach.

Political co-operation was very desirable for the Germans too. Bonn's ambivalent position between the views of Paris and the other capitals in the talks can be explained by the desire to expedite the policy's establishment. Political co-operation represented a potential contribution to *détente* in Europe, and was hence fully in line with German wishes. This was confirmed by Bonn's concern at the first political co-operation meeting in Munich on 19 November 1970 that the Six should study the proposed European Security Conference and relations with the Soviet Union. Furthermore, not only would political co-operation act as an aid and endorsement for the *Ostpolitik*, it would also potentially establish a very important arena for the development of Bonn's extra-European foreign policy. It should be recalled that only in 1973 did the Federal Republic join the United Nations. It can also be argued that Bonn's active desire for European backing for its Eastern policy (combined with the wishes of its partners to be kept fully informed of developments in this sensitive area), were major factors in enhancing the status of political co-operation. Finally, with bilateral Franco-German summits often taking their keynote from the topical issues of the day, one can suggest that the co-ordination of joint positions between Bonn and Paris at bilateral level helped to create wider consensus within the political co-operation talks themselves.

Conflicting French and German priorities were to make Economic and Monetary Union far more time-consuming an issue than political co-operation.[20] The two countries' different conceptions had already emerged clearly at the Hague summit. While the Germans felt that the co-ordination of economic policies should take the lead, the French emphasized monetary measures. This difference in priorities was to remain a leitmotiv of successive ministerial meetings and an ever-present obstacle to Community accord. The cleavage was very evident in the May 1970 interim report submitted by the working group set up under Pierre Werner, Prime Minister and Minister of Finance of Luxembourg. While the French, Belgians, and Luxembourgers argued that monetary measures should take precedence, the Germans, Dutch, and, to a lesser extent, Italians stressed the economic side. Although the Werner Group's Final Report of October 1970 produced a compromise, unsurprisingly arguing for parallel progress in the two spheres, this rift was now to be superseded by a new source of conflict.

The Werner Report had favoured the implementation of EMU by 1980, involving, *inter alia*, a considerable transfer of responsibility from national to Community levels, new institutions, and a revision of the EEC treaty. Though received favourably elsewhere, these major institutional changes, challenging national sovereignty, met with a very hostile reaction from the Gaullists. By all accounts, Pompidou was enraged by the Werner Group's findings. This explains the very abrupt shift in French policy towards EMU that now took place, with the sudden adoption of a much more hostile approach. The episode is worth keeping in mind as one of the rare instances of poor European policy co-ordination in France in the 1970s. French difficulties had stemmed partly from the fact that Clappier, France's representative on the Werner Group, was a keen pro-European who had been given no clear remit, and partly because Pompidou himself had been caught unprepared by the major changes that the Werner Group was to propose.

---

[20] For detailed analysis of EMU, see Tsoukalis, *European Monetary Integration*. See also, Robert W. Russell, 'Snakes and Sheiks: Managing Europe's Money', in Wallace *et al.*, *Policy-Making in the European Communities*, 69–90.

The dissipation of former French enthusiasm for EMU into a rearguard action following publication of the Werner Report led to a new quarrel with the Germans. France now proposed that the Six should postpone detailed discussion of institutional changes and instead concentrate on the first stage of EMU. The new stand was resisted by the Five, who were unwilling to divorce preliminary steps from final objectives. It is worth focusing on German reasoning. For the Federal Republic, it was necessary to spell out from the start the political aims and consequences of EMU, a prerequisite, as far as Bonn was concerned, for any progress on the first stage. The institutional aspect was part and parcel of Bonn's political and economic commitment to EMU, stemming from the Federal Republic's particular policy interests. Strong, centralized bodies were seen as vital to the co-ordination of economic policies, minimizing both the risk of imported inflation—that German *bête noire*—and the cost of the policy to the German exchequer, while also reinforcing political integration.

Clearly, French and German conceptions of EMU were fundamentally at odds, a view confirmed by the abortive meeting of foreign and finance ministers of 14–15 December 1970. The session stood out for Schiller's very firm approach towards his French counterpart. By the end of the meeting feelings were running very high on both sides. Schiller made no attempt to hide his bitterness at what he felt to be a French violation of Community principles and the spirit of The Hague. This determined, if not openly aggressive, stance recalled a similar line taken by Ertl in negotiations for a market organization for wine twelve months earlier. Certainly, both instances left no doubt as to the determination of these two very forceful German ministers to assert their views on what they felt to be key topics of Community policy.

It is worth looking more closely at the way in which the quarrel over EMU became increasingly identified as one between France and Germany. Two factors lay behind this trend: the inability to make progress at Community level, and the fact that discussions were often proceeding at bilateral Franco-German summits. Thus it was no surprise that attention should shift to the late January 1971 Franco-German meeting following the inconclusive results of the talks between Community foreign and finance ministers earlier in the month. Under these circumstances, Pompidou's major statement on his concept of Europe and its future at his press conference of 21 January 1971, coming shortly before the bilateral summit, can be partly read as an attempt to gain the initiative in the negotiations. Indirectly asserting the French position on EMU, the President explicitly underlined the primacy of inter-governmentalism in integration:

[Europe] can only mean building, on the basis of what exists, a confederation of States that have decided to harmonise their policies and to integrate their economies. And if one looks at it this way, one realises that the quarrel over supranationality is a false quarrel ... The idea of achieving it [Europe] on the basis of technical organizations, of commissions, is an illusion that has been swept away by the facts ... the government of Europe can only arise out of a gathering of national governments, joining together to take decisions that are valid for all.[21]

The Germans, listening attentively for any signs of movement on EMU, were disappointed. But Bonn appreciated this attestation of the President's European convictions and their underlying pragmatism. The sort of suspicions that had existed under de Gaulle had been dispelled, and Pompidou left no doubt as to his belief in the future of an integrated Europe—albeit one that would be created cautiously and along strictly inter-governmental lines.

The complexity of the German position on EMU contrasted with the much more straightforward approach in Paris. Significantly, the German Government was facing conflicting priorities and its stance towards the French was actually a good deal weaker than implied by Schiller. This distinction is important as it gives an indication of that lack of cohesion in German European policy during much of the Brandt Chancellorship which complicates clear analysis of the development of the Federal Republic's external posture. The Germans faced a dilemma. Bonn's desire for its views on EMU to prevail had to be balanced against the need for an active policy in the West and French support for the *Ostpolitik*. The importance of these factors was compounded by the domestic party political climate.

---

[21] Press conference given by President Pomidou, 21 Jan. 1971. French Embassy Press and Information Service translation, 3.

Brandt's Government, surviving on a slim majority, was already facing what would become a mounting barrage of criticism that Community affairs were being neglected in favour of the *Ostpolitik*. It was also claimed that the latter was being recklessly conducted independently of Bonn's allies.

Thus, his position weakened, the Chancellor went to Paris for the biannual summit on 25 January 1971 partly as political *demandeur*, seeking French backing for his Eastern policy. The compromise on EMU worked out in the talks with Pompidou—that France and Germany would reconcile their differences and aim to produce an agreed position in time for the Council of Ministers' meeting in early February—indicated the ascendancy in German policy of broader political concerns over more sectional economic interests. Brandt accepted Pompidou's strictly inter-governmental interpretation of EMU, and the Chancellor assured the President that Bonn was not insisting on any exaggerated 'perfectionism' in the creation of new European institutions. Rather, Brandt agreed to adopt a 'pragmatic' approach to the policy.[22] As *The Economist* wrote, 'Willy pays his price for the deal in the East.'[23] Brandt's flexibility was also picked up by an academic observer, who accurately noted the Chancellor's increasing preparedness to make concessions on European policy despite Cabinet opposition.[24] Though perhaps regarded by Schiller as defeats, such latitude was necessary to prevent the Community from running aground and to demonstrate the existence of an active *Westpolitik*. But the agreement reached in Paris was not to be without important domestic repercussions. Schiller complained that the compact represented a question of money—especially German money—involving a substantial transfer of German credit or resources.[25] The defeat over EMU was a first step in Schiller's gradual disenchantment with German Community policy, a process which culminated in the internal political differences over monetary policy and relations with France later in 1971 and his eventual resignation the following year.

---

[22] Quoted in 'Le Chancelier fédéral à Paris', *Documents* (Jan.–Feb. 1971), 13, and *International Herald Tribune*, 26 Jan. 1971.

[23] *The Economist*, 30 Jan. 1971.

[24] Joachim Besser, 'Die Angst vor den Deutschen', *Dokumente* 4 (1971), 263.

[25] For Schiller's comments and views, see 'Le Chancelier fédéral à Paris', 14.

As on many occasions in the past, the bilateral agreement reached in Paris opened the door to compromise at Community level. But although the Franco-German summit had given the green light, it could hardly be expected to resolve detailed technical issues. Therefore marked differences remained when the Community finance ministers met in early February. Agreement was restricted to the level of lowest common denominator. Political and institutional aspects of EMU stayed largely unresolved and concrete decisions were restricted to the monetary side. Matters of economic policy were left much more vague. The compromise that was reached hinged on the adoption of a 'safeguard' clause. This would enable a member state to withdraw from the monetary agreement if it felt insufficient progress had been made after three years to warrant moving to the second stage. The device had been specifically designed to minimize German fears of an open-ended financial commitment as a result of embarking on the first stage without any specific undertakings as to what would follow. It had been a key element in the talks between Brandt and Pompidou, giving the Germans 'a good excuse—some people might regard it as a sufficient guarantee'[26] for acceptance of the French point of view. Yet although Bonn had acquiesced to Paris on EMU—a consequence of the wider political considerations deriving from its unusual, particularly restricted, position in the constellation of states—it was patently clear that it was a Franco-German accord which had prepared the path for wider Community agreement, even at this limited level.

Franco-German dialogue

The Franco-German summit of January 1971 was by no means the only instance in the Brandt–Pompidou era when major bilateral agreement was reached on an issue of Community policy, although the breakthrough it permitted was certainly the most significant of the period from the Community's point of view. Other bilateral summits also played a valuable role in consolidating the *relance* which had been achieved at The Hague, and it is worth examining the first three of these more closely. Not surprisingly, there were few major topics of Community

---

[26] Tsoukalis, *European Monetary Integration*, 111.

policy to discuss at Brandt's first visit to Paris as Chancellor on 30–1 January 1970, with the meeting coming so soon after the EEC summit. On this occasion it was more a question of words than action. Both sides declared their resolve to push through the decisions reached at The Hague, and they agreed notably to co-ordinate their ideas on political co-operation, which would then be put to the rest of the Community. Though there is no clear evidence, this collaboration may well have facilitated the smooth passage and speedy establishment of the new policy.

As ever at Franco-German summits, some attention was paid to purely bilateral issues. Yet one can already discern signs of a change at this first meeting between the two leaders. In contrast to the past, when the actual results of foreign policy co-ordination between the two sides seldom lived up to the expectations raised, discussions between Brandt and Pompidou were of greater substance. The *Ostpolitik* must be identified as the main spur. At the summit in January 1970, East–West relations formed an important topic, with debate embracing the Berlin question and the issue of a possible European Security Conference. Talks on the *Ostpolitik* itself took up a sizeable share of the meeting. There is little doubt that such bilateral discussion (and particularly endorsement by the French) was keenly sought by the Germans, for whom it represented a bonus in the negotiations while also helping to disarm internal criticism. At the same time, one can point to a two-way process, with this dialogue in turn enhancing the value and status of the bilateral summits themselves. These had been tending to lose momentum under Kiesinger, the previous Chancellor.

Hence Brandt informed Pompidou of his policy plans in the East, although these were still in their early stages, and the Chancellor aimed to forestall any anxiety that the *Ostpolitik* might divert Bonn's attention away from the Community. Although it has been argued that French disquiet about the *Ostpolitik* began to increase at the start of 1970 at the latest, this date seems a little early.[27] For the time being, at least, Pompidou's attitude towards the German initiative was neutral.

With the spirit of The Hague still very much in evidence, French and German views on both Community and world affairs

---

[27] Nass, 'Incertitudes allemandes', 293.

were close. Relations were not yet marred by the friction in almost every field (political co-operation apart) that was to emerge once detailed negotiations on the summit's initiatives began in the Council of Ministers. This dichotomy provides a clear illustration of the distinction in Community decision-making between broad agreement on general principles of future policy at Head of State or Government level and the conflicts that can arise once detailed negotiations are broached among sectional ministers. The cordial atmosphere that prevailed at the first Brandt–Pompidou meeting was reflected in the media, with references to the summit as a 'Rendez-vous without conflicts' and 'La vie en rose'.[28]

By the time of the next bilateral summit in Bonn on 3–4 July 1970, the *Ostpolitik* had grown into the dominant feature. A clearer and less reassuring picture of the consequences of Brandt's *démarche* for the balance of power in Europe, especially regarding France and the Federal Republic, had taken root in Paris. This concern was heightened by Bonn's obviously determined pursuit of negotiations with the East.[29] Not only had Bonn patently outgrown its former status as a French subordinate in its dealings with Eastern Europe, the French also appreciated that they stood to lose economically as well as politically from the likely further development of Germany's eastern trade that would follow the *Ostpolitik*. Two events in particular can be highlighted in terms of their influence, one of a political, the other of a personal nature. Politically, Brandt's March 1970 meeting in Erfurt with Willi Stoph, the East German leader, was a concrete manifestation of inter-German *rapprochement*. The event was seen in France as being of the greatest significance. *Le Monde* referred to a 'major turning-point of the German nation'.[30] For some at least the meeting and the emotional scenes that accompanied it conjured up the spectre, however flimsy, of reunification—a theme that would grow in French calculations. In the West, too, Bonn's existing political stature and importance were confirmed by Brandt's April 1970

---

[28] *Die Zeit*, 30 Jan. 1970; *Neue Zürcher Zeitung*, 2 Feb. 1970.

[29] On the theme of rising French concern, see Nass, especially 293–4; Gilbert Ziebura, 'Frankreichs oder Deutschlands Ostpolitik—Konvergenz oder Divergenz?', *Dokumente* 1 (1971).

[30] *Le Monde*, 14 Mar. 1970.

visit to the United States. To French eyes, the Federal Republic appeared as America's privileged partner, a proximity which also rekindled traditional Gaullist fears that Europe's independence might be compromised.

On the personal level (and this must not be denigrated, Pompidou's attitude to Brandt the individual undoubtedly playing a significant part in his appraisal of the Federal Republic as a whole), the Chancellor's rapturous popular reception in both East Germany and the United States contributed to the President's growing resentment. Brandt's American tour, in particular, presented a sharp contrast with Pompidou's own far less successful visit the previous month. This had been marred by some very ugly public demonstrations.[31] Jobert goes so far as to suggest that the incidents that took place were influential in shaping the President's future unsympathetic attitude to Washington.[32]

Although on the eve of the July 1970 summit the French and German Governments both strenuously denied that the *Ostpolitik* was impairing their relations, there is little doubt that its negative repercussions were being felt in Paris. At the summit, the French voiced disquiet over two topics in particular: Bahr's secret diplomacy in Moscow, which they distrusted; and France's position as one of the occupying powers in Berlin, which they stressed and clearly did not want to see undermined.[33] Thus Schumann warned Scheel against thoughtless concessions to the Russians or against racing into legal recognition of the GDR, which might compromise the Allied position in the recently opened Four Power Talks on Berlin. The Bonn Government, which was actively engaged in negotiations with the Soviet Union, Poland, and the German Democratic Republic, for its part very much needed French backing, particularly as the Opposition's denunciations were growing increasingly voluble. The CDU–CSU was claiming that the Government was ignoring

---

[31] On Pompidou's and Brandt's American trips, see Kissinger, *White House Years*, 422–4. On the French President's visit, see also Roussel, *Pompidou*, 377–80.

[32] On this theory, see Jobert, *Mémoires*, 190–1. For a more reasoned view, see Grosser, *Les Occidentaux*, 340.

[33] For an indication of Bahr's views and the anxieties aroused, see Walter H. Hahn, 'West Germany's Ostpolitik. The Grand Design of Egon Bahr', *Orbis* (Winter 1973). As to the French position on Berlin, see Moersch, *Kurs-Revision*, 229–30. See also Baring, *Machtwechsel*, 277.

the Community and it was vigorously seizing on reports of French unease.

Thus, throughout the course of the wide-ranging discussions that took place at the July 1970 Franco-German summit, Brandt was conscious of the need to allay French anxiety. The Chancellor's success was not absolute. Although he managed to persuade Pompidou to speak out in favour of the *Ostpolitik*, and the President professed his country's 'moral and political support' for the normalization of relations with the East,[34] the French leader also highlighted the importance of Four Power rights in Berlin. This nuanced approach provided an early sign of a *décalage* that was gradually to develop between Pompidou's public statements and his private views on the *Ostpolitik*. This would grow into a major theme in bilateral relations, giving the clearest illustration of a continuing, historically-based, unease in French thinking *vis-à-vis* the Federal Republic. Generally, but by no means always, such doubts have been concealed by the façade of cordial and collaborative relations between France and Germany.

Community issues remained uncontroversial at the meeting of July 1970, while on the bilateral front both leaders repeated the usual intentions to strengthen the bonds between their two nations. At this summit the French and German ministers of science were also present to discuss the feasibility of a joint nuclear reactor project. Yet, as has been seen, the actual level of economic and technical co-operation, notably in the nuclear field, has seldom lived up to the grander expectations voiced on such occasions. This distinction well illustrates the contrast between the broad political will to co-operate in both countries and their frequent divergence of interests when such schemes have been put to the test in the form of detailed proposals, particularly at non-governmental level.

The economic side of the third Brandt–Pompidou meeting of 25–26 January 1971, which was notable for the agreement reached on EMU, has already been detailed above. It is the *Ostpolitik* aspect, forming the other half of the package, which will be tackled here. Brandt's policy had by now reached a crucial phase, with negotiations nearing their climax following

[34] Jobert, *L'Autre Regard*, 141.

the signing of treaties with Moscow and Warsaw the previous year. Yet, internally matters were growing increasingly acute. Opposition criticism was rising in pitch, while the ruling coalition faced defections, making the need for French backing all the greater. Yet as the *Ostpolitik* had accelerated so Paris had become more uneasy. Feeling was well captured by one newspaper, which observed that although France was undoubtedly behind the *Ostpolitik*, its views were not without a certain mistrust of German independence, 'which, for the French, appears to hold out incalculable prospects'.[35] There was also concern in Paris that Bonn might be negotiating recklessly. Yet, as has been seen, Pompidou was able to extract a high price for his endorsement of the *Ostpolitik*. The Chancellor's remarks made clear the interlocking interests involved. As Brandt states: 'In reality, Ostpolitik was one of our reasons for wanting progress in the West'[36]—the concession on EMU representing the concrete manifestation of such feelings.

As a result of Pompidou's press conference of 21 January, there was lengthy discussion at the 1971 summit about the future of Europe. The President reiterated the inter-governmental nature of his proposed European Confederation, while the Germans declared they would back his suggestion for Ministers for Europe, though Brandt pointed out some of the problems that this would entail. The question of relations between Europe and the United States, to be a major source of friction later in the year and especially in the winter of 1973–4, was also raised. Already, Pompidou underlined his opposition to any institutionalization of links between the Community and Washington. Brandt decribes the President's reservations: 'The Americans must not, he said, be led to believe that they could exercise a right of supervision over the European Community.'[37] It was to be exactly this impression that Kissinger's 1973 initiative for a New Atlantic Charter would provoke, with harsh repercussions for France, Germany, and the Community as a whole.

Finally, bilateral matters were also covered at the summit. Pompidou raised the question of language teaching and there was renewed discussion on the proposed nuclear accelerator. All

[35] *Süddeutsche Zeitung*, 25 Jan. 1971.
[36] Brandt, 254.
[37] Ibid. 259.

in all, the meeting of January 1971 was a more efficient, pragmatic affair than its two predecessors, and lack-lustre to some. This can largely be attributed to the difficult negotiations that had taken place on EMU, and also to the fact that as concrete issues increasingly came up for discussion, the novelty and public relations aspects of the summits between the two new leaders diminished and routine set in.

The *relance* of the European Community heralded by the Hague summit owed much to agreement between France and Germany. This was evident not just at the summit itself, but throughout almost the entire range of issues covered in the subsequent negotiations. Clearly, in a period of movement in European affairs, much depended on the co-operation of the Community's principal partners. Yet already certain difficulties had become apparent. First of all, a sharp distinction was visible between the collaborative and optimistic atmosphere of the Community's summit meeting and the problems and internal differences given expression once detailed negotiations began. This phenomenon was particularly evident regarding EMU. The problem has not, however, remained restricted to the 1970s. Subsequent experience has shown it to be endemic to Community decision-making as a whole.

Indirectly associated with this characteristic was the question of French European policy. Although Pompidou represented a significant break with the past, it was apparent by early 1971 that the force of continuity remained almost as strong in French calculations as that of opening. Pompidou's Europeanism was keenly tempered by a belief in the nation state and national sovereignty, tenets which, when they conflicted with new European developments, most notably the Werner Report, patently held sway. The result was often friction at Community level. Over-optimistic expectations, therefore, of a completely new direction in French European policy had to be revised in favour of a model in which progressive and conservative influences were much more evenly balanced. This would become clearer in the period covered by the chapter which follows.

In German foreign policy, too, some revision of expectations was necessary. Although the Hague summit had provoked speculation of a new balance in Franco-German relations more in Bonn's favour, it was clear that while the *Ostpolitik* was still in its negotiating phase and the Federal Government's Bundestag majority was slim, considerable constraints remained on the German side, affecting relations with France. Most conspicuously, the Brandt Government sought French endorsement of the *Ostpolitik.* This was important both internally, to stem mounting opposition criticism, and externally, in order to strengthen Bonn's hand in its talks with the Eastern bloc. The linked need for an active *Westpolitik,* which clearly depended on close co-operation with Paris, strengthened France's hand at bilateral and Community level. Only with the first fruits of the *Ostpolitik* and a more stable Parliamentary base would the balance between the two countries more obviously start to shift. In the meantime, as shall be seen in the next chapter, monetary instability would cloud these developments and create a new source of strain in bilateral relations.

5

A Period of Disorder

1971–1972

Introduction

In the sixteen months between May 1971 and the Paris summit of October 1972 monetary matters dominated Community affairs. Against the background of the Community's attempts to establish stable exchange relationships, the instability of the dollar, combined with the attractiveness of the Deutschemark as a safe refuge currency, resulted in serious economic and political divergence among the Six. With the benefit of hindsight, the highly charged and repetitive discussions that took place among the Europeans on the question of floating and, especially, on competitiveness and relative exchange rates, now seem ill-founded. Floating has come to be accepted in a way that seemed inconceivable in the early 1970s. More important, not only have there been much larger changes in parity levels since 1974, but these have also been accomplished without fuss and with surprisingly little damage. As a result, there has in fact been an evolution in government attitudes, with a greater readiness now to accept appreciations. This picture constrasts sharply with that of 1971–2.

A similar process has also taken place in the agricultural sector. With the CAP dependent on common prices, the exchange rate fluctuations of 1971–2 had severe repercussions on agriculture. Monetary and farm issues became closely inter-linked, and discussions among the ministers of agriculture were no less tense or repetitive than those between their financial colleagues. New mechanisms had to be devised to allow the continued functioning of the CAP, and each new bout of monetary instability resulted in further friction between the member states in the farm sector. Again, as with monetary affairs, the experience of protracted floating since 1974 and the institutionalization of a system of subsidies and border levies,

highly controversial at the time, have made this issue considerably less contentious.

Monetary unrest and its consequences

The monetary crisis in spring 1971 lay rooted in the previous
year's shift in American policy from controlling inflation to
stimulating growth and reducing unemployment, requiring a
reduction in interest rates.[1] This sparked off very large speculative outflows from the United States, predominantly drawn to
the Federal Republic by the high interest rates resulting from the
Bundesbank's anti-inflationary tight money policy and the
Deutschemark's appeal as a stable refuge currency. With the
Americans adopting a policy of indifference towards the drain of
funds in order to force the Europeans to act, the onus fell on the
Germans, as the major recipients of funds. Bonn faced a policy
dilemma. Economic controls were supported by Klasen, President of the Bundesbank, and a very wide section of business
opinion, which was anxious, as in the past, to avoid the
detrimental effects of a rise in the value of the currency on
exports. Yet a second faction pressed for an immediate joint EEC
float. Such a move was judged to be inevitable, and it would also
have the additional advantage of absolving the Federal Republic
from responsibility for supporting the dollar. It would also cause
least embarrassment to the Americans—an indication of the
continuing importance of this consideration for the Germans.
Floating would, furthermore, facilitate control of the domestic
money supply, and hence help combat inflation—the other
major influence on thinking.

These divisions were mirrored in the Cabinet, where ministerial positions reflected differing priorities, a cleavage that was
to remain over the next fifteen months. Schiller, doctrinally
opposed to any form of controls, put greatest emphasis on
relations with the United States. It is possible that he also saw in
the monetary crisis an opportunity to push the Community back

[1] On the crisis of May 1971, see Shonfield, i. 72–92, ii. 333–6; Susan Strange, 'The
Dollar Crisis 1971', *International Affairs* (Apr. 1972), 191–215; Panek, *Die Währungskrisen
von November 1968 bis Mai 1971 im politischen Prozess der Bundesrepublik Deutschland*; Gunter
Nagel, 'Mark flottant et unification monétaire', *Documents* (May–June 1971); Alain
Samuelson, 'L'Expérience du mark flottant, ses incidences jusqu'au réalignement des
monnaies', *La Revue d'Allemagne* (Jan.–Mar. 1972). For an insider's view of American trade
and monetary policy in 1971, see Kissinger, *White House Years*, 951–8.

towards an EMU on the lines he favoured. Thus the situation might provide a means of overturning the unattractive formula reached at the Franco-German summit of January 1971. By contrast, Scheel, concerned about maintaining good relations in the Community, and Ertl, worried about the effects of floating on the CAP and German farm incomes, both leant towards controls. Only at the Cabinet meeting on 7 May 1971 was it finally resolved that German strategy at the forthcoming Community talks would be to press for a joint European float, failing which Bonn would aim for 'toleration' of unilateral action.

This readiness to stand alone in defiance of the known views of Community partners is instructive, recalling earlier German policy at the Bonn Group of Ten meeting in November 1968. On that occasion, the CDU—dominated Grand Coalition, represented in the talks by the redoubtable duo of Strauss and Schiller, had staunchly refused to bow to heavy American, British, and French pressure to revalue the Deutschemark.[2] Despite the Federal Republic's desire and need for Community solidarity and the support of its European allies, in May 1971 the necessity to regain control of the domestic money supply, that decisive concern in German policy-making, combined with the desire not to offend the United States, overrode considerations of European unity and the certain criticism of Community partners, notably the French. Such thinking was indicative of the highly issue-based assertiveness that has remained a feature of German foreign economic policy to this day.

In the extremely tense Community talks on the crisis on 8 May, attention focused on France and Germany. Schiller passionately advocated the need for swift action on the monetary front, and he attempted to put a Community-minded face on the proposals he put forward for concerted floating. A wide variety of reasons explain the unattractiveness of his plans for the French. Economically, linking the weak franc to the Deutschemark would involve risks. It was also likely that the franc's value would be towed up in line with the German currency, involving a loss of competitiveness compared to non-Community coun-

---

[2] On the November crisis and conference, see: Panek, op. cit.; Ziebura, *Die deutsch-französischen Beziehungen*, 131–40; Seydoux, *Dans l'intimité franco-allemande*, 130–1; K. Schiller, 'Die Internationale Währungslage nach der Bonner Konferenz der Zehner-gruppe', *Europa-Archiv* 1 (1969); Shonfield, ii. 324–5; Baring, *Machtwechsel*, 139–47.

tries. Such competitive considerations would be highly prominent in shaping thinking in all the member states throughout the period. Politically, a joint float was also unacceptable to France, for the result would in reality be a Deutschemark zone, while German financial aid to the participants would only confirm the mark's leading role.[3] Such an appraisal well indicates the important role of national prestige in French thinking.

Most important for the French, however, was the American dimension, a notable illustration of the continuing importance of political concerns in French foreign economic policy. For Paris, the monetary crisis was of Washington's making. A joint float would lower European competitiveness towards the United States, and thereby benefit the Americans. Instead, Europe should put pressure on Washington to stem the monetary tide. Even more desirable would be an American devaluation by means of a rise in the price of gold, a long-standing French policy aim which would raise the value of national reserves. ,

Finally, floating would also damage the CAP, an aspect of Community policy particularly prized by Pompidou. The President's concern was made fully clear in September 1971, when he was to stress the protection of French agriculture and condemn European floating, which would signify, 'the death of the agricultural common market'.[4] The French were also unhappy about German handling of the monetary crisis. Not only was it felt in Paris that uncertainty in Bonn had encouraged speculation, there was also some suspicion regarding Schiller's motives during the crisis.[5] Such doubts give a good indication of the distrust that had persisted since his conduct in the 1968 and 1969 monetary turmoil, attitudes that would be intensified in 1971–2.

In the light of this profound rift between the positions of the Community's two major partners, it was hardly surprising that the Council of Ministers' negotiations were extremely laborious. The lack of effective economic policy co-ordination between the member states and the fact that the Six were not facing identical

---

[3] See Alfred Grosser, 'Après le referendum. Quelle politique extérieure?', *Études* (June 1972), 844.

[4] Quoted in *Le Monde*, 23 Sept. 1971. See also Pompidou's remarks at his press conference on 21 Sept. 1972, in *Le Monde*, 23 Sept. 1972.

[5] See Barre's comments on Schiller's role in *The New York Times*, 19 May 1971. On doubts about Schiller's behaviour, see Philippe Simonet, 'Pompidous europäische Gleichgewicht', *Dokumente* 2 (1971).

economic conditions, notably with differing inflation rates, exacerbated an already difficult situation. The talks, character-ized, as in previous negotiations, by the uncompromising attitudes of Giscard and Schiller, were only saved, *in extremis*, by Scheel's intervention. His moderating influence and assurance of Germany's European convictions provided the impetus for an extremely fluid compromise whereby it was agreed that the Council would tolerate a temporary Deutschemark float. Thus, although there was no acceptance of joint floating, the Germans had achieved their minimum aim. The decision represented a defeat for the French stance of total opposition to any increase in exchange rate flexibility. Paris responded by announcing a boycott on work on EMU, though the move was primarily a gesture, as little progress could in fact have been made in the duration of the float. One important by-product of the German action, however, was a reinforcement of the developing *rapproche-ment* between Paris and London.[6]

The May 1971 monetary crisis underlined a number of important differences between France and Germany. Of these, the most conspicuous was the dissimilar effect of the dollar's instability on the two countries. While the strong speculative pressures on the Deutschemark resulted in the Germans seeking immediate and comprehensive action, the much lower pressures on the franc allowed the French to adopt a considerably less urgent approach. Furthermore, the two countries' divergent attitudes to inflation and, in particular, their varying degrees of dependence on the United States, were spotlighted. It was clear that anxiety about losing control of the money supply and concern not to offend Washington were major influences on the German side. An interesting evolution would take place regard-ing the two issues over the coming months. While on inflation the French were to move closer to the German position, on relations with Washington Bonn would edge towards a more Gaullist view, at least until the 1973 Middle East war.

In May 1971, however, strategic considerations and the need to appease the United States weighed more heavily in Bonn's calculations. This was made clear by Brandt's comment of 9 May that floating was 'not a brutal reprisal against the dollar,

---

[6] On this theme, see Pierre Drouin in *Le Monde*, 23-4 May 1971, and Simonet, 135.

but a market-oriented answer, nothing more'.[7] The existing German dependence on the United States and the continuing clear link between the monetary and military sectors was intensified by the prevailing mood in Congress. In spring 1971, the Mansfield motion of halving the number of American servicemen in Europe in six months was under close scrutiny. In contrast to this firm German awareness of the military dimension, France's greater freedom of action on account of geographical factors, and consequently its lesser dependence on the United States, assisted in the adoption of a much more critical stance towards American monetary policy during the crisis.

French and German positions also differed on the question of inflation. For the Germans, control of the inflationary tendencies provoked by the inflow of dollars was absolutely vital. Floating obviated the need for the Bundesbank to intervene and buy dollars, allowing it to regain control of the money supply and tackle inflation. For the French, inflation's lower contemporary priority and, more important, the much lesser pressures on the franc compared to the mark, gave Paris considerably greater room for manœuvre in its response to the dollar inflows.

The repercussions of the German float on EEC policy were felt most immediately in the agricultural sector. This was illustrated by the timing of the 11–12 May emergency farm ministers' meeting, which highlighted the close connection between the monetary and agricultural sides. The increase in the value of the Deutschemark compared to its 'green' counterpart (used for calculating agricultural prices and incomes) meant that farm imports into the Federal Republic would become cheaper and exports dearer. To restore equilibrium and maintain a common price policy, a system of border levies and subsidies—the so-called Monetary Compensatory Amounts—would now have to be introduced and their size and method of operation resolved. The issue would be very bitter, with differences revolving around divergent French and German interests. While Bonn was preoccupied with maintaining farm incomes, Paris sought at all costs to protect the fabric of the CAP, which had already been shaken by the defensive measures taken by the Germans during

[7] Quoted in Rolf Kaiser, 'Die Interdependenz politischer und ökonomischer Interessen in der Weltwährungskrise 1971' (unpublished doctoral dissertation, Eberhard Karls Universität, Tübingen, 1976), 87.

the autumn 1969 monetary troubles. After a complex round of negotiations, based on France and Germany, a compromise was finally reached on MCAs. Again, the Germans achieved their objective of preventing the imposition of any time limits on MCAs, which were simply left open for monthly renewal.

Although a gradual softening of French hostility to the German decision to float can be traced over the course of the following two months, Pompidou was at first extremely angered by the move. His feelings emerged unequivocally at the press conference of 26 May, which closed his official visit to Belgium. The President vented his ire principally on Washington, then on Bonn. According to Pompidou, Europe should take on the United States for its mishandling of the international monetary system and establish its own monetary independence to bring about the end of the 'dollar standard'.[8] Such sentiments were strongly reminiscent of de Gaulle, and this political aspect would grow increasingly important in French emphasis on EMU. As to the German decision to float, this was 'an anti-Community step'.[9] It was not hard to discern a sharp trace of resentment in the President's words. According to Pompidou: 'The Federal Republic has problems of its own and sometimes tends to make them. We have been requested to approve certain solutions, and we did so—a little like approving a pact with the devil.'[10]

What explains the change of tack that took place in French thinking over the coming months following such acerbic comments? The fact that the float was not to prove as harmful as had been expected was a major consideration. Bilateral contacts also played a part. Perhaps most important, however, was the growing sensitivity to inflation in France. This could to some extent be countered by a slight rise in the value of the franc. Finally, a number of influential French figures had spoken up for the German policy. These ranged from Robert Marjolin and Raymond Aron to Jean-Marcel Jeanneney, a former minister and economic adviser to de Gaulle, who called for a concerted EEC float towards the dollar.[11] The extent to which thinking in some government circles had shifted was illustrated in Giscard's

[8] Quoted in the *Guardian*, 27 May 1971.
[9] Quoted in *International Herald Tribune*, 28 May 1971.
[10] Ibid.
[11] See *Le Monde*, 7 July 1971.

own comment that the Deutschemark float was, 'a decision which was perhaps necessary to normalize a certain situation.'[12]

Given the change of mood, it proved possible to outline a package deal on monetary policy at the 1 July 1971 Council meeting. Not surprisingly this revolved principally round France and Germany. Such an agreement would have been inconceivable barely two months earlier. French acceptance of the very principle of wider currency fluctuation margins was a breakthrough, though significantly it was tied to an agreement on an eventual return to fixed parities. Schiller's announcement of the introduction of measures to control foreign borrowing by German firms was as unexpected. This move had long been counselled by the Bundesbank (and it also represented the sort of controls sought by the French). But despite this progress, marked differences remained over the timing of the Deutschemark's return to a fixed parity. This continuing impasse, which again turned chiefly on the conflicting views of Paris and Bonn, had the effect of focusing attention on the Franco-German summit of 5–6 July—recalling the developments that had taken place on EMU at the last bilateral summit at the beginning of the year.

As in January, so in July money dominated the meeting between Brandt and Pompidou, taking up nearly half of their ten hours of talks. Yet unlike the previous summit, no common ground could be found. The two leaders and their finance ministers merely restated earlier positions with neither side as yet under sufficient pressure to give way. The French left Bonn disappointed at their failure to secure any guarantee on the termination of floating. In some French quarters the German stance was presented as a pursual of national interests rather than the common good—a criticism that would, before long, be echoed in the agricultural sector.

Other topics proved more fruitful, however, with discussions of European integration and enlargement, as well as wider world affairs, such as relations with the United States, the Eastern bloc, and the Berlin question. As ever, certain stock subjects recurred. At Schumann's visit to Bonn in May 1971, the question of language teaching—that particular preoccupation of Pompi-

---

[12] Quoted in *Le Monde*, 10 July 1971.

dou—had again been raised, with concern in Paris about the low status of French in German schools. Following changes made by the *Länder*, the French could now be assured that their language would be given the same weight as English and Latin. The Germans went out of their way to fête Pompidou, with whose sixtieth birthday the visit coincided, and the President was somewhat taken aback by the festivities and the enthusiasm of his hosts.[13] A boat trip down the Rhine emphasized the cordiality between the two nations. In addition, Brandt presented Pompidou with a canvas by Max Ernst, the President's favourite artist. Despite (perhaps because of) the failure to come together on the monetary front, great efforts were made to ensure the visit was a popular success.

The second phase

This calm in Franco-German relations was to prove short-lived. The highly restrictive trade and monetary measures announced by President Nixon on 15 August 1971, involving a ten per cent surcharge on a wide range of imported goods and the formal suspension of dollar convertibility, was to be the cause of renewed bilateral friction over Community policy and relations with the United States.[14] Once more, the influence of American action on European integration would be evident. As in May, French and German reactions to the American moves were substantially different. Bonn was again torn between European and Atlantic commitments. The latter aspect was greatly accentuated by security constraints, the balance of payments issue being very closely tied in American minds to the question of troop reductions.[15] Only a few days before the President's declaration, the Congressional Joint Economic Committee's Subcommittee on International Exchanges and Payments had stressed this link, arguing that steps towards solving the nation's balance of payments problem should include greater European

[13] See, for instance, the amusing account in Paul Frank, *Entschlüsselte Botschaft. Ein Diplomat macht Inventur* (Stuttgart, Deutsche Verlags-Anstalt, 1981), 37–8.

[14] On the development of American monetary policy in 1971 and 1973, see John S. Odell, 'The US and the emergence of floating exchange rates: an analysis of foreign policy change', *International Organization* (Winter 1979).

[15] On this aspect of German policy, see J.F., 'Bonn face à la crise monétaire', *Documents* (Sept.–Oct. 1971), 118.

participation in the costs of NATO. If the Europeans were unwilling to take on this extra burden, then the United States should reconsider its personnel levels in Europe accordingly. Given Bonn's constrained position as regards security, its response to Washington had to be careful and conciliatory. These considerations were reflected in an initial statement issued by the Finance and Economics Ministry on 16 August. Predictably, the reaction from Paris was very different. The French Government put out a critical statement in which it did not hesitate to point out the incompatibility of Nixon's moves with the rules of the IMF or GATT.

The American decision to suspend convertibility and halt currency swaps meant that all the Community countries would be obliged, partly or wholly, to abandon fixed parities. Yet, instead of coming together under this external pressure, the Europeans' divergent positions and interests were now glaringly exposed in the different strategies that were adopted. Although the situation seemed to vindicate Schiller's stand in favour of a joint float, as in May, this was not to French taste. Instead, on 18 August, Paris elected for a two-tier market, in which there was a fixed exchange rate for trade and official transactions and a second, floating, rate for the financial market. Pompidou made clear his displeasure towards the Americans by having his Secretary-General at the Élysée make public the announcement. As Jobert notes: 'It is thus that I emerged from the shadows, by chance and without pleasure.'[16]

The two-tier system, which was also adopted by Belgium and Luxembourg, was strongly opposed by the Germans on well-established lines of cost and *dirigisme*, as well as impracticality. It is interesting to note that, according to a source in a major Paris bank, forty per cent of the staff were involved in the double market during its period of operation.[17] In those two and a half years the French Government was repeatedly obliged to intervene directly in the foreign exchange markets to stem capital inflows. However, it was the fundamental political question of divergent attitudes towards the United States which towered over any such differences in economic thinking between France

---

[16] Jobert, *L'Autre Regard*, 181.
[17] Kaiser, 148.

and Germany. Matters rested on their dissimilar priorities between the Community versus the Atlantic level. As ever, the Germans were more conscious of the need to avoid antagonizing Washington. It is interesting to note here the evolution that took place in German attitudes by the later 1970s, by which time Bonn was adopting a much more critical approach towards American monetary policy. As shall be seen, dollar instability and consequent upward pressure on the Deutschemark caused by the early reflationary measures in the Carter presidency contributed to the allure of the EMS for Bonn.[18]

The central role of France and Germany, on whose agreement depended any joint European position towards the United States in 1971, was highlighted at the Community finance ministers' meeting on 20 August. As in May, the barriers to accord on monetary policy proved insurmountable and agreement was limited to a joint communiqué expressing concern at the American measures. Such a vague outcome was not entirely displeasing to the Germans, however. Though critical of the French decision to adopt a two-tier market (with hopes in some circles that the experiment would soon fail, and speculation in others that the Federal Republic might attempt to accelerate this process) Bonn was gratified by the authorization of floating it now received rather than its mere toleration as before. For the ardent European, however, the situation was depressing. The Community was now more divided than ever, and it appeared that the major beneficiary from this situation was the United States, which seemed to gain confidence from the obvious lack of any European cohesion.

In the aftermath of the Community's failure to unify, in what was beginning to form a familiar pattern, attention again shifted to the bilateral Franco-German level. Brandt informed Sauvagnargues, the French Ambassador to Bonn, of his readiness to hold talks with Paris at any time. Against a background of considerable diplomatic activity between the two capitals, Franco-German bilateralism was demonstrated in their joint opposition to the Benelux countries' plan for an additional Council meeting in early September to discuss the monetary crisis. As in the past, this display of Franco-German hegemony was ill received in the capitals of the smaller member states.[19]

Two developments in late summer were working against the French position on the monetary question: the Japanese decision at the end of August to float the yen; and the operational problems of the two-tier market. Signs in Paris of a greater readiness to compromise were lent credence by—hypothetical—discussion of the size of any putative Community revaluations. Chaban-Delmas's remark that France did not intend to make a doctrine of the two-tier system can also be read as an indication of the latter's operational difficulties and of a greater French tolerance.[20]

Yet the question of the franc's value, and therefore its competitiveness, was obviously going to prove a critical bargaining item. While Giscard asserted the policy of maintaining the present parity, Schiller gibed at the French for being too concerned with competitiveness, and he suggested instead that the franc could well bear a three to four per cent revaluation.[21] With the benefit of hindsight, the amount of time and energy spent on such arguments appears wasted. Certainly, the experience of protracted floating, a practice which has had surprizingly limited adverse consequences, has meant that governments have become considerably less sensitive to small upward parity adjustments. This evolution contrasts with the very great emphasis on maintaining competitiveness and, as far as possible, avoiding appreciations, that was typical of the early 1970s.

There were signs of movement on the German side too in early September 1971, with hints of a less pliant attitude towards the Americans. A number of factors were responsible, not least the temporary decline of the troop reduction issue in Washington. These developments in French and German positions helped to open the way for the substantial agreement that was achieved by the Community finance ministers at their meeting on 13 September. Although the accord can be criticized for being at a minimal level, it was perhaps unreasonable to expect anything

[19] Note, for instance, the angry Belgian press reaction quoted in *Le Monde*, 27 Aug. 1971.
[20] Reported in *Frankfurter Allgemeine Zeitung*, 3 Sept. 1971.
[21] Reported in *Le Monde*, 4 Sept. 1971, and *L'Express*, 6–12 Sept. 1971, 27.

more under the circumstances of continuing economic and political differences between the member states regarding the Americans.

The Six issued a renewed protest against the American trade and monetary measures, now calling for their retraction. Above all, they agreed on a series of joint principles to be followed at the Group of Ten meeting in London on 16 September. These comprised a return to fixed parities and the need for a realignment, from which the dollar could not be isolated. Although not in so many words, the Community as a whole was now officially demanding the devaluation of the dollar through a rise in the price of gold. In particular, the decision represented a major step for the Germans, who were now, albeit with reservations, significantly departing from previous policy. Bonn had never before called for an American devaluation, and the decision marked a sharp contrast with the compliance that had been evident in the earlier phase of the crisis. The move can well be seen as indicating the beginnings of a shift in long-term German attitudes towards Washington over monetary policy.

Although a step in the right direction, the Community's consensus on a series of general principles for international monetary reform was not enough. Accord on relative European parity levels, and between these and the yen, was the essential preliminary for any wider international arrangement. European agreement, in turn, centred on a decision on the relative values of the Deutschemark and franc. Bergsten captured the contemporary situation: 'Germany is reluctant to move more than 5% above France. Japan wants to move no more than 5% above Germany; and Italy, Britain, and some smaller Europeans will not move at all unless France does.'[22] Franco-German haggling, complicated by uncertainty and division in Bonn and exacerbated by renewed friction between Giscard and Schiller, was to prove the dominant feature of Community relations in the following weeks.

Pompidou's remarks at his press conference on 23 September indicated the extent of French intransigence—for the time being at least—on the question of parity adjustments. For the President, revaluation of the franc was 'absurd and unthink-

---

[22] C. Fred Bergsten, quoted in Kaiser, 183

able'.[23] In the period that followed, attempts to reach compromise emanated almost entirely from the Germans. Yet the position in Bonn was far from clear. As in the past, conflicting ministerial priorities led to marked divisions in the Cabinet. Scheel re-emphasized the importance of maintaining good relations with France, which had already been badly strained, partly on account of Schiller's aggressive tactics. Couve de Murville's remark on the monetary issue that 'In Germany, there is a certain indifference towards Paris'[24] gave an idea of the state of feeling in some French circles. The effect of such views would undoubtedly be to reinforce the growing tendency in France to place greater weight on relations with Britain.

Thus Scheel argued that European unity, which principally depended on an improvement in Franco-German relations, should be the main priority of Bonn's external policy. Schiller, on the other hand, continued to place relations with Washington above those with Paris. With competitiveness and exports firmly in mind, he pressed for any revaluation of the Deutschemark to be made conditional on a simultaneous moderate rise in the value of the franc. This ministerial rift emerged clearly at the Cabinet meeting in mid-October 1971, where a somewhat indecisive compromise was reached. For the time being, Brandt leaned more towards Schiller's point of view. After a stormy meeting, it was announced that 'The Cabinet confirms the previous attitude of the Federal Republic, and that it is the will of the Federal Government to achieve a result with its European partners which makes a discussion with others easier.'[25] This cryptic statement should be interpreted as meaning that the initiative had been left with Schiller, who had obviously made much of the wider economic and strategic factors involved; while at the same time, the Cabinet recognized the need for steps within the Six, principally towards France.

It is interesting to consider the Community finance ministers' meeting on 26 October 1971 in the light of these developments. The session was characterized by a surprising lack of friction

[23] Pompidou's press conference, 23 Sept. 1971. Text from French Embassy, London, Press and Information Service.

[24] Quoted in *Le Monde*, 17–18 Oct. 1971. See also Jobert's comments about Schiller in his *Mémoires*, 210.

[25] Quoted in *The Times*, 15 Oct. 1971.

between Schiller and Giscard, who had a half-hour tête-à-tête. Unfortunately, it is not possible to tell whether this cordiality on Schiller's part represented any reaction to possible Cabinet pressure to tone down his dogmatic stance, for the relative smoothness of the meeting stemmed partly from the fact that it was convened to deal with short-term economic policy co-ordination, a subject of considerable interest to Schiller, rather than more controversial monetary matters. What is certain, though, is that there were simultaneous indications that Brandt had now moved closer to Scheel's conciliatory approach. One cause may have been a greater appreciation of the fact that time was on France's side. The latter's considerably lower share of trade with the United States in terms of its total exports—in fact only about half as much in absolute terms compared to the Federal Republic—left France less vulnerable to the American import surcharge.[26]

Thus it was revealed that the Chancellor had sent Pompidou a letter suggesting a meeting in advance of the regular bilateral summit scheduled for January 1972 in order to discuss the monetary situation. It was illustrative of the Franco-German role in the Community that Brandt should have explicitly remarked in his letter on the necessity for accord between Paris and Bonn as a prerequisite for agreement among the Six. Additional evidence of a shift in the German line away from Schiller's position came in Klasen's remark that allowances would be made for those countries reluctant to devalue—indicating some relaxation in Bonn's demand for a revaluation of the franc.

Strain in bilateral relations

Pompidou's response to the Chancellor's suggestion for an early meeting was neither immediate nor over-enthusiastic. The German request was treated with a certain condescension, and Brandt was portrayed very much as *demandeur*—causing some annoyance in Bonn. For one German diplomat who spoke to the author this French behaviour was explicable in terms of a reluctance in Paris in any way to stray from the established pattern of the January–July meetings, regarded as de Gaulle's heritage, which it would be 'improper' to alter. The careful vigil

---

[26] This argument derives from Kaiser, 188.

kept by the orthodox Gaullists was adduced as an additional factor weighing on Pompidou.

Although this interpretation may constitute a fraction of the answer, it is clearly insufficient, and, while one should not exaggerate the incident, it was symptomatic of the more reserved attitude in France towards the Federal Republic, stemming from the strains of the monetary crisis and its agricultural repercussions. This link between the two sectors was very significant. Not only were the periodic increases in German MCAs a reminder of the Deutschemark's continuing float and thus an ever-present irritant; more important, Ertl's preoccupation with protecting farm incomes and his increasingly strident attacks on the CAP were beginning to cause a great deal of damage. Ertl's approach must be seen firmly in the context of domestic party politics; notably concern in the FDP, particularly in Bavaria, not to lose votes from the agricultural constituency. German farmers were growing steadily more disenchanted with small price increases and the effects of the rising value of the Deutschemark in depressing farm incomes.

A closer examination of Ertl's position is worth while, as it provides both a good idea of his own assertiveness and the basis of French criticism. In July 1971, Ertl publicly stated that he had always had doubts about the effectiveness and political practicality of the agricultural part of the Treaty of Rome, adding that the original construction of the common market in farm products had too obviously been based on the wishful thinking of the politicians then in power in France and Germany.[27] In another interview, he went further still, stressing the need for changes in the farm policy—although he conceded that it was still probably not possible to talk to the French about its revision.[28]

Such statements caused considerable alarm in Paris, where, in conjunction with the development of MCAs, they appeared to signal the disintegration of the CAP. As will be seen, by May 1973 this German position on Community farm policy would come to be interpreted in highly political terms by the French, intensifying growing doubts in Paris about the Federal Republic

---

[27] Reported in the *Financial Times*, 22 July 1971.
[28] Ibid.

and its future intentions. Although for the time being differences over the monetary and farm sectors were devoid of such wider political overtones the situation still provided a considerable source of tension, particularly as there was no end in sight to the German float. The French response was understandably bitter. According to the Secretary of State in the Ministry of Agriculture:

If the Federal Government was brought to a new Deutschemark revaluation, we would not be able to permit the continued existence of the compensatory levy system applied to agricultural trade. If the German Minister of Finance wants his currency to be the strongest in Europe, or indeed the world, he must realise that this cannot come about without consequences for his country's agriculture.[29]

Such acid comments amply illustrated the effect of the monetary unrest on bilateral relations and confirmed the importance to Paris of preserving the CAP intact.

Yet it was developments in the *Ostpolitik* even more than in agriculture that presented cause for French alarm regarding its Eastern neighbour. Brandt's meeting with Brezhnev at Oreanda on 16–18 September 1971 was taken in Paris as another ominous portent of Bonn's political ascent. Reactions to the Oreanda episode, not just among the French but also many of the Federal Republic's other Western partners, well illustrated the suspicions prevalent regarding Bonn's Eastern diplomacy.

Although Brandt records that, contrary to the general impression, it was Brezhnev who had sought the Oreanda meeting—an indication of Russian assessments of the Federal Republic's rising political and economic importance[30]—the summit evinced a very hostile reaction in France, accompanied by strong echoes of Rapallo. The Chancellor's remarks on departing for Oreanda, that 'we can act like the others. We are a state, an emancipated Government',[31] were in themselves viewed as maladroit, sparking off considerable criticism, especially in

[29] Quoted in *Le Monde*, 14 Oct. 1971.

[30] See Brandt, 343, 345.

[31] Quoted in Gerhard Kiersch, 'Frankreichs Reaktion auf die westdeutsche Ostpolitik', in Egbert Jahn and Volker Rittberger (edd.), *Die Ostpolitik der Bundesrepublik — Triebkräfte, Wiederstände, Konsequenzen* (Opladen, Westdeutscher Verlag, 1974), 185. The author gives the best account available of French reactions.

the right wing French press. Not only was this response indicative of the potent effect of the meeting, it also highlighted long-standing failings in information and mutual understanding in bilateral Franco-German relations. For *L'Aurore*, the Chancellor's visit represented the 'consecration of German rebirth under the beneficent patronage of Leonid Brezhnev through the second Yalta of 1971'.[32] The extract also re-echoes the pejorative overtones of Yalta in French thinking. *Combat* for its part spoke of 'King Brandt', claiming that the meeting bore witness to the Chancellor's position as the key figure in European affairs, the rise in Germany's prestige taking place at France's expense.[33] Oreanda aroused great fears that the Federal Republic was seeking to exploit its position as a fulcrum between East and West. Ertl's critical stance towards the CAP, demonstrating that Bonn was trying to distance itself from Community policy, lent credence to this belief. Subsequent events would confirm the existence of a close link in the French analysis between fidelity to the CAP, the *Ostpolitik*, and the future of Germany.

Reaction to the Oreanda meeting was extremely hostile within the French Government, an extension of the concern already voiced in Paris about reckless German pursuit of *rapprochement* with the East. Pompidou was incensed by the meeting, of which he had been given no prior warning, having only found out about it through the press. Information from a well-placed source shows that the entire French Cabinet meeting that day was dominated by the President's views and comments that Brandt had betrayed the West. This opinion was also expressed by officials at a high-level Franco-German meeting soon after.[34] Pompidou at once suspected a plot between Brandt and Brezhnev at the expense of Western Europe. It should, however, be stressed that France was by no means alone in nursing such doubts. Kissinger's memoirs make clear the disquiet being shared in Washington and London as a result of Brandt's diplomacy.[35]

[32] Ibid.

[33] *Combat*, 17 Sept. 1971.

[34] Ernst Weisenfeld, 'Geprägt von Monnet und de Gaulle. Frankreichs Aussenpolitik im Wandel', unpublished paper, July 1979. For Pompidou's earlier views on the *Ostpolitik* and the Soviet Union, see Roussel, *Pompidou*, 407–10.

[35] See Kissinger, *White House Years*, 410–11, 416, 422–3, 529–34, 828–9, 938, 963–4.

The French Government's anxiety was doubtless compounded by its highly pessimistic attitude towards the recently opened MBFR negotiations. For Paris, troop reductions called forth the prospect of 'special zones' in Europe, in turn evoking fears of German neutrality or, may be, reunification. This French unease was heightened and given substance by the belief that Bonn wanted to bring all-German questions into the MBFR arena. Pompidou appears seriously to have believed in the possibility that the Russian and West German leaders might have struck a deal at Oreanda, Bonn perhaps having given ground over troop levels in return for Russian promises on all-German affairs. Despite the unlikelihood of any such arrangement, these fears were very real to the President, giving a very good indication both of his character and of the failings in mutual understanding with the Germans. The episode underlines the continuing effect of traditional fears and stereotypes in French (and more widespread) relations with the Federal Republic, while also pointing up shortcomings in France's awareness of its partner's policy. As for Pompidou, suspicion about Germany, never kept wholly at bay, was to become increasingly evident. Although there certainly persist doubts about the future of Germany in official French circles, the moderated expression of such attitudes during the Giscard presidency testified to the more realistic foundations of bilateral relations that were established in the later 1970s.

At his press conference on 23 September 1971, Pompidou made clear his feelings towards the Federal Republic. He suggested that France would have expected to receive better advance notification about the Oreanda meeting. More important, the President stated categorically that the Federal Republic, 'believed at one stage that [gaining greater freedom in its relations with the East] was easier to achieve than was in fact the case'. In Pompidou's words: 'The German Government had been tempted ... to seek a Berlin solution solely via an inter-German dialogue.'[36] This was a telling public censure of Brandt's policy, indicating the President's displeasure. Pompidou's complaints were not entirely without foundation. As has been seen, the

---

[36] Pompidou's press conference, 23 Sept. 1971. Text from *Problèmes politiques et sociaux*, Supplement to Nos. 105–6, 9–10.

unexpected speed and secrecy of the Bonn–Moscow talks, combined with a possible lack of information at the outset, had raised doubts amongst all the Western allies, notably Washington.

Despite his comments, Pompidou's anger was largely suppressed. Rather, the President adopted a veiled approach. In the words of one commentator, 'support for the Ostpolitik was matched by warnings, the last word of the passage was "vigilance". While seeking to ease his countrymen's fears, the President of the Republic was playing a cautious game towards the German Chancellor.'[37] This restraint in Pompidou's remarks, which could have been much harsher, was appreciated by Brandt, especially in the light of the tense domestic political situation. Fear of causing too much damage may well have been one explanation for the President's reticence.

There is now little doubt that close links existed between French uncertainty about the *Ostpolitik*, the strain in bilateral relations created by the monetary crisis, and the growing *entente* between Paris and London. Such a connection is implied by Kissinger's recollection that at his 1970 visit to the United States, 'Pompidou even went so far as to ruminate on a London–Paris axis as a counterweight to uncontrolled German nationalism.'[38] The good relations and mutual respect between Pompidou and Heath aided this developing rapport, as did the pro-British feelings of influential French officials like Jobert, who had already established contacts with their senior British counterparts.[39] A number of high-level meetings had taken place, culminating in Heath's visit to Paris on 20–1 May and Schumann's trip to London on 11–13 November. Both occasions were marked by considerable warmth. This growing cordiality had already been given more solid expression in the decision to study construction of a Channel tunnel and the announcement of a royal visit to France in May 1972.

Towards resolution of monetary differences

German desire for *rapprochement* notwithstanding, differences between Bonn and Paris over monetary policy remained evident

[37] Alfred Grosser, 'Le Gouvernement Brandt à mi-parcours', *La Revue d'Allemagne* (Jan.–Mar. 1972), 13.

[38] Kissinger, *White House Years*, 422. Note also the comments by Poidevin and Bariéty, 337.

[39] See Jobert, *L'Autre Regard*, 176; Grosser, *Les Occidentaux*, 339.

in early November 1971.[40] Division over the Deutschemark float apart, the French wanted to be absolutely certain that reciprocal American action would follow any unilateral European concessions on monetary matters. The Germans, for their part, appeared ready to move some way towards French wishes on relative parity levels, and there continued the diminution in German calls for revaluation of the franc noted earlier. Signs of American willingness to give way sharpened the question of relative intra-European parity levels. Once again, interest concentrated on France and Germany, focusing attention, in the now familiar pattern, on the rescheduled bilateral summit.[41] Some preliminary discussion on exchange rates had already taken place at Scheel's visit to Paris in mid-November, and at their summit on 3–4 December 1971 Brandt and Pompidou were able to consolidate on this meeting. With domestic sentiment in both countries keen for a settlement, the two leaders were eager to resolve their monetary differences. Accordingly, they devoted their first day of talks to this and the linked issue of relations with the United States.

Accord on relative parity levels—so important at the time— took precedence. Cross rates between the franc and the Deutschemark had shifted by some twelve per cent since the beginning of May. This change was considered too large even by the French in view of the interdependence of the two economies. While Paris visualized an eight per cent margin, the Germans had in mind a five per cent maximum. That the latter figure eventually proved acceptable to the French can be attributed to two factors: the Germans made much of the fact that prolonged monetary unrest would damage their industry, meaning that any future Deutschemark revaluation made in a climate of recession would have to be smaller than one made at once; and Paris was growing increasingly restive about the effects of the monetary crisis on the CAP.

At the bilateral summit, Brandt and Pompidou co-ordinated positions for their forthcoming meetings with Nixon. The quid

[40] Note, though, that Alfred Frisch sees signs of the gap between Paris and Bonn already narrowing in October. See 'Face à la crise monétaire', *Documents* (Nov.–Dec. 1971).

[41] On the significance of the summit and the role of Franco-German relations, see Shonfield, i. 82–5.

pro quo for the French concession on parity levels took the form
of an understanding that preliminary agreement on the monetary issue would be announced by Pompidou at his summit with
Nixon in the Azores on 13–14 December 1971. This gave
Pompidou the kudos of appearing as Europe's spokesman *vis-à-
vis* the Americans. The incident provides another good illustration of the importance of prestige in French foreign policy. The
question of trade relations with the United States was also raised.
But the divergent positions adopted by the two leaders once
more testified to their two countries' differing political and
trading interests. While Brandt made clear the continuing close
link for the Germans between the economic and strategic areas,
Pompidou, in line with France's lesser dependence on Washington and its consequently greater freedom of action, took a
markedly different approach. According to Brandt's account,
'[Pompidou] appreciated what the American alliance meant,
just as I did, but he could not on principle accept that Europe
should finance America's military, political and economic
activities out of its own deficits—and that was just what we were
being asked to do.'[42] There is a strong similarity between this
approach of Pompidou to American policy and the critical
stance adopted by de Gaulle in the 1960s. Once again, one is
aware of a marked continuity in presidential attitudes despite
the change of power in 1969.

The Nixon–Pompidou summit had in fact been sought by the
Americans. Following their change of policy on devaluation,
they recognized that French resistance could still block a
settlement. By initially unveiling his monetary proposals before
the French President, Nixon gave Pompidou the public success
he desired—and perhaps also required in order to placate
orthodox Gaullist opinion. Joint discussions with the Americans
on the broad lines of an agreement would help portray France as
the leader of Europe. Yet there was a two-way process involved.
As has been observed, 'The prestige showered on the French to
be the first to know publicly of the United States decision was
paid in kind by President Pompidou's consent to trade talks
between the Common Market and the United States.'[43] As part

---

[42] Brandt, 257.
[43] Kolodziej, *French International Policy*, 223.

of the package, the American import surcharge would immediately be lifted in return for revaluations by Europe and Japan. The US would also raise the price of gold, representing an 8.57 per cent devaluation of the dollar. In return, the French would not insist on the restoration of convertibility as a precondition for a settlement, and would show flexibility over trade negotiations.

Details of the new parities among the Group of Ten were worked out at the Smithsonian conference on 17–18 December 1971. French emphasis on competitiveness was satisfied; the franc's revaluation was to be lower than the weighted average of the other European currencies and it was to be slightly devalued *vis-à-vis* the Deutschemark. The fortunes of the French and German currencies had well reflected the two countries' different economic strengths. While the franc's value had risen by seventeen per cent since its August 1969 devaluation, the mark had soared by forty-three per cent over the same period.[44] It is also interesting to observe the decline, despite illusions to the contrary, of Britain's role in international monetary affairs, confirmed by the Smithsonian talks. While the French and Germans had consulted with the British during the monetary turbulence and attempted to canvas London's support for their differing positions, it was clear that the 1971 crisis had been played out chiefly between America, Japan, France, and West Germany, with the latter pair dominating the European scene. The point has been underlined since 1978 in the central role of Bonn and Paris in the EMS, contrasting with Britain's non-participation.

Franco-German bilateralism

Settlement of the international monetary crisis allowed the resumption of progress within the Community on Economic and Monetary Union and farm matters in early 1972. Pending the introduction of EMU, the two areas remained closely interwoven. Decisions relevant to the agricultural policy, such as over the value of the unit of account, had to await developments on the Community monetary front. Thus, agreement to restore fixed parities by no means made way for the instant solution of the CAP's problems. Controversy over MCAs—focusing largely

[44] Ibid. 227–8.

on France and Germany—and the connected question of agricultural prices, dragged on well into the new year. As before, there were substantial differences in French and German priorities in both the monetary and agricultural sectors. At the same time, the eventual settlement in both areas owed in large part to bilateral agreement between Paris and Bonn.

This collaboration was most apparent regarding EMU. Taking up their commitment of December 1971 to revive the policy as soon as fixed parities allowed, Brandt and Pompidou reached substantial agreement at their summit in February 1972. There was a striking similarity between this meeting and its predecessor in January 1971. In both cases, preliminary agreement on EMU at bilateral level opened the way for subsequent accord in the Community as a whole. As before, the impetus came largely from Paris, motivated in both instances by the twin aims of protecting the CAP and presenting a coherent European stance towards Washington. For Brandt, the desire to demonstrate an active *Westpolitik* was the major incentive. In a package deal, Bonn accepted a narrowing of margins, and, in an important concession, agreed to introduce short-term capital controls if required by a monetary crisis. This was a significant departure from Schiller's free market doctrine—a lesson learned from the monetary unrest—and may well have contributed to his dissatisfaction, culminating in his resignation five months later. Brandt gives an entertaining view of Pompidou's feelings, illustrating also the differences in French and German economic philosophies: 'We ought, he said, to resume work on economic and monetary union. We could not manage without instruments for the control of short term capital movements. He wanted to tell me—"before Schiller comes"—that he did not believe in the feasibility of "total" economic liberalism.'[45]

This apparent lack of total conviction on the part of a Gaullist President (and an ex-banker at that) in market forces, which were being favoured instead by a Social Democrat, is doubly ironic. Not least, the contrast is instructive regarding the different policy perspectives of leading members of the two parties in France and Germany, a distinction which runs counter to the ideological cleavage that one might normally expect.

In return for German acceptance of narrower margins and the

[45] Brandt, 257.

principle of monetary controls, the French made a gesture towards Bonn's emphasis on economic policy. Paris now gave the go-ahead for the creation of an EEC steering committee for economic policy co-ordination. The decisions reached represented a significant demonstration of Franco-German bilateralism and highlighted the two countries' role in reopening the door to EMU. This was made explicit by Pompidou's statement: 'The Ministers of Economy and Finance and their staffs would, on the basis of the conclusions reached at the present meeting, draw up a common position, both on proposals which might be made to the two countries' partners and on the harmonisation of contacts to be opened with these partners ...'[46]

Yet in a stance once more reminiscent of his predecessor, Pompidou made clear the external dimension, principally regarding the United States, which underscored European action in the monetary field. For the President, a joint European line depended on 'a common attitude towards America'.[47] Despite the change of power from de Gaulle, it was clear that a tacit rivalry with the United States remained an inherent factor in French foreign policy. Differences had been brought to the surface for Pompidou by the aggressive American tactics on trade and monetary affairs. Although attenuated for the time being, the American strategy of 1973–4, which would correctly be interpreted in Paris as an attempt to secure political, and not just economic, control over the Europeans, would illustrate how much closer still was to become the similarity between Pompidou's stance towards Washington and that of his predecessor.

As at other bilateral summits, East–West relations were also aired. Brandt attempted to smooth French feelings over the *Ostpolitik* by stressing Bonn's Western commitment. However, one can detect a note of warning in Pompidou's remarks to the Chancellor during their private talks. According to Brandt, the President observed that 'the Europeans had to be extremely wary and present a firm front, thereby facilitating contacts and promoting détente in the best possible way.'[48] Talks were also held on political co-operation. The most interesting development here was the French Government's more flexible stance towards

---

[46] Quoted in *Keesing's Contemporary Archives*, 19–26 Aug. 1972, 25424.
[47] Quoted in *Le Monde*, 10 Feb. 1972.
[48] Brandt, 263.

the establishment of a small secretariat to supervise political co-operation. It should be recalled that this was not a new departure, but was, rather, in line with French policy dating from the Fouchet talks. Furthermore, Pompidou, like de Gaulle before him, stressed the strictly inter-governmental nature of political co-operation, which would extend to the proposed secretariat, from which the Commission would be excluded.

Throughout the summit, both sides strove to dispel any impression of a rift in their relations. In fact, the two leaders attempted to underline their countries' cordial links by breaking away from tradition and holding a joint press conference, a task normally relegated to the government spokesmen. This change, it was explained, stemmed from the importance and extremely positive results of the meeting. What lay behind the sudden paean to Franco-German friendship? Obviously, after almost a year of friction, the restoration of good relations suited both Paris and Bonn. For Brandt, the decision on EMU, with its repercussions on the CAP, would ameliorate relations with the French, and ease the tension surrounding Ertl and German farm policy. Yet internal considerations were probably pre-eminent for the Chancellor. The party political conflict in the Bundestag was growing ever fiercer as the ratification of the *Ostpolitik* treaties approached and the Government was being faced with the very real possibility of defeat. Matters were exacerbated by disaffection within both coalition partners. Two SPD deputies were to defect to the CDU in March. An active *Westpolitik*, demonstrating the Chancellor's 'Europeanism', was a valuable asset against at least some of his domestic critics.

The reasons underscoring Pompidou's behaviour are more difficult to judge. Undoubtedly, there was very great satisfaction on the French side that work on EMU could re-start, not least because of its benefits for the CAP. As has been seen, this had been under fire, principally from Bonn, but also from Rome, and, stranger still, even from within the Commission itself. In late January 1972 Commissioner Spinelli, with apparent backing from the Italian Government, put forward a plan for the replacement of the CAP's intervention mechanism with a British-style system of direct income subsidies to farmers through deficiency payments.[49] These proposals did not meet the instant hostility among the member states that might have been expected, and it was even reported that the idea would be discussed in Bonn.[50]

Yet there was more to the apparent warmth of French attitudes towards the Federal Republic than just satisfaction over the preservation of the CAP. First of all, renewed progress on EMU would be a means of binding Bonn more closely to the Six. Secondly, given Pompidou's concern with the Americans, EMU had an additional role to play, namely that of bolstering European independence and protecting the Community from American pressure. Finally, by stabilizing exchange rates and thus indirectly guaranteeing intra-European trade, EMU would also assist in France's own industrialization. Even more than for de Gaulle, France's industrial strength was of prime importance to Pompidou. The President's philosophy, no doubt with the Federal Republic partly in mind, was that only from a position of economic strength could France's views be heard by others in Europe when defending the Community—especially the CAP —or by the Americans, who were seeking to reassert their grip.

There was one final possible influence on Pompidou, though much more complex and by no means clear—his health. Jobert recounts an unusual incident at the Franco-German summit: 'Yet this time, on the occasion of the official luncheon, the President of the Republic disrupted the ritual of toasts and implored the Chancellor to bring forward Europe's destiny without rest and without weakening ... Maybe already, in the hour-glass of time, Georges Pompidou was seeing the weeks slipping by too quickly.'[51] It is not possible to make any certain judgements about the state of Pompidou's health at this time. That his illness and his awareness of the pressure of time did come to affect his views is no longer seriously in doubt. To what extent illness had taken hold as early as February 1972 is uncertain, though Jobert notes in retrospect the signs of ill health in the President by the summer, when he also made his will.[52]

---

[49] Reported in the *Guardian*, 27 Jan. 1972. Spinelli amplified his remarks the following year. See the report in the *Financial Times*, 19 Mar. 1973.

[50] See *Frankfurter Allgemeine Zeitung*, 29 Jan. 1972.

[51] Jobert, *Mémoires*, 223–4.

[52] Ibid. 231.

The bilateral nature of progress on EMU initiated at the Franco-German summit of February 1972 was underlined at a meeting of high French and German officials in Bonn on 3 March, in preparation for detailed discussion among the Community finance ministers soon after. Such directorial Franco-German collaboration on monetary policy was very badly received by the smaller states, and some at least took the resumption of progress as an opportunity for advancing their own particular policy interests. The Italians, for instance, now insisted on a regional aid programme, a long-standing aim, in return for their support for EMU. But despite these obstacles, substantial agreement was reached on a Community package deal. This was broadly on the lines of the settlement of March 1971, and a commitment was also made to the creation of a regional policy. Franco-German bilateralism in early 1972 was also evident on the agricultural side. After early disagreements on MCAs, there was a co-ordination of French and German views in reaching a conclusion at the March agricultural marathon. Though to a lesser extent than with EMU, Franco-German understanding had again largely underpinned the eventual settlement.

Domestic events and European affairs—the French side

Foreshadowing the pattern of 1973-4, the remainder of 1972 was characterized by a very marked interconnection between issues, though in 1972 it was internal matters rather than external events which were influential. The first of these was Pompidou's referendum on enlargement held on 23 April.[53] The referendum appeared to solve numerous problems for the President. It was made clear in the campaign that Pompidou did not see the vote as one specifically on enlargement, but rather as a wider mandate for his ideas on Europe. The occasion would also publicly demonstrate his own European conviction. These two factors indicated the continuing presidential use of referendums as means of enhancing personal prestige—a tactic initiated by de Gaulle.

[53] For analysis of the referendum and its consequences, see Michael Leigh, 'Linkage Politics—the French Referendum and the Paris Summit of 1972', *JCMS* 2 (1975-6); Berger, op. cit.; Rials, op. cit.; Grosser, 'Après le referendum'; A. Lancelot, 'Il ne faut pas jurer de rien. Le Referendum du 23 Avril 1972', *Projet* 67 (July-Aug. 1972).

Wider considerations also obtained. A successful referendum would assert and strengthen Pompidou's position not only in France, but also towards the other European leaders. Especially against the background of a future Paris summit, Pompidou would gain new authority and stand out as the leader of Europe. This motive was strongly implied by remarks he made on 11 April.[54] Internal party political considerations were no less important. The referendum offered a chance to break early signs of restored unity on the left by spotlighting the divergent views of the Communist and Socialist parties to the Community and enlargement. Thus it would place the Government in a very strong position for the legislative elections in March 1973. Lastly, the referendum would divert attention from various financial scandals affecting Gaullist politicians and it would help the party regain cohesion and prestige. A successful outcome would also improve Pompidou's control over the party and reinforce his more liberal stance, particularly over the orthodox Gaullists.

As it happened, the results did not live up to these expectations. The low turnout of 60.5 per cent reflected popular cynicism towards the referendum, which was hardly held on an issue of burning national importance. Of the valid votes cast, 68 per cent backed the President. With an above-average abstention rate, the Socialists claimed victory for their recommended strategy. Not all the abstentions should be seen as politically motivated, however; the figures could, in fact, be presented to suit all tastes. The support for Pompidou equalled that in the second round of the 1969 presidential election. Yet it was certainly not the massive 'yes' for which he had campaigned. Pompidou was extremely disillusioned. According to Jobert, 'his whole attitude was consumed by bitterness, and he was unable to shake this off'. Jobert notes elsewhere: 'In the following weeks he did not cease to remind his visitors of the blow he had dealt himself, of the error of judgement he had committed.'[55]

Opinion differs as to the extent of the referendum's effect on the President's policy. Certainly, it convinced him of the need to change Prime Minister, a move which also illustrated the enhanced power of the Gaullist old guard, who felt vindicated by

[54] Quoted in *The Times*, 12 Apr. 1972.
[55] Jobert, *L'Autre Regard*, 208 and *Mémoires*, 227.

the result. Hence the marked presence of traditional Gaullists in the new Government headed by Pierre Messmer. The outcome, undoubtedly also bore on Pompidou's European policy, particularly regarding the proposed summit. As Drouin notes: 'Its clearest consequence is that M. Pompidou will not be able to preside over the "Summit" in Paris next October with the authority he expected to gain from a "massive, clearcut, Yes".[56] One highly placed French official put a different slant on the argument, suggesting that Pompidou sought to rationalize the referendum result by claiming that it proved Europe did not interest the French. Yet, whether directly or indirectly, the referendum clearly affected the President's attitude towards the projected summit, making a successful outcome that much more important. Not only did the summit present an opportunity to further French policy aims, but it also offered a means of redressing Pompidou's weakened internal position.

The referendum cannot, however, be viewed in isolation. For just as it increased the importance of a successful summit for Pompidou, so too, at about the same time, did external pressures from France's partners seem to call that very outcome into question. These pressures were felt notably on institutional, but also on monetary, matters. Hence the change, from May 1972 onwards, in Pompidou's attitude to the summit, witnessed in his adoption of a much more defensive posture. The President grew increasingly reluctant to hold a conference whose agenda might not reflect his own policy priorities or, worse still, which might be dominated by discussion of institutional arrangements of a potentially supranational nature. These developments can be traced through the preparatory talks on the summit.

Pompidou first called for a conference of Community leaders on 18 August 1971, at the same time as the announcement of the French two-tier market. The main spur behind the proposal was the desire to emphasize European solidarity, particularly, as ever, towards the United States. This was confirmed by the timing of the original overture and corroborated by subsequent remarks.[57] The wish to protect the CAP was also influential. The

[56] Grosser, 'Après le Referendum', 835. See also the discussion in Rials, 137.

[57] See for example, *Le Monde*, 24 Dec. 1971; the President's television speech of 21 April 1972, in *Le Monde*, 23–4 Apr. 1972, and his press conference of 21 Sept. 1972, in *Le Monde*, 23 Sept. 1972.

link between European integration and a strong France was also underlined; Pompidou declared that the nation had to 'play a leading role in the creation of European independence and the defence of European interests'.[58] Hence too the importance for the President of a clear mandate in the referendum. The proposed agenda for the summit strongly mirrored Pompidou's policy preferences. Above all, it would concentrate on EMU. Jean-René Bernard, Pompidou's Economic and Financial Counsellor, accurately describes the importance this had come to assume for the President: 'Between the two 'pauses' of the Hague and Paris Conferences everything went by as if economic and monetary union between the member states of the Common Market was the avenue which should have led to our continent's independence.'[59] In addition, the summit would examine another of Pompidou's interests, the Community's external policy, notably towards the United States.

Yet despite French wishes, it was institutional matters that dominated discussion in the prelude to the Paris summit. These talks highlighted the divergence of opinion between France (and Britain) on the one hand, and the other member states on the other, over the institutional development of the Community. Two issues were uppermost. First, the proposed political co-operation secretariat, and secondly, the Commission's role in Community affairs.

Though the concept of a secretariat for political co-operation had been raised at the Franco-German summit of February 1972, nothing definite had been agreed. Most important, the question of its location remained open. Although Pompidou at his press conference on 16 March 1972 had voiced the hope that it would be situated in Paris, this wish was by no means universal. In fact, an interesting link was to develop between the question of the secretariat's location and the different conceptions of its role. Among the smaller member states, the French-inspired body was at first seen as a potential usurper of the Commission's influence. Such feelings were reinforced by Pompidou's emphasis on Paris as its base, which recalled Gaullist strategy in the Fouchet negotiations. Hence the Dutch, in

---

[58] Pompidou's television speech of 11 April 1972. Quoted in *Le Monde*, 13 Apr. 1972.
[59] *Le Monde*, 3 Apr. 1975.

particular, stressed that it should be located in Brussels, a tactic designed to minimize any anti-integrationist bias in the secretariat. By April 1972 the French had become isolated, the other member states all favouring the Belgian capital both politically and on simple grounds of practicality.

There were also preliminary signs of a rift over the Commission's function in Community affairs, notably political co-operation. While the Benelux countries, fearing domination by the larger powers, sought greater Commission participation, the French as usual stressed inter-governmentalism. One interesting by-product now was the onset of tacit support for the French position from the British—another sign of the developing alignment between Paris and London on many institutional questions. This relationship in the early 1970s well bears out some of the ironies in Benelux enthusiasm for British membership of the Community early in the previous decade, when it was eagerly believed that Britain would be a staunch upholder of the rights of the smaller member states.

French policy on the political secretariat grew increasingly forceful over the following two months. At a press conference in Luxembourg in early May, for example, Pompidou simply pointed out that the question of the secretariat's location had not appeared to constitute a threat to Europe at the time of the Fouchet talks (when Paris had been accepted as the site).[60] This and similar statements were part of a concerted French campaign on the secretariat. It was clear that the issue had come to assume considerable importance for Pompidou. The President's approach illustrated once again the prestige facet in French foreign policy (it has even been suggested that Pompidou's desire for French as the language of political co-operation was an additional reason for his enthusiasm for Paris as the secretariat's base).[61] More important, it also highlighted his hostility to supranationality with which Brussels, home of the Commission, was identified. Furthermore, with matters intensified by the referendum result, concern for the summit itself was becoming increasingly evident in the French position. Thus

[60] Pompidou's Luxembourg press conference, reported in *The Times*, 5 May 1972. See also Schumann's ideas, reported in *Le Monde*, 2–3 Apr. 1972.

[61] Pierre-Bernard Cousté and François Visine, *Pompidou et l'Europe* (Paris, Librairies Techniques, 1974), 45.

there were signs now of greater anxiety in Paris lest the conference and EMU, its major objective, should become overshadowed by institutional wranglings.

Matters reached a head at the foreign ministers' meeting on 26–7 May 1972, where the Commission took a stand on the issue of its participation in political co-operation and in the proposed secretariat. Obviously, political co-operation was often likely to involve Community institutions, and the French approach could not easily be defended. More important, there was discord among the member states regarding the Community's decision-making and institutional structures. In an important move, the Dutch circulated a lengthy document criticizing the present institutional arrangements and calling for changes to the Treaty of Rome and for direct elections to the European Parliament.

It is against this background of controversy over supranationality and institutions, threatening Pompidou's success at the summit, that his questioning of its future must be seen. The visit of a Benelux statesman to Paris at the start of June 1972 provided the President with the ideal opportunity for showing his hand. Pompidou made it clear that he would 'not take the responsibility of inviting nine Heads of Government if their meeting results only in vague declarations of interest, agreement on minor points, or worse still, badly camouflaged disagreements'.[62] Pompidou's timing was by no means fortuitous. His remarks were a direct consequence of the previous week's discussions among the foreign ministers. The President's dilemma was understandable. Not only was there strife on institutional topics inimical to Paris; worse still, this was obscuring matters dear to the French, notably EMU.

Reaction in the other member states to Pompidou's threats was generally restrained. Significantly, though, the Belgian Foreign Minister, Pierre Harmel, in a very clear echo of Belgian policy at the end of the Fouchet negotiations, adopted an extremely hostile stance obviously intended to signal to the President the unacceptability of any attempts to emulate his predecessor's tactics of undermining the Community by way of new institutions.[63] Once again, as in the 1960s, the smaller

---

[62] Quoted in the *Financial Times*, 3 June 1972. Note also Morgan, *From Summit to Council*, 15.

[63] See reports in the *Daily Telegraph* and the *Financial Times*, 8 June 1972.

member states showed a clear determination to block unacceptable developments.

More surprising, perhaps, was the obvious German antipathy towards Pompidou's strategy. This was largely explicable on account of domestic electoral reasons. Bonn's opposition focused not so much on the institutional side of the President's plans as the timing of the summit. Facing severe parliamentary problems and weakened as a result of the Baden-Württemberg elections, where the CDU had secured an absolute majority, Brandt could ill afford to put his *Westpolitik* at risk. The Chancellor's desire for an active and unified Community was heightened by his awareness that new federal elections would be necessary. (These were announced on 24 June.) Brandt clearly sought to capitalize on the party political advantages of a successful pre-election summit. Thus he opposed postponement, reasoning that the member states should concentrate on areas where agreement could be reached.

Confusion in the Community was increased by the British decision of 23 June 1972 to float the pound. The move dealt a serious blow to EMU, whose relaunching had formally been adopted by the Council (and the candidate nations) only three months earlier. The British decision placed both the future of the policy and the whole Smithsonian structure into doubt. Moreover, by threatening a major French policy objective, it added weight to feeling in Paris that the summit should be postponed. It is worth looking at the dissimilar French and German responses to the British action. These reflected not only their divergent policy preferences, but were also instructive as to the state of Franco-British relations. The British step was well received in Bonn, not least because it appeared to exonerate the Federal Republic's own monetary policy. Yet while Schiller expressed the warmest understanding, the French found themselves in a quandary. First reactions of hostility to this new obstacle to EMU and the CAP was soon tempered, however, by at least the outward display of understanding. This forbearance —in marked contrast to the French response to the German float in May 1971—bore witness to a desire in Paris to maintain good relations with London, as well as an appreciation that the British had been faced with little choice.

The German side

Although there was a considerable degree of Franco-German co-operation evident at the Community finance ministers' meeting called in the wake of the British float, internal problems in the Federal Republic prevented a repetition of the developing pattern of bilateral views on monetary policy being consolidated at summit level. The Franco-German summit on 3–4 July was heavily overshadowed by political difficulties in Bonn, contributing to the disappointing outcome of the talks.

Two factors were responsible. First of all, the Federal Government was, not for the first time, divided over monetary issues. On 26 June, Klasen had advised the Chancellor of the need to impose exchange restrictions. However, this measure was still resisted by Schiller. There resulted a clash between the two experts at the Cabinet meeting two days later. In the light of experience since May 1971, Schiller's doctrinal opposition to controls and renewed recommendation of concerted floating were now opposed by his colleagues. They were led, it should be noted, by Schmidt. The Cabinet now favoured some limited exchange controls. Expecting the Chancellor's backing and accustomed to having his own way in the Government, Schiller had misjudged the situation. His resignation, hanging over the Franco-German summit, was formally announced on 6 July. Brandt's comments are worth quoting: 'His grounds for resigning—a limited measure of control over foreign currency movements—were trivial. The fact was that he had managed to alienate nearly all his Cabinet colleagues.'[64] The affair well illustrated one facet of the personality conflicts besetting Brandt's Cabinet, complicating policy co-ordination and often impeding the emergence of a coherent government line. What was of special interest was the role played by Schmidt. The Defence Minister had been crossing swords with Schiller for some time and was instrumental in his downfall. The incident marked an important further step in Schmidt's steady emergence as probably the dominant figure in the Cabinet.

Deadlock in the Bundestag over the ratification of the *Ostpolitik* treaties was the second obstacle to firm action from

---

[64] Brandt, 438. See also the very good account in Baring, *Machtwechsel*, 670–2.

Bonn.[65] Though the treaties with Moscow and Warsaw had been signed in August and December 1970 respectively, their ratification had deliberately been made dependent on a Four Power agreement on Berlin. This was finally signed on 3 September 1971. Yet the climate in the Bundestag, which had been deteriorating steadily as the *Ostpolitik* gathered momentum, had worsened as ratification approached. The Opposition's hostility was attributable to many causes. These ranged from accusations of reckless negotiating and appeasement of the East, to insufficient consultation with Bonn's allies and neglect of Western affairs, especially the European Community. Above all, feelings were raised by nationalistic and emotional factors. These focused on Brandt's recognition of West Germany's post Second World War frontiers and acceptance of the GDR. Such concessions, it was claimed, would cement the division of Germany, negate the reunificatory aspects of the *Grundgesetz*, and weaken the Federal position in Berlin. There was also a strong ideological element in some quarters, with a deep hostility to Communism.

Party political considerations themselves were by no means absent. The CDU-CSU had adjusted badly to its new role as Opposition, and, for some of its leaders at least, the *Ostpolitik* represented an issue by which to overturn the Government. Those wishing to follow in detail the extremely complicated party manœuvrings that ensued are best directed to the footnotes. Suffice it to say here that, contrary to many expectations (Brandt and Scheel included), the Opposition's attempt on 27 April to unseat the Chancellor via a constructive vote of no confidence failed. Matters did not rest there, however. The following day there was deadlock on the second reading of the 1972 budget, the Bundestag dividing equally. Brandt now offered bipartisan talks on the Eastern treaties and there followed an extremely tense and somewhat chaotic interlude.

[65] On the course of the *Ostpolitik* and Opposition attitudes, see especially Moersch, *Kurs-Revision*; Ménudier, *L'Allemagne selon Willy Brandt*; Rainer Barzel, 'L'Intégration européenne et l'Ostpolitik', *Chronique de Politique Étrangère* (July 1971); Roland A. Höhne, 'Die Motive der ostpolitischen Opposition seit 1969', in Jahn and Rittberger, 53–70; A. Wiss-Verdier, 'La Crise d'avril–mai 1972', *Documents* (May–June 1972); Jérôme Vaillant, 'La Crise gouvernementale en RFA, *L'Allemagne d'aujourd'hui* (May–June 1972); Roger Morgan, 'Political Prospects in Bonn', *The World Today* (Aug. 1972). Most recently, see the very full account in Baring, *Machtwechsel*, 396–424.

Finally, after various prevarications from the CDU–CSU, ratification took place on 17 May.

The whole episode, a critical phase in the history of the Federal Republic, had demonstrated the lack of any stable majority in the Bundestag. Yet, on account of the special circumstances that had surrounded the framing of the *Grundgesetz* (which had been designed to guarantee stability and lacked provision for precipitating premature elections), the Government had to adopt the expedient of engineering its own downfall. This was brought about on 22 September. In the interval, policy-making in Bonn was effectively stymied.

The talks between Brandt and Pompidou at the July 1972 summit once again highlighted long-standing differences, notably on monetary policy and relations with the United States. That the two areas remained very closely linked for the French under Pompidou, as under de Gaulle, is shown by Brandt's account of the President's remarks, which also offer another indication of the pejorative connotations of Yalta. According to the Chancellor's record, Pompidou argued 'that the concerted floating currency system was leading to a sort of Yalta between the United States and Europe. The result would be a monetary partition of the world in America's favour.'[66] As with other monetary upsets, the timing of the British float had concentrated attention on the bilateral summit. In a renewed demonstration of the importance of EMU for France, Pompidou stressed the need for Britain to return to a fixed parity and for unity on monetary co-operation. This latter he presented as a precondition for holding the Paris summit.

On the institutional side, no agreement could be reached on the location of the political secretariat. There were signs now that the project would be stillborn. Pompidou's antipathy to Benelux policy on institutional changes emerges explicitly in Brandt's account: 'But there were proposals which, for all their sincerity, made him suspect that some people cherished vain illusions. There were also inordinate proposals obviously designed to cast France in the villain's role.'[67] The link for the French between renewed discussion of the supranational ques-

---

[66] Brandt, 260.
[67] Ibid. 258.

tion, the diminished position of EMU, and the future of the Paris summit is demonstrated in Brandt's record of Pompidou's remarks:

Information reaching him from the Benelux countries implied a revision of the Rome Treaties. France was not dogmatic, but she wanted no such amendments ... Pompidou did not want the Commission upgraded, nor did he at present wish to discuss direct elections to the European Parliament ... In view of the new dollar crisis, we should agree to throw our ideological or theological ideas overboard. Under present circumstances, it would be better to postpone the Summit by a few months.[68]

Clearly, not until the supranational issue was dropped and definite progress resumed on EMU would the French accept the original October date for the Paris summit.

Only in the bilateral realm was the generally despondent mood of the Franco-German meeting raised—though Pompidou's expressions of warmth for the Federal Republic may not have been uninfluenced by his anger with the Benelux countries for their institutional proposals and annoyance with the British for floating. It was obvious that the *entente* between Paris and London was now coming under strain. Not only had the British made plain that sterling would continue to float, but they had also linked their support for EMU to the creation of a regional fund for industry as well as agriculture, which they felt should take precedence at the Paris summit. Under these circumstances, there was perhaps an unusually searching note in the President's address to his German partners regarding the value of their bilateral co-operation. Little of a substantive nature was achieved at the summit, however, though the Germans, concentrating on the elections, put a brighter face on the outcome than the French. Yet the lack of concrete decisions, whether on policy or on the future of the Paris conference, was reflected by the fact that no joint communiqué was issued.

Steps towards agreement

Despite this apparent lack of progress at the meeting of French and German leaders, there were to be signs of a softening in French attitudes towards the Community summit in the coming

[68] Loc. cit.

weeks. German policy can be identified as a significant influence in this process. The prompt action by Schmidt, the new German Finance Minister, on capital controls—long recommended by the French—provided an indication of a more amenable German attitude to monetary questions, raising hopes in Paris for progress on EMU and undoubtedly influencing the French Government. This was followed by agreement in the EEC Monetary Committee on the creation of a Community Monetary Co-operation Fund, a scheme towards which the Germans had previously shown reluctance. There were even indications that Schmidt might consider introducing a two-tier market in the Federal Republic, though it is hard to see how this could be reconciled with former German policy.[69]

This growing *rapprochement* on monetary issues culminated in the meeting in Paris between Schmidt and Giscard at the end of July 1972. Giscard let it be known that there was now an almost complete identity of views on monetary matters on both sides of the Rhine. The contrast between this co-operative spirit and the difficulties that had marred relations with Schiller could not have been more sharply drawn. There is no doubt that the shared experience and like-minded views that now quickly developed between Giscard and Schmidt would bear fruit in the close Franco-German contacts of the later 1970s.

As institutional issues receded and agreement was reached on the priority of EMU at the 19–20 July Council meeting, so prospects for the Paris summit brightened. Notably, the Dutch dropped their controversial plans for changes to the Treaty of Rome. Yet, contrary to expectations, a decision on holding the summit was deferred, at French behest. The motives seemed twofold: Paris would have more time to ascertain the chances of success, and the President would potentially gain the advantage (and prestige) of making a pre-emptive announcement on the summit's future if he saw fit.

The prelude to the decisive Council session on the summit was occupied by a lengthy series of bilateral meetings, chiefly between the French, Germans, and British—a clear demonstration of the growing trilateralism in the Community. It is worth noting that the future development of this trend into a more directorial (and, by implication, inter-governmental)

---

[69] For this suggestion, see Tsoukalis, *European Monetary Integration*, 124.

Community structure appeared to be prophesied by Pompidou himself.[70] The meetings largely took place on French initiative. Pompidou obviously wanted to be absolutely certain of a profitable summit, while also perhaps seeking to wrest some last-minute concessions from his partners by means of continued wavering. It is worth quoting Brandt here: 'Pompidou's attitude during the prelude to the conference was vacillating, hesitant, and moody. I never quite discovered why the French delayed their invitation to the summit conference until autumn. (Did they hope to barter it for an acceptance of Paris as the headquarters of the Political Secretariat?)'[71]

Further developments in early September 1972 in the monetary and economic sectors provided additional indications of Franco-German unity and helped to ensure the summit's future. Though there remained conceptual differences between the two countries on the proposed European Monetary Co-operation Fund, the Germans were pleased by a clearly increased French concern with inflation. This was particularly timely as Schmidt was under domestic attack for paying insufficient attention to the subject—yet another indication of inflation's importance in Germany. Nor was Paris unaware of the diplomatic value of concern about economic policy co-ordination and inflation as a means of obtaining German acquiescence to the Monetary Co-operation Fund. With this influence no doubt partly in mind, Giscard announced that the Government would soon be taking the initiative in seeking the harmonization of Community economic policies, and he called for an urgent meeting of the EEC Economic Policy Committee to discuss inflation. In spite of the French interest, however, it is worth noting that the Committee's discussions once again laid bare the long-standing differences in political and economic philosophy and structure between France and Germany. While Paris favoured wage and price controls—*dirigiste* to the Germans—Bonn emphasized action in the monetary sector.

Decision on the Paris summit was finally reached on 12 September 1972. The large measure of agreement in the previous week's report by the Permanent Representatives had helped, as

[70] See Pompidou's remarks quoted in *The Times*, 12 May 1972.
[71] Brandt, 264.

had the considerable consensus shown by the four European nations on the United Nations Security Council over the Middle East. That this was read in Paris as a token for a more unified European foreign policy again illustrated the importance of a coherent European 'identity' for the French. There was considerable surprise at the extent of French flexibility in the Community's September talks. This development can partly be explained by French satisfaction with the COREPER document. Perhaps more important, however, was an awareness that Paris had obtained all it could and that a decision was now required. It can well be argued that matters had reached such a stage that postponement would have been more damaging for Pompidou than proceeding as planned. Had the President's prevaricatons justified themselves in terms of results? The gains were not spectacular. The supranational issue had been deflected and attention refocused on EMU, but the political secretariat had been effectively shelved, while the British had refused to give any commitment to the end of floating.[72]

As on other occasions, Pompidou's attitude at this juncture remained private. Certainly though, an underlying disappointment (by implication with his European partners) emerged clearly at his press conference in September 1972.[73] More interesting, an uncharacteristically self-revelatory remark confirmed the effect of the referendum: 'Maybe the French could have shown a little more enthusiasm for Europe, maybe this could have helped their government's policy.'[74] The referendum and its internal repercussions had clearly affected Pompidou's European policy. This had been seen most vividly in his vacillation over the summit. Pompidou's hesitation, combined with the wider international events of the period, notably monetary unrest, had surprisingly quickly created an atmosphere of suspicion and doubt surrounding the Paris summit more reminiscent of the days of de Gaulle. Certainly, the climate contrasted sharply with the optimism that had characterized the prelude to the previous summit at The Hague. This shift in French foreign policy would become much more evident in 1973–4.

[72] This balance was carefully scrutinized in the French press. See, for instance, *Le Figaro*, 13 Sept. 1972, and *Le Monde*, 14 Sept. 1972.
[73] Pompidou's press conference of 21 Sept. 1972. Quoted in *Le Monde*, 23 Sept. 1972.
[74] Quoted in Berger, 23–4.

6

The Balance Shifts

1972–1973

The Paris summit

The exhaustive preparations that had preceded the Paris summit left little room for surprises on 19–21 October.[1] Pompidou's emphasis on concrete action of a political as well as an economic nature was ever prominent. The marked contrast with his non-committal opening stance at The Hague indicated the President's very great concern now to assert European solidarity and counteract the divisive tendencies that had become particularly apparent since May 1971. Hence Pompidou's special stress on EMU and Europe's political destiny. As had been evident at The Hague, the two areas were not discrete for the French. EMU performed a dual function, presenting both a binding force for the Community and an expression of European independence, primarily *vis-à-vis* the United States. The considerable emphasis Pompidou placed on this latter aspect should be seen not simply as a continuation of long-standing French policy, but as an increasingly important preoccupation following the events of the monetary crisis. As the President observed, Western Europe 'must not and cannot sever its links with the United States. But neither must it refrain from asserting its existence as an original reality.'[2]

On institutional questions, there was a clear desire to avoid friction on the part of French and Germans alike. Hence Pompidou's apparent flexibility and pragmatism—rather surprising in view of previous events. The President now showed a willingness to contemplate change and new practices. However, too much should not be read into what was little more than a façade. Pompidou's approach was a clear attempt to head off

[1] On the Paris summit see Avi Shlaim, 'The Paris Summit', *The World Today* (Dec. 1972); Ulrich Everling, 'Die Europäische Gemeinschaft auf dem Wege zur Europäischen Union—Zu den Ergebnissen der Parisen Gipfelkonferenz', *Europa-Archiv* 23 (1972); Morgan, *From Summit to Council*, 14–17.

[2] Pompidou, quoted in French Embassy, London, Press and Information Service.

controversy. Thus inter-governmentalism remained his touch-stone, and Pompidou patently ruled out amendments to the Treaty of Rome. This view was mirrored by Brandt, whose circumspection on institutional matters indicated a shared desire to avoid controversy. Although the Chancellor called for improvements to the Council of Ministers' decision-making capacity and an increased role for the European Parliament, he took care to note that priority should be given to these developments until such time as direct elections were possible. Brandt's understatement of direct elections compared to his strong stand at The Hague is instructive. It testifies to his wish to avoid antagonisms, especially with the French, in order to ensure the summit's success, and to the experience of office. The Chancellor was clearly more conscious now of the barriers to direct elections on the French side.

Yet despite all the preventative efforts, there was a marked clash on Community institutions. In a familiar pattern, opposing French and Dutch views were at the forefront. However, Dutch pressure was insufficient to overcome what was principally a Franco-British alignment against institutional change—another indication of British attitudes towards the supranational ques-tion. Thus, plans on institutional matters were kept very vague. There was no reference to direct elections in the final communi-qué, nor was mention made of the political secretariat or Ministers for Europe. Both issues had been tactfully dropped in advance so as to avoid friction.

Although both Brandt and Pompidou took pains to stress the importance of the decisions to be reached in Paris, it is worth noting that they had somewhat different ends in mind. While Pompidou concentrated on EMU and external relations, infla-tion was at the forefront of German thinking. Brandt's emphasis on the issue once again bears out earlier observations regarding its particular, political as well as economic, significance for the Federal Republic. This close interconnection was made explicit in the Chancellor's statement: 'I am concerned about this development, for my government feels that strong inflationary tendencies may shake not only the economic, but also the social and political foundations of the Community.'[3] It is important to

---

[3] Quoted in *The Times*, 20 Oct. 1972.

bear in mind that internal considerations were at the forefront of the German approach. This was by no means the first time that an emphatic German Community policy was being influenced by domestic economic factors, of which inflation was pre-eminent. Rising domestic price trends, particularly salient in the prelude to the elections, were being singled out by the Opposition. Figures released by the Federal Statistical Office in October showed a one per cent increase in the cost of living index between mid-August and mid-September. At the end of the latter month, the Rheinisch-Westfälisches Institut, one of the country's leading economic research bodies, had warned of the threat of imported inflation on account of EMU, with the danger that all control over price trends might consequently be lost.[4]

What the Germans were looking for in Paris was a firm commitment to concerted Community action on inflation. Hence Brandt's emphasis that the summit should give expression to the common desire to create a 'Community of stability'. Renewed pledges from Bonn's partners on parallel action on economic policy—the *sine qua non* for an effective anti-inflationary policy as far as the Germans were concerned—underscored Bonn's own greater willingness to pool reserves in the European Monetary Co-operation Fund, which it was now agreed would be set up by April 1973. Brandt makes clear the importance of this economic–monetary link, especially in the light of domestic economic considerations:

Our 'iron rule' of parallelism between monetary and economic measures had nonetheless been reaffirmed. In resolving to set up the European Monetary Co-operation Fund ... we had taken care not to create a new source of inflation—nor the 'extraction plant' for German currency reserves to which our critics made irresponsible allusions at home.[5]

Understandably, the detailed anti-inflationary proposals spelled out by Schmidt were more controversial than the Chancellor's vaguer suggestions. The dichotomy illustrates once again the different focus of technical ministers on the one hand and Heads of Government on the other at summit meetings.

[4] Data from *The Times*, 11 Oct. 1972 and 27 Sept. 1972.
[5] Brandt, 266–7.

Most questionable was the German call for 'sizeable' across-the-board reductions in the EEC's external tariffs for at least six months. Such a measure, designed to reduce inflationary pressures, was closely in line with liberal German trading instincts, but hardly likely to appeal to the French. Though no major decisions were reached, the finance ministers were given an imperative mandate to adopt precise policies at their next meeting.

The Germans were little less forthright on their second preoccupation: relations with the United States. Brandt stressed the need for joint consultations and for a regular high-level exchange of views. This German emphasis was motivated by the fact that the increased tension in Atlantic relations had, as in earlier years, highlighted the potential political conflict in Bonn's dependence both on good relations with Washington and on a unified Community. Bonn had most to gain from any institutionalized consultative arrangements which would ease its exposed position and relax the tensions in the Alliance. Not surprisingly, however, the divergent positions of the member states on this issue gave rise to considerable differences at the summit. Both France, and more unexpectedly, Britain, opposed the German idea for a special body to handle relations with the Americans. It is worth bearing in mind in this context the shift in attitudes that has taken place in more recent years. Differences between the Europeans and President Carter in the late 1970s, and, most notably, signs of increasing European exasperation with the Reagan White House, particularly over economics and trade, have resurrected ideas for establishing some form of direct and permanent European input into the shaping of American economic policy.

Intra-Community differences in Paris were particularly acute over trade. As in the past, the French sought to avoid setting a precedent by giving the Americans the special concessions they desired. In a situation reminiscent of the conflicts over the Kennedy round of GATT in the 1960s, Brandt, motivated by political, strategic, and trading imperatives, was at the forefront of the controversy over references to trade relations with the Americans in the final communiqué. According to the Chancellor:

I thought it unwarrantable and improper that the French draft for a final communiqué should make no mention whatever of our relations with the United States and Canada. This led to an open dispute at the conference table. I could only construe the absence of any allusion to America as a snub, and ostentatiously declined to suggest any amendments. My point was taken, and the joint communiqué finally assumed a form acceptable to me in that it spoke of a 'constructive dialogue'.[6]

Problems regarding the drafting of the final communiqué were not limited to this issue alone. There were also differences between the British and French over the inclusion of a commitment to the establishment of a regional fund by 1974. The underlying cause of all these disputes rested on the system prior to 1974 of having the communiqué prepared by officials of the host country's Foreign Ministry. In recent years vesting responsibility for writing up the proceedings of European Council meetings in the Commission has tended to prevent such misunderstandings.

One rather unusual feature of the summit was the considerable attention paid to social policy. This is worth some comment, as the distinctive approaches adopted help one to differentiate between the characters of Brandt and Pompidou. The subject also provides another indication of the underlying sense of competition between the two leaders. Pompidou's motives for taking up the cause of social policy at the summit can be attributed partly to the public support to be reaped and the desire to improve the EEC's image following his own disappointing referendum result and the Norwegian decision not to join. Brandt's vociferous championing of the subject in the prelude to the summit may well have provided an additional spur to the President. The Chancellor's own stress on an electorally popular Community social policy could be attributed to a number of causes, not least the proximity of the federal elections. Brandt's impetus also worked to refute opposition claims of a lack of initiative in the Government's Western policy. Yet one should not be too cynical. Personal conviction played an important part. At the SPD conference in Saarbrücken in May 1970, the Chancellor had expressed the ambition of making the Community the most socially progressive area in the world within the

[6] Ibid. 266.

decade. Finally, though, it is worth bearing in mind the suggestion (from a source friendly to the Chancellor) that Brandt's emphasis on the social side was at least partly designed to distinguish him from Pompidou. So deliberate a course would testify to an interesting interaction between the two leaders' intentions and mutual expectations.

British and Italian enthusiasm for a regional policy was harnessed by the French as a lever to secure agreement on their own priority, EMU.[7] Thus, the financing of the regional fund from the Community's own resources would be linked to the start of the second stage of monetary union. German concern about controlling expenditure and inflation, to reach a climax in 1973, was already evident regarding regional developments. Brandt noted that he had to adopt an 'extremely reserved attitude rather than incur accusations from Opposition spokesmen at home that I was on the verge of giving away good German money'.[8] Yet the Chancellor's restraint was insufficient, and the events of the Copenhagen summit just over one year later would lend credence to the argument that Germany's willingness to sanction a regional policy in Paris was largely swayed by the fact that the size of its financial commitment remained nebulous. As detailed discussions progressed over the following months and the German Government, striving to control expenditure, adopted a more restrictive line, Brandt's commitment was to appear increasingly inopportune.

Probably the oddest feature of the summit was the concept of a 'European Union' raised by Pompidou. This notion remained vague throughout—perhaps deliberately so—the evocation of a grand and popular but undefined (and perhaps undefinable) ambition admirably suiting those present. It is worth recalling that as late as 1976 James Callaghan admitted to the House of Commons that he had no idea what 'European Union' meant. Pompidou's statement gave a good indication of some of the factors involved in Community summitry at the time and well illustrated the distinction between the detailed problems of 'low' politics and the grander, but vaguer, realm of 'high' politics. According to the President, 'To be sure, European

---

[7] On the regional policy, see Helen Wallace, 'The Establishment of the Regional Development Fund: Common Policy or Pork Barrel?', in Wallace *et al.*

[8] Brandt, 266.

Union is a vague formula, that was readily so in order to avoid
useless and paralysing doctrinal disputes.[9] Not surprisingly, the
Heads of State or Government preferred to restrict themselves to
such grand and uncontentious areas which were, additionally,
appealing in domestic electoral terms rather than involving
themselves in the detailed (and potentially controversial) negotiation of specifics. Although one German Foreign Ministry
official contacted by the author identified the tendency to adopt
vague guidelines and not saddle national leaders with the
negotiation of detailed issues as a particularly French practice,
it is clear that the habit on this occasion suited Brandt and
Heath no less. As *Le Monde* observed, 'European Union' diverted attention away from differences in other areas, notably
institutions, by opening up vast, but vague, vistas for the
future.[10] The concept was suitably all-embracing. While for the
French it was devoid of institutional overtones and it principally signified EMU, for the Benelux countries and Italy it
carried far more concrete, institutional connotations. Neither
side felt it in its interest, however, to define the concept any more
precisely.

Closer analysis of the Hague and Paris summits allows for
some interesting conclusions to be drawn about Community
decision-making and the motivations underlying national positions in the early 1970s. A gradual change in the function of
summit meetings is evident over the course of the decade. The
Community's early summits have rightly been described as
motors for integration and means of eliminating bottlenecks in
policy-making.[11] Yet in recent years the balance between these
two aspects has tended to shift from former to latter. The very
creation of the European Council and consequent diminution in
the role of the Council of Ministers, which has accentuated the
existing trend to inter-governmentalism, has augmented the
'problem-solving' function of meetings of Community Heads of
Government. Thus the European Council has increasingly been
obliged to tackle intractable problems handed up from below.
This was witnessed, for instance, in 1979–80, and again in

    [9] Quoted in *Le Monde*, 27 Oct. 1972. Jobert gives an amusing account of the birth of the
notion of 'European Union' in *L'Autre Regard*, 164.
    [10] *Le Monde*, 22–3 Oct. 1972.
    [11] Juliet Lodge, 'The Role of the EEC Summit Conference', *JCMS* 3 (1973–4), 337–45.

1982–84, in the attention devoted to the British budget contribution, or in early 1981, to a common fisheries policy.

By contrast, it was new policy-making, generally very well prepared in advance (the Copenhagen summit would be a notable exception), which was uppermost in the Community's early summits. These were presented as rather special 'events', at which new initiatives were expected in an atmosphere of considerable public attention. The public relations (and novelty) aspects of the Hague and Paris conferences have rightly been highlighted.[12] It can well be argued that the public relations side was particularly evident at the Paris summit, whose wide-ranging but diffuse tone contrasted with the greater sense of urgency apparent at The Hague. As one observer stated, the Paris gathering 'did little more than salute, in somewhat vague and pompous terms, the desirability of creating a more agreeable and better co-ordinated Community, thus avoiding any precise commitment by heads of state themselves.'[13]

Various factors explain this disparity between the Hague and Paris summits. The latter's very nature was different; it was more of an 'occasion', designed to celebrate enlargement. Despite setbacks, notably in the monetary field, by October 1972 the Community had gained confidence. The uncertainty about its future that had been partly reflected at The Hague was now very much abated. Completion and enlargement had been achieved, and considerable progress had been made on deepening. Hence the somewhat self-congratulatory air of the Paris meeting, compared to the leaner atmosphere at The Hague. The public relations aspect of the Paris summit was sharpened by a shared appreciation of the need to assert the success and vigour of the EEC. This concern, reflected in many of the speeches, was intensified by the French and Norwegian referendum results. The prevarications and difficulties which had preceded the conference, building up a sense of expectation, heightened this general desire to make the summit appear a success.

More important, domestic requirements contributed to a convergence of interests between the Community's three major countries. The French, German, and British leaders were all

[12] Morgan, *From Summit to Council*, 56.
[13] Ibid. 17.

looking for a public relations success in Paris. Pompidou needed a boost to his prestige after the referendum; Brandt faced elections the following month; and Heath sought justification for his European policies. Despite the Prime Minister's pro-Market feelings, such enthusiasm was not shared throughout the country, and some tangible gains from membership were accordingly highly desirable. Hence the shared need, applicable to all summits, but particularly marked in Paris, to make the meeting appear a major achievement—a consideration reflected in some of the grand, but unrealistic, expectations raised. Outstanding in this respect was the proposed 'European Union'.

The very marked co-operation between the French, German, and British sides prior to the summit reflected this mutual requirement, and calls for some comment here. Brandt and Heath met on the eve of the summit, mainly to discuss procedural matters, while the Prime Minister also paid a one-and-a-half-hour 'courtesy call' on Pompidou, with talks on the summit's agenda. Such collaboration, foreshadowed by earlier contacts at official level, indicated both a nascent trilateralism and a shared interest among the three leaders, for the reasons given above, to eliminate difficulties and ensure the conference's smooth functioning. Partly on account of the fact that some exchange of French and German interests had already come about at Council of Ministers level, it was a Franco-British alignment which was most evident at the summit.

Hence, in his opening speech Pompidou noted that Britain's entry added 'a new dimension to our Community'.[14] Throughout the meeting there was a clear recognition of mutual interests. In order to avoid friction with London, Pompidou did not make an issue of sterling's return to a fixed parity by 1 January 1973, and he showed an appreciation of the emphasis Heath placed on a regional policy. Once sure of the President's support for the latter, the British leader took care not to offend French sensibilities. Thus Heath backed Pompidou's opposition to any institutionalizaton of links with the United States, and he supported the French position on development aid.

The lack of British support for the Dutch stand on institutions

---

[14] Quoted in French Embassy, London, Press and Information Service. Opening speech by President Georges Pompidou at the Paris summit, 19 Oct. 1972.

was particularly interesting. It both reconfirmed the close Franco-British alignment on this issue, and further increased the disillusionment with the United Kingdom in federalist circles that would reach a zenith later in the decade. Certainly, the Paris summit appeared to prophesy a very close *entente* between the French and British over the future of Community institutional policy—one cut short by the British change of power in February 1974 and subsequent differences over a range of issues. Although Schaetzel overshoots in arguing that Heath's emphasis on good relations with France and deference to Pompidou 'persisted beyond the point where this policy could be excused as a tactical imperative to successful negotiations',[15] it is interesting to note that the major conflict to emerge in Britain's relations with its Community partners between the time of the Paris summit and Heath's downfall a year and a half later was not one, as has generally been the case in subsequent years, with France, but rather with the Federal Republic.

Changing bilateral relationships

Reflecting German priorities, it was anti-inflationary policy that took pride of place in the Community's post-summit negotiations. A number of proposals, resembling Schmidt's ideas, had already been put forward by the Commission. These included a temporary reduction in the external tariff, farm price freeze, and examination of the use of direct income subsidies. Such recommendations were highly unattractive to some of the member states. Notably, the Germans themselves, in another example of poor policy co-ordination, were very obviously divided. Dissimilar priorities meant that two of the Cabinet's major figures, Schmidt and Ertl, took opposing views. Schmidt's idea for lowering some farm prices was bitterly contested by Ertl. The FDP minister, with electoral considerations firmly in mind, was more anxious than ever to placate the farm constituency, particularly in Bavaria, where the FDP's hold was tenuous.

In addition, indicating the divergence in French and German trading interests, the idea for tariff reductions was strongly opposed by the French. It was felt that the scheme would weaken

---

[15] Robert J. Schaetzel, *The Unhinged Alliance. America and the European Community* (New York, Harper and Row, 1975), 30.

the Community's stand in the forthcoming GATT negotiations, while hardly influencing consumer prices. Bonn and Paris were also at odds over the Commission's proposal for a twenty per cent rise in industrial import quotas (textiles apart). This was viewed by Giscard as a needless concession to the United States prior to the trade talks. Thus, although the Community finance ministers were agreed on the need to restrict national expenditure and monetary growth, and united on common action against short-term capital inflows, differences in national economic policies prevented accord on more contentious matters. The Germans opposed the price surveillance put forward by the Commission, while the French resisted any moves on tariffs or import quotas. For the German Government, faced with an opposition strategy of drawing attention away from the *Ostpolitik* by concentrating on inflation, the decisions were disappointing. French comment, by contrast, bore witness to the continuing dissimilarities between the two countries' economic preferences. Thus, Giscard expressed satisfaction that the anti-inflation measures would not damage expansion.

At their meeting on 22–3 January 1973, Brandt and Pompidou surveyed the range of Community policy in the light of the summit. Since the last bilateral meeting two events, the Federal election result and the conclusion of a Basic Treaty between the two Germanies, had noticeably tilted the balance between Paris and Bonn in the latter's favour. In the elections, where an above average 91.1 per cent turn-out had reflected the high emotional content of the issues involved, notably the *Ostpolitik*, the SPD had increased its vote by 3.1 per cent compared to 1969, making it, for the first time, the biggest group in the Bundestag.[16] With the FDP registering similar gains, the coalition now seemed secure against the vicissitudes which had plagued it over much of the past year. This new strength of the Chancellor contrasted with the doubts hanging over the Gaullists in the French legislative elections in March 1973.

As to the Federal Republic's relationship with the GDR, on 8 November 1972 Bahr had initialled a *Grundvertrag*, signed on 21 December, establishing the basis of relations between East and

---

[16] On the German elections, see: William Paterson, 'The West German Elections', *The World Today* (Dec. 1972); R. E. M. Irving and W. E. Paterson, 'The West German Parliamentary Elections of November 1972', *Parliamentary Affairs* (1973–4).

West Germany. In a statement on 7 November, Brandt made clear the significance of what had taken place: 'We are on the eve of an important event ... Much will become possible which until yesterday was unimaginable.'[17] The normalization of relations with the GDR, the high point of the *Ostpolitik*, would put an end to many former difficulties. It would greatly increase the room for manœuvre in Bonn's foreign policy, and to some extent reduce its dependence on the European Community. Certainly, Bonn could now take a wider interest in international affairs and assume its place in the United Nations. Publicly, the French Government had reacted with enthusiasm. Yet Jobert's comment, though undeniably partial, gives what is probably the truer picture. 'Germany was already dreaming of the future; of a neutrality which would prevent anything compromising the future of the entire German people; of a close bond with the United States which would free it from Europe and lend it weight *vis-à-vis* Moscow.'[18] The remarks were ominous, indicating the strain that was to impair Franco-German relations within a few months. Reports of bilateral differences in January 1973 over trade with the GDR in the light of the *Grundvertrag* can well be seen as a harbinger of what was to come. Following the normalization of inter-German relations, it was reported that Pompidou, anxious about German economic weight and wanting to close a loophole, felt that the free access for East German goods into the Community negotiated by Adenauer's Government in the late 1950s had now become redundant. Instead, the GDR should be treated as any other non-EEC country.

The lengthy discussions on East-West relations at the January 1973 Franco-German summit illustrated the dominance of topical issues in the bilateral talks. Thus Pompidou reported on his meeting with Brezhnev earlier in the month in Minsk. The stress placed on economic co-operation at the latter meeting could well be read as a French response to the danger of losing ground to the Federal Republic in East European trade. Politically, Paris had been gratified by the fact that the talks with the Russians had not dispelled the image that it was still Moscow's privileged partner in the West. Brandt and Pompidou

---

[17] Quoted in *Keesing's Contemporary Archives*, 16–23 Dec. 1972, 25622.
[18] Jobert, *L'Autre Regard*, 256.

also spent a considerable amount of time discussing the Helsinki Conference and MBFR. The former had been a major topic in the President's talks with Brezhnev. That Pompidou had raised the question of the future of Germany in these discussions intimated his growing concern with France's neighbour across the Rhine.

On the Community side Brandt and Pompidou were in full accord on the question of a regional policy and inflation. The two leaders also renewed their commitment to the Monetary Co-operation Fund and EMU. However, familiar differences re-emerged on relations with the United States, where the Germans continued to seek some institutionalization of links. Though both sides agreed that a constructive dialogue was necessary with the Americans, the usual French scepticism was evident. Pompidou again strove to emphasize European independence, stating that 'Europe was not simply an outpost of the United States'.[19] On trade, in line with the differing national priorities cited above, Brandt and Pompidou remained divided. While the French sought harmonized tariff reductions at GATT (involving high rates being reduced by larger margins than low ones), the less protectionist and more internationally minded Germans favoured linear cuts (which would entail a greater overall reduction in the Common External Tariff).

With the summit marking the tenth anniversary of the Franco-German Treaty, bilateral relations occupied an un-usually large part of the talks. Exceptional efforts were taken to veil differences and make the summit appear successful. Neither side wanted public disagreements, and hence the silence over the question of East Germany's trading position *vis-à-vis* the EEC. The size of the German delegation, comprising seven Federal Ministers and the Premier of Baden-Württemberg, emphasized the importance and cordiality of the bilateral bond. Unparal-leled stress was placed on public relations. Brandt and Pompi-dou gave each other their countries' highest medals and the Chancellor laid a wreath on the tomb of the Unknown Soldier, an honour previously reserved for Adenauer alone. Yet, while both leaders were effusive in praising their countries' friendship, and the meeting certainly provided a very sharp contrast with the much cooler atmosphere of its predecessor in 1968 which had

[19] Brandt, 261.

marked the treaty's fifth anniversary, it was ironic that this testament to the improved climate and better understanding in bilateral relations was so soon to be belied.

As ever, the contrast between grand declarations of intent at bilateral summit level and the actual results of co-operation remained sharp. However, one should not be surprised that on this occasion at least more than usual was achieved. Agreement was reached on marketing the Airbus. Furthermore, on French persuasion, there was accord on the construction of a heavy rocket launcher. Paris also pressed for greater co-operation on arms procurement. While the economic, cultural, and humanitarian benefits that had come about as a result of the Franco-German Treaty and the youth exchange programme received considerable attention and praise, Pompidou once again raised the question of the status of the French language in German schools.

To forestall any impression of excessive Franco-German proximity consequent on the occasion (which might be misread by others) both sides took care to stress the non-exclusive nature of their collaboration. (It is worth noting that, following the intensification of bilateral co-operation under Giscard and Schmidt, this concern came to be given even more attention.) Both sides underlined the fact that *entente* between them served not just the construction of Europe, but *détente* throughout the continent. Brandt also drew attention to the fact that the Franco-German Treaty had made for greater interpenetration between the two countries while promoting European integration and permitting the *Ostpolitik*.

The return of monetary instability

In February 1973 a massive influx of dollars into Europe brought monetary issues back to the fore, calling into question the Smithsonian accord. Once again, it was the Deutschemark which had exerted the greatest pull. Despite the increased use of controls since Schiller's resignation, the mark's position, as in 1971, as a stable refuge currency once more made it the prime target of this floating capital. Between 1 and 9 February, the Bundesbank took in 5.9 billion dollars.[20] It is interesting to

---

[20] Figure from Emminger, *The D-Mark in the conflict between internal and external equilibrium*, 36.

compare German reactions in 1973 with those of May 1971. Bonn's response now was to arrange a meeting in Paris between Schmidt, Giscard, and Barber, the British Chancellor of the Exchequer. This was an obvious evolution in German policy. Mindful of the intra-Community differences of May 1971, Bonn was now clearly more anxious than ever to achieve a European consensus on monetary policy in advance of a crisis. This development can be attributed both to experience and to the close working relationship established between Schmidt and Giscard. Fear of upsetting the market, and perhaps other Community partners as well, esplained the great secrecy surrounding the meeting. Clearly, the Germans wanted to be sure of firm action and to avoid the arguments that had been so obvious in May 1971. Both aims were most likely to be achieved by a prior co-ordination of views between Bonn and its two main partners. However, although the event offered a further indication of budding trilateralism, one should bear in mind Brandt's remarks which implied that the meeting had originally been conceived on a bilateral Franco-German basis.[21] Even in 1973, and to a far greater extent later in the decade, economic problems constrained Britain's position *vis-à-vis* France and Germany, notably in areas directly affected by the United Kingdom's relatively weak economy, such as monetary policy.

As might be expected, the reaction of the other member states to the meeting was very hostile. The Italians pointed out that a European solution could only come about through a full meeting of the Nine. It is worth noting, though, the way in which Rome's exclusion forcefully illustrated both its position on the fringe of the Community's major powers and the lira's weakness. The Benelux countries too, as in the past, voiced great concern at the turn of events. The meeting also provided another example of the politicization of monetary issues in the 1970s, and it offered further evidence of the erosion of the Commission's role. This trend would reach a peak in the later 1970s and early 1980s, and was undoubtedly accelerated by the inter-governmental nature of discussions on monetary policy and reform in the early 1970s.

The trilateral meeting was soon followed by a gathering of all nine Community foreign ministers in the wake of the American

---

[21] Brandt interviewed in *The Times*, 27 Feb. 1973.

decision to devalue the dollar on 12 February 1973. Undaunted by the floating of the lira on 22 January, they reaffirmed their commitment to the Monetary Co-operation Fund and looked to accelerated progress on EMU. In spite of Barber's opposition at the Paris meeting, Schmidt repeated his call for a joint float in any future monetary crisis. German concern had increased since mid-February. Following the mounting monetary pressure at the end of the month, which culminated in the Bundesbank's purchase of nearly 2.7 billion dollars on 1 March,[22] the question of British participation in any concerted action took on an additional significance. Thus the issue formed a major topic at the Chancellor's talks with Heath in Bonn on 1–2 March.

Brandt made an unprecedented offer to the British Prime Minister in order to secure his backing for a joint float. He writes:

I let it be known that we were ready to pay a high price—in other words extensive support for Britain in particular—if a European solution could be found. The first prerequisite would have been a universal freeing of exchange rates. Like us, Heath saw a chance to emerge from the crisis by means of a major forward step. We conferred with our experts late that evening at Schloss Gymnich and next afternoon at my office. That was as far as we got. On the British side, political determination failed to overcome the ifs and buts of the experts. Our own experts, and above all the gentlemen of the Bundesbank, probably heaved a sigh of relief as well. They regarded the risks as great, although they were prepared to go a long way ... to render possible a support operation of unprecedented scope.[23]

Brandt's offer to underwrite the sterling balances was highly significant. It represented a use of financial clout that testified to the economic and political power now at the Federal Republic's disposal, and demonstrated German determination to act forcefully on those issues—principally economic—where major interests were felt to be at stake. The tactic would be repeated in January 1974, in the offer of a huge loan to the French to persuade them to stay in the Snake. However, it should be borne in mind that it was only under Chancellor Schmidt that economic strength became more widely and systematically used to further Bonn's foreign policy objectives.

---

[22] Figure from the *Daily Telegraph*, 2 Mar. 1973.
[23] Brandt, 251.

Brandt's offer to the British was extremely controversial. The incident represented one of the most salient examples of poor German policy co-ordination in the period. When Heath later sought to take up the Chancellor's proposal, the Germans presented great barriers at the technical level. Although on the one hand it was interpretable as a courageous and imaginative step, on the other hand Brandt had not acquainted himself sufficiently with the difficulties involved when making the original offer, nor had he consulted adequately with the German interests concerned. In addition, the proposal had caused annoyance in Italy, no less weak financially than Britain. Rome's participation had not been invited. The incident well illustrated the distinction between high and low politics and, while it demonstrated the Chancellor's considerable political imagination and his readiness to go beyond his technocrats, it can at the same time be argued that the offer highlighted a lack of knowledge and appreciation of the detailed side of economic policy on Brandt's part. The contrast with Schmidt was telling.

British support for a joint float remained a problem throughout early March 1973. Perhaps deliberately, so as to block the step, Barber set stringent preconditions. The French position was also ambivalent, with suggestions that participation would depend on the British. Despite all Bonn's efforts to secure prior agreement, therefore, the similarities with May 1971 remained striking, indicating the continuing effect of outside circumstances beyond the Germans' control. Thus French concern about competitiveness was once again a major influence, as was the much lower speculative pressure on the franc compared to the Deutschemark.

This German failure to secure agreement was followed by a distinct hardening of positions, an illustration of Bonn's greater self-assurance in 1973. The Germans stepped up their campaign for joint action. Schmidt threatened a unilateral Deutschemark float if necessary and warned that in such an event the burden of speculative inflows would fall mainly on the other European nations.[24] Nor was such assertiveness reserved for the Europeans alone. There was also a considerably more forceful German line towards the dollar, with strong emphasis on the need for American action. How does one account for this contrast with

[24] See Schmidt's interview with *Die Zeit*, 9 Mar. 1973.

Bonn's relative docility of May and August 1971? Various factors were responsible—notably the first fruits of the *Ostpolitik* and the climate of *détente* evident in the first half of 1973. Though one should take care not to exaggerate the degree, both of these factors allowed the Federal Republic a greater margin of manœuvre in its foreign policy and reduced its dependence on Washington, where the troop reduction issue had also abated— for the time being at least. Schmidt's character also played a part. Though an Atlanticist like Schiller, under the present circumstances he placed greater weight on controlling the domestic money supply than on supporting the dollar. Finally, one should also note that while Schmidt's threat in 1973 of a unilateral float was chiefly a tactical move designed to put pressure on the other Europeans (and was discounted by Brandt and Friderichs, the Minister of Economics), the incident demonstrated Schmidt's authority and his growing strength in the Cabinet.

The Community's eventual decision on 11 March 1973 to undertake a joint float was undoubtedly grounded on a Franco-German accord. The move had been sketched out at a meeting between Schmidt and Giscard the previous week. No announcement had then been made, however, pending the outcome of the French legislative elections. Agreement between the two ministers over a three per cent revaluation of the mark had played a major part, alleviating French fears of a loss of competitiveness as a result of linking the franc to the German currency.[25] The French Government's retention of its majority in the second round of the elections, which coincided with the Council meeting, vouchsafed the joint action, which had also been greatly assisted by the good relations between Schmidt and Giscard. Schmidt had expressed special praise for his counterpart's 'co-operation'. The bilateral component behind the float was underlined by Britain's non-participation, an indication of its handicapped position *vis-à-vis* France and Germany even within three months of Community membership.

The float was, in reality, a Deutschemark zone. What is more, it would in time incorporate non-Community countries such as Sweden, Norway, and Austria, closely associated with the

[25] For the factors influencing the French to join the float, see Kolodziej, *French International Policy*, 228–9.

German economy. Despite the outward unease in the smaller member states towards the Federal Republic's authority, it is interesting to note the argument put forward to the author by one eminent German economist, who stated that, despite their complaints, countries like the Benelux were happy to link their economies to the mark. (It should also be recognized that they had little alternative.) This association (it was suggested) would augment their political weight and impose necessary economic discipline, while also improving their terms of trade. The comments are illustrative of the strong didactic streak in German foreign economic policy that became increasingly evident in the later 1970s.

Agricultural repercussions

Parallels between the troubles of March 1973 and May 1971 were not limited to the monetary side. As in 1971, there were naturally also repercussions for agriculture. Decisions on new prices had to be postponed and, true to fashion, in late March and April, a series of tense meetings took place. France and Germany were the main antagonists. The similarity between national positions in 1973 and those of the later 1970s and early 1980s is also striking; while the British, concerned about inflation, sought a total price freeze at the 27 March 1973 Council meeting, and James Godber, the British Minister, attacked the CAP, Chirac, the new French Farm Minister, demanded substantial rises. In addition, in line with French emphasis on maintaining a unified agricultural policy, he backed the 2.76 per cent cut in MCAs proposed by the Commission. The choice for Ertl was more difficult. Confronted with the conflict between farmers' demands for price rises on the one hand and government policy to tackle inflation on the other, he adopted the expedient of seeking only a small price increase while totally opposing any reduction in MCAs. In this way, inflationary pressures would be kept to a minimum, while the principle of MCAs would be upheld. This stress on the continuation of MCAs was shared by the British, who were conscious that their abolition would only reinforce pressure for higher prices. This point of view remains part of present-day British policy; similarly, Chirac's criticisms of the time have no less familiar a ring, especially when one recalls the arguments of

1980 over Britain's budget contribution. Addressing an admittedly partisan audience at the FNSEA Congress on 12 April 1973, he censured the British for their 'uncooperative' attitude, and noted, in words remarkably similar to those of the early 1980s, that the United Kingdom's repeated requests for concessions 'cast doubt on its ability to be a market member'.[26]

Though certain aspects of the conflict centred on France and Britain, it was the dispute between France and Germany, on the well-worn ground of MCAs, that was dominant. Ertl remained adamant in refusing MCA cuts. Meanwhile for Chirac, it was Germany, for purely monetary reasons, which was the cause of all the trouble. This lengthy wrangling was only cut short in mid-April by the Danes, whose tightly controlled negotiating mandate—an indication of the Folketing's very considerable degree of authority over the Government in Community policy—prevented them from overstepping the Commission's compromise proposals without prior parliamentary approval. The issue of accountability had come to a head in a Danish censure motion two months earlier.

French and German positions in the meantime continued to harden, and the Germans made a number of strong statements emphasizing the monetary link in farm pricing.[27] As often in the past, relations with the United States provided an additional cause for division. However, on this occasion there was an ironic reversal of the usual French and German attitudes. Chirac now criticized Bonn for seeking a grain price rise on the eve of trade talks with the Americans, who were pressing for a freeze on grain prices and areas under cultivation.

French and German positions at the ensuing Community meeting on 28 April 1973 were manifestly confrontational. Ertl remained very firm, and no agreement was reached by the end of the first day. In Godber's inimitable words, 'some of us felt that we might have been better employed watching football'.[28] Chirac accused the Germans of wanting to throw the Community into a crisis on the eve of the trade talks, and—foreshadowing future developments—implied that Bonn was more interested in policy towards Eastern Europe than the EEC. Ertl responded furiously,

---

[26] Quoted in *International Herald Tribune*, 13 Apr. 1973.
[27] See the reports in the *Financial Times*, 26 Apr. 1973, and the *Guardian*, 27 Apr. 1973.
[28] Quoted in the *Sunday Telegraph*, 29 Apr. 1973.

declaring to the press 'that's a load of rubbish. I think it's time he underwent psychiatric treatment'. The German minister later elaborated that he had 'never spoken ill of a colleague'.[29] Such animosity, exceeding even that shown between Schiller and Giscard at their worst, underlined the extreme importance that the MCA issue had come to assume in both Paris and Bonn.

After negotiations, lengthy even for the farm ministers, a compromise was finally reached. The most controversial aspect of the package was the dual pricing of milk. This would rise by 5.5 per cent, except in Germany and the Benelux countries, where the figure would be 4 per cent. The decision represented an important precedent, marking a heavy blow for countries, like France, which were eager to maintain the CAP's façade of uniformity. The Germans had remained steadfast throughout. The agreement on milk and on a further one per cent increase in some prices as soon as fixed parities were restored represented the full extent of their concessions for the continuation of MCAs. In addition, Bonn won a decision on a review of the CAP and on a joint meeting of the farm and finance ministers to discuss the implications of the monetary situation for the agricultural policy. This was also a major achievement for Bonn, which had consistently asserted the importance of taking into consideration the monetary element in farm pricing.

Though it was Ertl who was in charge of the negotiations there is little doubt that the determined German stand owed as much, if not more, to Schmidt. It is to the former that Bonn's increasingly hostile attitude at this time to certain aspects of the CAP must largely be attributed. Numerous factors were responsible. In a climate of domestic inflation, partly countered by sizeable cuts in public expenditure, 'wasteful' spending on the farm policy was increasingly drawing the Finance Minister's attention. Much of the contemporary philosophy of Bonn as the 'paymaster' of Europe emanated from Schmidt and his close colleague Apel. Furthermore, in the country as a whole a change of mood had become apparent, perhaps attributable to the slightly more difficult domestic economic circumstances. Subsidized sales of surplus Community butter to the Soviet Union had attracted considerable adverse comment, while there was also

---

[29] Quoted in *The Times*, 30 Apr. 1973.

increasing resistance to high food prices, with the farm lobby coming under attack. Eugen Loderer, President of the Metal Workers Union, complained at the level of food price rises and its effect on inflation. He also disputed the long-standing assumption that farmers needed special treatment.[30] Changes in the composition of the Bundestag were an additional influence. The Government's comfortable majority meant that the former policy of appeasing the farmers, increasingly regarded as fruitless, was now being given a lower priority, at least by the SPD.

On the French side, the outcome of the Council meeting occasioned a mixed reaction of resignation and hostility. Many speculated gloomily on its significance for the future. Notably, there was considerable comment on the further decline of France's position in the Nine and the threat to the CAP now posed by the Federal Republic.[31] While pleased that the farm policy had survived one of its severest tests, the French Government was clearly disturbed. Though in his speech before the National Assembly Chirac tried to highlight the positive aspects of the negotiations, he admitted that despite the agreement, the EEC was heading into difficulties. Misgivings, possibly founded on the spectre of an Anglo-German alliance, focused on the planned review of the CAP. It was not surprising, therefore, that in the ensuing period both Chirac and Pompidou rallied to the policy's defence.[32]

The proposed review cast a shadow over Franco-German relations in the following months. This was heralded in mid-May by the tart exchanges between Chirac, who played down its significance, and Ertl. At the end of the month, the German minister very forcefully reiterated Bonn's emphasis on the need for co-ordinated action on farm prices and monetary policy.[33] Reform was necessary, he reasoned, and this should include structural measures and action on surpluses in order to eliminate waste and control the Federal Republic's financial outlay. While stating that he did not want to replace the intervention price

---

[30] Reported in the *Financial Times*, 17 May 1973.

[31] For instance see *Le Figaro*, 2 May 1973, and *Le Monde*, 3 May 1973.

[32] See reports of Chirac addressing the National Assembly in the *Guardian*, 5 May 1973, and also Pompidou's remarks reported in *Le Monde*, 5 May 1973.

[33] See Ertl's interview with *Süddeutsche Zeitung*, 26–7 May 1973.

system, it is interesting to note that Ertl showed a willingness to consider the use of direct payments as an extension of the farm policy. Taken together, these dangerous sentiments on a key French priority—one dear to the President—would greatly reinforce the existing doubts in Paris about the Federal Republic's future intentions.

Atlantic relations and European affairs

While these differences were simmering at Community level, major new developments were also in the offing on the Atlantic front. Following preliminary soundings earlier in the year, on 23 April 1973, Henry Kissinger announced the Administration's proposal for a 'New Atlantic Charter' between the United States and its NATO partners. This document would form the corner-stone of an American plan to make 1973 the 'Year of Europe' during which Atlantic relations would be reasserted by an Administration at last able to divert more of its attention away from Vietnam. Therefore, taking its initiative from Pompidou (so Kissinger claims)[34] Washington would seek a reconfirmation of Atlantic co-operation on defence, trade, and political issues. That matters would not be as simple as Kissinger might have hoped, nor American motives as selfless as he strongly implies in his memoirs, would become increasingly clear in the course of the year. Certainly, much of the Community's attention over the coming months was to be occupied by the American initiative. This challenge was not always to be adequately or uniformly met by the Europeans, whose differing political positions would be exposed by the tight links Washington would try to establish between political, economic, and military affairs.

What was the rationale behind the American *démarche*? One cannot deny that all was not well in the Alliance. Atlantic relations had suffered as a result of American trade and monetary policy in 1971 and 1973, while the Administration for its part continued to resent many aspects of Community trading policy and the CAP. Not least, European attitudes to Vietnam, and especially the bombing of the North at Christmas 1972, had

---

[34] Henry Kissinger, *Years of Upheaval* (London, Weidenfeld and Nicholson/Michael Joseph, 1982), 130.

caused grave dissatisfaction in Washington.[35] Kissinger's second volume of memoirs, *Years of Upheaval*, is the obvious work to consult for any closer understanding of feeling within the White House. Yet even the most casual reader cannot fail to be struck by the sense of self-righteousness and implied criticism of most European intentions and policy-making procedures that characterize its pages. It is hard to dispel the impression that Kissinger's recollection, though undoubtedly a central document, forms only a partial record.

Various factors underlay American policy towards the Alliance in 1973. Uppermost amongst these was a determination to reassert the primacy of Atlantic interests over more regionally minded European or Japanese concerns. Above all, there was the desire to keep in check steps towards a more coherent and independent European political posture, which, it was feared, might potentially compromise Washington's own diplomacy. This emphasis on American political priorities emerged unequivocally in Kissinger's statement announcing the initiative:

In economic relations the European Community has stressed its regional personality; the United States, at the same time, must act as part of, and be responsible for, a wider international trade and monetary system.... The United States has global interests and responsibilities. Our European allies have regional interests. These are not necessarily in conflict, but in the new era neither are they automatically identical.[36]

In his memoirs, Kissinger has expressed regret at his formulation of these differing interests and stated that his intentions were widely misinterpreted in Europe.[37] Despite such protestations, the mass of evidence lends weight to the view that the fundamental motive behind American policy was to re-establish some degree of authority over the Europeans. Thus the Community was seen as a group increasingly ready to assert its political independence from the United States, and thereby potentially cause considerable embarrassment or additional

[35] On the bombing, see ibid. 137. On trading problems, see 135, and *White House Years*, 425–6.

[36] Quoted in 'Z.' 'The Year of Europe', *Foreign Affairs* (Jan. 1974), 240, and Kissinger, *Years of Upheaval*, 153.

[37] See Kissinger, op. cit. 152–3, 161.

difficulties to America in its world diplomacy, particularly *vis-à-vis* the Soviet Union, and later the Arab states.

With this in mind, the subordination in the Year of Europe of wider Alliance concerns to common (though American-defined) aims was firmly underpinned by Kissinger's dual strategy: first of all, of expanding the Alliance's range of interests far beyond its original scope; and, secondly and far more compellingly, of 'demanding linkage from the allies and a quasi-right of American participation in West European decision making'.[38] By taking the initiative and linking the monetary, political, and strategic sectors, Kissinger intended to reconfirm Washington's control over the Alliance and nip in the bud any potentially damaging moves towards independent European political action. At the same time, Washington could discourage Allied interference and opposition by constantly reminding its partners of its primary contribution to their security.

The European response to Kissinger's proposal was generally one of puzzlement and suspicion. The latter applied particularly to the French on account of their long-standing sensitivity to any suggestion of American hegemony. Such traditional policy preferences would place France at the forefront of opposition to the American plans in the coming months.[39] Jobert describes the French reaction. The American *démarche* surprised the Europeans 'who had hardly been consulted about the evolution and taking in hand of their destiny'.[40] Interestingly, Kissinger's account explicitly contradicts this statement, suggesting instead a substantial degree of preliminary contacts. This is by no means the only occasion on which the two statesmen's published records significantly differ. In this instance, it is Kissinger's account which is the more convincing. Elsewhere, however, his portrayal of a cat and mouse diplomacy between the United States and Europe during much of 1973, in which America emerges as the innocent, well-meaning partner regularly crossed by European, and especially French, cunning and equivocation is unpersuasive, and often leaves the reader with the impression that either too much, or too little, is being said.

[38] This argument stems from Stanley Hoffmann, *Primacy or World Order. American Foreign Policy since the Cold War* (New York, McGraw-Hill, 1978), 48–9.

[39] Note, for instance, Kissinger, *Years of Upheaval*, 164, 187, 704.

[40] Jobert, *L'Autre Regard*, 288.

Furthermore, with the benefit of hindsight, one can well concur with Jobert's appraisal of Kissinger's scheme as indicating the Administration's desire 'to organize the Western camp in the perspective of a world strategy'.[41] Others too note that aspect of Kissinger's tactics whereby Washington could use its alliances as stilts with which to tower over Communist rivals or other blocs that might challenge the United States.[42] Finally, and again with the benefit of hindsight (although firm evidence is lacking), perhaps it was not so far-fetched of Jobert to insinuate, as he repeatedly did, that Nixon's European initiative was not entirely unconnected with his growing domestic problems. Though strenuously denying such claims, Kissinger himself concedes that the Administration's persistence with the Year of Europe in the face of allied reluctance was partly affected by domestic considerations.[43]

The political differences that would soon arise among the Europeans over relations with the United States were exacerbated by divisions over trade. In early April 1973 the Commission had put forward preliminary ideas for the Community's stand at GATT, involving 'substantial' tariff cuts and the removal of some non-tariff barriers. Serious discussion and stimulation of farm trade was also stressed. This latter was a major American preoccupation. Schaetzel identifies 1970 as the key date from which the CAP came to be viewed by the Administration not just as a prospective menace to American farm trade, but as a specific obstacle. This negative image was intensified by Nixon's concentration on the farm vote in 1970. Hence, 'Washington's aversion to the Community's agricultural policies became an obsession.'[44] Little less contentious was the question of Community agreements with the Less Developed Countries, where European goods were gaining a preferential treatment much resented by the Americans. There was no doubt that such economic considerations strongly reinforced the political motives underlying the proposed 'New Atlantic Charter'.

---

[41] Loc. cit.
[42] Hoffmann, 49–50.
[43] For Jobert's claims, see *L'Autre Regard*, 381, and Jobert's interview with the *Washington Post*, reported in *The Times*, 15 Feb. 1974.
[44] Schaetzel, 53–4.

These American complaints were not without substance. But, as has been remarked, the Community can often appear more powerful and resolute to outsiders than to those within. Certainly, it should be noted that the Nine were not always of one mind about their trading policy. While in March 1973 the French sought reverse preferences (exactly the type of reciprocal benefits that the Americans condemned) in the Community's trading regime with the Mediterranean area, this was resisted by the British, Germans, and Dutch. They all sought freer international trade, for both traditional trading and economic reasons, and also, perhaps, on account of sensitivity to American wishes. Nor were intra-Community differences limited to the industrial sector. At the Council meeting on 14–15 May 1973, Jobert, the new French Foreign Minister, launched a stinging attack on the Commission's trading suggestions, and emphasized the total unacceptability of advance concessions on topics that were not negotiable, notably agriculture. There was little doubt that anxiety in Paris over pressure for external concessions on the CAP interacted with the internal confrontations that had already taken place among the farm ministers, all serving to increase French resistance.

The question of the Community's stand at GATT once again exposed and turned on long-standing differences between the member states' trading policies, ideologies, and political preferences. In contrast to the French, most of the Nine welcomed the conciliatory Commission document, especially those, like Germany and Britain, with more outward-looking trading orientations. In particular, Franco-German differences were revealed over Bonn's apparent support for the elimination of industrial tariffs. This contrasted with the French view that such a step would turn the Community into a free trade area. There were also considerable differences over the CAP. Notably, Jobert claimed that London wanted to use GATT to change the farm system. The suggestion clearly illustrated the interconnection between the external and internal dimensions of Community policy for the French.

Discussions on relations with the United States continued among the Community foreign ministers on 4–5 June 1973. Procedurally, it is worth noting that the portion of this meeting devoted to political co-operation was conspicuous for a rigid

French enforcement of the distinction between topics for inter-governmental political co-operation, and Community affairs. This demarcation would be taken to extremes the following month. As to the French stand on GATT, there appeared to have been a slight relaxation in Paris. The change can be attributed to an American willingness to play along with France at this stage. Many observers have commented on the fact that, as with monetary policy in late 1971, the French were regarded by the Americans as the linchpin for European approval of their political proposals. This special relationship is made explicit by Kissinger.[45] Thus there had been provisional American accep-tance at the Nixon–Pompidou summit in Reykjavik of French opposition to any linked talks on political, economic, and military co-operation, with concentration instead on bilateral contacts. It should be noted, however, that Kissinger in his memoirs offers a somewhat different interpretation of the outcome of the talks than was understood on the French side.[46]

The Franco-German element

With international matters at the forefront of Community affairs, the Franco-German summit on 20–1 June 1973 took its keynote from the topical issues of the day. Thus the meeting concentrated on international questions, notably that of rela-tions with the United States.[47] Both Brandt and Pompidou had been involved in a round of meetings, the Chancellor having visited Washington at the start of May and received Brezhnev later in the month, and Pompidou having first met Heath and then Nixon. The difference of opinion that was apparent between Bonn and Paris regarding the 'Year of Europe' was hardly surprising in view of their dissimilar policy interests. As was to be expected, Brandt took a much more accommodating line to the American plans. (One should bear in mind first, however, that the Chancellor's more sanguine assessment was not mirrored throughout the SPD;[48] and secondly that Kissinger offers a rather different picture, with Pompidou presented as the

---

[45] Kissinger, *Years of Upheaval*, 129, 163.

[46] Ibid. 180.

[47] For a general survey of the summit, see, A. W[iss]–V[erdier], 'La Rencontre Brandt–Pompidou, ou l'Europe des incertitudes', *Documents* (July–Aug. 1973), 6.

[48] See Dieter Dettke, *Allianz im Wandel* (Frankfurt, Alfred Metzler Verlag, 1976), 159.

inspiration for the American policy and France and Germany portrayed as equally indifferent to ensuring its realization.)[49]

The Franco-German talks did not bring about a change of view in either country, though there was, according to Scheel, some *rapprochement* on GATT. The two Governments were, however, in unison on monetary matters; in line with French wishes, the two sides quite reasonably decided that major specific issues could perfectly well continue to be handled by the appropriate bodies such as the IMF rather than in an independent forum with the Americans.

Pompidou was clearly preoccupied with security issues. These had formed an important element in his talks with Nixon in Reykjavik at the end of May 1973. In response to the specific wishes of the American President, who was under renewed pressure from the Mansfield lobby, Pompidou had formally requested the continued presence of American troops in Europe, which he felt to be a matter of 'extreme importance.'[50] Jobert records Pompidou's comment that 'having turned everything down, I could hardly let Nixon leave without this basic satisfaction'.[51] Yet there is no doubt whatsoever that the request was also fully in line with the French President's own wishes. Continued deployment of American troops had been desired by the French since the early days of the *Ostpolitik*, both as a safeguard for France and to avert the danger that the German policy might strengthen isolationist tendencies in the United States. The Mansfield lobby had already made use of the *Ostpolitik* as an additional argument for American troop reductions.[52] Thus, as early as February 1970, Pompidou had declared:

Unfortunately, all is still not perfect, and that is why we think that an American presence is useful and even necessary at this point in time, and we feel that this presence, whose weight it is not for me to measure, should be significant and not simply symbolic.[53]

There is an interesting irony in the contrast between this wish of Pompidou and the eschewing of the deployment of American

---

[49] Kissinger, *Years of Upheaval*, 130, 151–92.

[50] See Jobert, *L'Autre Regard*, 294.

[51] Loc. cit.

[52] See Kissinger, *White House Years*, 399.

[53] Pompidou before the National Press Club. Quoted in *Notes et Études Documentaires*, 26 May 1970, No. 5693.

troops by de Gaulle prior to 1968. The change can be attributed to the very different climate in international affairs in 1973, notably regarding European security and the position of the Federal Republic.

The questions of American international diplomacy, troop levels, and French attitudes to Germany were all closely interwoven in the Élysée. First, there was little doubt that the Nixon Administration's increasing pursuit of bloc diplomacy, expressed most vividly in its developing *détente* with Russia, was one of the major causes for the return to a more fundamental Gaullist multipolarity in Pompidou's foreign policy. On 22 June 1973, Washington and Moscow signed an Agreement on the Prevention of Nuclear War. Jobert's remarks before the National Assembly that the accord resembled a 'return to Yalta' bore witness to the force of the blow in Paris.[54] Such independent action by the superpowers emphasized the exclusion of France and Europe from world policy-making. Yet, although the significance of what had taken place was primarily political, the strategic dimension was little less important. This was elaborated by Jobert in a clash with Kissinger later in the year, when the French Foreign Minister rightly observed that the agreement with Russia had reduced the credibility of the American nuclear guarantee over Europe.[55] Hence too Pompidou's stress in 1973 on the continued presence of American troops.[56]

Secondly, it was felt in France that the military implications of this superpower *détente* bore major potential ramifications for the future of Germany—Pompidou's pessimistic analysis almost certainly also coloured by ill health at this stage.[57] The *rapprochement* between Washington and Moscow brought to the surface underlying contradictions in Pompidou's policy towards the Federal Republic. On the one hand, in line with the

[54] Quoted in Grosser, *Les Occidentaux*, 348.

[55] See James O. Goldsborough, 'France, the European crisis and the Alliance', *Foreign Affairs* (Apr. 1974), 549. For Pompidou's view of the agreement, see Kissinger, *Years of Upheaval*, 167.

[56] For further evidence of Pompidou's uneasiness about the policies of the two superpowers, see Brandt, 261. See also Pompidou's remarks in Teyssier, 479; Jobert, *L'Autre Regard*, 179; Kissinger, *White House Years*, 420.

[57] It is suggested in 'Un récit du dernier conseil des ministres présidé par M. Pompidou', *Le Monde*, 9 Apr. 1974, that the President appeared very ill before his trip to Iceland. It should be noted, however, that this account has been contested. In this context, see also the comments in Kissinger, *Years of Upheaval*, 129, 175.

principle of multipolarity, the President felt that the improved relations between the superpowers increased the need for joint European action on defence. This concern had been illustrated a few days earlier by Jobert's comment that, 'day by day Europe's defence will increasingly appear to have an individual personality'.[58] Thus, discussion of European security issues formed an important part of Pompidou's talks with Brandt at the June bilateral summit. Yet traditional differences of emphasis over defence policy prevented anything substantial arising out of their deliberations. While the French stressed the need for joint European action, the Germans—sceptical, as in the 1960s, about France's independent defence posture—stressed the role of NATO and the Eurogroup, in which they argued France should participate.

On the other hand, *détente* intensified French anxiety about the future of the Federal Republic. There were real fears in Paris—given substance, it was felt, by MBFR—of an understanding between the superpowers regarding troop reductions and demilitarization in Central Europe. Such an agreement would profoundly affect the position of West Germany. The latter's European commitment was already coming under closer scrutiny among the French as a result of its greater stress on national interests in Community affairs. These factors go much of the way to explain the difficulties in bilateral Franco-German relations that would come to the fore in August. Pompidou and Jobert were growing extremely concerned about the future possibility (however remote) of a neutralized, and perhaps even reunified, Germany, and were very much reading Bonn's European policy in this light. It is ironic that Pompidou should have arrived in Bonn for the bilateral summit on the very day that the Basic Treaty between the two Germanies came into operation.

Jobert's remarks in an interview with *Der Spiegel* in early June 1973 are particularly revealing in this regard, unequivocally illustrating the prevailing mood in Paris.[59] Though as Foreign Minister Jobert was—at the very least—an idiosyncratic figure, and one not renowned for his self-effacement, and while his

---

[58] Jobert before the National Assembly, 19 June 1973. Quoted in *Le Monde*, 22 June 1973.

[59] *Der Spiegel*, No. 24, 11 June 1973, 92–4.

views on Germany became markedly less restrained while out of office between 1974 and 1981, in terms of content his remarks did not deviate substantially from the pattern of thinking in high government circles, notably the Élysée. (Similar feelings could also be said to apply in Washington and London.)[60] It is unfortunately not possible to summarize Jobert's interview and his comments, pregnant with innuendo, to a manageable length for quotation. Yet their overwhelming import was that the *Ostpolitik* had greatly increased the opportunities open to Bonn, and the question of reunification, which Jobert appeared glibly to accept, 'depended on Germany'.

The studied nonchalance and insinuations in the Foreign Minister's remarks and his apparent matter of fact acceptance of options in German foreign policy which were ruled out in Bonn, such as reunification or a possible severance of the Federal Republic's political links with Western Europe, received widespread and hostile coverage in West Germany. That such opinions were not Jobert's alone is corroborated by Brandt's own account of his summit meeting with Pompidou. Noting that 'many of Pompidou's pronouncements at our last two meetings ... had a testamentary flavour',[61] indicating an increasing preoccupation with long-term policy issues as the President's life drew to a close, Brandt recalls a question posed by his counterpart:

How do you see Germany's future in the light of what is happening? Don't think me indiscreet, but much depends on this from France's point of view. My question doesn't refer to the sort of German future you would *like*. If the GDR ceased to be Communist and reunification followed, France would applaud, but this is surely improbable. Recognising the attitude of the United States and the Soviet Union, and viewing matters in the light of your policy and your relations with the countries of the East, how do you visualise Germany's future *then*? That's the question as I see it. I am asking you

---

[60] On the very interesting theme of foreign misgivings about the *Ostpolitik*, see Kissinger, *Years of Upheaval*, 129, 144–6; Roger Morgan, *The United States and West Germany 1945–1973. A Study in Alliance Politics* (London, RIIA/OUP, 1974), 211–16, and 'Washington and Bonn. A Case Study in Alliance Politics', *International Affairs* (July 1971), 489–90; Henry Brandon, *The Retreat of American Power* (London, The Bodley Head, 1973), 74. For German views, see Brandt, 284, 288–9; Moersch, 225–6; Baring, *Machtwechsel*, 260–3, 283–4.

[61] Brandt, 269.

to interpret a policy which must necessarily be more complex than the French.[62]

In his reply, Brandt affirmed his country's European commitment, both for the present and the future. The Chancellor records Pompidou's response that regarding the *Ostpolitik*, 'there are memories that might have prompted me to feel concern', and his comment that:

You have tried, with some success, to banish such memories. Since you have referred to a constant factor in Germany's new policy, I would draw your attention to two fixed magnitudes in that of France. One is that France could not fail to be extremely alarmed by the neutralization of Central Europe—even if unarmed—and all that might conduce to it.[63]

These remarks clearly indicated the tenor of Pompidou's thought in 1973, with only, under the circumstances, the depth of his disquiet veiled.

Strained relations at the Franco-German summit extended to Community and bilateral policy. The Germans were visibly both more self-assured than in the past and readier to show their irritation about the recent differences that had arisen on agricultural policy and relations with Washington. Bonn appeared to be playing down the meeting; for the first time, an official German spokesman had stated in advance that the summit would be difficult.[64] Jobert's remarks to *Der Spiegel* had not helped. The Foreign Minister had also expressed disappointment in his interview at the altered and less exclusive nature of Franco-German summits. This development, he had implied, had stemmed from the *Ostpolitik* and the widening of German perspectives in its wake. This sense of change was echoed in much of the French press. *Le Monde*, for instance, reported talk in Bonn of a new 'realism' in relations with France, and commented on what it saw as a shift in the attitude of German policy-makers.[65] In turn such reports did not go down well in the German capital, where they increased the existing strain in bilateral relations.

---

[62] Loc. cit.

[63] Ibid. 270.

[64] Reported in *Le Monde*, 22 June 1973.

[65] Ibid. See also the suggestions of deliberate German intransigence in *Le Point*, No. 44, 23 July 1973.

Some progress was made at the summit. Notably, there was a compromise on MCAs, which the French no longer insisted should be abolished and whose link with EMU was accepted, in line with German wishes. In the bilateral sphere, there was accord on the reorganization of the Franco-German Youth Office, and on language teaching. Yet though, as usual, the two leaders praised the results of their talks, the outcome was disappointing. In Germany the blame was squarely placed on the French, with much of the press claiming that Paris was blocking further integration. This was accompanied by hints of French jealously at the Federal Republic's strength. These comments indicate the mistake in viewing chauvinism in bilateral relations as an exclusively French characteristic. In sum, greater German self-confidence had brought about a more critical appraisal of its partner, whose concern about misinterpreted trends in Bonn's foreign policy had caused it to adopt a more defensive posture, which was in turn further straining relations.

Renewed differences over trade policy, and especially the CAP, exacerbated matters. At the Council meeting of 25–6 June 1973, France and Ireland—two of the farm policy's major beneficiaries—strove to ensure that agricultural protection would not be diluted in the Community stand at GATT. As before, the other member states sought by contrast a more conciliatory approach towards the Americans. The eventual Community agreement, whereby neither the 'principles' nor the 'mechanisms' of the agricultural policy would be open for discussions at the trade talks, favoured the French approach, as did the joint position reached on tariffs.

Discussions on trade and political relations with the United States continued to occupy the foreign ministers the following month. However it is for procedural reasons rather than any special controversy over Atlantic relations that the meeting of 23–4 July 1973 has remained notorious. The session stands out for the rigid French adherence to the distinction between political co-operation—discussed in Copenhagen in the morning, and Community affairs—tackled in Brussels by the same group of men that very afternoon. The sluggish pace of the talks was partly attributable to Jobert's introduction of a link between GATT and monetary reform. Yet accusations of obstructiveness must be weighed against the more constructive attitude shown by the French Foreign Minister towards political relations with the United States. The change could be ascribed both to an apparent shift in American views and to signs of greater British backing for the French position. (It should be noted, though, that Kissinger takes a much less sanguine view of the meeting).[66]

American responses to the British stance, which seemingly ran counter to the established concept of a 'special relationship' between London and Washington, are of considerable interest. Yet even at this stage, though well before the British return to a more pro-American alignment later in the year. Kissinger exaggerates in suggesting that: 'We faced in Heath the curiosity of a more benign British version of de Gaulle.'[67] In his *Years of Upheaval*, Kissinger goes further still in implicitly criticizing Heath's Europeanism—which is presented as having been necessarily at odds with the principle of close relations with Washington—and in suggesting dissatisfaction with the Prime Minister's allegedly strong pro-French feelings.[68] Though a conflict of interest is possible, it is undoubtedly a mistake (born usually of an excessively US-orientated perspective) automatically to assume that tightening European links necessarily involved any damage to London's Atlantic outlook.

That the French were clearly still optimistic about achieving Community solidarity towards Washington on their own terms is demonstrated by Jobert's remarks: 'Provided that we did not lower our guard, we were well on the way to showing our unity on most of the issues at stake, commercial, monetary, and political.'[69] Thus the member states, seeking to temporize, followed French wishes in agreeing to draw up a 'constructive' response to the American plans, and to base their future negotiations with Washington on a document setting out a 'European identity'. This decision was highly unpalatable to Kissinger, chiefly on account of the slow pace of such an exercise in Community foreign policy-making, especially over the summer period. Yet Kissinger is probably right to suggest an additional, and growing, obstacle, namely the fact that as the

[66] Kissinger, *Years of Upheaval*, 188.
[67] Kissinger, *White House Years*, 964–5. See also Schaetzel, 30.
[68] Kissinger, *Years of Upheaval*, 141–2, 163, 189.
[69] Jobert, *L'Autre Regard*, 314.

Watergate scandal broadened, so the European governments became increasingly reluctant to associate themselves with an obviously beleaguered President. As he states of the 'Year of Europe': 'Even those sympathetic to the concept felt an understandable disinclination to rally round a reaffirmation of the moral unity of the West put forward by the tarnished Nixon Administration.'[70] However, as will be seen, while the Nine were able to achieve a considerable measure of unity towards the United States in the relaxed atmosphere of mid-1973 (with the initiative for a New Atlantic Charter playing the role of external integrator), the tension in world affairs that would arise by October would have precisely the opposite effect.

Franco-German strain and the role of the Ostpolitik

It was friction over the agricultural policy, exacerbated by the 5.5 per cent revaluation of the Deutschemark on 29 June 1973 (a further blow to the myth of uniform farm pricing) which was the ostensible cause of the storm that was about to break in Franco-German relations. But agricultural and monetary differences constituted only one symptom of a deeper *malaise*, embracing French suspicion of an economically powerful Germany, liberated politically by the *Ostpolitik*. German concentration in 1972–3 on combating inflation, combined with a greater self-assurance, was bound to lead to a more critical appraisal of certain policy commitments. A clash with the French was perhaps inevitable given the widespread mood of suspicion in Paris. Conflict between the two partners had already been intimated at the agricultural marathon of April 1973 and the June bilateral summit, as well as in the negotiations over GATT. The German revaluation had worsened matters. Under these circumstances, Pompidou's lengthy paean to the agricultural policy before the French Cabinet in late June represented a response to these developments and an unequivocal assertion of French priorities.[71]

Yet in the Federal Republic attitudes to the CAP were hardening. Schmidt, responsible for combating inflation, was

---

[70] Kissinger, *Years of Upheaval*, 154. See also 123, 153–5, 191, 193, 702, 734.

[71] Pompidou's statement to the French Cabinet, 28 June 1973. Reported in *Le Monde*, 30 June 1973.

particularly outspoken. Addressing a major agricultural rally in Stuttgart in early June, he strongly criticized the financial burden on the German exchequer imposed by unjustifiable aspects of the agricultural policy.[72] Such statements provide an interesting parallel with the British stance of the late 1970s and early 1980s, and they have fuelled the regular speculation about a joint Anglo-German initiative for the reform of the CAP. Such a move has yet to materialize, however, its likelihood impeded, not least, by the substantial benefits German farmers have come to derive from the workings of the CAP's green money system.

According to Schmidt, producers of surpluses should be made responsible for their financing, while subsidized butter sales to Russia only illustrated the absurd workings of the CAP. Schmidt was especially bitter about the magnitude of Germany's share of the Community budget, and he singled out the lack of Parliamentary control or accountability of the EEC's financial bureaucracy. It was thanks to German pressure, he declared, that the farm policy would be subjected to a fundamental critical re-examination in the autumn. Such statements were hardly likely to be welcomed in Paris, where unease over German intentions was growing. French feelings were intensified by fears of possible Anglo-German collusion over changes to the farm policy in the forthcoming review.

The rising tension in Franco-German relations was finally unleashed by the leak of a secret German report on agriculture, commissioned by Ertl from his ministry's independent advisory council, which had been given the brief of studying possible changes to the CAP in the light of the October review. The experts came up with a number of options, one of which entailed the abandonment of the unified price system in favour of a renationalization of agriculture along the lines of a permanent border tax mechanism. This was seen as the most effective way of dealing with distortions to farm competition.[73] In the public controversy that resulted, the official German position was to maintain that this option, along with many others (including the former British-style deficiency payments system) had been rejected.

---

[72] Reported in *Süddeutsche Zeitung*, 7–8 July 1973. Note also Ertl's June press conference, reported in *Süddeutsche Zeitung*, 6 June 1973.

[73] For accounts of the German report, see *Le Monde*, 8 Aug. 1973, and the *Financial Times*, 10 and 16 Aug. 1973.

Yet the very fact that pulling out of the CAP—a corner-stone of the EEC and of relations with France—had even been considered by the Germans reflected, in descending order of magnitude, their sense of disillusionment with certain aspects of the Community, the emphasis on combating inflation, and the country's greater self-confidence towards its European partners. Despite the German denials (which have been convincingly confirmed to the author), it is none the less interesting to speculate as to whether the recommendation on renationalizing agriculture would have been pursued any further had it not been for the premature and adverse publicity received.

Chirac seized upon the affair. It vindicated, he believed, his earlier accusations of German disinterest in the EEC. His consequent remarks on the Federal Republic's policy in an interview with *Le Point* caused uproar.[74] Asked to comment on the state of the Community, Chirac replied:

I am pre-occupied by Germany on account of the distance it is taking from Europe. This has become more and more evident to me over the last year at Brussels. At first I had thought that it was purely a question of Mr Ertl's personal position. Lately, accompanying M. Pompidou to Bonn, I ascertained that it was in fact that of Mr Brandt's government.[75]

Chirac's remarks provoked a mixture of bewilderment and anger in Bonn. The incident was seen as grossly exaggerated, orchestrated primarily for the benefit of the French farm lobby, with electoral pay-offs firmly in mind, and representing an opening shot prior to the review of the CAP.[76] The Federal Government responded officially by issuing a statement reasserting its European aims and convictions, and calling Chirac's comments the very opposite of the true position. Interviewed by *Le Point*, Ertl described the German agricultural report as a means of finding, in a period of monetary fluctuation, a provisional solution prior to EMU.[77] Germany had no intention of questioning the fundamental principles of the CAP. Ertl did point out,

---

[74] *Le Point*, No. 47, 13 Aug. 1973, 18–19.
[75] Ibid. 19.
[76] For a very good account of the German reaction, see A. W[iss]–V[erdier], 'La Perturbation entre Bonn et Paris', *Documents* (Sept.–Oct. 1973), 14.
[77] *Le Point*, No. 48, 20 Aug. 1973, 24–6.

however, that after ten years, a review of the farm policy was not unreasonable. Characteristically, Apel was more outspoken: 'I find it a little odd that a French minister does not conduct himself more circumspectly.'[78] It was totally unrealistic to imagine a German drift to neutrality, he declared, and he asserted rather that Bonn's policy was based on its commitment to a European Union made at the Paris summit. As to the blame for the present friction, Apel's comments elsewhere regarding the French gave what was probably the most accurate representation of contemporary feeling in Bonn: 'For them, a short-sighted and silly national egoism is put above the long-term vital interests of all the West Europeans to come together and decide their fate for themselves without the tutelage of East or West.'[79]

There are strong reasons to suppose that Chirac's outburst, though made on his own initiative, was representative of the prevailing mood in the Élysée.[80] The Minister of Agriculture was a *protégé* of Pompidou, and his own words in the interview implied presidential approval for his policy in Brussels. Collard notes that Chirac was a 'very orthodox Pompidolian well in favour at the Élysée'.[81] In Pompidou's memoirs (a work not noted for its complimentary portrayals of the great majority of the figures who populate its pages) there are many warm and touching references to Chirac, whom Pompidou obviously regarded as a close and trusted younger friend.[82] Not least, Chirac had proved his worth during Pompidou's period in the wilderness between 1968 and 1969.

Thus it is unlikely that Chirac would have gone so far had he been unsure of the President's tacit sympathy with his views. It was not coincidental, therefore, that there should now have appeared a flurry of reports alleging Pompidou's anxiety about West Germany and his fear of its drift to neutrality.[83] In the words of one unnamed source: 'At the Élysée, every conversation

---

[78] Loc. cit.

[79] Quoted in *The Times*, 23 Aug. 1973.

[80] See especially Marc Ullmann, 'Security Aspects in French Foreign Policy', *Survival* (Nov.–Dec. 1973).

[81] Daniel Collard, 'Convergences et Divergences Politiques', *Documents* (Mar.–Apr. 1974). The article provides a good study of contemporary Franco-German differences.

[82] Pompidou, 264, 271–2, 274.

[83] See *L'Express*, No. 1153, 13–19 Aug. 1973; *Le Nouvel Observateur*, No. 459, 27 Aug. 1973; *Der Spiegel*, No. 34, 20 Aug. 1973; Ullmann, op. cit.

about foreign policy, no matter how it starts, always ends up conjuring up the German problem.'[84] Though exaggerated in style, these reports were fundamentally accurate. The political, economic, and strategic consequences of the *Ostpolitik*, coupled with Pompidou's ill health and the influence of advisers, and aggravated by poor relations with Brandt, had combined to coalesce the President's concern with the Federal Republic into a much deeper anxiety.

Suspicion of Germany was hardly a new theme in French history. In Pompidou's own words: 'The Germans must act tactfully, for one does not have to scratch too far for the French once more to uncover an old aversion.'[85] French unease focused on the *Ostpolitik*. While *rapprochement* with the East had been a policy long counselled by de Gaulle, and the French Government had criticized the German Grand Coalition's early moves as insufficient, it was perceptively noted at the time that, 'one is already aware of a certain jealously in the face of the first successes of the Ostpolitik and a certain fear before the new economic weight and independent action of the Federal Republic'.[86]

After 1969, such ambivalence in France developed in tandem with the Brandt Government's resolute pursuit of its political normalization with the East. While Pompidou at the outset cautiously backed Brandt's moves, and could hardly oppose the pursuit of a policy advocated by his predecessor, he remained suspicious and sought as far as possible to shape it in accordance with French wishes. French anxiety increased as the *Ostpolitik* gathered momentum, matters aggravated by a lack of German consultation at the start. This occurred notably with regard to Bahr's secret talks in Moscow, a source of unease to probably all the Allies.[87] Concern in Paris grew as a result of the Federal Republic's increasingly independent approach to its dealings with the East and its growing *entente* with Moscow. According to the Gaullist Deputy Raymond Bosquet, following its treaty with the Soviet Union, West Germany had taken its place 'among the

---

[84] Quoted in *L'Express*, No. 1153, 13–19 Aug. 1973, 8.

[85] Pompidou, quoted in Jobert, *Mémoires*, 73.

[86] Pierre Hassner, 'Les Politiques envers l'Est. Rivalitées et Convergences', in Grosser (ed.), *Les Politiques extérieures européennes dans la crise*, 66.

[87] See, for instance, Kissinger, *Years of Upheaval*, 145–8, and Baring, *Machtwechsel*, 280.

autonomous actors in world politics'.[88] Bonn, rather, than Paris, had become Moscow's privileged partner, contradicting all de Gaulle's efforts, and to some extent sparking off instead competitive tendencies in French and German *détente* policies.[89] Under these circumstances the French became increasingly preoccupied with the political and military implications of the *Ostpolitik*. Bonn's closer relations with the East opened up the possibility of a reduced German commitment to the West, whose security guarantee would no longer be so important for the Federal Republic. The result might well be a drift towards neutrality, seen by many in Paris as more in line with German interests.[90] Thus at the Nixon–Pompidou summit in Iceland, the French leader had commented on the Federal Republic, which was 'beginning to talk of its two options and proclaim its attachment to the West as it is being pulled into the specific German problem which turns it to the East'.[91] Such a drift appeared all the more plausible given the existence of a Socialist Government in Bonn, comprising what many French leaders regarded as nationalist elements—notably the redoubtable Bahr.

Furthermore, unlike de Gaulle, who believed Russia sought to preserve the post-war European status-quo, Pompidou felt that German neutrality was a prime Soviet objective intended to bring about the withdrawal of American troops from Europe. Hence the President's special stress on their continued deployment, and his deep concern that *détente* in Europe would reinforce the position of the Mansfield lobby, whose very existence, to Pompidou's mind, might encourage Bonn to look to the East. Such an appraisal helps to explain Pompidou's strong stand on the troops issue at his visit to Washington in 1970 and his emphasis on possible future instability in Europe.[92] In a press conference in 1969, he had already stated that 'the problem of

[88] Quoted in *Journal officiel de la République Française, Débats parlementaires. Assemblée Nationale*, 5 Nov. 1970, 5213.

[89] On these themes, see Roland Delcourt, 'Ein Fall von Schizophrenie. Deutsche Ostpolitik aus Pariser Sicht', *Der Monat* (Aug. 1970), 54; Kissinger, *White House Years*, 422–3, and *Years of Upheaval*, 146, 176.

[90] For an appraisal of this topic early in the *Ostpolitik*, see Gilbert Ziebura, 'Neue deutsche Ostpolitik in Pariser Sicht', *Dokumente* 5–6 (1969), 367.

[91] Pompidou, quoted in Kissinger, *Years of Upheaval*, 177.

[92] See, for instance, the ideas suggested by Dieter Dettke, 'Westmächte', in *DGAP* iii. 21–2.

Germany is at the centre of the European problem'.[93] Similarly, Schumann's assertions that the *Ostpolitik* should not affect the Four-Power status of Berlin and his emphasis on French rights in the city reflected French reasoning and policy, which was aimed at preserving the status quo and ensuring that France would not be excluded from any possible future negotiations between Moscow, Bonn, and Washington. Internal politics also played a part. Pompidou felt less secure after the 1972 referendum, especially when compared to Brandt's electoral success. In addition, Germany's Eastern policy and its ramifications gave rise to conflicting pressures on the President. While seeking to maintain good relations with Moscow, partly in order to keep the French Communists and Socialists divided, Pompidou did not at the same time wish to appear too compliant towards the Russians.

By 1973, French anxiety regarding the *Ostpolitik* had surged, particularly as a result of Brandt's Oreanda trip and the Basic Treaty between the two Germanies.[94] Serious concern now began to be voiced about the possibility of German reunification. For Jobert, 'In order to preserve the unity of the German people, the Federal Republic will never directly confront Soviet Russia, and will seek to demonstrate, via neutrality, its dynamism, its usefulness, and its power of attraction.'[95] Closer German scrutiny of Community policy, notably the CAP, was taken as evidence of Bonn's desire to loosen ties with the EEC. There were also French doubts, about the continuing value of the Franco-German Treaty and bilateral co-operation, which, it was argued, had reached their limits.[96] *Détente* between Washington and Moscow, exemplified by MBFR, SALT, and the talks for a European Security Conference, intensified French misgivings about the possibility of some arrangement between the super-powers on disarmament in Central Europe, and the opportunities that this would grant the Federal Republic. Hence Pompidou's continued emphasis at his meeting with Nixon in

[93] Pompidou's press conference on 10 July 1969. Quoted in Rials, 136.
[94] See especially Kiersch, 'Frankreichs Reaktion auf die westdeutsche Ostpolitik', 187.
[95] Jobert, *L'Autre Regard*, 348. For all their differences over Atlantic relations, it is worth noting the similarity of views—more precisely suspicions—between Jobert and Kissinger regarding West Germany.
[96] See, for instance, the conclusions drawn as early as 1970 by Nass in 'Incertitudes Allemandes'.

1973 on maintaining the American military presence in Europe, and his concern that Watergate would make the President more susceptible to pressure from the Mansfield lobby and less able to resist any Russian plans or German ambitions. French fears were not alleviated by the disappointing outcome of Brezhnev's visit to Paris in June 1973, which contrasted sharply with his trip to Bonn the previous month. In sum, the trends in West German foreign policy, in the words of one source formerly extremely close to French external policy-making, 'did not please us at all'.

The economic side

Pompidou, perhaps even more than de Gaulle, laid great weight on France's economic development—though arguably he placed greater emphasis on its internal benefits than its external function of underscoring the country's foreign policy. This background of Pompidou's attitude towards industrialization is important in understanding the difficulties that arose in relations with Bonn. Emphasis on industrial development was a major element of Pompidou's presidential programme, featuring in his message to Parliament on 25 June 1969 and in Chaban-Delmas's Government Declaration on 16 September 1969. Furthermore, in his press conference on 22 September 1969, Pompidou declared that a major task in the coming years would be to make France 'a real economic power'.[97] Pompidou looked to successful economies, such as the United States or West Germany, as examples. The Federal Republic, in particular, given traditional French attitudes, appeared both as a threat and a challenge. Redressing the economic balance between the two countries had been a long-running French objective, for economic, political, and electoral reasons. As early as 1964, Pompidou had stated that 'the life of the Common Market presupposes the economic balance between the six countries and especially ... between the French economy and the German economy.'[98] In January 1969, he stressed that 'the industrial weight of Germany poses a problem ... for us'.[99] In the early 1970s, Pompidou was undoubtedly very gratified by the Hudson

---

[97] Pompidou's press conference on 22 Sept. 1969, in *Le Monde*, 24 Sept. 1969.
[98] Pompidou's television address on 24 Mar. 1964. Quoted in *Le Monde*, 26 Mar. 1964.
[99] Quoted in *Le Monde*, 19–20 Jan. 1969.

Institute Report, commissioned by the Government, which reached the conclusion that the French economy was already the most dynamic in Europe and suggested that in ten years it would be the continent's strongest in production terms.[100]

Against this background, there is little doubt that the commercial consequences of the *Ostpolitik* and the competitive factors it unleashed between the French and German economies contributed to Pompidou's pessimistic appraisal of the Federal Republic's future. Such fears could be given historical justification. In the 1930s, Germany had been the dominant economic power in Central and Eastern Europe, while the Nazis had skilfully manipulated the economic dependence of neighbouring countries as a tool in their expansionist policies. In the post-war period, not only was the fact that the Federal Republic was more capable and better placed than France to trade with the East a source of rivalry, but economic forces were also seen in Paris as further influences impelling Bonn towards Eastern Europe. Thus, it was widely felt in France that German industry was at the forefront of the *Ostpolitik*.[101] Such opinions were disseminated in the French media, particularly the right-wing press—a further demonstration of the failings in information and bias in bilateral relations. On the day of Brandt's first Government Declaration, *L'Aurore* claimed that Bonn was seeking to 's'entendre pour vendre'.[102] Notably, Scheel, regarded as the closest political representative of German industry in the governing coalition and the leader of a party long recommending *rapprochement* with the GDR, was seen as a powerful actor behind the *Ostpolitik*.[103] This is ironic in view of his image in Germay where, despite his party's established leanings towards a normalization of relations with the East, he was often derided, in the early phases of the *Ostpolitik* at least, as a weak and frequently circumvented figure. Long-term German credits to Moscow and expanding trade lent further weight to the French analysis of Bonn's economic

---

[100] Edmund Stillman *et al.*, *L'Envol de la France dans les années 80* (Paris, 1973). It is worth noting that the inaccuracy of these prognostications has been borne out by experience. The report's findings were already questioned by other studies within a short time of its publication. See e.g. Menyesch and Uterwedde, 'Wirtschaftliche und soziale Strukturen in der Bundesrepublik und in Frankreich', 65–6.

[101] See, for instance, Jobert, *Mémoires*, 262.

[102] *L'Aurore*, 28 Oct. 1969.

[103] See *Aspects de la France*, 13 Aug. 1970; *Perspectives*, 10 Jan. 1970.

motivations, while the Basic Treaty between the two Germanies appeared to confirm Bonn's privileged position as a fulcrum and broker between East and West. Furthermore, the Basic Treaty drew attention to the GDR's special status in Community trade, and rekindled fears of the economic might of a unified Germany.

Yet the *Ostpolitik* did not represent a totally new departure in West German trade with Eastern Europe. Rather, it accelerated previous trends.[104] Between 1965 and 1969, West German exports to the Eastern bloc and China had risen by some 90 per cent, compared to a 62 per cent increase in exports globally.[105] By contrast, French sales to the East rose by 65 per cent, and 49 per cent world-wide. The share of the Federal Republic's sales to the East as a percentage of total exports was also accelerating beyond that of France, having risen from 5.4 per cent in 1965 to 6.3 per cent in 1969. The comparable figures for France were 3.6 per cent in 1965 and 4.0 per cent in 1969. In value terms, German exports to the Eastern bloc totalled 3.4 billion dollars, compared to 1.1 billion for France. Paris had long sought to redress the balance, and had established a number of co-operative bodies with some of the East European countries in order to boost bilateral trade. However, the *Ostpolitik* merely reinforced Bonn's advantage with the state trading nations (see Tables 1 and 2). Though West German exports to the GDR admittedly diminished as a proportion of total exports, their rise in value terms was still substantial. Moreover, by 1974 West German exports to Russia and Eastern Europe (excluding the GDR) had risen to 6.25 per cent of total exports, while for France the comparable figure was only 3.56 per cent.[106]

Personal considerations

There was more to French attitudes towards West Germany than just political and economic influences. Personality factors also played an important part. Pompidou's reasoning towards France's Eastern neighbour was based on the premiss that reunification was the Federal Republic's destiny and its ultimate

[104] For analysis of the economic factors behind the *Ostpolitik*, see Michael Kreile, 'Ostpolitik Reconsidered'; and 'Ostpolitik und ökonomische Interessen'.

[105] All figures from Ziebura, 'Frankreichs oder Deutschlands Ostpolitik', 33.

[106] Source: OECD Foreign Trade Statistics, Series B, Jan.–Dec. 1974.

Table 1. *German exports by value to state trading nations (excluding GDR)*

Year	Million DM	Increase (1962 = 100)	% of total exports
1962	2,143	100	4.05
1969	5,081	237.1	4.47
1970	5,400	252.0	4.31
1971	5,825	271.8	4.28
1972	7,660	357.4	5.14
1973	10,814	504.6	6.06

Source: Helmut Gröner, 'Die westdeutsche Aussenhandelspolitik', in Schwarz, *Handbuch*, 409.

Table 2. *West German trade with East Germany*

Year	Exports to GDR		Imports from GDR	
	(Million DM)	% of total exports	(Million DM)	% of total imports
1960	1,030.3	2.15	1,007.3	2.36
1969	2,077.8	1.83	1,656.1	1.69
1973	2,938.2	1.65	2,688.1	1.85

Source: Ibid., and Klaus Körner, 'Die innerdeutschen Beziehungen', in Schwarz, op. cit. 620.

foreign policy aim, however veiled. For the President, steeped in French nationalist tradition and lacking (in line with many of his advisers) a wider appreciation of the constraints operating on the Federal Republic, such a wish on the part of its people was self-evident. Pompidou frequently recalled the example of the 1972 Olympic Games, when the Munich crowd had so warmly applauded the East German athletes, and he dismissed Brandt's doctrine of 'two States in one Nation' as harmless philosophizing. Rather, 'one must reckon with Brandt's extraordinary nationalist passion, with the Chancellor who is not a Rhinelander but a German'.[107] The President had indicated his feelings as early as June 1970, speaking of German economic strength and 'the existence of the German Nation'.[108] Bahr's secretive negotiations in Moscow compounded such French misgivings.

Pompidou's character also had a role in shaping his views. The

[107] Quoted in Jobert, *L'Autre Regard*, 165.
[108] Speech in Strasbourg, June 1970. Quoted in Nass, 'Incertitudes Allemandes', 293.

President was a cautious and suspicious man. The picture given by Seydoux, French Ambassador to Bonn at the start of the *Ostpolitik,* encompasses a number of important themes:

On 30 January precisely, Egon Bahr had his first conversation with Andrei Gromyko; it went on for six hours. The President of the Republic did not conceal from me how closely he was following the exercise. The Russians were showering him with attention, which did not reassure him. Hadn't the Chancellor been almost too friendly towards him? ... It seemed to me that Georges Pompidou was unable to shake off a secret unease.[109]

While for de Gaulle relations with the Federal Republic had a special, emotive significance, Pompidou, while respecting his predecessor's ideals, originally regarded West Germany with some dispassion.[110] Hence his evocation of Franco-German relations as 'exemplaire', compared to the epithet of 'privilegié' used by de Gaulle.[111] Thus it would be wrong to accept the exaggerated picture given by de Saint Robert of the President as a man holding a particular grudge against the Germans from the outset.[112] Rather, Pompidou's attitude to the Federal Republic by mid-1973 was a considered response on his part to the situation as he saw it, resulting in the firm conviction that West Germany could abandon the Western Alliance and drift instead towards the East. It is well worth bearing in mind that such misjudgements were not restricted to government circles, but, with an element of prejudice, particularly on the left, were widespread in France.[113] At a press conference on 12 July 1973, Mitterrand had called into question the attachment of some countries (implying West Germany) to the European Community. On a previous occasion, the Socialist leader had stated that

---

[109] Seydoux, *Dans l'intimité franco-allemande,* 170.

[110] Ziebura remarks on this attitude early in the Pompidou presidency, in *Die deutsch-französischen Beziehungen,* 164.

[111] See Chaban-Delmas's Government Declaration, 27 June 1969, and Ménudier, *L'Allemagne selon Willy Brandt,* 139.

[112] De Saint Robert, 141, 149, 152–3, 156–7.

[113] For opinion poll data regarding French attitudes towards the Federal Republic, see Kiersch, 200, and the SOFRES poll in *L'Express,* No. 1159, 24–30 Sept. 1973, 118–19.

'Germany is growing as Europe contracts.'[114] Not surprisingly, there has been an enforced change of attitudes (at least on the surface) since May 1981.

There is strong evidence to suggest that ill health played a considerable part in influencing Pompidou's attitude to Germany by 1973 (if not before). The President's illness had made itself felt long before his death. Kissinger in particular leaves no doubt as to the signs that were visible during the 1973 Nixon–Pompidou summit:

The change in Pompidou even in the two weeks since I had seen him last was likewise striking—or perhaps the monarchical environment of the Élysée Palace had obscured it. He was bloated from cortisone. Though his courtesy never flagged, it seemed to require a massive effort to maintain it. He had that withdrawn appearance of cancer patients, as if the private battle in which he was engaged made irrelevant the matters at hand.[115]

On 5 June 1973 it was announced that there would be a reduction in the President's representative activities. Information from sources close to the Élysée suggests that ill health was influential in two, related ways. First of all, Pompidou was becoming very tired and often irascible, and his illness undoubtedly contributed to the pessimistic view he came to take of international affairs by summer 1973. To quote Kissinger once again:

No doubt Pompidou's suffering contributed to the increasing irritability of French policy. It was a tall order to ask him to be a partner in launching a new initiative of undefined duration when he was contemplating his own demise.... But now his lack of confidence in potential successors ... compounded Pompidou's native scepticism and caused him to avoid new courses that in other hands might lead to unpredictable and perhaps deleterious results.[116]

Another observer also describes the President's extreme pessimism and predictions of an unsettled future for Europe at a lunch

---

[114] Quoted in *Le Nouvel Observateur*, No. 459, 27 Aug.–2 Sept. 1973. On the purely humanitarian side it is worth adding that Mitterrand caused no little controversy in the later 1970s by his backing for a committee to supervise the protection of civil liberties in the Federal Republic. See François Mitterrand, *L'Abeille et 'architecte* (Paris, Flammarion, 1978), 184, 191–2, 201–2.

[115] Kissinger, *Years of Upheaval*, 175, See also 129. Most recently, Roussel gives a good analysis of Pompidou's ill health and its effect: Roussel, *Pompidou*, 473, 497, 503–12.

[116] Ibid. 175–6.

for journalists at the beginning of July.[117] The second influence of ill health was that Pompidou was deeply conscious of the pressure of time. This was especially marked as he was convinced that much needed to be done in order to correct what he saw as dangerous tendencies in Europe, notably regarding Germany and Russia. These considerations help explain French policy towards the Federal Republic in mid-1973 and also the line later adopted towards the United States, particularly over energy policy.

Lastly, one less certain consequence of Pompidou's illness concerns the extent to which he came to rely on close advisers, notably his foreign minister. Jobert had worked with Pompidou since 1963, and had been the President's Secretary-General at the Élysée before his promotion to the Quai d'Orsay.[118] Despite the predominant presidential role in foreign policy-making in the Vth Republic, the circumstances of 1973 were exceptional. Opinion differs about the extent of Jobert's involvement during Pompidou's last year. However, many sources suggest that he became increasingly influential in shaping French foreign policy. A parallel has frequently been drawn between his role and that of Henry Kissinger. It is interesting to note that there was a close intellectual bond between the two former back-room advisers. Kissinger himself leaves no room for doubt as to his assessment of the state of affairs. Summing up the course of French foreign policy in 1973–4, he writes:

Jobert was a great talent, who might have thrived had his President not been stricken just when he reached prominence. Pompidou was essentially measured, careful, and balanced. I cannot believe that he would have let matters slide so completely out of control had he been healthy.[119]

However, this is dangerous ground, with Kissinger's judgement coloured by the special circumstances of the 'Year of Europe' in which Jobert was his principal adversary. Indeed, the whole Kissinger–Jobert relationship and the role of these two highly intelligent, opinionated, and egocentric men at the forefront of

---

[117] Teyssier, 474.
[118] Note the entertaining sketch provided by Kissinger in *Years of Upheaval*, 164–6.
[119] Ibid. 166.

their respective countries' foreign policies at a time of marked decline in their mentors is one which cries out for special study. Certainly, the link between Pompidou and his foreign minister was exceptionally strong. It is amusing that Pompidou should refer to Jobert as 'Mon Kissinger à moi',[120] while Jobert himself declared after Pompidou's death that 'my life with him had been a boundless accord'.[121] Elsewhere, Jobert has written of the unusual freedom of action he enjoyed as a result of the mutual understanding and confidence between himself and the President.[122]

Jobert's opinions do appear to have had an impact on French policy towards the Federal Republic in 1973. His firm belief in the possibility of neutrality or even reunification probably exceeded in scale Pompidou's own doubts.[123] Jobert's feelings were most clearly defined in his writings during the mid-1970s. On his policy in 1973, he has stated: 'I have never concealed the fact that Germany's vocation for neutrality—if there is no change in the division of power between the two super-powers—seems to me to be inscribed on the horizon.'[124] Given Jobert's senior position in 1973 and his close relations with Pompidou, it is not unreasonable to suppose that his views were influential in reinforcing the President's own opinions, and thus affecting French relations with Bonn.

Conclusion

The perception of the European scene as outlined above helps explain some of the inconsistencies in French foreign policy in 1973, especially regarding defence and Community affairs. As Ullmann accurately sums up, 'France's foreign policy is based on an attitude of trust towards West Germany, whereas her defence policy reflects an attitude of distrust of that country.'[125] In the military sphere, although Pompidou

---

[120] Goldsborough, 'France, the European Crisis, and the Alliance', 545.

[121] Quoted in *Le Monde*, 17 Apr. 1974.

[122] Jobert, *L'Autre Regard*, 361–2. Note also Jobert's role in the preliminary negotiations with the British prior to membership.

[123] Kiersch, 195, draws useful comparisons between the views of Jobert and his predecessor Schumann. For Jobert's opinions, see his interview with *Der Spiegel*, No. 24, 11 June 1973, 92–4; *Mémoires*, 15–16; and, above all, 'De l'Allemagne'.

[124] Jobert, *L'Autre Regard*, 348.

[125] Ullmann, 263.

keeps talking about defending the independence of Western Europe vis-à-vis the United States, he at the same time tells Mr. Nixon that America must continue to maintain her troops in West Germany. Equally paradoxically, although he talks about the dynamic progress of *détente*, he has also many times shown his distrust of any positive changes in the political and military future of Europe that could result from the conferences in Helsinki, Geneva, and Vienna.[126]

Under these circumstances, which could potentially have led to a neutralized Central Europe, France would be isolated. Hence Pompidou's increased emphasis on the development of the *force de frappe*. As for his European policy,

the French government aims at maintaining co-operation with West Germany but at the same time wants to keep its hands free in case this co-operation should break down. By the same token it also blocks the path that could lead to the creation of a truly European government.[127]

Although in its severity an isolated episode in the Brandt–Pompidou era, the friction that arose in summer 1973 testified to some of the major problems that existed in bilateral Franco-German understanding and information—failings not removed by the 1963 treaty between the two countries. From the French point of view, de Gaulle's observation of 1965 that 'il y a l'Allemagne qui se transforme et dont nous ne savons pas, absolument pas, où vont les ambitions' remained apposite. Given the major changes that were taking place in the relative positions and foreign policies of France and Germany between 1969 and 1974—a transitional process which arguably reached its peak in 1973—some difficulties of adjustment in bilateral relations were by no means surprising. It was inevitable that this process should have been felt more acutely on the French side, where it involved the recognition and acceptance of a more confident and assertive West Germany, and hence of a new balance in bilateral and European relations. The friction of summer 1973 marked the clearest expression of these difficulties of adjustment during the Brandt–Pompidou years.

---

[126] Ibid. 265. See also Uwe Nerlich, 'West European defence identity: the French paradox', *The World Today* (May 1974).

[127] Ullmann, 263.

7

Energy and Other Issues

1973

A return to normality in bilateral relations

The German Government's public reaction to the accounts of suspicion and unease emanating from Paris was one of restraint, although there were reports that Brandt was awaiting a clarification from the French President. Certainly Sauvagnargues, the French Ambassador to Bonn, was called for a private meeting with Frank, one of the State Secretaries in the Auswärtiges Amt, who conveyed the Government's feelings. Brandt himself remained reserved. One of his few public utterances on the issue came in a speech on 22 August 1973, when he remarked that one member state should not make another bear the brunt of its own internal difficulties. In comments to *Le Monde* about the crisis, Scheel, for his part, was conciliatory, though characteristically Schmidt and Apel reacted more vigorously.[1] Furthermore, as on occasions in the past, some of the German press comment bore witness to a distinct national chauvinism. Hostile reaction was not, however, limited to the German side; there was criticism in some French circles too of the Government's suspicion of Germany and inaction over European policy.[2]

There was a long delay before any official French denial of Chirac's remarks or the reports of Pompidou's feelings about Germany was issued. *Der Spiegel* did, however, allude to a communication from the President to Brandt stating that Chirac had been speaking in a private capacity.[3] By the end of August, it was obvious that both the French and German Governments

[1] *Le Monde*, 25 Aug. 1973. For Schmidt's remarks, see the Bonn newspaper, *General Anzeiger*, 22 Aug.; Apel's words are reported in *Süddeutsche Zeitung*, 18 Aug. 1973.

[2] See Joseph Rovan, 'Brandt m'a convaincu que...', *Le Point*, No. 50, 3 Sept. 1973; and *Le Monde*, 14 Aug. 1973.

[3] *Der Spiegel*, 20 Aug. 1973.

were trying to defuse the crisis, which clearly suited neither side. Ertl also sought to smooth the waters, though, like Brandt, he suggested that Chirac's remarks had been made for internal rather than external reasons. Notably, the Agriculture Minister was careful now to refer to the German plans for a return to a national farm price system as a 'middle course', which did not interfere with the CAP's basic principles, and he stressed that Bonn did not approve of extreme measures to reform the agricultural policy, but rather sought its 'further development'—the Government's new euphemism, according to the *Frankfurter Allgemeine Zeitung*, for changing the CAP.[4]

The friction of August largely explains the limited mention of the CAP review at the farm ministers' meeting on 26 September 1973. Chirac's suggestion on this occasion that there seemed little reason to warrant discussion of basic changes to the farm policy went unopposed. With the Germans reserved, for fear of upsetting relations with Paris, the British were reluctant to press the issue. What is more, the French were clearly mounting a campaign, aimed primarily at the Federal Republic, to minimize pressure for change. At his press conference on 27 September 1973, Pompidou accentuated the fact that France was not an unduly large beneficiary from the farm policy.[5] As regards that other main German topic of complaint—agricultural over-production—the President added that French farm output had only increased by about 93 per cent since the foundation of the EEC, as against a Community average of 96 per cent and a Dutch rise of approximately 150 per cent. Pompidou correctly pointed out that Dutch farmers had received about five times as much as their French counterparts in direct aid from Brussels over this period. Nor did the President forbear to stress the Federal Republic's own gains from the Community, most notably in the industrial sector. Pompidou sought to equate these with the French position on agriculture. The President was surprisingly candid regarding the *Ostpolitik,* his remarks indirectly confirming earlier suggestions about his outlook. Confronting the issue head on, Pompidou stated that 'given the

---

[4] Reported in the *Financial Times*, 1 Sept. 1973.
[5] Pompidou's press conference on 27 Sept. 1973. Reported in *Le Monde*, 29 Sept. 1973. See also the report in *Frankfurter Allgemeine Zeitung*, 28 Sept. 1973.

German situation, this policy can hardly allow some possibilities to go unperceived. Denying it would be absurd.'[6]

Despite Pompidou's *plaidoyer* for the agricultural policy, there was no easing of German pressure, emanating especially from Schmidt, for a reduction in Bonn's financial contribution. In a speech on 9 October 1973, the German minister criticized the CAP's cost, and claimed that in the last ten years Germany, Italy, and Belgium had borne a disproportionate share of the expenditure, while France, Luxembourg, and the Netherlands had received an inequitable share of the benefits.[7] In his struggle to control government expenditure, the CAP was an obvious target for Schmidt. Once again, his complaints bore a striking resemblance to Britain's policy in similar circumstances in the late 1970s and early 1980s.

Despite Schmidt's stand, the fact that so little was to result from the CAP review of November 1973 was attributable to a number of causes, chiefly the high current level of world food prices, which made many European products cheaper than those on the world market. The emergence of other, more pressing, issues, notably the Middle East and oil, also served to obscure agricultural reform and increase the need for Community solidarity. In addition, difficulties in reconciling the different national objectives on the CAP were perhaps now more clearly perceived. Finally, Schmidt notwithstanding, German desire for agricultural reform had to some extent been tempered by the clash with the French, while the British, the other advocates for change, were now concentrating more on regional policy and directing their diplomatic efforts towards Paris, making them reluctant to antagonize the French.

International affairs

After a lull over the summer (caused not least by the winding down of the Community's diplomatic machinery over the holiday period, much to Kissinger's chagrin) the question of Euro-American relations regained prominence in September.

---

[6] Collard, 96, comments on the unconvincing nature of Pompidou's expression of confidence in the Federal Republic at the press conference.

[7] The German position was reinforced at a special meeting between Brandt and several of his ministers, including Schmidt, on 11–12 October. See the *Financial Times*, 11 Oct. 1973.

Existing differences were now to be greatly intensified by the Middle East war the following month. This situation further challenged the Community, and, as after the 1967 Arab–Israeli conflict, highlighted French and German divisions stemming from their different policy preferences and limitations. Matters were clear cut for the French. Their policy of multipolarity— strongly reinforced by Pompidou's and Jobert's own feelings towards the superpowers in 1973—was now directed towards asserting European identity and solidarity independently of the United States, with whom the French were additionally in conflict over their sympathy with the Arabs.

Matters were much more complex for the Germans. While the *Ostpolitik* had widened Bonn's room for manœuvre in foreign policy and resulted in a greater self-assurance, the renewed climate of international tension vividly re-exposed the Federal Republic's particular constraints and vulnerabilities. As had happened, for instance, over Vietnam and the Middle East in 1967, Bonn was once again torn between solidarity with Washington and—to an unprecedented degree—sympathy with French emphasis on European cohesion and independence. However, even more problematic was the fact that the Middle East conflict created a far greater moral and political dilemma for Germany than for any other European country. The Federal Republic's pro-Israeli stance, a corner-stone of its external policy since its foundation, had now somewhat uncomfortably to be reconciled with its interest in maintaining good relations with the Arabs in the face of the oil threat. The particular intensity of this problem for Bonn, a legacy of the Third Reich, highlighted one facet of the special constraints that still restrict its external relations.

During summer 1973 work had progressed slowly on the Community's document setting out a 'European identity', on which the Nine had decided to base their relations with Washington. In the meantime, however, the divergence of interests between Europe and the United States had been widening. In August the Americans, increasingly concerned about autonomous European action, had presented a draft for the New Atlantic Charter. This had been unacceptable to the Europeans, and the British, with French backing (another indication of the alignment between the two), had responded by producing an alternative text. While recognizing Europe's political and military solidarity with the United States, this document also laid weight on the latter's recognition of the Community's unity and position in the world. Paris had also shown willingness to approve a text on the political and military solidarity of the Alliance. This decision was attributable to the still good relations between Kissinger and Jobert, and to French concern about the state of international affairs. Kissinger ironically contrasts this desire to proceed on defence issues—a subject of interest to the French—with their reluctance to make progress on the question of closer political and economic co-operation.[8] 'It was vintage Gaullism' in the American diplomat's view. Obviously, though, separating defence from economic and political co-operation into two texts stymied Kissinger's tactic of linking military matters with other issues as a lever for obtaining concessions. Both documents were adopted by the Community foreign ministers at their political co-operation meeting on 10–11 September 1973.[9]

Not only were these European proposals strongly disliked by Kissinger, but the fact that Andersen, the Danish President of the Council of Ministers, brought them to Washington on 25 September as the Community's representative seemed to symbolize that very European cohesion and determination in international affairs which the Secretary of State sought to keep in harness. Kissinger's reaction was hostile. The European plans were viewed as an undesirable expression of independence—a concern that would come to a climax in November—and he described the situation as an 'event of the greatest significance'.[10] By way of response, Kissinger's counterproposal at the end of the month reasserted inter-dependence and very much diluted the references in the Community's document to its autonomous role in world affairs.

However, it was the outbreak of hostilities in the Middle East on 6 October 1973 and the associated renewal of international

[8] See Kissinger, *Years of Upheaval*, 704–6.

[9] For a fuller account of the meeting, see Dettke, 160–4; also Andrew J. Pierre, 'What Happened to the Year of Europe?', *The World Today* (March 1974); and especially, for an analysis focusing on Jobert and the French position, Jacques-Guillaume Leroy, 'Le Petit Homme, la France, et l'Europe', *Contrepoint* 15 (1974).

[10] Kissinger's press conference on 26 Sept. 1973, quoted in Dettke, 161.

tension, rather than any American action, that in the end dissipated European cohesion and restored the initiative to Washington. This reversal was by no means instantaneous. In fact, the Community's conspicuous exclusion from the Middle East scene and the peace process acted as an additional politically unifying factor at the outset. Once again, France was at the forefront, the latest events accelerating the return to Gaullist first principles provoked by the New Atlantic Charter and the events of the summer. French emphasis on the need for European identity and independent action was exemplified by Jobert's offer of French help to calm the Middle East conflict before the United Nations on 10 October. It was also announced that the Franco-German summit would be brought forward from January 1974 to November 1973.

Yet European determination to stand united proved to be short-lived once subjected to closer scrutiny and particularly, by mid-October, to increasing use of the oil weapon. Though 'tired of being mute, powerless, and forgotten', in Jobert's words,[11] the weakness of the Community's mid-October call for a ceasefire in line with UN Resolution 242 testified to the differences between the Nine regarding Israel and the Arabs. This divergence of opinion revolved principally around France on the one side, and Germany and Holland on the other. The French position was straightforward, clearly cast in the mould of de Gaulle's post-1967 approach. As Jobert replied to a question in the National Assembly on responsibility for the Middle East conflict: 'Does trying to return home necessarily constitute an unforeseen aggression?'[12] For the Federal Republic, by contrast, inherent sympathy for Israel had to be balanced against oil dependence.[13]

The insecurity of the German position was underlined by friction in relations with Washington in late October 1973. In an incident reminiscent of American use of German bases in the Lebanon crisis of 1958, it was discovered that two Israeli ships were loading American military supplies in Bremerhaven. There was an angry German response, and even suspicion in Bonn that,

---

[11] Jobert, *L'Autre Regard*, 343.

[12] Jobert, 8 Nov. 1973. Quoted in Grosser, *Les Occidentaux*, 350.

[13] For the problems facing the Germans, see A. W[iss]–V[erdier], 'La Guerre israélo-arabe et les suites', *Documents* (Nov.–Dec. 1973), 134.

maybe deliberately, adequate precautions had not been taken—
perhaps in order to cause embarrassment and give the impression that the Federal Republic was aiding the Israelis. Brandt
comments on this American high-handedness:

I was not merely dismayed that nobody had seen fit to inform us (the
US Embassy was not overcommunicative even when confronted with
the report from Bremerhaven). What I failed to understand was why, if
the shipments were considered so vital, they had not been put aboard
vessels flying the US flag. It seemed unfair to me that such manifold
doubts should be cast on our official expressions of non-partisanship ...
What we could not accept was an initial reluctance to tell us the truth
(evinced by American uneasiness) when we detected some arms
deliveries from an unspecified source. Washington began by reacting
fiercely to our enquiries. It was even intimated to our representatives
that the Federal Republic enjoyed only limited sovereignty in
American eyes ...[14]

A number of additional factors straining US–German relations
have been posited. These included differing priorities over
MBFR and CSCE and, in (muted) echo of French attitudes,
dissatisfaction regarding a lack of consultation over the June
1973 US–Russian agreement.[15]

Matters deteriorated further following the full American
nuclear alert of 24–5 October 1973. This came as a surprise to
most of the Europeans, and was viewed with considerable
suspicion in some quarters. There were even suggestions that it
was designed to divert attention away from Watergate. In turn,
Washington responded very angrily to what was felt to be an
uncooperative European attitude. In his press conference on 26
October, Nixon attacked European policy on the Middle East,
while Kissinger complained to a group of Community parliamentarians that the Europeans had 'acted as though the
Alliance did not exist'.[16]

In view of its traditional policy preferences, it was hardly
surprising that France should now have taken the initiative
among the Nine in seeking to redress the balance in Atlantic
relations following the Middle East hostilities. Similarly, it was
Paris which tried to unite the Community around a coherent

[14] Brandt, 316. See also the authoritative account in Frank, 267–72.
[15] Morgan, *The United States and West Germany*, 241–4.
[16] Quoted in 'Z.', 237.

independent posture. Hence Pompidou's call in November 1973 for a Community summit.[17] At his press conference on 27 September, the President had already suggested regular summits in order to improve political co-operation and map out common European foreign policies. The events in the Middle East, which had demonstrated Europe's political eclipse (and had given rise to calls in France for action), had concentrated this desire. As Pompidou noted, attempts to end the fighting had taken place 'without the slightest participation of Europe'.[18]

Reaction in the other member states was generally favourable to the President's summit proposal. Significantly, there was immediate support from the Germans, who were particularly keen to back any initiative likely to reduce the tension. Notably, though, there were doubts among some of the smaller member states regarding Pompidou's plans for regular summits comprising only Heads of State or Government and excluding the Commission. These clearly recalled de Gaulle's tactics. As usual, it was Holland's voice which was loudest. Dutch opposition focused not just on the institutionalization of summits, but also on the tendency of France, Germany, and Britain to work together. In this context, one should bear in mind the suggestions that the unilateral Dutch revaluation of September 1973 without prior consultation was a response to the secret February meeting between Giscard, Schmidt, and Barber.

A large part of the explanation for the failure of the EEC's Copenhagen summit can be put down to the fact that the meeting had been proposed and was to take place just at a time when intra-Community differences on the Middle East were widening. This was principally as a result of increased Arab use of the oil weapon in the wake of the Middle East war. However, the tide had been turning against the oil consumers for some time: the equilibrium between demand and supply had shifted steadily (the share of oil in Western Europe's total primary energy consumption had risen from 32.4 per cent in 1960 to 59.2 per cent in 1970).[19] Furthermore, this trend had been accom-

---

[17] For Pompidou's motives in calling the summit, see Morgan, *From Summit to Council*, 17–18.

[18] Quoted in the *Financial Times*, 1 Nov. 1973.

[19] Source: OECD Statistics on Energy (Various years).

panied by a more militant attitude on the part of many oil producers since the late 1960s and early 1970s, notably Libya.

By autumn 1973, Arab political pressures following the Middle East hostilities coincided with these commercial factors, bringing matters to a head. The pace of developments was to be very rapid. On 16 October, six Gulf states decided to increase the price of their oil by 70 per cent, from $3.01 to $5.12 per barrel. The next day, Arab members of OPEC announced a monthly five per cent cutback in production, to last until such time as Israel pulled back from the territories occupied since 1967 and Palestinian rights were observed. On 17 October, Saudi Arabia went one step further, announcing a ten per cent cutback until Arab political demands were met.

Matters were exacerbated following President Nixon's request on 19 October for a $2.2 billion military aid package for Israel. The Arab response was swift. On 20 October, Saudi Arabia and other Arab nations announced a total oil embargo on the United States. This measure was also extended to Holland, a country viewed as pro-Israeli by the Arabs. For the other Europeans, the step exacerbated an already developing *sauve qui peut* attitude. France and Britain were at the forefront of the scramble. Each sought to capitalize on existing favoured links with certain oil producers. (Both countries had been granted 'friendly' political status by the Arabs.) For those other member states less fortunate, notably the Dutch themselves, the situation was regarded very differently. For them, a joint Community stand appeared to be the only solution.

But a common energy policy had proved intractable for the EEC long before the present crisis. Energy had been the subject of various abortive initiatives since the 1960s.[20] Not even the strong premonitory signs of a more militant OPEC attitude in 1973 had managed to provoke results. Although Simonet, the EEC Energy Commissioner, had called for discussions between the Nine and other oil consumers on energy issues, the meeting of EEC energy ministers in May 1973, the first such session since

[20] For the background to European energy policy, see Robert A. Black, Jr., 'Plus ça change, plus c'est la même chose: Nine Governments in Search of a Common Energy Policy', in Wallace *et al.*; Guy de Carmoy, 'The Politics of European Energy Policy', in Martin O. Heisler (ed.), *Politics in Europe* (New York, McKay, 1974); Louis Turner, 'The Politics of the Energy Crisis', *International Affairs* (July 1974).

1969, had failed to establish a consensus. Agreement had been limited to a national commitment to bring in 'crisis management' legislation on oil.

Many factors divided the Nine. Primarily these concerned divergent economic and political philosophies and practices. By early 1974, dissimilar susceptibilities to American pressure would also play a part. These divisions should be examined more closely. On the economic side there were marked differences in thinking. The French, for instance, pursued a highly controlled domestic oil policy: preferential treatment was given to French companies and to crude oil from the franc zone, while restrictions were placed on foreign firms and prices were tightly controlled. The British, Dutch, and Germans, by contrast, had long adopted a much more *laissez-faire* approach, with matters largely left in the hands of the international oil companies. Britain and Holland, furthermore, themselves had domestic oil majors. The picture was additionally complicated by the Nine's heterogeneity regarding energy resources (with the British, notably, having access to North Sea oil) and their differences over nuclear power.

Political considerations were inextricably intertwined. It was not just for economic reasons that the French favoured a *dirigiste* Community policy on energy: according to the French conception, the Nine should also aim to discriminate in favour of certain sources, such as associated states like Algeria. By contrast, most of the other member states preferred a free market approach—or at least its façade. Political differences were also highly evident on the procedural side. The French had opposed giving Simonet a mandate to consult with the Americans (something which had been welcomed by the majority of Community capitals), on the grounds that this was an intergovernmental matter and the EEC should first prepare its own energy policy before entering into talks with outsiders. There is little doubt that the French stance was to some extent influenced by its attitude to the wider question of political relations with the United States, as well as its long-standing antipathy to Anglo-Saxon domination of the international oil industry.

Although new proposals for a Community energy policy had been submitted by August 1973, discussion was overtaken by events in the Middle East. The Community's growing disarray in autumn well illustrated some of the conflicting interests of its members. By late October, Luxembourg had banned oil outflows, while France and the Netherlands had stipulated licensing for oil exports to non-Community countries. Matters further deteriorated by early November, with the Commission, backed by Bonn, claiming that the Italian and Benelux oil licensing schemes were incompatible with the Treaty of Rome, as was the French plan to allocate market shares to foreign oil companies.

It was against this background of public accusations among the Europeans and private rumours of secret deals with the Arabs that the Community foreign ministers met on 6 November. Tension was greatly raised by the embargo on Holland. Rather than being met, the Dutch demand for a joint stand and oil-sharing merely served to intensify existing intra-Community differences. The Dutch posture was viewed with great distaste in London and Paris for fear of damaging privileged links with the Arabs. (At the meeting of Arab oil ministers on 5 November, France and Britain had been spared the 25 per cent cutback on September levels announced for the other EEC countries. The two 'friendly' nations had, instead, been promised supplies at the level of the first nine months of 1973.)

Under these circumstances it was hard to see how the Council of Ministers could reconcile the problem of simultaneously reassuring the Dutch without offending the Arabs. However, economic realities finally got the better of moral qualms, and the Nine blatantly bowed to Arab pressure. All the member states (the Dutch included) now agreed on a British-inspired resolution on the Middle East which went beyond their earlier restatement of Resolution 242. The EEC now more assertively referred to the legitimate rights of the Palestinians and called on the Israelis to withdraw to the ceasefire lines of 22 October.[21] Significantly, this apparent temporary closing of European ranks in the face of economic necessity was very badly received by Kissinger. Not only, as in September, did it offer further proof of budding European political cohesion, but it was now also interpreted as an—at the very least unhelpful—

---

[21] The text of the Community's resolution can be found in *The Times*, 7 Nov. 1973. For a closer account of the meeting, see Turner, 409–11.

interference in the Secretary of State's Middle Eastern diplomacy.[22]

Certainly, the fact that the Nine's foreign ministers had managed to reach agreement suggests that, at this stage at least, the centripetal influence of the oil threat—expressed in the Community's outward political solidarity over the Middle East—still exceeded the centrifugal tendencies that were also being provoked. Only gradually would the latter take precedence. It would be interesting to learn whether the Dutch agreement to the joint resolution on the Middle East had come about as a result of a preconsidered and independent shift of policy in The Hague, or whether—and perhaps this lies closer to the truth—some compromise had been struck among the Council of Ministers. Conceivably, those member states most closely aligned with the Arabs, namely France and Britain, might have suggested (by no means altruistically) that the 'reward' for a pro-Arab stance would be the removal of the oil embargo. At the very least, the possible proposal of French and British good offices towards the Arabs might have played a part in bringing the Dutch round. In either case, such tactics would only have been partly successful. Although the Arab oil ministers announced on 19 November that the Community would be exempted from the next five per cent cutback in supplies scheduled for December, they retained their sanctions on the Dutch. However, it should be noted here that, largely as a result of the multinational oil companies' policies of transhipping supplies, the victims of the embargo were not, in fact, affected as badly as had been expected.

The French remained at the forefront of pressure for European political solidarity in the coming weeks. Jobert, addressing the National Assembly on 12 November, gave perhaps the most eloquent exposition to date of the restored Gaullist strain in French external policy resulting from the circumstances of middle and late 1973 (the quotation defies translation):

Traité comme une 'non-personne', humiliée dans son inexistence, l'Europe, dans sa dépendance énergétique, n'en est pas moins l'objet du deuxième combat de cette guerre du Proche-Orient. Victime oubliée

---

[22] See here Jobert, *L'Autre Regard*, 343–4; Leroy, 79.

du conflit, mais victime tout de même, alors qu'elle n'avait cessé de dénoncer les périls, son désarroi et son amertume sont évidents. Mais elle a aussi constaté qu'elle était un enjeu, plus encore qu'un instrument ou un appoint dans l'arbitrage des Grands. Elle peut, elle doit en tirer une essentielle leçon. Bien des peuples attendent, non son sursaut, mais sa naissance![23]

That Brandt, speaking before the European Parliament in Strasbourg the following day, should have adopted so similar, though understandably more muted, a stance, testified to the effect, in Bonn little less than in Paris, of Kissinger's bloc diplomacy of 1973, and also to the present strain in bilateral relations between Bonn and Washington.[24] The Chancellor called for a common European foreign and defence policy and demanded equal treatment from the United States. As influential on the Federal Republic as American policy was the sense of frustration in Germany at the country's inability to sway the course of events. Such feelings were intensified by the expansion of the Federal Republic's foreign policy interests in the wake of the *Ostpolitik*.

Yet it was an indication of the moral and political constraints still facing West Germany (and an indirect confirmation of the overriding economic determinants) that Brandt should have admitted to the Parliament's Socialist group that he felt that the Nine had gone too far in their previous week's resolution on the Middle East.[25] At the same time, however, the breadth and authority of the Chancellor's speech also bore witness to the expansion of German foreign policy interests in 1973. In September, the Federal Republic had finally entered the United Nations.

At their meeting on 20 November 1973, the Nine retained a surprising degree of cohesion on oil and the Middle East. This was in spite, or perhaps because, of Dutch threats to reduce natural gas supplies to Community partners. Yet that there had definitely been some movement on the Dutch side was confirmed by the Community's agreed restatement of its standpoint of 6 November and its accord on the need to speak to the oil

[23] Jobert, *L'Autre Regard*, 344.
[24] Brandt, reported in *The Times*, 13 Nov. 1973. Moersch hints at German doubts about Kissinger's plans, 225–6.
[25] Reported in the *Financial Times*, 14 Nov. 1973.

producers with one voice. This was in line with Jobert's plans for a conference between Europe and the Arabs. It was also agreed that the Community would seek new contacts with the oil producers and try to convince them of a change in the Dutch attitude. Community membership was now undoubtedly providing a highly convenient cloak for the Dutch (and Germans), shielding them from unpopular individual choices. In both countries, public opinion sympathized strongly with Israel, and there was very great resentment at what was seen as Arab blackmail over energy.

Bilateral discussions

Not surprisingly, energy policy took pride of place at the Franco-German summit on 26–7 November 1973. The Germans put extremely strong emphasis on a common European policy, which they had come to regard as a symbol of the Community's will to unite. But there was much more than just ideology to the German posture. For the Federal Republic, joint action on energy represented the best expedient in a very complex situation. Lacking privileged links with the Arabs, and greatly constrained in its Middle East policy by its special relationship with Israel, the Federal Republic, unlike France, had everything to gain from a common energy policy. Hence Brandt's repeated assertions at the summit that Franco-German solidarity now had to prove itself in the light of the crisis facing Europe, and his stress on joint Community action on energy. In the Chancellor's words, 'we are all equally affected and none of us has the right to leave the other alone with its worries. By accepting the weakening of one country, we are in reality weakening the Community itself, and, thereby, each of its members.'[26]

Yet a sharp cleft was evident between this stance and Jobert's much more jaundiced approach. According to the French minister, Brandt

was dreaming of a sort of European crusade on oil: pooling of stocks, savings shared out equally ... 'Solidarity! Solidarity!' proclaimed the Chancellor in his talks, annoying Georges Pompidou, who saw nothing there but an internal policy manœuvre, alerted by all the international press. 'Yes, yes,' grumbled the President of the Republic, 'solidarity,

[26] Quoted in *Le Monde*, 28 Nov. 1973.

but not just for oil, for everything else as well. Then they won't shout so loudly. Let the Germans join Eurodif—for producing enriched uranium—and then I'll start to shout solidarity.'[27]

French interests were very different from those of the Germans. With an even greater dependence than the Federal Republic on imported oil (comprising 71.3 per cent of French energy needs as against 51.8 per cent for Germany)[28] France remained extremely reserved on any joint energy policy for fear of jeopardizing relations with the Arabs. Rather than proceeding on a Community basis, Paris saw greater benefits in pursuing a bilateral diplomacy with long-cultivated Arab states. This option was to be energetically put into practice by Jobert in a bout of peripatetic Middle East diplomacy, opening the way to a series of large deals in early 1974. Such a course would certainly bolster France's position in the difficult economic years ahead and set the pattern for a new generation of arms for oil barters, helping the balance of payments and building up a thriving and strategic French armaments industry.[29]

However, it could well be argued in 1973 that there was an inherent contradiction between the assertively independent French stance on energy and the simultaneous demands Paris was making of its Community partners for a common European line towards both the United States and the Middle East. Ostensibly, the French were trying to get the best of both worlds. This paradox was not lost on the Germans, who did not cease to allude to it in the prelude to the Copenhagen summit. It was clear from the French approach that Community solidarity was desirable—but not on a global basis. In any conflict between Community and national aims, particularly on an issue as sensitive as energy, it was the national interest which outweighed the European commitment. In fairness, it should be stated that this order of priorities did not apply to France alone. The British

[27] Jobert, *L'Autre Regard*, 349.

[28] Figures from Wallace, 'Old States and new Circumstances', 32.

[29] On French arms sales, see Edward A. Kolodziej, 'France and the Arms Trade', *International Affairs* (Jan. 1980). See also the articles in *The Economist*, 16 Jan. 1982; the *Financial Times*, 1 Mar. 1982 and 17 Jan. 1984. For interesting comparison with the contemporary German position, see Hans Rademacher, 'Une nouvelle industrie', and Walter Schütze, 'La République fédérale d'Allemagne et le marché international des armements', both in *Documents*, 1 (1976). See also the *Financial Times*, 26 Aug., 13 Oct. 1983, 15 Feb. 1984.

too, though slightly less vocal advocates of a common European political stance towards Washington and the Middle East, were themselves pursuing a similar approach on the oil question.

Under these circumstances, it was ironic that Brandt's visit to Paris for the bilateral summit should have coincided with the presence in the French capital of the Algerian and Saudi oil ministers. The lack of any firm decisions on energy at the Franco-German meeting was unremarkable in view of the complexity of the topic and the divergent interests involved. Against this background it was hardly surprising that the meeting's conclusion on a note of vague, face-saving long-term plans for energy, allowing ample scope for national differences, should have been so closely mirrored at the wider Community summit in Copenhagen three weeks later.

Two side-issues arising out of the Franco-German meeting deserve closer attention. First of all, Jobert's remarks on Brandt's attitude quoted above indicate the level of French disappointment at the lack of wider support for Eurodif, their uranium enrichment venture. The British, Germans, and Dutch had decided to co-operate on a rival scheme. This had obviously caused annoyance in Paris, and it arguably influenced French thinking on a common energy policy. The lack of co-operation also highlights earlier observations regarding failings in Franco-German economic collaboration. Secondly and more important, Jobert's comments indicate a very biased attitude towards the Dutch. There is strong reason to believe that similar opinions were held elsewhere in the French Government. Brandt, for example, records Pompidou's remark that the Dutch 'had never been paragons of solidarity'.[30] At the Franco-German summit, the President no doubt pointed out Holland's former opposition to any common energy policy (at least along the lines envisaged by Paris). There also appeared to have been a more fundamental cause for French resentment of the Netherlands, perhaps rooted in the long-standing friction between the two countries over the question of supranationality and the Community's institutional structure. The Dutch revaluation in September 1973 had also been censured in Paris.

---

[30] Brandt, 468. For further indications of hostile French attitudes towards Holland, see *Le Monde*, 28 Nov. 1973; Jobert, *Mémoires*, 305; de Saint Robert, 128.

Franco-German differences were not limited to energy. The circumstances of middle and late 1973 had undoubtedly contributed to a greater shared emphasis on the principle of increased European co-operation on defence. However, this *rapprochement* tended to break down under closer scrutiny, with the two countries' divergent priorities becoming more apparent. At the WEU Assembly meeting in Paris on 21 November, a sharp distinction, highly reminiscent of the Franco-German differences of the early 1960s, was discernible in the contrasting positions taken up by Georg Leber, the German Defence Minister, and Jobert. While the latter, evoking the need for Europe to stand alone, and attacking the so-called *détente* between the superpowers, put forward WEU as a framework for a common European defence policy, the German minister stressed the role of the NATO Eurogroup and expressed the hope for a link between the activities of the Alliance and the European Community.[31] Just as at the time of the Franco-German Treaty, for the Germans, an independent European defence posture was inconceivable outside the Atlantic Alliance. Both Brandt and Pompidou sought to play down this rift at their summit and show greater flexibility. Yet it was a measure of their divergent outlooks that accord was limited to the minimal level of agreement on the importance of the American nuclear deterrent.

In sum, the bilateral summit of November 1973, like its predecessor in July, had not been an easy occasion. Once again, the result had testified both to the greater German self-confidence and stress on national policy objectives that had arisen, and, more important, to the very complex nature of some of the issues involved, notably energy. This problem was to become more acute by the time of the foreign ministers' meeting on 3–4 December 1973, called to prepare for the Copenhagen summit. With the oil embargo not lifted and no sign of joint European action, the Dutch, planning to introduce petrol rationing by January, were more determined than ever to implement a common policy and mutual assistance. Their demands were accompanied by threats to obstruct other areas of Community affairs and suggestions of a ban on oil and natural

---

[31] Leber's comments are quoted in *Europe-Archiv* 6 (1974), D131–5. See also Jobert, *L'Autre Regard*, 345–7, and Nerlich, 195–7.

gas exports from Rotterdam. Lines of division between the member states had grown more marked: while the French and British temporized by adopting a placatory façade (without commiting themselves to any firm action), the Federal Republic became increasingly cast as the spokesman for the smaller Community countries, with whose interests it was most closely aligned. The possibility of losing supplies from Rotterdam was an important additional influence on the Germans. In the end, although the British and French managed to postpone an open breach over oil and the Nine restricted themselves to discussing plans for joint action on the crisis, antagonisms had most certainly not been reduced. They would soon find expression in Copenhagen.

The Copenhagen summit

Circumstances had forced the scope of the summit to be widened far beyond Pompidou's original conception of a 'fireside chat', between Europe's leaders. Yet its character remained different from earlier meetings, and more akin to the present European Council.[32] There would be no major speeches, nor grand ceremonies, but rather a concentrated discussion of the pressing issues. Arguably, though, it was precisely that lack of consensus on just what those issues were that largely accounted for the ultimate failure of the talks. While for most of the member states the key topic was undoubtedly energy, for the French both on account of traditional policy interests and antipathy to oil-sharing, the focal point was European political solidarity—principally, as ever, towards the United States. Throughout the meeting, Pompidou's assertion that political co-operation, rather than energy, was the summit's main aim and the focus for any expressions of solidarity bore witness to the continuing French distinction between the two areas noted earlier.

Yet while Paris wished to view energy and political co-operation separately, for most of the other member states—Germany and Holland in particular—they remained intimately linked. A common European political attitude towards Washington and the Middle East were part and parcel of a joint

[32] On the Copenhagen summit and its position in the evolution to the European Council, see Morgan, *From Summit to Council*, 17–19, 38–9, 47–8.

approach to the energy issue. The Germans made plain that for them it was joint action on energy which was the very symbol of that solidarity that Pompidou sought to isolate and emphasize elsewhere. Hence, according to Brandt, failure to work out a common policy on oil would mean that 'the Rome Treaty is not worth the paper it's written on'.[33] Addressing the Bundestag before the summit, the Chancellor had dwelt on this indivisibility of solidarity.[34]

In Copenhagen, this theme was championed by Schmidt in particular. His post made him especially conscious of the economic repercussions of any oil shortage, and the underlying competitiveness between the Nine. Thus Schmidt spelled out Bonn's major contribution to the Community's policies and asserted that 'we are perfectly in the right to request and make clear that in the energy crisis no one must come out better than his neighbour'.[35] The implicit threat to other Community programmes underlying this German emphasis on a fair allocation of energy resources reflected both Bonn's greater self-assurance and the overwhelming importance of the energy issue for the Germans. Yet, while this approach was shared by the Dutch and Danes, there was no change in the French or British camps. Both countries continued to favour the path of secret diplomacy to any potentially provocative Community action.

Two additional factors intensified this intra-Community rift. First was the influence of American policy. At the NATO Council meeting on 10–11 December 1973, Jobert had reiterated his country's stress on independent European action in the light of the US–Russian agreement and the Middle East war. In particular, he had made clear that France would resist American proposals for joint action by the major oil consumers.[36] Much more appealing for Paris in view of its multipolar doctrine was the idea of a direct dialogue between Arabs and Europeans—a strategy which would effectively circumvent the superpowers. It is worth noting here, however, the subsequently established Euro-Arab dialogue's failure to live up to expectations. At the

---

[33] Quoted in the *Sunday Times*, 9 Dec. 1973.

[34] Reported in *Le Monde*, 14 Dec. 1973.

[35] Quoted in *Le Monde*, 11 Dec. 1973.

[36] For Jobert's account of the meeting, see *L'Autre Regard*, 350–1, and *Mémoires d'avenir*, 307.

outset the Community's exclusion of political matters from the discussions and the active American role in Middle East diplomacy, particularly under Kissinger, were the main causes. Only in the later 1970s and early 1980s, with the Community's decision to launch an independent Middle East initiative, did the policy gain momentum—although concrete results remain unlikely to materialize.

American attitudes towards the Community had hardened in late 1973. At the Pilgrims Society dinner in London on 12 December, Kissinger once again played on the now familiar themes of the dearth of European co-operation and consultation with the United States:

> Europe's unity must not be at the expense of the Atlantic Community, or both sides of the Atlantic will suffer. It is not that we are impatient with the cumbersome machinery of the emerging Europe. It is rather the tendency to highlight division rather than unity with us which concerns us. I would be less than frank were I to conceal our uneasiness about some of the recent practices of the European Community in the political field.[37]

The Community's joint stand on the Middle East—especially its declaration of 6 November—was the main culprit here, France and Britain being Kissinger's prime targets. The Secretary of State observed that the Community's attitude 'seems to attempt to elevate refusal to consult into a principle defining Europe's identity'.[38] Yet the other European countries, notably those showing reluctance to assist in American arms shipments to Israel or to allow overflights during the Middle East war, were also squarely within Kissinger's sights.

Most important, the energy crisis was now seen in Washington as unreservedly demanding that cohesion entailed in the New Atlantic Charter which had so far effectively been resisted by the Europeans. With the benefit of hindsight, Kissinger's proposal for a Joint Energy Action Group, comprising the United States, Canada, Western Europe, and Japan, clearly emerges as a further manifestation of his bloc strategy. Certainly, the critical French appraisal of the plan as a means of splitting the world

---

[37] Quoted in *Keesing's Contemporary Archives*, 14–20 Jan. 1974, 26293. Note also Kissinger's own comments in *Years of Upheaval*, 899, 901, 926.

[38] Quoted in *Keessing's Contemporary Archives*, loc. cit.

into oil producing and consuming blocs, and of enshrining American hegemony, would not be proved wide of the mark. Already, the American plans were having the effect of dividing the Europeans, separating France from Britain.

The second factor complicating talks in Copenhagen was the presence of the Foreign Ministers of Algeria, Tunisia, and the Sudan, and the representative of the United Arab Emirates. These four had been delegated by the Arab summit of late November 1973 to communicate the Arab position on the Middle East to the Europeans and enlist their support. Their arrival, playing 'the role of Banquo at the feast',[39] was a major distraction and source of tension. The visit eclipsed debate on the first day, and caused a breach among the Nine (accurately reflecting their policy differences) as to how the delegation should be received. While the British and French sought some measure of dialogue with the visitors, the Germans, Belgians, and Dutch felt that at most a hearing could be granted. Brandt's comments bear witness to the special position of the Federal Republic:

Our reception of them may have been over-constrained. In any case, I felt bound to insist that the Israeli Ambassador was likewise offered an interview by the Danish chairman. I only succeeded in overcoming stubborn French resistance by hinting that, if the worst came to the worst, I would invite the Israeli Ambassador to meet me independently.[40]

Friction between the Nine was by no means limited to the question of how to treat the visiting delegation. There were suggestions from some of the smaller member states that the visitors had in fact been secretly invited by the French.[41] It was also rumoured that France and Britain were indulging in covert negotiations. That such claims were circulating testified to the extraordinary mood of suspicion and recrimination generated by the energy issue. The charges appear unfounded, although there is no firm evidence either way. Even Jobert has described the visit as untimely.[42] That the British and French should have

[39] Wallace and Allen, 238.
[40] Brandt, 276.
[41] This view is repeated somewhat bitterly by Kissinger, *Years of Upheaval*, 727, 898.
[42] Jobert, *L'Autre Regard*, 353–4.

wished to make use of the opportunity for a real exchange of views was understandable and not in itself proof of any complicity. Jobert provides an entertaining reply to the rumour that he and the British Foreign Minister were taking part in late night meetings. He writes, 'one had gone to bed while the other was holding a public meeting with the press'.[43]

Not at all surprisingly, the agreement reached between the Nine on energy fell far short of a common policy—a highly predictable outcome in view of the differences evident at the 3–4 December Council session. At Copenhagen the member states were prepared to agree on considering measures in general, but were obviously divided on doing anything in particular. Thus although the Commission was given instructions to formulate a wide range of plans by the end of January 1974, there was no commitment to any immediate (or precise) action.[44] The compromise reached on Kissinger's proposals was cast in a similar mould. The Community considered it 'useful' to study ways of dealing with short- and long-term energy problems with other consuming countries. But on the question of institutions it was agreed, doubtless primarily at French behest, that any talks should take place within the framework of the OECD rather than in a new organization as desired by the Americans. At this stage, it was clear that while the Nine were unwilling openly to rebuff the American proposals, they were not eager to fall in line either.

While the value of the summit's decisions on energy may well be questioned, what little was achieved can in large measure be attributed to pressure from the Federal Republic. The latter was the only one of the Community's three major member states actively interested in a common policy. German influence also made itself felt on the Middle East, with reports of opposition from Brandt to French and British wishes to go beyond the Community's declaration of 6 November.[45] Certainly in their final communiqué the Nine restricted themselves to restating their earlier stand.

At least other issues proved somewhat easier. There was considerable agreement on political co-operation, with the Community adopting the prepared text on a 'European iden-

[43] Jobert, *Mémoires*, 315.
[44] Copenhagen summit statement on Energy, *The Times*, 17 Dec. 1973.
[45] See the *Financial Times*, 17 Dec. 1973.

tity'. This document bore clear witness to the French influence, seen in the assertion that relations between Europe and the United States 'do not conflict with the determination of the Nine to establish themselves as a distinct and original entity'.[46] This was precisely the approach to which Kissinger objected so strongly. Yet there is little doubt that the Americans read too much into these European moves. The declaration's vagueness testified to the differences between the member states. While praising its style, Brandt is correct to note that 'Its claims may have been too remote from reality for it to gain the attention its careful phrasing deserved'.[47]

Pompidou's plans for closer political co-operation were also discussed, and the President again proposed more frequent summit meetings. It was this idea, subsequently taken up by Giscard, which formed the basis for the present European Council. Perhaps most surprising was Pompidou's suggestion for the creation of a body of senior national civil servants who would be responsible for crisis management—a group bearing marked similarities to the ill-fated political secretariat. The muted presentation of the new proposals could probably be ascribed to a desire to avoid a recurrence of the friction that had beset the previous initiative. This problem has still not been resolved. Even in the 1980s, the Community lacks an effective crisis management mechanism. Major events, notably the tardy Community response to the Soviet invasion of Afghanistan, have highlighted the omission, and led to renewed calls for the establishment of such a group.

Franco-German co-operation, so evident at the Hague and Paris summits, was in Copenhagen largely restricted to the monetary side. Though international events and other Community plans had diverted attention away from EMU, a number of developments had taken place over the latter half of the year. Both Bonn and Paris had grown less enthusiastic about reserve pooling, scheduled to begin on 1 January 1974. More important, there had been a convergence of interests on the need to postpone the transition to the second stage of EMU. While for

---

[46] Document on the European Identity published by the Community foreign ministers, 14 Dec. 1973. See *Bulletin of the European Communities* (Dec. 1973), 118–22. For comment, see Wallace and Allen, 238.

[47] Brandt, 276.

Paris the exclusion of Britain and Italy from the Snake was the obstacle, Bonn as ever blamed the lack of progress on economic policy co-ordination, notably regarding inflation.

There had also been a *rapprochement* between the two countries' monetary policies. The instability set off by the Dutch revaluation in September had necessitated considerable German support buying of the franc, resulting in a $2,200 million French debt to Germany. Significantly, this had played a major part in the increased French willingness to accept a reduction in the role of gold in national reserves, witnessed at the IMF meeting in September 1973.[48] The result was a closer alignment between the French and the German positions.

Community difficulties were clearly brewing over the regional policy. Matters turned on the growing German reluctance, apparent during the discussions in October and November 1973, to subsidize a massive regional fund sought by the British and others. Typically, the Copenhagen summit avoided detailed negotiations on figures, which were left to the foreign and finance ministers. But, to a much greater degree than at the Paris summit the previous year, Brandt now found himself in an uncomfortable position. There had been a difficult German Cabinet meeting prior to the Copenhagen conference, at which Schmidt insisted, and the Cabinet agreed, on a 150 million unit of account maximum German offer. Accordingly, in the Danish capital Brandt was obliged to disappoint British expectations regarding the size of the fund.[49] In view of the friction that was soon to emerge on this issue, it is worth mentioning here the opinion of one German official who felt very strongly that the Chancellor had inadequately explained at the summit just how small the German offer actually was. If this view is accurate, the omission could be attributed to a personal failure on Brandt's part, or, more likely, to a wish to maintain European unity and avoid immediate embarrassment in the hope of finding a later compromise. The vague nature of discussion on specifics at summit meetings may also have been responsible. All these factors most likely played some part. Yet the episode also provided another indication of poor policy co-ordination on the German side.

[48] For this meeting and the effect of the currency crisis on French policy, see Kolodziej, *French International Policy*, 216.
[49] Brandt, 276–7.

How should one estimate the outcome of the Copenhagen summit? Undoubtedly, little was achieved. One commentator has even stated that the summit was 'inconclusive on every single issue'.[50] But it would have required a minor miracle in Copenhagen to have produced major decisions of a detailed nature, particularly on energy, in view of the climate of intense internal Community division and external pressure. Nor had the speed of events helped. It had not been possible to make the sort of lengthy preparations that had preceded the Hague and Paris summits. The host government's defeat in the recent elections cast an additional shadow over proceedings in Copenhagen. What did come about was a temporary papering over of the cracks, allowing each delegation to return home with some measure of success. No one side achieved anything approaching all its aims, but at least each member state gained some superficial satisfaction.

This dichotomy between national aims and end results emerges clearly when one considers the differing French and German positions. As suggested earlier, Bonn and Paris had highly disparate aims on energy policy. Neither country achieved quite what it wanted. For the French, Pompidou had managed to deflect pressure for immediate joint action over energy, and thus gained time. But the President had failed to bring about any firm assertion of European political unity. Pressure from France's partners on energy had transformed the summit from the small and private gathering to affirm Europe's political cohesion that the President had originally intended.[51]

For the Germans too the results of the summit were similarly mixed. Certainly, the meeting had achieved some symbolic unity on energy policy—enough at least for the Government to show at home that it had started to bring about the Community solidarity long demanded of its partners. But despite such claims of success, there was no denying that the consensus reached was at the level of lowest common denominator. Bonn's dilemma lay in the fact that nothing more could be achieved on a joint energy policy in the face of French and British opposition short of

---

[50] Morgan, *From Summit to Council*, 19.

[51] Jobert gives an indication of the President's disappointment that the nature of the summit had changed, in *Mémoires*, 313–14, and *L'Autre Regard*, 352–4.

provoking a Community crisis. Even then the desired results could not be guaranteed. Therefore for the Federal Republic too the outcome of the summit was temporary and largely cosmetic. With no shift in French and German attitudes towards energy, the likely rupture on the issue had not been averted, but merely postponed.

8

Brandt and Pompidou—
The Final Months
1974

In the aftermath of the summit

The parallel session of Community foreign and finance ministers of 17–18 December 1973 was not the occasion for post-summit consolidation and progress that might have been expected. Rather, it formed the venue for a severe clash of views and one of the most conspicuous instances of German assertiveness in the Brandt–Pompidou era. This time, though, it was not the French who were directly involved in the argument, but the British. At the meeting, the finance ministers reached quick agreement on the transition to the diluted second stage of EMU—whose change of name, from 'the' second stage to 'a' second stage, barely revealed the downgrading involved.[1] But the foreign ministers' detailed talks on regional policy and energy proved much more acerbic. The contrast between these negotiations and the Copenhagen summit's restrained tone and avoidance of specifics says much about Community summitry at the time. Understandably, the Heads of State and Government had preferred to restrict themselves to broad questions of 'high' politics and to relegate technical or contentious issues of 'low' politics, such as haggling over the size of the regional fund, to their ministers.

The vigour of German opposition to the Commission's proposal for a 2,250 million unit of account regional fund was telling. Deputizing for Scheel, Apel put forward a figure little more than quarter the size. Though open to review in mid-1975, it would only be raised in the light of satisfactory progress towards integration—notably EMU. The extent of British disappointment was reflected in the scale of its reaction; London now vetoed further discussions on energy and monetary union.

---

[1] On what the change meant, see Tsoukalis, *European Monetary Integration*, 151–4.

The quarrel, though largely excluding the French, is worth looking at in more detail, as it marks an interesting episode in the Federal Republic's evolution in the early 1970s and is a good illustration of some of the failings on the German side. Various factors underscored the determined German position on the issue. Characters indirectly played a part. Apel, like Schmidt, was an outspoken figure who represented a new and more self-assured generation of German politicians less amenable to pressure from Community partners. For example, when asked whether his country's stance would lead to a crisis, Apel replied that, while the Federal Republic had been afraid of crises in the past, this was no longer the case.[2] Bonn would not bow to pressure or be overcome by attrition. Rather, 'the shadows of the past are forgotten now'.[3] Though there was undoubtedly an element of bluster in his stand, such statements indicated the combined influence of economic strength and the *Ostpolitik* in creating a more forceful German political posture in the Community in late 1973.

Economic concerns lay at the heart of the German position. The state of the domestic economy had, by winter 1973, increasingly obliged Schmidt to emphasize controlling inflation and reducing government expenditure. 'Wasteful' Community spending was an obvious and popular target: there is little doubt that domestic electoral considerations (and, not least, Schmidt's own rising position within the government) played an additional part in shaping his priorities on the question of spending cuts. Hence Schmidt's populist depiction of Germany as the 'paymaster' or 'treasurer' of Europe. It was in this vein that Apel had pointed out that under the Commission's plans for the regional fund Bonn would contribute 28 per cent of the cost in return for a mere 8 per cent of the benefits. Acquiescence to such a distribution and to the British tactics would, in Apel's words, be like 'paying your wife for being faithful'.[4]

Failings on both British and German sides were responsible for the fracas that ensued. Expecting opposition from the French capital, London had focused its diplomatic efforts on Paris and

    [2] Reported in the *Financial Times*, 18 Dec. 1973.
    [3] Quoted in the Guardian, 20 Dec. 1973. See also the reports in *The Times*, 19 Dec. and *Frankfurter Allgemeine Zeitung*, 20 Dec. 1973.
    [4] Quoted in *The Times*, 18 Dec. 1973.

had inadequately appreciated the growing hostility in Bonn to subsidizing a new policy. German critics were not entirely wrong in claiming that their country's financial backing tended to be taken for granted by its European partners. Moreover, the British Treasury's view of the fund as a means of balancing the nation's contribution to the Community budget had increased opposition on the German side. British antipathy to a common energy policy had worsened matters.

Yet there were major shortcomings in Bonn too. As on other issues in the past, poor policy co-ordination was a major culprit. At his visit to Chequers in October, Brandt had signalled support for a large regional fund. Yet his own subsequent remarks about his stand at the Copenhagen summit illustrated the scale and suddenness of the German shift. On the failure in German policy co-ordination and the confusion caused, one observer accurately comments: 'The rather fragmented structure of government and absence of effective central coordination impeded the clear definition of policy on the RDF and obscured its articulation in Brussels. Characteristically the German attitude became known only late in the day ...'[5]

The quarrel over the regional policy also gave an insight into the state of German internal politics. Apel's stand in Brussels brought home the extent of Schmidt's influence in the German Cabinet, a development which would have important ramifications for Brandt.[6] The Chancellor had already been forced into an embarrassing volte-face over the regional fund. One can also speculate on whether the talks in Brussels might have gone more smoothly had Scheel not been absent. In May 1971, his last-minute contribution had been decisive.

In what was to emerge as very skilful diplomacy, contrasting with earlier errors, the Germans changed tack at the start of 1974. Bonn postponed the Council meeting for 7 January and sought to play down the rift with Britain by reshaping the regional fund in slimmer form. It was now that the French became directly involved. Any narrowing of the fund would affect France in particular. Thus, under the suggestions put forward by Apel to Olivier Guichard, the French Minister for

[5] Wallace, 'The Establishment of the Regional Fund', 151.
[6] On this theme, see Baring, *Machtwechsel*, 594–600, 623, 702–8.

Regional Development, Paris should now contribute 23 per cent
of the cost in return for 8.1 per cent of the benefits (as against the
21 per cent proposed by the Commission). The Federal Republic
would now pay 28.2 per cent and receive 5.7 per cent.[7] With
simultaneous comment on the size of French gains from the
CAP, the German move was tactically very adroit, shifting
responsibility to the French. They, caught unawares, responded
by linking any changes to the fund to a satisfactory agreement on
farm prices. In a speech on 29 January 1974, Pompidou parried
the German sally on the farm policy by defending the CAP. The
President reverted to his strategy of noting the advantages of the
industrial customs union for other Community countries.[8] The
German Government, in the meantime, appeared ready to bide
its time.

Under these circumstances, it was at first glance surprising
that on 23 January the Germans should announce their readiness
to double their previous offer on the regional fund to 1,200
million units of account. Two related factors were responsible.
Scheel's voice undoubtedly played a major part. His presidency
of the Council of Ministers increased his sense of responsibility
for taking the initiative. Yet the German offer had only come
about as a result of a majority Cabinet decision. Within the
Government there was growing tension, notably around Schmidt
and Brandt.[9] Scheel was more adroit at dealing with Schmidt
than the Chancellor, who was reluctant, especially by this stage,
to impose his views. In contrast to Schmidt's restrictive attitude
to Community spending, Scheel, as in his clash with Schiller in
1971, placed wider political factors above purely financial
considerations. The two occasions provide good examples of the
potential conflict of interest between the more sectoral outlook of
a forceful minister of finance and the broader perspective
required by a foreign minister. In both cases, Scheel's position as
leader of the junior coalition partner was an important
additional factor in overcoming opposition.

The need to maintain unity in the EEC in the light of divisive
trends was the second, related, motive behind the German

[7] Figures from the *Financial Times*, 8 Jan. 1974.

[8] Pompidou's speech reported in the *Financial Times*, 11 Jan. 1974. The President's
remarks can be likened to his approach at his 27 Sept. 1973 press conference.

[9] For contemporary problems in the Cabinet, see Baring, 594–600.

concession. Apel remarked that the improved offer had been made in respect of the 'symbolic value of the Fund to Britain', expecially considering the country's current problems.[10] No less an influence, however, was the French decision on 19 January 1974 to float the franc, damaging EMU. The move was fully in line with the traditional priorities of French foreign economic policy. Although provoked by renewed speculative pressure and exacerbated by the oil price rise, the float was chiefly designed to keep French industry competitive in the new climate of high oil prices. There was a certain similarity between the French decision and the British float of August 1972. Both—symbolically as well as materially—set back EMU, the one occurring six weeks after the decision to launch the European Monetary Co-operation Fund, and the other within almost three weeks of the transition to the policy's second stage. As will be seen, financial problems continued to constrain the economic side of French European policy into the mid and later 1970s and beyond, though to a much lesser extent than for the British. Thus economic initiatives, notably the EMS, tended to come from Bonn. This situation has been markedly highlighted since May 1981, with French foreign economic policy becoming much more of a holding tactic.

As with Brandt's proposal to underwrite the sterling balances, the last-minute German offer of a massive loan to keep the franc in the Snake highlighted Bonn's increased readiness and ability to use economic strength to advance specific policy aims, generally of an economic nature. This clout was aggressively underlined by Schmidt's grandiose description of the proposed $3,000 million loan as 'certainly the greatest currency support any single country has ever offered'.[11] Yet, as with the German proposal of financial help in May 1971, reasons of prestige, as much as avoiding undesirable economic commitments to the Germans, influenced the French refusal to accept the offer and its implied recognition of the Federal Republic's economic prowess.[12] Rather, the French Government's decision on 31 January to raise a $1,500 million loan laid bare some of the

[10] Quoted in the *Financial Times*, 24 Jan. 1974.

[11] *Deutscher Bundestag*, 7. Wahlperiode, Sitzung. Bonn, Wed. 23 Jan. 1974, 4733.

[12] In this context, the comments of Ándré Boulloche, a French Socialist, are most interesting. See Grosser, *Les Occidentaux*, 356.

political realities behind the constant declarations of bilateral economic co-operation. Against this background, the announcement in April 1981 of a joint Franco-German initiative to raise a £2,700 million credit can be seen as one of the more impressive confirmations of the bilateral *rapprochement* that took place in the Schmidt–Giscard era. However, it should be noted that following Mitterrand's election the future of this scheme had been left uncertain. While Bonn has decided to go ahead, the French have suspended action.

One interesting by-product of the French float of January 1974, illustrating a strong pragmatic streak in French policy not always wholly to the fore, was Chirac's call at the farm ministers' meeting on 21 January for the introduction of MCAs for France. Hostility to those mechanisms, previously regarded as anathema, was now forgotten. Ertl can perhaps be forgiven for not being able to resist the temptation of pointing out the value of MCAs, so often vilified, in cushioning the blow of the French float on the CAP.

The French move brought home the fallacy of any lasting stable links between all the EEC currencies and highlighted the implausibility of 1980 as the target date for EMU. Rather, within one month of the transition to the second stage, five of the Community's currencies were floating together and four independently. The decision to float also pointedly confirmed the nature of the Snake as a Deutschemark zone and offered further evidence of the Federal Republic's economic predominance. At the meeting of the Snake finance ministers on 21 January 1974, the Germans were very much the main actors. By contrast, the Commission remained on the sidelines, again illustrating the erosion of its position as a result of the monetary instability of the early 1970s.

Energy problems

The German Government's attempts to minimize the damage caused by the French float to bilateral and European relations, and its plans to bolster Community solidarity through the new offer on the regional fund, were being increasingly frustrated by Community differences over energy. As the Heath Government aligned itself more closely with the American position on oil and grew preoccupied with internal difficulties, notably the increasing unrest in the coalfields, this dispute came to focus on Bonn and Paris.

On 9 January 1974, the White House had followed up Kissinger's initiative of December 1973 with invitations to an energy conference in Washington. In line with their divergent priorities, the American *démarche* called forth widely different responses in France and Germany. While the Germans welcomed the suggestion, the French vehemently opposed what they once again perceived as a blatant American attempt to compromise European independence. Rather, in line with the renewed strain of multipolarity in French foreign policy and its anxiety not to offend the Arabs, Paris favoured an international conference on energy under UN auspices. However, the French, who were at this point probably still optimistic about winning round their European partners, appeared unwilling to precipitate any open Community conflict. Their decision to temporize was evident in Jobert's arguments at the Council meeting on 14–15 January 1974 that Nixon's proposed date of 11 February was unduly early. The French did not, however, block agreement in principle between the Nine to accept Nixon's invitation, and Scheel and Ortoli, Presidents of the Council of Ministers and Commission respectively, were appointed as the Community's representatives at the conference.

National positions on oil were far from straightforward or static, however, despite the outward harmony of mid-January. The Federal Republic in particular was beginning to show signs of wavering under economic pressure. As with the French and British, so now with the Germans, emphasis on a joint energy policy had increasingly come to be weighed against self-interest, in the form of protecting the domestic economy. In contrast to the Benelux countries, the other main proponents of a common energy policy, the German economy was of sufficient size and international importance to warrant emulating the French and British examples of bilateral arrangements with the oil producers. Paris had been surrounded by speculation in December 1973 regarding further sales of Mirage fighters and military equipment to Saudi Arabia beyond those already agreed two months earlier. Moreover, in January 1974 the French announced a twenty-year oil supply agreement with the Saudis—the preliminary, it was stated, to a much larger deal.

In mid-February, a long-term Franco-Libyan co-operative agreement was also concluded. Similarly, the British finalized a major commercial package with Iran in late January.

Apel's comment that bilateral agreements were fair provided they were not pursued at the expense of European partners gave some indication of the influence of these events on German thinking.[13] The statement also illustrated the reduced constraints on the Federal Republic, contrasting with its position in the 1960s. The limited German forays at this stage into bilateral agreements, even at the cost of antagonizing the Americans (Washington had indicated its strong disapproval), testified to the greater independence and self-assurance in Bonn's external relations. Furthermore, although Jobert's oil policy was open to criticism, his castigation of American hypocrisy was not entirely ill-founded. Although under considerably less pressure than Europe on account of its lower dependence on imported oil and constrained by its relationship with Israel, Washington would before long be following the European example of seeking bilateral deals with the oil producers.

Yet the German position was far from straightforward. There were strong reasons preventing Bonn's systematic emulation of the French and British policies over oil deals. Closer examination of these factors highlights a number of the determinants influencing the Federal Republic's foreign policy, while bringing into sharper relief certain contrasts with France. First, as has been indicated, the Germans did not enjoy the same flexibility in their relations in the Middle East as did the French. Bonn's hands were tied by its commitment to Israel and its identification with American policy in the region. Hence Paris was better placed to exploit its good relations with the Arabs. However, it is worth bearing in mind that the Germans had themselves been seeking to cultivate better links in the Middle East for some time.

Secondly, despite the lowered constraints on German dealings with the United States, Bonn remained more susceptible than Paris to the very strong American pressure that was being brought to bear on energy. One source very close to German foreign policy-making at the time has intimated that it was not so much American pressure that was decisive in shaping German

---

[13] Apel, reported in the *Daily Telegraph*, 11 Jan. 1974.

attitudes, as the fact that Bonn felt that a solution could only come of a joint approach and Washington was seen as the only party able to influence the Israelis. Whichever force was the stronger, it is interesting to note how much German attitudes have evolved since early 1974. By the later 1970s and early 1980s, Bonn was firmly backing the Community's independent Middle Eastern initiative in spite of Washington's disapproval.

The effect of American influence on Bonn in early 1974 was by no means negligible. Not only did the Germans wish to avoid a recurrence of friction with Washington after the difficulties of October 1973, they were also highly conscious of the need for strong allies and solidarity at a time of crisis. Such considerations can clearly be understood in terms of Bonn's greater political and military vulnerability than Paris. These considerations were reinforced by internal factors. Both private comment and the public events at the Washington conference place Schmidt, a confirmed Atlanticist at this stage, at the forefront of German opposition to what was seen as a French pursuit of independence totally out of key with the circumstances. Just as in the heyday of de Gaulle's autonomous policy over defence, so now political links between Bonn and Washington were reinforced by the failure of the French to offer the Germans a realistic alternative. Rather, Bonn was pushed closer to the United States.

Thirdly, with a definite feeling of uncertainty in early 1974 regarding future Arab policy on oil and its consequences for the West, co-operation between the oil consumers seemed for many Germans the best response to the oil producers' cartel. Joint action would offer a countervailing force and would help to overcome any competition for supplies or costly overbidding. While all the Europeans, and not just the French, were conscious of the need to avoid the impression of a confrontation with the oil producers, collaboration between the oil consumers appeared a more sensible option than the *sauve qui peut* attitude adopted by Paris and others. Thus, within the Community, the Germans had already come out strongly in favour of collaboration on oil. Closely associated with these arguments was a firm awareness of underlying economic and competitive dangers. As matters stood, France, with its privileged access to oil, had the definite advantage over Germany, with obvious ramifications for the two economies. An oil consumers' bloc would bring all the Western nations closer into line. Historical factors possibly also played a part, with the Germans seeking to prevent any reversion to the competitive devaluations and damaging nationalism of the 1930s—fears certainly kindled by the French decision to float the franc.

This growing rift between the French on the one hand and the Germans and Americans on the other was emphasized by Jobert's trip to Saudi Arabia, Kuwait, and Syria on 24–9 January 1974. Despite his claims of limited aims and denials of direct negotiations as trade deals, the tour was undoubtedly undertaken with pressing economic and political interests in mind.[14] As Jobert himself declared in Damascus, 'Some malicious people might suggest that selling arms was one of the objects of my tour. I won't hide from you that we did come to examine such questions.'[15] Discussions over long-term oil supplies took place in all the capitals visited. Significantly, within a few days of Jobert's departure, the Kuwaitis announced the purchase of Mirage fighters and other military equipment. Throughout his tour, Jobert stressed the importance Paris placed on a joint Euro-Arab conference and very much sought to distance France from the American plans on energy. This was all part of the strategy of maintaining French links with the Arabs in order to guarantee oil supplies (and, it has been suggested, to encroach upon American political and commercial interests in the Middle East[16]). Hence Jobert explicitly declared in Syria, 'the positions of France and the United States are completely opposed.'[17]

By the time of the Council of Ministers' meeting on 30 January 1974 (which had been specially called to discuss the regional policy) a number of other issues, notably energy and monetary affairs, were becoming acute. Conversely, the situation regarding the regional fund had eased. The British had reacted favourably to the improved German offer and consequently lifted their veto on energy and EMU. French opposition now remained the hurdle. On energy, differences also revolved around conflicting French and German positions. It was not

[14] For Jobert's disclaimers, see *Mémoires*, 319 and *L'Autre Regard*, 368–9.

[15] Jobert, quoted in Grosser, *Les Occidentaux*, 356.

[16] Turner, 'The Politics of the Energy Crisis', 411.

[17] Jobert, quoted in Grosser, op. cit. 356. See also Messmer's remarks, quoted in the *Financial Times*, 31 Jan. 1974.

hard to read implied criticism of France in the stress on solidarity
in monetary and energy policy contained in Brandt's Government Declaration on 24 January. With the French approach
doubtless in mind, the Chancellor was forthright:

We shall only be able to keep energy, monetary, and international
trade problems under control if there is no relapse into self-sufficiency
and narrow-minded nationalism. For this reason we also welcome the
initiative of the United States in calling an oil conference ...[18]

Hostile to the French line on energy, the German Government
stepped up its campaign to bring about a united Community
posture. According to one minister, Bonn would 'emphatically'
be using its presidency of the Council of Ministers to this end.
Schmidt was even more explicit, calling for co-ordinated
European action rather than independent measures to meet the
oil crisis.[19]

In view of the size of the gap between the French and German
positions, it was surprising that a compromise could be reached,
allowing the Nine to establish a joint mandate for attendance at
the Washington conference. Under the circumstances, the very
nature of that agreement must arouse some doubts. It can well
be argued that the differences between the Nine—chiefly the
French and Germans—exhibited at the foreign ministers'
meeting on 4–5 February presaged the rift that would emerge in
Washington. Though it undoubtedly reflected the French
approach, the Community's mandate—a fusion of French and
German draft proposals—was a more flexible document than the
French cared to recognize. At the same time, however, it by no
means justified Scheel's subsequent stand in Washington.

What brought about the apparent reconciliation between the
opposing French and German views? For the French Government, increasingly on the defensive by the time of the Council
meeting, opposition to the Washington conference had to be
weighed against the desire for European political solidarity. This
had been damaged not least by France's own decision to float the
franc. Thus, although the French acquiesced to Community
attendance at the conference, it was only on the strict proviso

---

[18] *Deutscher Bundestag*, 7. Wahlperiode, 76. Sitzung, Bonn, Thurs. 24 Jan. 1974, 4770.
[19] Statements reported in the *Daily Telegraph*, 28 Jan. 1974, and the *Guardian*, 30 Jan.
1974.

that the EEC's mandate should not contradict established national policy—and thereby cause embarrassment for France in its dealings with the Arabs. Hence Jobert's constant stress at the Council meeting on a very precise Community stand, which would make clear that European participation in Washington was not intended as a confrontation with the oil producers. It is in fact highly unlikely that the French actually wanted anything to come out of the Washington meeting from which they had virtually nothing to gain. Thus, French participation was largely explicable by the desire to maintain an aura of European political solidarity, especially towards the Americans. These circumstances explain Jobert's insistence on a very precise Community mandate and, no less, his readiness to provoke a crisis in Washington once that precision had been undermined.

The second aspect of Jobert's stance at the foreign ministers' meeting harked back to French policy the previous year towards Kissinger's 'New Atlantic Charter' proposals. Thus Jobert stated that the Nine should oppose the creation of any new bodies to follow up the Washington conference. Instead the Community should insist that co-operation be restricted to existing institutions such as the IMF. Greater weight has rightly been placed on this political aspect of the French approach than on the purely energy side.[20] Paris correctly perceived that the Americans would seek to use the energy issue as part of their strategy of regaining authority over the Europeans by linking co-operation over oil with political, economic, and military matters. The French Government felt strongly that one aspect of Kissinger's motives for creating new institutions was to impose, through the back door, precisely that American preponderance over Europe that the Community had so far successfully avoided. Hence Jobert's emphasis that the Community mandate should specifically exclude discussion of economic and monetary affairs, and his rejection of a German suggestion that the Washington conference should tackle the implications of oil price rises for the international monetary system. An additional consideration (though this was not stated by the French) was the fact that new institutions might also be construed as offensive by the Arabs.

---

[20] Turner, 'The Politics of the Energy Crisis', 412. This is confirmed by Jobert's interview with the *Washington Post*, reported in *The Times*, 15 Feb. 1974.

For the Germans, by contrast, the energy crisis pushed aside earlier doubts and intensified the need for precisely that dialogue with the United States that was being so strenuously opposed by the French. It was the forced amalgamation of such profoundly dissenting views that largely explained the pliability of the Community's joint mandate.[21] While clearly circumscribing the Washington conference's purview, the compromise accepted broad aims. Opposition to the notion of the conference developing into a 'permanent organism' for the discussion of energy matters contrasted with acceptance of the possibility of establishing 'short-term working groups of appropriate composition' in certain areas. It was reported, however, that this clause had only been sanctioned by Jobert on the understanding that such groups would not be considered a continuation of the conference itself, and would be open to the developing and oil-producing nations. Furthermore, the Community would not take part in them before having reached agreement on their remit.[22] Under these circumstances, with only the thinnest of veils being drawn over the divergent French and German positions, the rift that was to take place in Washington, where the Nine were subjected to extremely strong American pressure, should not be seen as a great surprise.

The Washington conference

The Washington meeting stands out for its unprecedented demonstration of intra-Community differences, principally between France and Germany. The British, by this stage, had adopted a much lower-keyed approach. Though ostensibly provoked by a disagreement over Scheel's interpretation of the Community mandate, the split that arose between the French and the Germans lay rooted in their conflicting views on energy policy and, fundamentally, in their divergent outlooks towards the United States. A sharp clash of personality between Jobert and Schmidt provided an added edge.

There was little genuine movement in the American stand on oil. The concessions suggested by Kissinger in his opening speech

---

[21] Jobert gives an interesting picture of the negotiations preceding the mandate, in *L'Autre Regard*, 375–6, and *Mémoires*, 322.

[22] This position was repeated in an official French statement on 6 February, which also reiterated the aim of establishing contacts between the oil producers and consumers.

stemmed less from recognition of Community solidarity than endeavour to overcome French opposition.[23] Though the Secretary of State appeared to accept the European view that many aspects of co-operation could be tackled within the framework of existing bodies, there seemed little difference between his new notion for a co-ordinating body for energy policy and the earlier proposal for a Joint Energy Action Group. Criticism of bilateral oil deals also continued unabated.

Controversy centred on Scheel's reply for the Community. His offer of broad support for the Americans and mild criticism of bilateral arrangements aroused an angry response from Jobert. Although not present at the previous night's meeting of Community foreign ministers, the French delegate had seen, and objected to, Scheel's draft text. Jobert quite correctly claimed that it represented a departure from the Nine's agreed mandate (at least as construed by Paris). His comments convey both the fervour of his feeling and the restored Gaullist tenor of French foreign policy. According to Jobert, although Scheel had appeared willing to consider changes, 'he didn't go far! Everyone thought it would be possible gently to get France's representative first of all to see his isolation, and then to fall into line with the rest of the troop.'[24] By way of confirmation, it is worth noting here the repeated suggestions in Kissinger's account that the other Europeans were ready and waiting to go against France, hesitating only on account of fear regarding a possible Franco-American compromise on energy policy behind their backs.[25]

Given the French reluctance from the outset to attend the conference, it is certain that Jobert's stance was hardened, at least in tone if not in content, by Scheel's apparent betrayal of the Community's mandate. Hence the extremely critical character of Jobert's speech, notably regarding American intentions and Scheel's stand. Nor were French suspicions of Nixon's motives in calling the conference and regarding energy policy as a whole played down. The theme was amplified in Jobert's remarks before the National Assembly Foreign Affairs Committee on his return: 'Energy hardly interested Henry Kissinger and

[23] Jobert relates that Kissinger had a private meeting with him prior to the conference in an attempt to win him round. See *L'Autre Regard*, 379.

[24] Ibid. 378–9.

[25] Kissinger, *Years of Upheaval*, 907–8, 917–19.

his President; they wished to group their world around them and control its evolution as they pleased.'[26]

These comments corroborate earlier suggestions about the priorities in French policy with regard to attendance at the conference and American intentions. Nixon's own remarks that 'security and economic considerations are inevitably linked and energy cannot be separated from either',[27] confirm the accuracy of the French fears regarding the Administration's aim of linking energy to other matters and thereby asserting control over the Alliance. Kissinger has since contended that Nixon's comments were not, as was generally believed at the time, a deliberate 'pressure play' by the President: 'It was in fact vintage Nixon, spontaneous and all the more noteworthy because he was truly its sole author.'[28] But irrespective of the origins of Nixon's remarks, they must surely have reflected the underlying trend of American thinking.

It was in this light that Jobert attacked Kissinger's plans which, he claimed, sought to impose a new energy order on the world. Instead he stressed France's multipolar doctrine, drawing a sharp distinction between American and European interests. Nor would France participate in any follow-up to the conference outside the framework of established organizations. As for Scheel, his interpretation of relations with the United States had exceeded the agreed mandate: to the National Assembly Foreign Affairs Committee Jobert subsequently alluded to the action of France's partners in Washington: 'At our next meeting I shall say to them—with a smile of course—Good morning traitors.'[29]

A caucus between the Nine foreign ministers on the first evening of the conference failed to restore unity. The gulf that was now exposed between Community positions proved too wide to paper over. In fact, intra-Community wrangling (eventually

---

[26] Jobert, *L'Autre Regard*, 378. This view was widely held at the Quai d'Orsay. See, for instance, Gergorin's comments in DFI, *Deutschland, Frankreich und die europäische Krise*, 45–6. See also Jobert's remarks to the National Assembly, quoted in *Le Monde*, 23 Feb. 1974, and A.-M. Walton, 'Atlantic Bargaining over Energy', *International Affairs*, (Apr. 1976), 186, 188.

[27] Quoted in Walton, 189.

[28] See Kissinger, *Years of Upheaval*, 915–6.

[29] Jobert, *Mémoires*, 326.

coming to occupy eighty per cent of the proceedings) held up the plenary talks and resulted in a one-day extension. Despite their lengthy deliberations, the Nine were unable to make progress on a joint stand. The question of post-Washington institutional developments proved the stumbling-block. This fricton between France and its partners was exacerbated by Schmidt's uncompromising approach.

Characteristically, Schmidt took a highly Atlanticist view— an attitude which contrasted with his more nuanced approach in the later 1970s.[30] He questioned the very foundation of the French position, doubting that the Europeans could deal with the Arab oil producers independently of the United States. Overall, Europe needed to rely on America's 'goodwill and co-operation'.[31] Drawing on past experience as Defence Minister Schmidt accepted the American link between security and energy. But he was unduly provocative in stating that co-operation with the United States rated more highly for the Federal Republic than relations with the Community. The remark illustrated both the level of his Atlantic commitment and his frustration with the apparent misconceptions of the French position as well as his relatively narrow perspective as Minister of Finance. The latter was of necessity to be widened on becoming Chancellor.

Schmidt's comments on intra-European relations bore witness not only to his own forceful nature, but also to the increased German weight in world affairs. His candour, paralleling Apel's stand earlier in the year, offered a sharp contrast to the more restrained opinions usually identified with West German statesmen in the past. Not even during the difficulties in Franco-German relations under Chancellor Erhard had Bonn been so outspoken. As has been recognized:

The resentment against the French had been building up, and the unashamedly aggressive stance of Herr Helmut Schmidt, the West German Finance Minister, towards France's intransigence in Washington was a plain sign that the Germans were at last gaining the

---

[30] It is also worth bearing in mind the strong suggestions of unilateral American inducements to the Germans in Washington. Schmidt had talks with Schulz, the American Treasury Secretary, just before the conference on the subject of offset costs. The situation recalled similar American tactics in August 1971.

[31] Quoted in *International Herald Tribune*, 13 Feb. 1974.

self-confidence in diplomatic affairs which befits their economic strength.[32]

Not only did the Germans launch a direct attack on the French in Washington; more important, they were now prepared to ignore them when they refused to compromise. Just as the authority of Brandt's stance at the Hague summit had suggested new perspectives in German foreign policy, so Schmidt's conduct in Washington confirmed and extended this trend. Jobert, personifying to the Germans the delusions in French policy, was the butt of Schmidt's anger.

The evidence suggests that an element of personal animosity deepened the already wide gulf in thinking between the two men. Schmidt, no less than Jobert, was extremely forthright. He openly admitted that the fundamental intra-European conflict that had blocked the conference was one which transcended energy policy—'it is clearly not just an energy question'[33]—there were underlying political issues as well. Though impassioned by the heat of the moment, Schmidt's warning that the Nine's failure to agree 'could have very grave results' for the future of the Community was illustrative not just of his own character but also of the readiness of a new generation of German leaders to speak out.

The clash of personality came out fully in Jobert's disparaging response. He writes:

We had some laboured sessions between Europeans; my colleagues did not know how to overcome our resistance, and I led them back untiringly to the promises they had made. Helmut Schmidt proved particularly unpleasant, and, for him too, I chose to respond with a cold indifference.[34]

The tenor of Jobert's public remarks in Washington illustrated both his character and the influence of popular attention on his views—or at least their manner of presentation. As Grosser notes of Jobert's elevation to the post of Foreign Minister, 'arrival at

[32] Louis Turner, 'The Washington Energy Conference', *The World Today* (March 1974), 92. See also Roger Berthoud's report from Brussels in *The Times*, 13 Feb. 1974, and the *Financial Times*, 14 Feb. 1974.

[33] Quoted in *International Herald Tribune*, 13 Feb 1974.

[34] Jobert, *L'Autre Regard*, 380.

centre stage did not incline Michel Jobert to underestimating himself'.[35] Kissinger is understandably less oblique. Writing of Jobert at the Washington conference, he notes: 'He could be charming and insinuating; his mordant wit was as entertaining as it was perceptive. But once engaged—especially before an audience—Jobert did not seem able to maintain self-control.'[36] It was also possible, though there is no firm evidence, that Jobert's performance in Washington was additionally influenced by his own, maybe already nascent, political ambitions.

Jobert's stand requires closer attention. Two quotations, their provocative manner helping to explain Schmidt's acrimony, illustrate the French minister's attitude. He warned his colleagues against being too dogmatic or moralistic on the question of bilateral oil deals, claiming to know of at least seven countries which were pursuing such arrangements.[37] In a quotation that cannot be translated if its full favour is to be retained, he added:

M. Schmidt a dit qu'il ne fallait pas que chacun cherche à sauver sa peau et j'observerai, certes, que quand tout va bien les démarches sont élégantes et que, quand tout va mal, chacun cherche à sauver sa peau. Mais on n'a pas tous la même peau. Certains l'ont bien tendue et luisante, d'autres sont minces et s'inquiètent de la nourriture de demain. Tenons-en compte avant de prononcer des condamnations d'ordre moral.

To reporters Jobert rejoined: 'I am perfectly calm. I will not budge from my position ... My tone was very diplomatic. I even added some compliments for the Americans at the beginning of my speech.'[38] This almost exaggerated self-possession calls into mind Jobert's interview with *Der Spiegel* the previous year.

French opposition to the American plans was unmoved by a private meeting between Jobert and Kissinger on the second day. Thus, the eventual final communiqué of the conference one day later took the form of an agreement from which the French stood partly aside. In line with his stance at the earlier Council meeting. Jobert refused to accept those passages involving economic and financial measures or institutional developments.

[35] Grosser, *Les Occidentaux*, 339.
[36] Kissinger, *Years of Upheaval*, 913.
[37] Jobert, *L'Autre Regard*, 380.
[38] Both statements quoted in *Le Monde*, 13 Feb. 1974.

That Jobert remained somewhat aloof from the general mood of conciliation that followed bore witness to the continuing importance for the French of the conference's political ramifications. As Kissinger pithily observes: 'It was in Jobert's interest to downplay the conference, it was in ours to downplay the controversy.'[39] Jobert's remarks made clear this political primacy for the French. He noted that the other member states had forgotten that the EEC was 'still an economic institution and not a political one',[40] adding, in muted echo of the students' rallying call of 1968, that 'it so happens that ... imagination has taken part in this conference.'[41]

But despite all their efforts, the French had failed to counter Kissinger's strategy, which had triumphed over the other member states and left France isolated. Only with the benefit of hindsight can one see that Kissinger's success came too late. The Americans were to grow increasingly involved in the domestic preoccupations of Watergate during the first half of 1974, and the 'New Atlantic Charter' was to be left to one side. Only in June 1974 was a document finally produced. As for European relations, Jobert's barbed comments and innuendos regarding the Germans were inauspicious. One wonders about the future course of bilateral relations had Jobert remained in office after May 1974.

The French stand in Washington struck a popular chord at home. Jobert's views resoundingly echoed de Gaulle's policy. The General's desire for a European Europe, independent of the United States, was explicitly evoked in Jobert's interview with the ORTF.[42] A similar attitude was taken up by de Lipkowski, deputizing for the indisposed Foreign Minister, before the Cabinet.[43] Asked elsewhere whether he had deliberately set out to disrupt the conference by refusing to agree to any follow-up machinery for purely political reasons, Jobert replied, 'Yes, it is a good conclusion.'[44] Such jingoism appealed to a wide spectrum of French opinion. In a poll, 52 per cent of those asked approved of

---

[39] Kissinger, *Years of Upheaval*, 923.
[40] Quoted in *International Herald Tribune*, 14 Feb. 1974.
[41] Loc. cit.
[42] Jobert's interview with ORTF, reprinted in *Le Monde*, 16 Feb. 1974.
[43] Reported in *The Times*, 21 Feb. 1974.
[44] Jobert's interview with the *Washington Post*, reported in *The Times*, 15 Feb. 1974.

their country's refusal to follow the American line on energy.[45] Jobert himself, commenting on his treatment by the National Assembly Foreign Affairs Committee after the conference, felt that, 'in general, the reception there was friendly'.[46] Certainly, the restoration of a firmly Gaullist foreign policy was indirectly implied by the approval of some of the party's old guard. Messmer was delighted, 'rejoicing' in France's isolation in Washington, which took him back to the days of de Gaulle. [47] Debré seemed no less pleased.[48] Less partisan sources, however, took a more realistic view. *Le Monde* for instance was critical both of Jobert's motives and of his manner in Washington.

For the Germans, Scheel was characteristically conciliatory. He sought to play down the impression of a principally Franco-German rift in Washington, attempting to restore the Community to an even keel. The latter concern was accentuated by his presidency of the Council of Ministers. Thus, in a clever play on words, Scheel suggested that the split that had taken place in Washington was one between France and the Eight, with the Federal Republic on the latter side, rather than an exclusively Franco-German conflict.[49] Yet Scheel also dwelt on the need for co-operation with the United States. This theme was amplified by Schmidt, whose caution regarding new developments in the Community and hints of German reluctance to subsidize the balance of payments deficits of neighbours unwilling to display a minimum of solidarity indicated the beginnings of a German strategy of linkage. [50]

As with the events of mid-1973, the Washington conference raises important questions about French policy formation at the end of Pompidou's presidency. Although opinion differs as to the extent of Jobert's freedom of action in Washington, the evidence strongly suggests that he was clearly following instructions —though he was not loath to give the impression of a measure of leeway. Pompidou was in full control of French policy at the conference. A number of authoritative sources have suggested

[45] SOFRES poll in *Le Figaro*, reported in *The Times*, 23 Feb. 1974.
[46] Jobert, *L'Autre Regard*, 382.
[47] See the *Financial Times*, 15 and 25 Feb. 1974.
[48] See *Le Monde*, 16 Feb. 1974.
[49] Reported in *The Times*, 16 Feb. 1974, and *Latest from Germany*, 19 Feb. 1974.
[50] Reported in *Le Monde*, 14 Feb. 1974, and *Latest from Germany*, 19 Feb. 1974.

that his attitude to American intentions was even more hostile than Jobert's own.[51] At a Cabinet meeting after the conference, the President was reported to have shown considerable opposition to American actions and to have described the behaviour of France's partners as a rout before the United States, with France as the sole defender of the European faith.[52] Such sentiments were indistinguishable from those of de Gaulle. Jobert's stance in Washington bore the distinctive stamp of Pompidou's views at this stage. Leroy points out the excessive pessimism and suspicion of partners and the tendency to overdramatize and present ultimatums that characterized French policy towards the close of Pompidou's presidency.[53] This emerged, for instance, in Jobert's constant suggestion (mirroring Gaullist policy of the 1960s) that the Federal Republic could somehow choose between Europe and America.

There were other signs too that Jobert was doing Pompidou's bidding in Washington. In a radio interview, for example, Messmer stated that French policy had been fully discussed in the Cabinet prior to Jobert's departure, the Foreign Minister having been given a written brief.[54] Jobert did not, however, attempt to contradict the impression held by some of France's partners that he was in a position to negotiate—thus allowing the President more room for manœuvre if required. Just before the end of the conference, Jobert telephoned Paris, reporting the possibility of a mediocre outcome, *sans éclat*, and was told rather to stick to his instructions—resulting in his refusal to accept the final communiqué in its entirety.[55]

The German stand at the conference also requires further attention. A distinction must be drawn between Schmidt's fervent championing of close relations with the United States and the more Community-minded attitude represented by Scheel and others (who, of course, were themselves not opposed to the idea of co-operating with the Americans). Such a ministerial difference of emphasis was hardly novel in German

[51] This section draws heavily on interview material. Note also Jobert's record of Pompidou's comments about American policy, in *L'Autre Regard*, 294–5.
[52] See reports, based on a French Cabinet leak, in the *Financial Times*, 15 Feb. 1974.
[53] Leroy, 81.
[54] See reports in *Le Monde*, 13 Feb. 1974, and *The Times*, 14 Feb. 1974.
[55] Interview material. Teyssier confirms that the refusal to accept stemmed from Pompidou.

policy. But Schmidt's views at this time should not be taken as fully representative; again, it is interesting to note the broadening of perspective that took place as a result of his accession to the Chancellorship.

As with the Middle East, so with energy, the Federal Republic found itself in a very complex position in Washington. A degree of disillusionment with the United States and awareness of Kissinger's intentions had to be set against a consciousness of the inaptitude of the French line for a country in Germany's position. The Middle East war, oil crisis, and subsequent American policy on energy, all demonstrated that, *Ostpolitik* notwithstanding, the Federal Republic remained constrained and was not always able to steer a clear foreign policy course. Occasionally, a consistent line was further obscured by personal differences and division within the Cabinet. Principally, its continued, though attenuated, dependence on American military support meant that Germany remained more susceptible to American pressure than France. Hence the greater French freedom of action, allowing Paris to reassert its doctrine of multipolarity and European independence, in a model in which Schmidt's commitment to close relations with Washington represented one extreme, and Jobert's espousal of European autonomy another. Only in the later 1970s, largely under the more moderated policies of Giscard towards the United States on the one hand, and the difficulties in relations between Schmidt and Carter on the other, was it possible for the two countries to draw closer together in their foreign policies and collaborate more effectively.

The end of an era

There was remarkably little sign of the Community's rift in Washington spilling over into other areas of its activity following the conference. The strain was largely confined to the foreign ministers—though it lasted some time. In the short term, this containment can largely be ascribed to the desire of most member states, outwardly at least, to maintain the impression of unity. In the longer term, the domestic upheavals that were soon to take place in London, Paris, and Bonn were chiefly responsible.

Already, at the mid-February farm ministers' meeting, attention focused on the forthcoming British elections. The circumstances proved useful for Britain and Germany alike. While domestic electoral considerations reinforced London's desire to see minimal price rises, Bonn's orientation with the British harmonized with the national trend towards greater consumer and trade union resistance to large food price rises. A recently published government report had shown a 19 per cent increase in farmers' incomes in 1973, and an average rise of 13.3 per cent over the past five years. This compared with an average of 12.6 per cent during the period for the work-force as a whole.[56] Faced with severe differences between the member states, the Council eventually decided to postpone further discussions on farm prices until after the British and Belgian elections.

The finance ministers' meeting on 18 February 1974 was also free from post-Washington friction. Here again, however, decision—on the revaluation of gold reserves—was put off. As with the farm ministers' meeting, it is interesting to speculate on whether there was any connection between the French position as *demandeur* in both cases and the lack of strain at the meetings. Whatever the answer, it is worth noting that although Giscard remarked on intra-European relations after the Washington conference that perhaps the best way to help Europe at the moment was to 'make it pass through a period of calm', this view did not appear to be fully representative of the Government as a whole.[57]

This was made clear at Jobert's meeting with Scheel on 1 March 1974. The French Foreign Minister appeared undeterred by the Washington fracas, and he returned to the theme of European independence from the United States and contacts with the Arabs.[58] The French were patently trying to salvage some remnant of Community solidarity along the lines they envisaged from the ruins of the Washington meeting. Given Scheel's concern to restore normality in the EEC, it was not entirely surprising that at the foreign ministers' meeting on 4 March—three days after the bilateral tête-à-tête—the Nine should have returned to the French view, agreeing on a joint initiative towards the Arabs. The decision appeared directly to

---

[56] Figures from the *Financial Times*, 19 Feb. 1974.
[57] Quoted in 'Europa', *The Times*, 5 Mar. 1974.
[58] See Jobert's account of the meeting in *L'Autre Regard*, 383.

contradict the Community's acceptance in Washington of American opposition to precisely such an approach. Certainly, the move was very badly received by Kissinger.[59] But he was probably mistaken in attributing the blame entirely to the French. Rather, it would appear that, while ready to bend to American pressure in Washington, once back in Europe the Nine returned to a more independent course. The end result—acceptance of Kissinger's proposals on the one hand, and adoption of at least that part of the French strategy concerning an independent dialogue with the Arabs on the other—looked very much like the best of both worlds. Even Schmidt hinted at German acceptance of these new standards (an indication of the commercial pressures on the Federal Republic). Yet he also strongly implied his disapproval for the former unrelenting French stand. Thus, although Bonn would prefer a common policy between consumers and producers, this framework would not preclude bilateral deals. However, 'The alternative, which we don't like too much is that, with no regard to what your neighbour does, you try to solve your own problems by bilateral deals and refuse to co-operate with the rest of the oil consumers.'[60]

Although the agreement on a Euro-Arab conference represented the achievement of half of France's aims, the question of relations with the United States, the other half of the package, continued to plague the Community. The issue taxed the Nine's foreign ministers at a difficult meeting in Luxembourg on 1–2 April 1974. Differences, mirroring those of 1973, resurfaced between France and the other member states. In the familiar pattern, while France's partners (Britain and Germany in particular) sought regular contacts with the Americans, the French argued that the Community should simply inform the United States of any relevant matters after discussion by the Nine.

There were clear signs at this stage of growing German frustration with certain aspects of Community affairs, and, by implication, with French policy in particular. These had already been made evident in the Bundestag debate on Europe on 28

[59] For Jobert's impressions, see ibid. 384, and *Mémoires*, 328–9. See also Turner, 'The Politics of the Energy Crisis', 413.

[60] Quoted in *International Herald Tribune*, 11 Mar. 1974.

March where Brandt, painting a sorry picture of the EEC, had put considerable weight on relations with Washington.[61] Yet it was a reflection of the shift in the German position since mid-1973 that the Chancellor, listing the problems facing the Nine, should have included—in undoubted reference to the French—incomprehending jealousy of the US–Russian dialogue. One should not forget to what extent the Germans had formerly shared France's unease on this score. That Bonn appeared disillusioned and frustrated by Community bickering, and perhaps genuinely feared the disintegration of the Nine, was additionally indicated by Scheel's uncharacteristically pessimistic appraisal.[62] The Foreign Minister's expression of disappointment in his country's failure to use its presidency to better effect owing to the general difficulties facing the Nine also gave an indication of the constraints on German European policy. It was in this vein that Scheel noted a hesitancy in Bonn to take the lead.

However, this air of stalemate in Community affairs was already beginning to clear, although the change owed less to any individual act of will among the Nine than to the effect of developments in the Community's internal political make-up. The British election results of 28 February 1974 provided the first influence. A Labour Government was returned, pledged to renegotiating Britain's terms of entry. Bonn in particular was sympathetic to the British case—especially on agriculture. The alignment partly reflected the Federal Government's desire to show solidarity with Socialist colleagues. Later chapters will show the strain that would develop in bilateral relations. For the time being, however, the change rang in the new and offered the prospect of novel possibilities.

The situation in France provided the second cause for uncertainty, with increasing speculation as to Pompidou's health. There had already been a Cabinet reshuffle at the end of February 1974. On 12–13 March, the President had undertaken a trip to the Black Sea for talks with Brezhnev—'The unnecessary Calvary of Pitsounda' according to Jobert, who also records

---

[61] See *Deutscher Bundestag*, 7. Wahlperiode, 91. Sitzung, Bonn, Thurs. 28 Mar. 1974, 6096–101.
[62] See reports in the *Financial Times*, 29 Mar. 1974, and *The Times*, 29 Mar. 1974.

that Pompidou was suffering badly by this stage.[63] Twenty days later, on the evening of 2 April, the President died.

With France (and also Belgium) in flux, the political co-operation meeting on 20–1 April 1974 at Schloss Gymnich was very restrained. The climate of uncertainty was hardly conducive to conflict. The atmosphere was also influenced by the deliberately relaxed format of the meeting. In contrast to their earlier differences, the Nine now reached a compromise on relations with the United States. This development was facilitated by the reduced American pressure as a result of the Administration's increasing pre-occupation with Watergate. Jobert, whose future lay in doubt following the death of his mentor, captured the mood of the meeting. In his words, 'with calm and common sense we can arrive at quieter and even happier days.'[64]

However, one further event remained to shake this relative tranquillity. On the night of 6 May, Brandt's resignation was announced. This followed the arrest on 24 April of his personal aide, Günther Guillaume, on spying charges. There is an ironic parallel between Brandt's fall on account of East German espionage and that of Erhard, the architect of the German economic miracle, as a result of the recession of 1966.[65] Brandt attributed his decision solely to the Guillaume affair and its potential consequences.[66] Speculation about the motives has, in fact, grown into a popular feature of subsequent academic and biographical studies. The most recent and substantial of these confirms the Chancellor's decision to resign on the Guillaume issue and the rumour of associated scandals.[67] But although it is

[63] Jobert, *L'Autre Regard*, 15. See also 386–7. See also *Le Monde*, 9 Apr. 1974; Kissinger, *Years of Upheaval*, 728, 733.

[64] Quoted in the *Financial Times*, 22 Apr. 1974.

[65] The example is drawn in Morgan, *The United States and West Germany*, 253. On Brandt's resignation, see Brandt, 230–1, 443–50; Ménudier, *L'Allemagne selon Willy Brandt*, 186–9, 205, 217; Joseph Rovan, *Histoire de la social-démocratie allemande* (Paris, Seuil, 1978), 392–3, 411–23; Wolfgang Wagner, 'Kanzlerwechsel in Bonn. Der Rücktritt Willy Brandts und das neue Kabinett Schmidt–Genscher', *Europa-Archiv* 11 (1974); A. W[iss]–V[erdier], 'La Conjoncture politique', *Documents* (Mar.–Apr. 1974), 134, and 'La Fin de l'ère Brandt', *Documents* (May–June 1974), 67.

[66] See, for instance, Brandt's television broadcast of 8 May giving reasons for his decision. Reported in *Keesing's Contemporary Archives*, 10–16 June 1974, 26557. Note also Brandt's comments in Ménudier, *L'Allemagne selon Willy Brandt*, 17–18.

[67] Baring, *Machtwechsel*, 715–62. As to developments in Brandt's mood after the 1972 elections, see 509–10, 519–20, 566, 594–600.

convincingly shown that Brandt had begun to reassert himself after a lengthy period of lassitude, the wind had, in fact, been turning against the Chancellor for some time.

A variety of factors were responsible. The SPD's comfortable Parliamentary position following its 1972 election success had allowed for a loss of discipline. Notably, there was friction between the vociferous and radical Young Socialists and the party's right wing (a situation paralleled in some ways in 1981-2). Differences between the coalition partners—increasingly linked to the slow progress of the Government's social programme—and criticism of Brandt within the higher echelons of the SPD also came into play. In late September 1973, Herbert Wehner, a senior party figure and growing detractor of Brandt, had publicly criticized the Government's handling of certain aspects of the *Ostpolitik* while in Moscow.

In the country as a whole, rising inflation and the worsening economic climate of winter 1973-4, the absence of new developments in the *Ostpolitik*, lack-lustre performance of the EEC, and problems in Atlantic relations, all contributed to the mood of discontent and consequent fall in Brandt's prestige. At the beginning of 1974, industrial unrest, in open defiance of the Chancellor's own recommended pay norm, exacerbated matters. The Government's eventual climb-down further contributed to the public sense of weakness and division in Bonn.[68] Such feelings were confirmed in election results in the first quarter of 1974, with the Social Democrats' losses in Hamburg on 3 May regarded as especially significant.

Brandt himself had been increasingly tired, irritable, and remote in 1973 and—until an eleventh-hour revival—much of early 1974. Exhaustion from the twin jobs of Chancellor and party Chairman, and criticism from within the SPD, took their toll. In addition, there was perhaps an element of disappointment with affairs of state, notably regarding the Community and East-West relations. These factors no doubt affected the Chancellor's mood, contributing in turn to the criticisms of isolation and lack of leadership. The increasing importance of matters of a detailed economic nature in both domestic and

[68] See Jèrôme Vaillant, 'La Grève des services publics en RFA', *L'Allemagne d'aujourd'hui* (Mar.–Apr. 1974), 30-4. For a good survey of the elections in early 1974, see A. W[iss]-V[erdier], La Conjoncture politique'.

international affairs—much more in Schmidt's domain—rather than the broad foreign policy issues that were Brandt's forte undoubtedly also played a part. In sum, although Brandt could probably have weathered the Guillaume storm, he would certainly not have been the ideal Chancellor for the difficult period ahead.[69] With the benefit of hindsight, his resignation probably represented the best solution for all concerned.

Thus, within almost a month, Germany and France lost the men who had led them since 1969. On 16 May 1974, Schmidt was voted Chancellor. This was followed three days later by the election of Giscard d'Estaing as President. A new phase had opened for the two countries individually and for the Community as a whole.

[69] Note here Baring, 760.

9

The Schmidt–Giscard Years—
Picking up the Pieces
1974–1977

Introduction

The change of power in France and Germany offered the Community new hope for escape from the impasse in which it had found itself at the end of the Brandt–Pompidou period. Unlike their predecessors, both the new French and German leaders were experienced economists. This quality, above all others, was to be a prerequisite for the effective guidance of both national and EEC affairs in the immediate aftermath of the oil crisis. Furthermore, although no one expected an instant improvement in bilateral relations under the prevailing circumstances, it was true that Schmidt and Giscard did at least possess a proven record of friendly and effective co-operation as ministers of finance.

Despite these advantages, there was at first to be little scope for the dynamic bilateral collaboration that was to become such a feature of the European scene later in the decade. Until the end of 1974 at least, Paris and Bonn had to address themselves principally to the urgent (and seriously mooted) problem of preventing the possible disintegration of the EEC. Hence the widespread contemporary comment about performing a 'salvage operation' on the Community. Only once the major cracks had been shorn up would there be some scope for breaking new ground, a development heralded by the Paris summit of December 1974. Even then, however, both bilateral and Community business would remain at the mercy of international economic circumstances, and, to a lesser extent, the internal problems of more recalcitrant member states such as Britain.

Economic policy

Two themes dominated European relations in the first months of the Schmidt–Giscard period: the need to combat inflation, and

the danger of protectionism. Both trends were direct consequences of the fourfold increase in oil prices that had taken place
in winter 1973–4. Substantial cost inflation was an obvious by-
product of the oil price rise, which had by now begun to feed into
other key areas. The drift towards protectionism was more
complex, representing an attempt by certain Western oil-
importing countries to bolster their now heavily burdened
balance of payments by at least reducing the level of imports.
Accordingly, both Denmark and, most seriously, Italy had
imposed trade restrictions. Under the Italian scheme, introduced
on 7 May 1974, importers of some 400 manufactured and
agricultural products were obliged to make a six-months
interest-free deposit covering some fifty per cent of the value of
their goods.

Both the inflationary and protectionist trends were viewed
with the greatest concern in Bonn given traditional policy
preferences. While the former put at risk the stable money policy
followed by successive German governments, the latter threatened the Federal Republic's dominant export sector. The
Germans themselves were in a comparatively favourable position: German inflation rates were relatively low, standing at 7.2
per cent in the year to March 1974, as against 12.2 per cent for
France and 13.5 per cent for Britain.[1] On the balance of
payments too the Federal Republic stood out in facing a
substantial surplus in comparison to the large deficits of its
neighbours.

Yet the level of German concern underlined an established
irony in the country's post-war economic success, namely its
reliance on a stable world economic and trading system. Under
the present circumstances, the Germans were deeply concerned
about the threats being posed to that very stability, and
consequently to their own economic well-being. It was hardly
surprising, therefore, that Bonn should have led the opposition
to the Italian import restrictions. Similarly, Schmidt chose to
concentrate on the twin themes of inflation and protectionism at
his first meeting with Giscard on 31 May–1 June 1974.

Bonn's principal concern was to prevent any French emulation of the Italian example, which would have both added

---

[1] OECD figures, in the *New York Times*, 31 May 1974.

respectability to the practice and severely affected German trade. In the event, such fears were misplaced. The hastily convened Franco-German meeting marked a considerable success for the Chancellor and was a harbinger of what was to come. Giscard fully accepted the German view that economic recovery in Europe should not be brought about by protectionism.[2] Probably even more important for the Germans, he was also in accord that firm action should be taken to prevent inflation. The agreement indicated the similarity of views now to be expected from the French and German leaders. Furthermore, there was a strong joint political commitment to work together to revive the Community. Already, the contrast with the Brandt–Pompidou period was marked.

This shared emphasis on the need for common action to minimize the repercussions of the economic crisis was developed at the Franco-German summit on 8–9 July 1974. While their earlier meeting had mainly been an occasion for an exchange of views, by now Schmidt and Giscard had both introduced comprehensive anti-inflationary programmes of their own. As usual, it was the Germans who led the way. Schmidt underlined the need to control inflation and maintain internal activity. Significantly, though, in contrast with the past, these priorities were now being wholeheartedly echoed by the French President. Giscard had already taken steps to reduce domestic demand and restrict credit amid widespread comment that French economic policy appeared to be taking on a distinctly German slant. Interestingly, Giscard himself conceded the likeness.[3] Only later in the decade would the President grow more reluctant to draw such parallels, under attack from Gaullists and Opposition alike. But in mid-1974 at least, this similarity of views was no embarrassment but rather a bonus in domestic political terms and a welcome change from the bilateral divisions of the past. There is little doubt, in fact, that close collaboration between Schmidt and Giscard in the economic field was an established practice from the early to mid-1970s, long before it became more popularly recognized later in the decade.

With the benefit of hindsight, one can well claim that the

[2] See e.g. Giscard's speech quoted in *Le Monde*, 4 June 1974.
[3] See *Le Monde*, 10 July 1974. As to Schmidt's approval, note, for instance, the remarks in Giroud, 49.

deflationary policies of 1974 spearheaded by Germany and France were carried to extremes.[4] Certainly, within only a year, it was not so much the question of fighting inflation as that of combating recession and unemployment which was dominant in Franco-German economic conversations. At both their bilateral summits of 1975, Schmidt and Giscard dwelt on this problem. Yet the change of emphasis reflected not just the economic contraction that had taken place. More positively, it also illustrated the fact that Giscard had experienced some success in reducing French inflation to a level closer to that of the Federal Republic. The President had also brought about an improvement in the country's balance of payments.

At their summit in July 1975, therefore, the two leaders were freer to concentrate on restoring growth. Both sides were by now planning substantial reflationary programmes. Thus their meeting provided an important opportunity for exchanging ideas and co-ordinating policies. The fruits of the summit were made evident in the announcement of a synchronized programme of economic revival.[5] Yet details were left sketchy—much in line with past practice—and the move should be seen more as a symbol than a concrete set of policies. Two factors were responsible. First, the declaration marked a statement of intent rather than one of precise proposals. These would follow later at national level. Secondly, there is no doubt that both Schmidt and Giscard were anxious to discuss their reflationary ideas with their partners in the Snake before proceeding further. This later aspect is important; although criticism would mount throughout the decade regarding over-exclusivity in Franco-German relations, it must be recognized that the two leaders generally took pains to keep their partners informed of their intentions, precisely so as to avoid such an impression.[6] Whether they were always successful, however, is more doubtful.

Despite the interest aroused by the joint Franco-German declaration, it can well be argued that it was not so much this

[4] See e.g. the conclusions drawn in *France* (Paris, OECD, January 1976), 5, regarding underestimation of the economic downturn.

[5] See *Le Monde*, 29 July 1975. For a less optimistic appraisal of the reflationary plan, see *The Economist*, 2 Aug. 1975.

[6] For the action taken after the July 1975 summit, see *Frankfurter Allgemeine Zeitung*, 28 July 1975.

step as Giscard's acceptance of the priority of economic over monetary policy co-ordination which was in fact the summit's outstanding feature.[7] The move represented a major shift in French thinking (one only has to recall the heated and seemingly endless debates over priorities in EMU in the early 1970s), and it was instrumental in the subsequent rise of Franco-German economic policy co-ordination later in the decade. Giscard's decision was not, however, altogether surprising; by mid-1975 monetary union—at least in the form envisaged in the Werner Report—had become widely recognized as unattainable.[8] Economic policy co-ordination had to take precedence. Thus Giscard's decision in June 1975 to rejoin the Snake was a positive step. But, in the aftermath of the oil crisis, with substantial, and in some cases widening, differences between the member states, no one seriously believed that concrete progress towards EMU could be resumed in the immediate future.

French acceptance of the priority of economic policy co-ordination remained highly salient both at bilateral and Community level in the following months. Internally, too, France's economic policy came increasingly into line with that of the Federal Republic. This evolution was particularly marked after August 1976, when the new Prime Minister, Barre, made reducing inflation a prime target of national policy. Bilateral co-operation undoubtedly gained from the change, with matters reaching a zenith at the Franco-German summit of February 1977. Barre's anti-inflationary measures had already won approval in the Federal Republic, and the Chancellor himself now offered fulsome praise.[9] As a sign of their growing identity of views, the two sides announced an escalation of their system of economic policy co-ordination. In future, meetings between the French and German Ministers of Finance and Economics would take place quarterly. In view of their wish to avoid the impression of exclusivity, it was significant that both capitals took care to present the move as a preliminary to a more frequent pattern of Community-wide talks. Once again, though, it was a Franco-German initiative which led the way.

---

[7] See *Le Monde*, 29 July 1975.

[8] See, for instance, the conclusions reached in the Marjolin Report of March 1975. European Communities Commission, *Report of the Study Group 'Economic and Monetary Union 1980'*.

[9] See the *Financial Times*, 4 Feb. 1977.

The gesture should not be underplayed. In this instance it represented much more than just a palliative to the other member states. The bilateral decision to increase the frequency of talks indicated a more fundamental aim, namely to prepare the ground for a closer harmonization of Community economic policies. Hence Schmidt and Giscard announced that their governments would be presenting new proposals to their European partners by the end of the year.[10] More important, this step was in turn intended to be the curtain-raiser for a still more ambitious target; the restoration of progress towards economic and monetary union. The culmination of all these moves would be the advent of the European Monetary System the following year. What should be borne in mind here, though, is the specific Franco-German role in preparing the ground for closer economic policy co-ordination among the Nine some time before the much more publicized events of 1978.

Monetary policy

As suggested above, conditions in the mid-1970s were far from ideal for achieving closer European monetary co-operation. What discussion there was tended to be concerned with third parties, notably, as ever, the United States, and wider international monetary problems. On both counts France and Germany were closely aligned, unlike the case so often in previous years. This evolution was partly attributable to the shared backgrounds of Schmidt and Giscard in economic and monetary affairs, experience which lent them a knowledge and weight lacking not only in their immediate predecessors but also in the majority of their contemporary Western partners.

The problem of American monetary policy, and particularly the Ford Administration's apparent neglect of the dollar, was uppermost amongst the issues confronting the two leaders. The question of American indifference to the damage caused by the instability of the dollar was hardly unfamiliar from the Nixon era. As will be seen, it would recur as a unifying factor in Franco-German relations in the 1980s. In each case, restabilizing the dollar's value was viewed by Bonn and Paris alike as one of the keys to solving wider problems in the world's monetary system.

---

[10] Joint Franco-German declaration reprinted in *Le Monde*, 6–7 Feb. 1977.

By 1975, this had been additionally burdened by the repercussions of the oil price rise. Hence monetary issues were well to the fore at the Franco-German summit of July 1975. The meeting confirmed the similarity of French and German views regarding American responsibility, not only for stabilizing the value of the dollar, but also for providing the lead out of the recession. The development in German thinking in comparison with earlier years was particularly striking. The critical appraisals of American monetary policy now being made by Schmidt—one facet of a growing German readiness to criticize its dominant partner—would become increasingly prominent as the decade progressed and would provide a good barometer of the rising German self-confidence, based on economic and growing political strength, that was a hallmark of the Schmidt Chancellorship.

The bilateral summit of July 1975 also gave a clue as to another major development in Franco-German relations. This concerned the growing role of monetary differences with the United States as a unifying, rather than divisive, issue between Bonn and Paris. This was in marked contrast to the divisions witnessed earlier in the decade and would be particularly striking in relation to the EMS in 1978, and also in bilateral relations in the early 1980s. Finally, one additional feature of the meeting, illustrating the new alignment of views on both sides of the Rhine, was Schmidt's support for Giscard's initiative for a major Western conference on monetary reform. With this backing, the idea would gather pace in the coming months, culminating in the Rambouillet summit of November 1975, the first of an annual series.[11] The initiative was important in forming part of the process of 'personalization' of international economic affairs in the 1970s, one factor behind the emergence of economic policy into the realm of 'high' politics.

In discussing monetary policy between France and Germany, something must also be said about the rising political status of the Federal Republic in the period between Brandt's downfall and the later 1970s. As has been seen from earlier chapters, the process had been under way for some time. Only under Schmidt, however, did the transition of West Germany's economic might

---

[11] On the economic summits, see Georges de Ménil, 'De Rambouillet à Versailles: Un bilan des sommets économiques', *Politique Étrangère* 2 (June 1981).

into a more assertive political stance come out fully into the open. There would be regular examples of German economic, and political, prowess during the mid-1970s. Most notable was Schmidt's offer in August 1974 of a $2 billion bilateral credit to Italy. The move was significant not so much for its size, though that in itself was telling considering it came at a time when most European states had little enough money to spare, as for the economic, and, by implication, political strings attached.

The German credit was surprising in view of Bonn's former reluctance to give financial aid to Rome. The step, when it came, was undoubtedly taken in part response to the Italian Government's decision to embark on a more deflationary economic strategy—a course long counselled by the Germans. More important, the loan represented a recognition in Bonn that German interests (notably in the export sector) would not be served by a further Italian drift into protectionism or beggar-thy-neighbour policies. Thus, although the Germans were able to extract tough terms from the Italians, the offer, like those made earlier to Britain and France, represented not so much a commercial arrangement on Bonn's part as a broader manœuvre, indicating the more cogent foreign economic policy being pursued by Schmidt.[12] As the 1970s progressed, it would become increasingly evident that the Federal Republic would be willing to use its considerable financial resources as an instrument in its foreign economic policy in a much more coherent way than in the past. This would form a valuable instrument in achieving desired economic and political ends, or, as in the case of the Italian loan, preventing undesirable ones.

Further evidence of the Federal Republic's enhanced position in the international political economy came in the consistent pressure on Bonn, notably from the United States, to take a leading role in reflating out of the recession. This insistence was evident at almost every major economic gathering of the period, and it offered a mirror image of Bonn's own view that it was the United States which should take the initiative in reflating. The American attitude, shared by most of Bonn's partners, gave a good indication of the pivotal position now occupied by the

---

[12] Note the instructive comments on the loan by Gebhard Schweigler, 'A new political giant? West German foreign policy in the 1970s', *The World Today* (Apr. 1975), 138.

Federal Republic (and Japan) in the expectations of other Western nations. By contrast, the Germans strenuously denied such a role. Such abnegation stemmed both from political reasons, to avoid any incremental antagonisms provoked by such a position, and also from sound economic grounds. Both the desire not to jeopardize internal stability and the long-standing reliance on export-led growth explained Bonn's counter-arguments in favour of a co-ordinated international reflation.

The French position in this debate is worth attention. Unlike Washington and London, Paris was somewhat less insistent on a German reflation. During discussions on world economic issues at the bilateral summit of February 1977, for instance, the French President adopted a restrained approach. Various factors explained Giscard's reticence. He was conscious of the close economic inter-linkages between the French and German economies, and he also shared Schmidt's fear of rekindling inflation through peremptory action. Furthermore, the two leaders had only just agreed on co-ordinating their economic policies more closely. Thus Giscard was doubly reluctant to press as openly as other Western statesmen for the Federal Republic to be the 'locomotive' pulling the West out of recession, and his restraint served to underline the growing alignment of views in Bonn and Paris.

Energy policy

The energy sector was one of the foremost areas of change in French policy from Pompidou to Giscard. Under the new President, France moved away from its earlier confrontational strategy to a considerably more accommodating line. Although Giscard, like his predecessor, held a strong commitment to the development of close links with the oil and other major raw material producing nations, he did not seek to pursue this aim at the cost of co-operation with France's Western industrialized partners. In this respect, his policy was grounded on a firm sense of pragmatism and clear conception of Western economic interdependence. This contrasted with the more ideologically-based aim of distancing Europe from a seemingly hegemonic United States that had guided Pompidou's closing months.

The change in French thinking was of immense benefit to Franco-German relations in two related ways. First, while differences with the Germans over energy policy remained, these were no longer of their former magnitude. Secondly and most important, the wider question of relations with the United States, which had so overshadowed energy matters in early 1974, had now receded as a divisive issue between France and Germany. The shift in American priorities away from international affairs to domestic concerns, notably Watergate, was the prime cause for this, the change to a more pragmatic French approach under Giscard the subsidiary reason. As a result of these realignments French policy would no longer be so single-mindedly aimed at weaning Bonn away from Washington, nor at presenting the Germans with impossible choices as had been the case in the latter days of Pompidou and Jobert.

The new realism in French thinking quickly bore fruit in terms of improved relations with Bonn. There were already strong signs of a reduction in bilateral tension on the energy front at the Franco-German summit on 7–8 July 1974.[13] Giscard did not announce any sudden reversal of his predecessor's boycott of the Energy Co-ordinating Group established at the Washington conference, nor did he suggest any relaxation of Pompidou's emphasis on a united European approach to energy questions. But it was obvious that a substantial change of tone had come about in bilateral discussions, with a much less rigid French stance and a greater willingness to consider subjects which might previously have been regarded as taboo. Above all, there was a strong hint of future French plans in the reported suggestion that Paris might consider a fusion of the Energy Co-ordinating Group into OECD as an acceptable compromise forum for future participation in Western energy talks.[14]

This twin track approach to energy along both novel and traditional lines remained a hallmark of French policy throughout the Giscard presidency. That Giscard was edging towards closer co-operation with other Western oil consumers was confirmed at his summit meeting with Ford in Martinique in December 1974, where the principle of advance co-ordination was accepted by the French. Yet such concessions were not to be

---

[13] See *Le Monde*, 10 July 1974. On the development of energy questions in 1974, see Walton, 'Atlantic bargaining over energy'; Henri Simonet, 'Energy and the Future of Europe', *Foreign Affairs* (Apr. 1975).

[14] See report in *Le Monde*, 10 July 1974.

at the cost of better relations with the oil producers. At his press conference on 24 October 1974, Giscard had already proposed a tripartite gathering of oil producers and of industrialized and non-industrialized consumers. The Martinique meeting set the seal on this initiative, with American backing for Giscard's plans coming as the quid pro quo for France's greater flexibility on preliminary Western collaboration.

It is likely that these twin developments proved highly satisfactory to the Germans, offering them the best of both worlds. First of all, Giscard's acceptance of a more open relationship with the Americans and his readiness to participate in Western energy co-ordination satisfied long-standing German wishes. One only has to recall Schmidt's position at the Washington conference. In addition, though, the Germans undoubtedly saw attractions in Giscard's initiative for a dialogue between oil producers and consumers. Bonn had been moving towards better relations with the Arab world for some time. Provided it was not conducted to the detriment of relations with the United States and Israel, the French impetus would serve as a valuable extra diplomatic tool.

Hence the extremely cordial tone of discussions on energy at the February 1975 Franco-German summit—a far cry from the lack of communication familiar from the end of the Pompidou era.[15] At their meeting, Schmidt and Giscard reached agreement on a number of points, notably the calendar for the preparatory talks and for the major conference Giscard envisaged. As so often in the past, the bilateral summit proved highly opportune in its timing, coming only days before the reopening of the energy dossier at Council of Ministers level.

Quite whether the results of the North–South conference, eventually held in Paris in December 1975, lived up to Giscard's original expectations is debatable.[16] That the scope of the meeting progressively widened to embrace issues such as raw materials, development, and finance was more an irritation to the Americans than the French. Yet the dilution of the conference's impact via the establishment of specialized commit-

[15] See *The Times*, 5 Feb. 1975, and Giscard's television speech, reprinted in *Le Monde*, 6 Feb. 1975.

[16] On Giscard's policy towards North–South and Third World issues, see Charles Zorgbibe, 'La France: les initiatives d'une "puissance moyenne"', *RfSP* (Aug. 1976).

tees, which only completed their studies in June 1977 coalesced with the generally disappointing conclusions they reached to create a strong sense of disillusionment and anticlimax. The Western industrialized countries did not gain the guarantees on oil supplies and prices that they had wanted, while the developing states failed to achieve their desired moratorium on debts or indexation of raw material prices.

This question of raw materials and, more particularly, the establishment of special stabilization funds deserves closer attention. The issue was the focus of an important difference of opinion between the French and Germans, who were otherwise closely aligned in their views on the conference and its proceedings. While the French supported the idea of stabilization funds as a means of assisting the developing states and regulating the market, the Germans were wholly opposed to the notion. This was chiefly on grounds of cost, and also because the scheme might only benefit the richest of the raw material producers.[17] Such a dichotomy in French and German thinking brought to mind earlier cleavages in the two countries' foreign policies, with Paris primarily interested in the political aspects of a problem and Bonn more concerned with questions of cost-effectiveness. Though Schmidt and Giscard sought to overcome their differences via the establishment of a joint committee in 1975, the impasse was only broken in April 1977, when at the European Council meeting the Germans agreed to a modified stabilization scheme, thereby opening the way to Community accord at the North–South conference.

European issues

It was not only in the energy field that French policy underwent a marked transformation under Giscard. In Community affairs, too, the change of power in Paris opened the way for a more pragmatic and considerably less doctrinaire approach, with a reduced stress on national independence and a shift away from the legalistic formulas and strict demarcations observed by Pompidou. Giscard's prime foreign policy objective on reaching power was to revive the European Community. However, against the background of the 1973–4 economic crisis, with all

---

[17] For bilateral differences, see reports in *Le Monde*, 8 July 1976 and 4 Feb. 1977.

the member states concentrating on economic problems, progress on this aim had largely to be limited to the political field. As will be seen, although it was the French who took the lead, almost every move was made in consultation with the Germans.

Revitalizing the EEC formed an important topic of discussion at both of the meetings between Schmidt and Giscard in June and July 1974.[18] At their July summit especially, this objective was carried to the extent of an agreement to work towards a full-scale Community conference in Paris at the end of the year. A third meeting with Schmidt at the beginning of September provided an additional fillip to bilateral co-operation. Such regular face-to-face contacts, supplemented by frequent telephone conversations, illustrated the degree of co-ordination prior to the Paris summit of December 1974.[19] Active diplomacy between the French, Germans, and, to a lesser extent, British conformed to the existing pattern of holding prior consultations. Yet in mid- and late 1974, this scheme of preliminary soundings was taken to new lengths in view of the shared perceptions of the need to revive the Community. In this sense, the importance of the Paris summit can rightly be compared to that of the Hague conference in 1969. Not only were the usual questions of prestige at stake, but under the present economic circumstances, Schmidt and Giscard also firmly felt that some powerful demonstration of the Community's cohesion and its future prospects was especially desirable. Above all, it was essential to avoid a repetition of the previous year's fiasco in Copenhagen.

These goals were largely met in Paris. Despite their economic problems, and the additional diversion of Britain's renegotiation campaign, the Nine, under Franco-German guidance, achieved a signal advance. The results of the summit came in three categories: the resolution of outstanding policy differences; joint measures to tackle present economic difficulties; and optimistic steps towards the Community's future political cohesion. The first of these areas proved surprisingly easy. Most notably, the member states finally agreed to the establishment of a regional

[18] Note the joint statement in *Le Monde*, 4 June 1974 and the report in *Frankfurter Allgemeine Zeitung*, 10 July 1974.
[19] On the Paris summit, see Roger Morgan, 'A new phase in European summitry', *The World Today* (Jan. 1975); Pickles, *Contemporary French Politics*, 82–4; *The Economist*, 14 Dec. 1974.

fund, and to the size of the contributions and benefits to be given. It was more in relation to immediate difficulties that the extent of Franco-German groundwork made itself felt. The decisions reached by the Nine on avoiding protectionism and moving towards reflation followed on closely from what had already been agreed at Franco-German level.

Above all, though, it was institutional progress which stood out. A number of new initiatives were launched. In almost all of these, the French played a primary role.[20] Thus the member states agreed to Giscard's wish for an institutionalization of summit meetings, in the form of the newly created European Council. This development has rightly been seen as a descendant of the existing pattern of institutionalized Franco-German co-operation. However, as has been shown, the move was not entirely original, having long been sought by Pompidou as a means of improving decision-making and asserting the inter-governmental nature of integration. That the idea was no longer blocked by the smaller member states bore witness not only to their now greater sense of urgency regarding the need for regular top-level consultations, but also to the fact that French policy under Giscard no longer evoked the same degree of suspicion as in the past.

Yet the question of the new President's Europeanism was one that would recur over the coming years. Despite Giscard's progressive image, even at the Paris conference, some of the institutional decisions reached were kept deliberately ambiguous, partly to suit the French. For instance, although much was made of Giscard's acquiescence to greater flexibility in majority voting, it is arguable whether the form of words devised actually meant much in practice. Less ambiguous was the decision to fix 1978 as the date for direct elections to the European Parliament. This move had long been sought by the Germans and the smaller member states, but, as has been seen, had been consistently blocked by the French. Giscard's acquiescence represented a breakthrough. Yet it remains unclear whether the President, who was surely aware of the domestic political pitfalls involved, merely believed that these could be overcome

---

[20] On this early phase of Giscard's European policy, see Michael Leigh, 'Giscard and the European Community', *The World Today* (Feb. 1977).

in the interval, perhaps by way of the realignment of the governmental majority that he sought. Some observers, by contrast, have claimed that Giscard's agreement was largely cosmetic. It is argued that the President knew he could afford to bide his time, being well aware of the opposition that a significant rise in supranationality would engender in countries such as Britain and Denmark. Certainly, one should not take Giscard's Europeanism entirely for granted.[21] At the same time, though, one should also bear in mind the major domestic obstacles the President faced.

Institutional developments

In view of the closeness of Franco-German co-operation prior to the summit, it is surprising that there should have been so little evidence of discussion at bilateral level on the Community's institutional structure in the subsequent twelve months. Franco-German summits in 1976 were taken up, rather, with economic issues and the question of British renegotiation. Various explanations can be put forward for this absence. First, it was clear that both Schmidt and Giscard were anxious to avoid the impression of prejudging the institutional issues under consideration. Rather, negotiations were very much left to specialized groups reporting directly to the Commission or European Council. Yet this bilateral restraint did not just stem from a regard for the feelings of the other member states. It is also likely that it originated from a desire not to derogate authority from the Council itself, a body which was, after all, Giscard's brain-child.

Secondly, there was the fact that some of the institutional matters raised at the Paris summit remained the subject of lengthy detailed study. The question of 'European Union' was one such example. As has been seen, this ill-defined concept, supposedly to be enacted by 1980, had first raised its head back in 1972. By the 1974 Paris summit, however, few Community leaders appeared to be any the wiser as to what exactly it meant. Hence their decision to entrust the task of defining European Union and recommending concrete steps towards its realization to Leo Tindemans, the Belgian Prime Minister. The presentation of his report at the end of 1975 coincided with and

---

[21] On this theme, note Leigh, 'Giscard and the European Community', 74, 76.

contributed to the revival of talks on institutional questions between the French and Germans.[22] Unfortunately however, this development did not simply reflect the wider attention now being paid to institutional issues. It also stemmed from the fact that both the Tindemans Report and, to a lesser extent, the slightly later Community negotiations on direct elections exposed a marked dissimilarity in French and German views.

Differences over Tindemans's findings were relatively straightforward—recalling earlier disagreements on Community institutional matters. In fact, it was surprising, given the change to a more liberal French stance under Giscard, that the cleavage should have been along such traditional lines. It was not Tindemans's suggestion for a two-tier Community integrating at different speeds—the most controversial of his ideas—that divided Bonn and Paris, so much as differences over the Report's institutional implications. The Germans were enthusiastic about the proposals for increasing the powers of the Commission and boosting the role of its President. They were no less pleased about the suggestion for the European Parliament being given the right to initiate and not just rubber-stamp policy. All these ideas, however, were unacceptable to the French, who took a minimalist view. While Paris was gratified by Tindemans's approval for the European Council, his recommendations for wider powers for the Commission and Parliament were seen as highly undesirable, smacking much too strongly of supranationalism.

Much more appealing to the French than any such federalist options was the notion of a political directorate to guide the Community. This well-worn scheme resurfaced in government circles in February 1976, partly, perhaps, in response to the Tindemans Report.[23] Though never put forward officially, Paris appeared to have in mind a group comprising two or three of the larger member states, and one smaller one possibly participating by rotation. What was striking about this kite was the way in which it harked back to a much earlier theme in French

[22] Leo Tindemans, 'Report on European Union', *Bulletin of the European Communities*, Supplement, 1/76. See also E. Moxon Browne, 'The EEC after Tindemans: the institutional balance', *The World Today* (Dec. 1976); Pickles, *Contemporary French Politics*, 90–6.

[23] See report in *Le Monde*, 10 Feb. 1976.

European policy, one most familiar from the days of de Gaulle. It was a firmly inter-governmental Europe that Paris—and presumably Giscard himself—had in mind. More precisely, this was to be a Community dominated by France, Germany, and perhaps Britain, in which there was to be no question of an intrusive Commission nor, for that matter, of an excessive influence for more federally minded member states like the Benelux countries. In reverting to so archaic an institutional structure for the Nine, Giscard again invited doubts about the depth of his European convictions. The President had undeniably shown a firm and pragmatic commitment to the Community and its development. Yet, just as in the early days of Pompidou, so with his successor, it soon became clear that, whatever the increase in pragmatism from one French President to the next, on the fundamental question of institutions French policy remained decidedly evolutionary.

Giscard's views, both on the Tindemans Report and on a European directorate, caused some differences with the Germans. Bonn was not impressed by the President's taciturn response to Tindemans's findings, nor especially by the idea for a directorate.[24] Schmidt made plain his coolness towards the latter scheme at the bilateral summit of February 1976.[25] It is worth considering the reasons for this attitude, which might at first glance appear to be contrary to Bonn's own interests. Though the Federal Republic had undoubtedly grown more favourable to inter-governmentalism in the EEC since 1974, this did not stretch to backing an idea which would both patently disadvantage the smaller member states and also throw an unwelcome political spotlight on Bonn. The Federal Republic's economic and political rise in the 1970s was incontrovertible, as was the fact that France and Germany were the Community's two key partners. Emphasizing this, however, was something the Germans were keener to avoid. As has been seen, a variety of constraints (and an element of self-interest) underlay this attitude. The result remains that, except in certain special circumstances, the Germans have preferred to play down their political ascendancy in the Community, frequently adopting instead a policy of almost deliberate restraint.

[24] See reports in *Frankfurter Allgemeine Zeitung*, 12 Feb. 1976, and *Süddeutsche Zeitung*, 16 Feb. 1976.
[25] See report in *The Times*, 14 Feb. 1976.

In view of German disinterest, and the outright hostility of the smaller member states, it was clear at the Franco-German summit of February 1976 that Giscard had had second thoughts about the directorate, and was likely to let the idea drop—at least for the time being. This was confirmed in April 1976 at the European Council, when both the directorate, and, more important, the Tindemans Report were put to one side. Reasons behind the failure to act on Tindemans's findings were complex. Although all the member states had found something of value in the report, it had failed as a whole to kindle sufficient interest. Differences on specifics had greatly outweighed overall approval, while other preoccupations, notably economic—though also institutional, in the form of wrangling over the details for direct elections—had been of greater concern.

The problem of direct elections was complex, particularly as it became interwoven with difficulties in French domestic politics. On the question of Parliamentary seat distribution, for instance, Giscard could only be certain of Gaullist support provided he adhered to the principle of strict proportionality and to the precepts of the Treaty of Rome. Such domestic impediments held up Community agreement for some time. Yet the breakthrough, when it came, owed much to Franco-German co-operation. No decision was reached on the distribution of Parliamentary seats at the European Council meeting of April 1976, and there followed a considerable flow of diplomacy between Bonn and Paris. These soundings bore fruit at the bilateral summit on 5–6 July, where Schmidt and Giscard were able to prepare the ground for a Community agreement. Thus, at the European Council meeting of July 1976 the member states took up the compromise package put forward by the Germans at their previous week's summit with the French, and the Community now agreed to a compromise which went some way towards reconciling the conflicting French demands for proportionality with those for fairness to the smaller member states.

It was now that French domestic politics seriously began to intrude on the Community's plans. The differences that arose both between the Government and the Communist Party, and within the majority itself, have been well documented in the literature.[26] Only by turning the issue into a vote of confidence in 1977 was Barre finally able to guarantee Gaullist support. What is of primary interest here, though, is the need to explain the surprisingly limited damage of these internal manœuvrings on Franco-German relations. The Germans were hardly likely to have been indifferent to the events in France, which, after all, threatened one of their longest-standing European policy aims. Yet the question of direct elections was hardly mentioned at bilateral summit level in 1977 or 1978. A number of reasons can be advanced to explain this omission. First, it is possible that there remained a reluctance to broach Community institutional topics at bilateral level, as had happened after the 1974 Paris summit. More telling, though, is the argument that Bonn was anxious to steer clear of a highly charged French internal problem. Chance remarks by Schmidt on French domestic politics had already been taken amiss in certain circles,[27] and it is most probable that the Germans were resolved to be especially careful under the present circumstances. Such prudence was all the more advisable in view of the internal political climate in France. In early 1977 at the latest, debate became increasingly overshadowed by thoughts of the following year's legislative elections which many expected the Opposition to win. Hence the Germans would have been especially cautious not to appear to meddle in French domestic affairs, nor, at the same time, to cause Giscard any unnecessary embarrassment by dwelling on sensitive topics.

Problems with other partners—the British

As suggested earlier, the return of a Labour Government after the 1974 British general elections raised a new and hitherto untackled problem in Community relations, that of renegotiation.[28] The issue was to prove both time-consuming and

[26] See Leigh, 'Giscard and the European Community'; Julian Crandall Hollick, 'France under Giscard d'Estaing—a retrospect', *The World Today* (June 1981); R. E. M. Irving, 'The European Policy of the French and Italian Communists', *International Affairs* (July 1977), 419–20; Pickles, *French Contemporary Politics*, 21–2.

[27] On this theme, see Pickles, 87–8; *Frankfurter Allgemeine Zeitung*, 7 July 1977; *Le Monde*, 7 July 1977.

[28] On this theme, see, Simon Z. Young, 'Britain and the Community: the meaning of renegotiation', *The World Today* (Sept. 1974); John Pinder, 'Renegotiation: Britain's costly lesson?', *International Affairs* (Apr 1975); Pickles, *Contemporary French Politics*, 81.

contentious. Gradually, there was to develop a Franco-German understanding on the subject, and a strengthening of bilateral bonds in close proportion to the decline in relations with the British. The United Kingdom's size and economic and political importance meant that it would always retain a major say in Community policy-making. But the difficulties posed by renegotiation, combined with signs of British intransigence and demands for special treatment, resulted in a gradual deterioration in London's relations with its major European partners after 1974. As Jobert tartly observed, while Heath was 'a man of the Rhine', Wilson 'is a man of the Scilly Isles'.[29] This British introspection, combined with the country's economic difficulties, was to cause the progressive replacement of the developing trilateral model of Community leadership familiar from the Brandt–Pompidou era with a bilateral mould based squarely on France and Germany.

The positions adopted on renegotiation in the interval between Britain's first presentation of its case in June 1974 and the December Paris summit were only to alter slightly in the weeks of talks ahead. Throughout, Bonn and Paris were London's major interlocutors. Yet while the French appeared unsympathetic from the outset, the Germans adopted a far more pragmatic line. Why Paris should have been so inflexible from so early a stage is hard to tell. French views were highly complex; the need for rigorous observance of the rules of membership was the reason most frequently cited. Yet this explanation veiled deeper and more established concerns, comprising fears for the CAP, which the British wanted to see reformed, and wider political worries about possible British plans for a dilution of the Community's international role. Just as important were questions of cost. Britain's demands focused on the excessive size of its budget contribution. It was here that the French were adamant, their opposition based chiefly on the desire to avoid any unnecessary call on their exchequer. It is striking how closely this adversarial pattern between London and Paris has been repeated in subsequent budgetary disputes. The upshot has generally been to reinforce Franco-German co-operation and to impede any meaningful British intervention.

[29] Quoted in *The Economist*, 24 Jan. 1976.

As for the Germans, the role of go-between adopted by Bonn paradoxically reflected both the country's strengths and weaknesses. The fact that Germany, as the Community's major economic power, would have to end up paying the lion's share of any budgetary compromise was another acknowledgement of its economic prowess. Yet that Bonn was so anxious to bring about a settlement also illustrated its continuing concern to avoid unnecessary friction in Community relations, from which it had nothing to gain. Thus, beneath Bonn's concern to resolve the renegotiation dispute lay a continuing dependence on a smooth functioning Community. This requirement was steadily diminishing under Schmidt, but it certainly remained in play during the renegotiation period. Naturally, other factors were also involved. The Germans were sympathetic to the British case on its merits, and they also wished to show some solidarity towards a fellow Socialist government, whose membership of the EEC they were keen to preserve.[30]

All these influences coalesced in the considerable personal role played by Schmidt in helping to solve what was principally an Anglo-French dispute. It was on the Chancellor's advice that Wilson visited Giscard shortly before the Paris summit to discuss the British case. Schmidt was particularly well placed to intercede in this way. He was both conversant with the French position and also sympathetic to the British stand. However, this active German diplomacy did not make a solution a foregone conclusion. In fact, the outcome of the Paris summit seemed a good deal less certain than French acceptance of British membership at The Hague back in 1969. What the Germans did achieve was to bring the opposing parties closer together, perhaps easing the way by giving some preliminary indication of their readiness to help restructure the budget. Thus the Community leaders eventually agreed in Paris to set up a 'correcting mechanism' to iron out irregularities in Britain's contribution. Even this concession, however, was hard fought, with a lengthy Anglo-French wrangle over the wording of the final communiqué. Yet the net result was that Britain gained recognition for its budgetary anomaly, an outcome in which German help had played a major part.

[30] Note e.g. Schmidt's speech before the Labour Party Conference, reported in *The Economist*, 4 Dec. 1974.

This pattern of German moderation compared to French rigidity was based on a fundamental difference of perceptions. Whereas Bonn was genuinely worried about the possibility of British withdrawal from the Community, the French seemed less concerned. There is no reason to believe that Giscard actively wanted British withdrawal. The reasons in favour of continued participation still by far outweighed those for encouraging London's departure. Yet there were obviously very strict limits to the extent of French flexibility. It was this restricted room for manœuvre which was explored at the European Council meeting in Dublin in March 1975—the first of its kind. Major changes to the CAP were out of the question as far as the French were concerned. Hence the compromise struck on this area of the British demands was of necessity vague. The CAP was already in some turmoil, and Britain's wishes were satisfied by the agreement to organize a further review of the policy's operations.[31] On the budgetary side, it was the Germans who filled the breach, and although Giscard might have been unhappy about some of the concessions made in this field, he clearly did not view the issue as sufficiently serious to warrant blocking the deal. Hence the renegotiation issue was finally settled, largely thanks to Franco-German compliance.

Although the dispute over renegotiation caused friction between Britain and its European partners, it was not the sole cause for the realignment in the pattern of relations between Bonn, Paris, and London under way in the mid-1970s. This was a slower process, in which renegotiation was a major, but by no means solitary, influence. While the referendum of June 1975 finally settled the question of the United Kingdom's membership of the Community, a series of problems, small in themselves but cumulative in effect, led to a further deterioration in relations with France and to a growing sense of frustration among the Germans. The upshot of these developments was to be a gradual Franco-German re-evaluation of London as a viable partner, and a further strengthening of bilateral bonds as a result.

The first of these contributory incidents concerned the British

---

[31] For the difficulties facing the CAP and the intrusion of the British element, see Trevor Parfitt, 'CAP—beginning to take stock', *The World Today* (Nov. 1974), and 'Keeping the CAP on', *The World Today* (Mar. 1975).

demand for separate representation as an oil producer at the Paris energy conference. This desire for independence caused a marked rift at the European Council meeting of December 1975.[32] The Germans in particular were irritated by the British move. To their eyes, the lengthy wrangle that ensued was not only a distraction from more pressing economic issues, but also a confirmation of London's lack of Community spirit. This was especially galling in view of the efforts Bonn, above all Schmidt himself, had taken over renegotiation. Thus the Chancellor was reported to be extremely angry with the British.[33]

Although there were widespread expectations that matters would improve under Wilson's successor, Callaghan, such feelings were to be short-lived. Problems with London persisted, being concentrated in the British presidency of 1977.[34] Various issues were involved. These included differences over agricultural prices and fishing policy,[35] doubts about Britain's commitment to the timetable for direct elections, a protracted dispute with the Germans over the site for the Joint European Torus project, and the beginnings of renewed trouble over the budget. Finally, there was the broader question of Britain's handling of the presidency itself. There were accusations of too partisan an attitude, with much of the criticism falling squarely on John Silkin, the Minister of Agriculture.[36] The upshot of all these differences was threefold: to cause general disenchantment with Britain's European policy and commitment to the Community; to create additional antagonisms, particularly amongst the Germans, who were growing increasingly exasperated with their British partners; and finally, and most important, to contribute to a tightening of Franco-German links as a result of this shared dissatisfaction.[37]

[32] See *The Economist*, 6 Dec. 1975. For Franco-British differences, see Neville Waites, 'Britain and France: towards a stable relationship', *The World Today* (Dec. 1976), 454–5.

[33] See *The Economist*, 6 Dec. 1975.

[34] For a good survey of the British presidency, see Geoffrey Edwards and Helen Wallace, 'EEC: the British Presidency in retrospect', *The World Today* (Aug. 1977).

[35] On agricultural difficulties, see Trevor Parfitt, 'Bad blood in Brussels', *The World Today* (Jun 1977). On fishing, see Angelika Volle and William Wallace, 'How common a fisheries policy?', *The World Today* (Feb. 1977).

[36] Note the comments in Parfitt, 'Bad blood in Brussels', 206, and Edwards and Wallace, 285.

[37] See, for instance, the suggestions in *Le Monde*, 4 Feb. 1977.

Relations with other partners—the Americans

It was not only differences with the British that brought Bonn and Paris closer together in the mid-1970s. Difficulties in relations with the United States provided almost as strong a motive for greater bilateral co-operation. As will be seen in the next chapter, the prime cause was monetary. Yet other influences were also involved. There were profound uncertainties on the political front regarding Carter's foreign policy, particularly towards the Soviet Union and human rights. Both issues came to a head in 1977. At the impromptu dinner meeting between Schmidt and Giscard in July that year, the Administration's emphasis on human rights in its Eastern policy formed a major theme. While the French and German leaders were sympathetic to the moral questions involved, they were both extremely concerned about the political dangers to *détente* inherent in Carter's approach. It is striking how consistent this fear has been in European attitudes to American policy, a result of differing degrees of vulnerability to the Soviet Union. Such divergences have reached a peak under Ronald Reagan.

Both Schmidt and Giscard had been highly critical of Carter's stand on human rights. The Chancellor's low estimation of the American President was one of the open secrets of contemporary international diplomacy, while Giscard for his part had publicly accused Carter of jeopardizing *détente*.[38] Rather than the counter-productive American method of frontal attack, the French President had counselled a strategy of secret contacts. Such shared Franco-German anxieties over *détente* were instrumental in helping to cement the rapport between Schmidt and Giscard. Hence the two leaders carefully co-ordinated their positions on the issue in order to present a united front towards the White House. Yet, with the benefit of hindsight, one cannot help but feel a certain irony in their complaints about Carter's policy. In comparison with the Reagan Administration's much more bellicose approach, Carter's moralistic stand appears less alarming.

The second major issue upsetting relations between France, Germany, and the United States was that of civilian nuclear

[38] The interview was carried in *Newsweek*, 23 July 1977. See also the substantial reports in *The Times*, 18 July 1977, and the *Financial Times*, 19 July 1977.

technology exports.[39] The problem had first arisen in 1975, when the Americans had shown disapproval for a comprehensive German contract to sell nuclear equipment to Brazil. It was only in 1977, however, that matters grew more serious. Concerned to minimize proliferation (and, it was felt on the German side, to protect commercial monopolies) the Carter Administration had decided in September 1976 to suspend sales of enriched uranium to France and Germany on account of the Brazilian deal and a similar French nuclear contract with Pakistan. According to the Americans, neither arrangement had adequate safeguards against military exploitation of the technology on offer.

Both the French and German Governments responded angrily to the decision, seen as an unnecessary interference in their trading policies. Reflecting this joint concern, discussion on nuclear exports formed a central topic at the bilateral summit of February 1977. Yet although the two countries' views were similar, they were not identical at this stage. Contrary to the usual picture, it was Paris which was more responsive to the American position than Bonn. The French had already bowed to American pressure in December 1976 and agreed to suspend sales of reprocessing plants on completion of their contract with Pakistan. There were even suggestions that the French themselves were uneasy about the German decision to sell Brazil a similar facility, though on what grounds it is hard to tell, considering that this type of plant had formed part of France's own deal with Pakistan.[40]

Despite these differences, the American uranium embargo did much to coalesce French and German views. There were shared objections to the moratorium, and a strong joint commitment to the rights of developing countries to acquire nuclear technology for peaceful purposes.[41] The scope for French and German firms in supplying such equipment was an unspoken theme. Although the Germans gave no commitment to suspending sales of reprocessing plants, the two sides found much common ground. Most notably, in stating their respect for the dangers of proliferation while at the same time emphasizing the right of

[39] On this theme, see the article by Karl Kaiser, 'The Great Nuclear Debate: German American Disagreements', *Foreign Policy* 30, (Spring 1978).
[40] See report in *Le Monde*, 5 Feb. 1977.
[41] Franco-German joint communiqué, reprinted in *Le Monde*, 6–7 Feb. 1977.

states to acquire nuclear technology for civilian use Bonn and Paris were able to show solidarity with Washington while simultaneously indicating their joint readiness to act independently if necessary.

This determination should be seen as an important symbol of tightening bilateral bonds in the mid-1970s. As in the past, it also provided a clear demonstration of the integrative function of external pressure under certain circumstances. The joint statement was particularly significant on the German side, where it testified to the more critical and autonomous line now being pursued by Schmidt *vis-à-vis* Washington. The Germans had steadfastly refused to cancel their contract with Brazil in deference to Carter's wishes. This firmness coincided with a growing appreciation of the value of closer co-operation with the French. Giscard's own greater pragmatism in international affairs formed the major influence here, making bilateral collaboration considerably more practicable than in the past. There is little doubt that the understanding reached on nuclear policy was an important step in this process. Certainly, as far as the bilateral summit of February 1977 was concerned, the nuclear agreement, in conjunction with that reached on closer economic co-ordination, marked an important stage in the developing Franco-German *rapprochement* under Schmidt and Giscard.

French and German views on nuclear exports were to become even more closely aligned by June 1977. This resulted from Bonn's unexpected decision to follow the French lead and suspend sales of reprocessing plants upon completion of the Brazilian deal. It is hard to pinpoint the exact causes behind this step. American pressure had certainly played a part. Yet the timing of the German announcement to coincide with a bilateral Franco-German summit strongly suggested the influence of other factors, such as wanting to offer an explicit signal to the French regarding the value of close co-operation.[42] Bonn's move could reasonably be seen as the logical consequence of the official dialogue on nuclear policy that had been set up following the previous bilateral meeting. The fact that the meeting of

[42] It is worth noting, however, that the Bonn correspondent of one French newspaper took a more cynical view, associating the timing of the German shift principally with domestic considerations. See *Le Monde*, 19–20 June 1977.

June 1977 also marked the thirtieth Franco-German summit may also have provided a symbolic influence. Whatever the reason, Bonn and Paris were now following identical paths on nuclear sales. Although they had acknowledged American wishes, neither government had in the end succumbed and abandoned its existing contracts. Both had demonstrated their independence and had gained from each other's support. As will be seen, this pattern would continue into the next phase of the Schmidt–Giscard era, when all the influences already experienced, notably monetary policy and relations with Britain and the United States, would further work to strengthen bilateral bonds.

10

The Schmidt–Giscard Years—
Progress Restored
1977–1981

Introduction

It was in the period after 1977 that co-operation between Paris and Bonn reached its zenith and talk of a Franco-German 'axis' in Europe became most commonplace.[1] The reasons for this situation were manifold. They arose partly out of developments already seen, and partly out of new factors. Of the latter the rise of closer monetary co-operation, culminating in the creation of the European Monetary System, was the prime example.

Bilateral co-operation was almost equally evident in the other main areas of Community activity. On economic policy, French and German views remained closely aligned. Considerable progress was also made on direct elections and enlargement. Furthermore, Bonn and Paris once more played a key role in the dispute over Britain's budget contribution, which resurfaced after 1979. It should be remembered, though, that their views on this topic were not always to be wholly convergent. In fact, on the budget, the positions of other member states, notably the Dutch, marked an important extra dimension. International affairs too, and East–West relations in particular, were also more complex. The events in Afghanistan and Poland at the end of the decade put new pressures on Bonn and Paris, exposing differences of perception and necessitating compromises. As will be seen, not all issues were adequately resolved by the end of the Schmidt–Giscard period.

The exigencies of domestic politics also began to leave a bigger mark. The Social Democratic–Liberal coalition in Bonn survived the 1976 legislative elections and went on to win a comfortable majority in 1980. Yet in France Giscard's foreign

---

[1] See, for instance, Simonian, 'France, Germany and Europe'.

policy was to become increasingly affected by the aptly named 'permanent election campaign' that developed between the 1978 legislative elections and the presidential contest three years later.[2] These domestic concerns would intrude into bilateral relations, and create additional strains.

Economic policy

Continuity was to be the keynote of both Franco-German and Community economic policy in the later 1970s. Although there was some improvement in trading conditions compared to the situation a few years earlier, the second oil crisis of 1979 once again created turmoil. None the less, certain themes remained constant. Principally, the close alignment of French and German economic policies continued much as before. At the bilateral summit of February 1978, for instance, there was talk of the 'greatest parallelism' between the two countries, and of steps towards even closer co-ordination in the future.[3] Probably the best example of such co-operation came in the announcement on April 1981 of a joint Franco-German scheme to raise some £2,700 million in order to help modernize the two countries' economies. The venture highlighted the like-minded approaches being pursued in Bonn and Paris.

Yet such collaboration was not without its problems. These stemmed not so much from the governmental side as from internal political manœuvrings in France. Close co-operation with the Germans had long been an object of irritation for many politicians of the extreme left and right, whose feelings were largely based on traditional animosities. In the lengthy prelude to the presidential elections, the ranks of this group swelled to include more centrist members of the Opposition and even some Gaullists. It was not so much Giscard's close relationship with the Chancellor that came under fire as Barre's unpopular economic policies, which were widely identified with the Federal Republic. Hence the frequent accusations of imported German ideas and subservience to Bonn. Chirac's attack on the President in December 1978 provided a good example of this trend, with

[2] On this concept, see Pickles, *Contemporary French Politics*, 14–26; Frears, *France in the Giscard Presidency*, 51–2.
[3] See Ludlow, 198.

the former Prime Minister going so far as to dub Giscard leader of the 'parti de l'étranger'.[4]

Such pronouncements would have cut less ice had Barre's economic policies been more popular and more tangibly successful. One must, in fact, question how well suited his measures actually were to the French model. That emulation of the Federal Republic lay behind the Government's programme was undeniable. The Barre plan of 1976 was designed to reduce inflation and the level of state subsidies by means of tight monetary controls and an end to deficit spending. The removal of price controls in 1978 and steps to reduce the Government's role in industry marked a similar attempt to transpose German economic methods to France. For many observers, however, such efforts were only partially successful. While the balance of payments certainly remained stable, monetary targets were not met and inflation stayed persistently above German levels. Nor, for that matter, did much of domestic industry adequately respond to the challenge of greater competition offered by the Government. These findings were well catalogued in the OECD's annual reports of the later 1970s.[5]

Despite such failings, it can be argued with the benefit of hindsight that Barre's record was actually a good deal more positive than many of his critics maintained. Even if not wholly successful, the Premier's tough economic measures did at least manage to preserve the level of activity during a very difficult period. The value of the franc was upheld, and growth also preserved. The contrast with the early phase of Socialist rule is striking, when both inflation and unemployment soared. Thus, although some of Giscard's detractors might have exploited the 'Germanic' nature of French economic policy for political purposes, the fact remains that the measures adopted, even if unpopular, were instrumental in preventing a serious decline in the French economy. By way of contrast, it is instructive to note the successive bouts of—appreciably less popular—austerity measures that the Socialist Government has gradually been forced to introduce.

---

[4] Quoted in Frears, *France in the Giscard Presidency*, 59.
[5] See e.g. *France* (Paris, OECD, February 1979), 52–4, and *France* (Paris, OECD, May 1980), 52–6, 67–9.

As for the Federal Republic, the later 1970s were a period of continuity, confirming earlier trends. Principally, there was further evidence, should any be required, of the country's economic pre-eminence. Just as earlier in the decade, other Western powers continued to look to the Germans to provide a lead in reflating their economy. At the Western economic summit of July 1978, for instance, this course was once again strongly advocated by the Americans. Yet, as before, it was vehemently resisted by the Germans on mixed grounds of provoking inflation and, a newer motif, the argument that Bonn had already done all it could. The greater publicity given to the latter view could be taken to represent both a growing exasperation in Bonn with the demands of its partners and a greater readiness now to voice this feeling.

Even more telling an indication of the Federal Republic's economic strength, and this asset's transition into a stronger political posture, was the 1979 Guadeloupe summit. For many observers, German participation at this meeting alongside France, Britain, and the United States set the seal on the country's political coming of age. Although Schmidt sought to play down the occasion, it undoubtedly represented a milestone for the Germans, marking not only international recognition for their growing place in world affairs, but also (in a nice touch) providing an opportunity for them to sit for the first time as equals in the West's highest political counsel alongside their former occupying powers.

Monetary policy

It was undoubtedly in the monetary field that bilateral Franco-German co-operation was most evident in the later 1970s. Above all, the birth of the European Monetary System in July 1978 came of a clear convergence of French and German interests, confirming the two countries' leading roles in the Community. The venture would never have been possible without joint Franco-German agreement. Nor, for that matter, would progress have been so rapid had it not been for the close personal relationship between Schmidt and Giscard, which permitted easy mutual access and a greater facility for overcoming domestic obstacles.

The complex background to the EMS has been well covered in

the literature.[6] The present account will accordingly concentrate on the specifically Franco-German dimension. Earlier chapters have shown how existing economic divergences, exacerbated by the first oil crisis, combined with institutional problems to scupper EMU. Yet interest in closer European economic and monetary co-operation did not end there. Rather, it featured in a number of authoritative reports in the mid-1970s.[7] As with EMU, both economic and political aims were involved. The growing level of intra-Community trade made co-ordinated European economic and monetary measures obviously more sensible than purely national actions. Furthermore, as in the past, closer monetary links were also seen as a way of boosting the Community's flagging political cohesion, already damaged by the differing economic remedies being followed by the member states. Yet it should be noted that none of the ideas now put forward envisaged the sort of master plan originally intended in the Werner Report. Both the benefit of experience and the unpropitious economic circumstances meant that whatever new policies were adopted would of necessity be of a gradualist and highly pragmatic nature.

This was the background to the discussions on closer Community monetary links that took place in 1977. Giscard made a major political move when, at the end of January, he reaffirmed the decisive role he felt EMU should play in European integration, and he called for a special European Council meeting at the end of the year to discuss steps towards its revival.[8] A number of factors underscored this enthusiasm. The President was known to have been keen on the idea of creating a European zone of monetary stability for some time, for reasons that were not dissimilar to those which had motivated Pompidou back in 1969. Even more important, however, Giscard felt that by linking the franc to stronger

---

[6] On the EMS see above all Ludlow, *The Making of the European Monetary System*. See also Geoffrey Denton, 'European monetary co-operation: the Bremen proposals', *The World Today* (Nov. 1978); Jocelyn Statler, 'The European Monetary System: From conception to birth', *International Affairs* (Apr. 1979); Paul Taylor, 'Interdependence and autonomy in the European Communities: The case of the European Monetary System', *JCMS* (June 1980) Tsoukalis, 'Economic and Monetary Union', gives a good idea of the background.

[7] For details, see Ludlow, 3–4; Denton, 437–8.

[8] *Le Monde*, 30–1 Jan. 1977.

currencies like the Deutschemark French inflation could be kept in check. This was one illustration of the President's wider philosophy that France's economy could emulate that of Germany and benefit from greater exposure to it. As in the past, anxiety about the Federal Republic's elevation to the first rank of world economic powers may also have played a part.[9] Improving monetary links would not only strengthen the bonds between the French and German economies, but also bind the Federal Republic more closely to Europe.

While the French position was understandable, the fact that Schmidt had not dismissed Giscard's ideas out of hand was more surprising. Both the Bundesbank and the Ministry of Finance retained their traditional opposition towards any schemes that might tie down the value of the currency and consequently constrain the use of exchange rate policy as a means of maintaining internal stability. Schmidt himself had opposed the suggestions for economic and monetary progress set out in the Tindemans Report. Unfortunately, deference towards Giscard's views is the most satisfactory explanation that can be given for the Chancellor's indulgence, failing any more substantial evidence.

It was astounding, therefore, that by the time of Schmidt's meeting with the President at Rambouillet on 2 April 1978 he had come to adopt a far more positive approach to new monetary measures. This new interest emerged more fully at the European Council meeting in Copenhagen a few days later, when the Chancellor unveiled an ambitious plan for closer European monetary links. A large number of factors were responsible for Schmidt's change of heart, which was extraordinary in view of his former position. It should be stressed, however, that the initiative at this stage was very much the Chancellor's own.[10] Matters had not been co-ordinated with the Cabinet or bureaucracy, and major difficulties with both the Bundesbank and the Ministry of Finance were to follow.

Pre-eminent among the Chancellor's motives was the state of

---

[9] See Tsoukalis, 'Economic and Monetary Union', 246.

[10] See Ludlow, 92. Both this author, 17–18, and Edwards and Wallace 'Germany in the chair', 4, also draw a connection between the EMS initiative and the German presidency of the Council in the second half of 1978.

relations with the United States. The heavy fall in the value of the dollar between 1977 and 1978 had given rise to great unease in the Federal Republic.[11] Matters were exacerbated by the profound doubts about the Carter Administration's willingness and ability to reverse the slide. As in the early 1970s, the Deutschemark was once again the most attractive refuge for funds coming out of the United States. Thus, not only did the declining dollar hamper German exports to America, but, by upsetting parity relationships within the Snake itself, it also threatened the monetary stability on which much of Germany's European trade was based. Furthermore, again just as in the early 1970s, differing speculative pressure on the currencies of the Nine worsened existing economic and monetary divisions. There was also a wider question of uncertainty. Despite determined American attempts to restore stability in December 1977 and January 1978, the dollar had again begun to tumble by February. With no sign of an end to the unrest, the Chancellor had obviously become more receptive to new ideas. Finally, there was the strong desire, for both economic and political reasons, to prevent the Deutschemark from turning into a reserve currency, a trend that was already well under way.[12]

Wider economic and political forces also played a part. Again, problems with the United States predominated. The frictions that had arisen in relations with Carter have already been described. As has been seen, these were influential in altering Schmidt's perceptions and bringing him round towards a more European and less Atlanticist approach. German resentment at the pressure being brought to bear to reflate the economy was also instrumental. The Americans (and some Europeans too) were seen as the major culprits here. There was a strong sense in Bonn that Washington, as in the past, was tending to disown responsibility for the economic crisis and failing to put its own house in order. At the same time, however, the need for some German response to the external pressure was also understood. Thus, as relations with the United States became more difficult,

[11] On American monetary policy, see Miles Kahler, 'America's Foreign Economic Policy: Is The Old-Time Religion Good Enough?', *International Affairs* (Summer 1980). For an alternative view, see T. de Vries, 'Saving the dollar', *The World Today* (Jan. 1979).

[12] On this theme, see *The Economist*, 15 July 1978; Ludlow, 8.

so co-operation with France appeared more attractive and the idea for a new European monetary initiative gained weight in Schmidt's mind.

Certain European factors were also responsible. As with EMU, the arguments for the Federal Republic's participation in closer monetary integration were by no means wholly negative. The Snake had worked well for the Germans, helping to maintain some stability in parity relationships and thus benefiting trade. Extending the scheme might provide an additional boost to German exports. Furthermore, tightening monetary links might also help to guard the Federal Republic from imported inflation, while restricting the use of devaluation policy would increase pressure on economically weaker member states to pursue less expansionist economic policies. These were persuasive arguments on the Chancellor.

All these factors had coalesced by the time of Schmidt's meeting with Giscard on 2 April 1978. Matters were additionally helped by the removal of certain internal obstacles.[13] Principally, the French Government's survival in the legislative elections on Mary 1978 had lifted a major barrier for Giscard. Thus the way was now clear for a joint Franco-German impetus. This bilateral role, which would become increasingly prominent in the following months, was already evident in the timing of the Franco-German meeting, which had been deliberately scheduled in preparation for the European Council session shortly after. Schmidt and Giscard now put the finishing touches on the Chancellor's monetary proposals and carefully co-ordinated their positions. This close co-operation was entertainingly illustrated in Giscard's reported reply to a question about the new monetary scheme's parentage. Quoting Napoleon, the President remarked: 'En matière de paternité, Monsieur, il n'y a que des hypothèses.'[14] Though principally German in origin, the EMS could not have progressed without French inspiration, nor, for that matter, without a final spell of grooming in France.

In the round of open and secret negotiations that followed the meeting of April 1978, the role of bilateral co-operation was to become paramount. This was particularly true as the British

---

[13] For the German side, see Ludlow, 77–80.
[14] Ludlow, 98.

increasingly cooled to Schmidt's ideas. As is observed of the secret tripartite talks established after the European Council meeting, 'Indeed, much of the significance of this episode lies precisely in the fact that it undermined a serious effort to create a directorate of three and confirmed a tendency, which was already strong, towards a directorate of two.'[15] By the time of the meeting between Schmidt and Giscard on 24 June 1978, this bilateral function had clarified. Any further progress from here would have to come from France and Germany, the British having effectively removed themselves from the debate.

As had occured before the European Council session of April 1978, so the June meeting between Schmidt and Giscard in Hamburg opportunely preceded the full European Council in Bremen the following month. Once again, the timing of the bilateral meeting was deliberately designed to smooth the way to full Community agreement. The French and German leaders discussed a document on monetary co-operation prepared by their representatives in the secret talks. This in turn formed the basis for the proposals put forward by Schmidt in Bremen.[16] Unremarkably, the overwhelming evidence now of a guiding Franco-German duopoly created some antagonism among the other member states. Yet although there were strong objections to the secret discussions (notably those including the British too) that had earlier taken place, such complaints were overcome by the importance of the proposals being put forward.[17] This uneasy compromise between opposition to Franco-German co-ordination and understanding of its value has been a consistent policy characteristic especially amongst more European-minded member states like the Benelux countries.

The Bremen summit accepted almost every aspect of the proposals that had been agreed between Schmidt and Giscard. Even the ambitious timetable, which envisaged a final decision being reached on the EMS by December, was approved. There now followed detailed discussions between expert groups. Yet even against this background of open negotiations at Community level, it was not long before attention shifted back to the

[15] Ibid. 105.
[16] See *The Economist*, 15 July 1978; Ludlow, 126–7.
[17] On this theme, note *The Economist*, 15 July 1978; Ludlow, 112–15.

Franco-German side. This was as a result of the differences that had arisen between the Nine on the detailed question of operating the EMS. Two rival schemes had been put forward: a parity grid system, supported by the Germans; and a basket method, backed by the French. The former appeared advantageous to the Bundesbank in particular as it would spread the burden of intervention for any rise in the Deutschemark's value between all the participating countries. Under the basket scheme, by contrast, the burden of intervention would fall more squarely on the authorities in the country whose currency had moved out of line. Hence, in the case of upward pressure on the Deutschemark, the Bundesbank would be obliged to intervene much more strongly, with consequent dangers of stimulating inflation. As it had been the mark which had most regularly deviated in the Snake, it was precisely for this reason that the French preferred the basket system, laying responsibility for controlling changes principally on the Bundesbank.

Only at the Franco-German summit in Aachen on 14–15 September 1978 was this division, along with a number of other technical differences, finally resolved. The breakthrough came as a result of a French change of heart, with Paris now deciding to back the parity grid. The reason for the shift was simple, namely a growing awareness that the basket scheme as it stood might be technically unfeasible. The joint agreement reached in Aachen was significant for a number of reasons. Most obviously, it once again underlined the role of Franco-German co-operation as a vital element in wider Community accord. As in January 1971 and February 1972, when bilateral discussions on EMU had cleared outstanding obstacles, so in September 1978 the decision by Schmidt and Giscard to present a joint paper on the EMS to the forthcoming meeting of Community finance ministers removed a number of serious barriers to the new monetary venture.

Two other aspects of the agreement were also of note. First of all, the outcome of the meeting once more testified to the close personal relationship between Schmidt and Giscard. This was probably at its height at this stage, with major differences yet to come. There is no doubt that the friendship between the two leaders played a substantial part, not just in the birth of the EMS, but also in the smooth and rapid pace of subsequent negotiations. Secondly, both leaders alluded to the symbolic role of Aachen as the venue for their meeting. Though the location of the summit was hardly the major cause for the accord that was reached, it undoubtedly played an incidental part. Both sides made much of Charlemagne and of the city's role as a common link in their history and culture. There were even overtones of an earlier Franco-German meeting in a cathedral city—that between de Gaulle and Adenauer in Rheims in 1962, when the bilateral treaty of friendship between the two countries had been sealed. Though circumstantial, such echoes should not be underestimated, and they certainly worked in favour of a breakthrough at Aachen.

Against this background of close bilateral co-operation, reaffirmed at an unscheduled Schmidt–Giscard meeting at the beginning of November, it is surprising how swiftly and unexpectedly differences on the EMS sprang up. Though originally intended as the venue to finalize arrangements for the scheme, the European Council meeting in Brussels on 4–5 December 1978 was instead the occasion for a testy confrontation.[18] It is not easy to unravel the large number of separate strands that had become interlaced by this stage. To put it most concisely, the dispute revolved round two main themes: the size and distribution of resources from richer to poorer member states that was to accompany the EMS; and the outwardly unconnected but technically linked question of the future of MCAs. In both areas, matters were greatly exacerbated by Giscard's preoccupation with domestic politics, with the result that the President adopted a highly inflexible line.

These domestic considerations were most evident in Giscard's stand on MCAs. There had been growing objections in France to the benefits which certain countries, notably the Federal Republic, had derived from the CAP as a result of the agri-money system. These had been accompanied by a new bout of agricultural unrest in late 1978. Under the circumstances, the President very much wanted to be seen to be putting French farmers' interests to the fore. Such an approach would also rob Gaullist critics, and notably Chirac, who had long courted the agricultural constituency, of a powerful weapon, which had been brought increasingly into play in the slow prelude to the following year's European elections. Hence Giscard's insistence at the European Council meeting that the Nine should use the introduction of the EMS as an opportunity to start dismantling MCAs, and his decision to make this a precondition for French agreement to the scheme.

Whereas the French stand on MCAs was more in the order of a domestic symbol and a negotiating ploy, to be likened to similar moves by Pompidou in the past (or Mitterrand in the future), Giscard's line on the question of transferring resources to Italy or Ireland was much more serious. Two major influences were at work here. First, there was a fundamental French reluctance, for purely budgetary reasons, to offer the two countries anything like the sums they wanted. Secondly, domestic factors worked to reinforce this stand. With the issue of direct elections and French sovereignty becoming increasingly sensitive, Giscard did not wish to accede to any measure which would appear to give way to a concurrent campaign by the European Parliament to increase the size of the regional fund. As greater regional spending was one of the means whereby resources were to be transferred to Italy and Ireland, the two issues became interwoven.

Despite strenuous efforts by Schmidt to bridge the differences between the French, Italians, and Irish, the Brussels summit eventually broke down in disagreement. Only after a new offer—led, it should be noted, by the Germans—did the Irish finally agree to participate in the EMS. The Italians, for their part, acceded soon after. However, with no solution to the MCA dispute in sight, the EMS remained stalled. Perhaps the pattern had become so familiar that the absence of any last-minute intervention by Schmidt and Giscard in itself caused some surprise.[19]

Unlike the Aachen meeting, the Franco-German summit of 22–3 February 1979 proved unable to resolve bilateral differences. Giscard still appeared sufficiently swayed by domestic considerations to remain unwilling to sanction the EMS.[20] Hence

---

[19] Note the comments in Ludlow, 279.

[20] On the limited discussions on the EMS at the bilateral summit of Feb. 1979, see reports in *Le Monde*, 24 Feb. 1979, and 25–6 Feb. 1979.

the bilateral summit was a far cry from its predecessor. Neither side seemed at all keen to broach the subject of MCAs, and indeed, both countries were at pains to emphasize the Community nature of the problem. Considering how little this had intruded on discussions in the past, such delicacy undoubtedly indicated a joint assessment that raising the issue would not be advisable at this stage. The Germans, well aware of Giscard's domestic political difficulties, most likely felt it best to let matters rest for the time being. This relaxed approach was indicated by the suggestions from Bonn that a solution might not even be found before the European elections in June.[21]

Despite such a long-term approach, the eventual resolution of the MCA dispute was as sudden as its onset. At the Community farm ministers' meeting on 5–6 March 1979, the French unexpectedly backed down, for reasons that remain unclear. Perhaps Giscard felt that he had made his point, and that further obstruction would now be disadvantageous. Whatever the motives, the removal of French opposition meant that the EMS could begin operations on 13 March 1979, two and a half months late.

Even the dispute which had held up the system's inauguration had had its roots in a predominantly Franco-German disagreement. In fact, the clash between the two countries' farm ministers at the decisive Council meeting on 17–18 December 1978 harked back evocatively to earlier arguments over MCAs in the Brandt–Pompidou era. Yet despite the scheme's delayed start, its subsequent course has confirmed the central Franco-German role. It is ironic, though, that in winter 1980–1 there should have been a marked (albeit temporary) reversal of positions, with the franc the strongest and the Deutschemark the weakest member of the EMS. As the next chapter will show, this was to be but a passing phase before the return of a more familiar pattern, reconfirmed especially after May 1981.

Energy policy

Energy issues had subsided as a topic of discussion at Franco-German level in the mid-1970s, reflecting the measure of stability that had returned to the oil market by this period. Yet

---

[21] The comment was made by Lambsdorff and was reported in *Le Monde*, 22 Feb. 1979.

the revolution in Iran and the second oil crisis of 1979 led to a swift reversal. In contrast to the situation after 1973, however, the later crisis witnessed a much more united Franco-German approach.[22] The prime contributor to this was the evolution in French thinking under Giscard already noted in the previous chapter. In the face of reduced supplies and substantial price increases, Paris was to figure amongst those capitals most determined to adopt a co-ordinated international strategy. The contrast with thinking in 1973–4 could hardly have been more striking. A number of factors were responsible. Pre-eminent was Giscard's greater pragmatism and appreciation of Western economic interdependence. Unlike his predecessor, the President was well aware that France could not isolate itself from the consequences of energy decisions made elsewhere, nor from the wider influence of international demand and supply, irrespective of any attempts to strike selective bilateral deals. The limited success of the Paris North–South conference and the Euro–Arab dialogue may well have consolidated such feelings.

Ironically, it was the Germans who had if anything shifted slightly from their former enthusiasm for wide-ranging international co-operation on oil. Though by no means opposing such arrangements, Bonn had come to place rather more emphasis on bureaucratic and *dirigiste* drawbacks than in the past. The Federal Republic had undoubtedly also gained confidence in its own ability to act more independently thanks to its economic strength and thus make its own arrangements.

Yet such developments only occasionally marred bilateral co-operation with the French.[23] Otherwise, examples of close co-ordination between the two sides were frequent. At the bilateral summit of February 1979 for instance, both countries were in agreement on the need to concentrate on energy at the following month's European Council session in Paris. That meeting in turn stood out for a further demonstration of the greater French flexibility on energy policy under Giscard. Though still not a member, the French agreed to the target of a five per cent

---

[22] For a good survey of French and German positions in the second oil crisis, see Robert J. Lieber, 'Europe and America in the world energy crisis', *International Affairs* (Oct. 1979).

[23] See, for instance, the differences on how interventionist an energy policy the Community should operate that emerged at the European Council meeting of June 1979, reported in *The Economist*, 30 June 1979.

reduction in oil consumption in 1979 that had been proposed by
the International Energy Agency. Bilateral co-operation was
confirmed at Barre's unexpected trip to Bonn at the beginning of
June, a visit primarily designed to allow the co-ordination of
views prior to a number of impending international exchanges.
All in all, such co-operation provided a striking contrast to the
differences of view and personal animosities that had been
witnessed during the last months of the Brandt–Pompidou era.
Most notably, the joint European stand on energy policy at the
July 1979 Tokyo economic summit stood out sharply against the
ruptures that had marred Community solidarity in Washington
in February 1974.

Community affairs

While the establishment of the EMS was undoubtedly the most
impressive feature of Franco-German co-operation in the second
half of the Schmidt–Giscard period, progress towards the
Community's second enlargement and settlement of the renewed
British budgetary dispute were also major achievements. On
enlargement, the role of France and Germany was less collaborative than independent, with the Federal Republic the most
consistent advocate of new membership in general within the
Nine, and France alternating between favouring and opposing
the claims of the three candidate nations.

The return to democracy in Greece, Spain, and Portugal in the
mid- to later 1970s was swiftly followed by energetic attempts in
the three countries to establish firmer political ties with the EEC,
ideally in the form of full membership.[24] It was not just economic
advantages that were sought, but also a wider political recognition of newly established democratic credentials and return to
the mainstream of European political practice. Certainly, it was
this aspect which featured most prominently in the assessments
made by the existing member states.

France's role in the enlargement debate was distinctly mixed.
Paris took a clear line on Greek membership, with Giscard

---

[24] On enlargement, see Loukas Tsoukalis, *The European Community and its Mediterranean
Enlargement* (London, George Allen and Unwin, 1981), especially 132–51; David Rudnick,
'Spain's long road to Europe', *The World Today* (Apr. 1976); Michael Leigh, 'Mediterra-
nean agriculture and the enlargement of the EEC', *The World Today* (June 1977).

consistently presenting himself as the country's principal partner in Europe. The President sought to maintain excellent relations with Athens, an aim greatly facilitated by the fact that Greek agriculture did not present any serious threat to the farmers in the south of France. The same could not be said of Spanish membership. Giscard's line towards Madrid was most inconsistent, marking a rare example of poor French policy coordination. Though Spanish membership was welcomed at the outset, with a belief that it would help to redress the geographical imbalance in the Community from North to South, more careful consideration of the detailed implications led to a marked reassessment. Broad geopolitical advantages increasingly gave way to detailed agricultural drawbacks, especially once the grievances of France's Mediterranean farmers began to be taken up by the Gaullist and Communist Parties.

Hence Giscard's volte-face on Spanish membership and the French Government's increasing use of delaying tactics on the issue. In early 1977, Paris began to insist on a reform of the Community's Mediterranean farm policy as a precondition for sanctioning enlargement.[25] Such a course would both delay matters and perhaps also mollify France's southern farmers by offering potential financial benefits in the future. The President also began to draw attention to the detrimental effects of enlargement for the Community's decision-making processes. In September 1978, Giscard put forward the idea of establishing a committee of 'three wise men' to consider the functioning of Community institutions after enlargement. Although such tactics failed to achieve any unified agreement by the Nine to delay new membership, they did effectively postpone consideration of the Spanish application. As will be seen, a similar approach would also be adopted by Mitterrand once he was installed as President.

The place of Portugal in French thinking was a good deal less clear. Lisbon's fate came to be bracketed with that of Madrid, although for reasons that remain uncertain, as the two countries' positions were by no means similar. Portuguese agriculture posed nothing like so great a threat to the French, while the country's underdeveloped industrial sector could hardly be said to be a

---

[25] On this topic, see Leigh, 208, and, for Giscard's arguments at the European Council meeting of July 1977, *The Economist*, 2 July 1977.

rival. Rather, political factors appeared to underlie Giscard's lack of enthusiasm for Portuguese membership. The President's limited sympathy for the Portuguese Socialists and the revolution were partly to blame, as were, perhaps, the fact that the country was perceived more as an Atlantic than a European nation and was closely associated by tradition with the United Kingdom, thereby diminishing its interest for France.

German attitudes to enlargement were much more clear cut. Bonn consistently concentrated on the political aspects of new membership, placing special weight on the idea of bolstering fledgling democracies. Almost as much emphasis was placed on the major trading advantages to be derived. It should not be forgotten that all three candidates were important German export customers. Hence, despite an increasingly critical attitude towards the size of their contribution to the Community budget, the Germans recognized and accepted the fact that they would have to carry a large part of the additional burden following enlargement.

Such an appraisal provided further acknowledgement of the Federal Republic's enhanced role in international affairs under Schmidt. Again, there was a much more coherent use of the country's economic resources as a means of securing desired political ends. Financial assistance provided the instrument to further Bonn's desire for stability and democracy in southern Europe (while such help additionally served to demonstrate the Federal Republic's own espousal of similar qualities—one aspect of a didactic streak in Germany's external stance that has been usually reserved for economic policy issues). The trend was shown in the SPD's support for Socialist parties in Spain and Portugal, and in government financial aid both to the Portuguese and especially to Turkey, where Bonn had consistently taken the lead. In both the Turkish and Spanish examples German interest was particularly strong, as political and strategic interests overlapped, with Bonn seeking to ensure Ankara's continued membership of NATO while keenly anticipating Spanish participation.

Further problems with the British

Difficulties in Britain's relations with the European Community were not to end in 1977. In fact, it was the issue of renewed budgetary differences with London that provided the third main area for Franco-German contacts in the Community in the later 1970s. It should be noted, though, that on the budget question it is more accurate to speak of a conscious French and German attempt to manage differences rather than any automatic identity of views. Bonn and Paris were obliged to co-ordinate positions in the light of the British demands, but this certainly did not mean that their preferences were always the same. Rather, the two capitals had differing reasons for maintaining the existing system. Furthermore, while the present account concentrates on the Franco-German role, it should be stressed that, on the highly complex budget issue, the views of the other member states, notably the Dutch, provided an important additional element.

Despite Britain's successful renegotiation, by early 1979 the question of the United Kingdom's budget contribution resurfaced in Community talks. As before, Schmidt and Giscard were the main agents responsible for bringing about an eventual solution. Once again, however, this was to be at the political cost to Britain of a further deterioration in its relations with Bonn and Paris. For, in the longer term, the new budgetary dispute finally removed any remaining trace of a trilaterally guided Community, and contributed instead to a further intensification of bilateral Franco-German collaboration. This arose both out of necessity and as a result of shared frustration with the British.

The 1979 budget dispute lay rooted in the failure of the 1975 'correcting mechanism' to perform as planned. Instead of removing the irregularities in Britain's budget contribution, these had increased, to the extent that Britain, the third poorest member state, was now contributing some fifty per cent of the net EEC budget.[26] The anomaly arose out of the fact that the corrective mechanism had been designed to operate in line with Britain's gross payments to the budget rather than its net position. The fact that any refunds were also linked to the country's balance of payments intensified British feelings of injustice. With North Sea oil making an increasing contribution, the size of reimbursements was likely to be limited.

Though the matter had been forcefully raised by Callaghan in

---

[26] Figure from *The Economist*, 17 Mar. 1979.

early 1979, it was only after the May general elections that differences really developed. At the Strasbourg summit of June 1979, Mrs Thatcher won both personal plaudits and some recognition for Britain's grievances. Yet it was precisely her determination which was soon to prove one of the barriers to agreement. At the December European Council meeting, by which time more detailed assessments of the British position had been made, the Prime Minister's demands for a £1,000 million rebate and frequent references to Britain's 'own money' created a great deal of ill feeling amongst the French and Germans.[27] While Schmidt in particular had a certain sympathy for the British predicament, Mrs. Thatcher's abrasive style and apparent readiness to embark on obstructionist tactics created a highly prejudicial effect.

Both Schmidt and Giscard were adamant that they could not bridge the gap between the British demand and the £350 million already offered by the other member states. Giscard made it plain that this was a final figure as far as he was concerned, while Schmidt made great play of the fact that the Federal Republic would have to bear the brunt of the additional costs involved. As in 1974–5, other Community business had to be pushed aside on account of the dispute, much to the irritation of most of the other member states, while relief at the departure of recalcitrant Labour ministers like Silkin was now replaced by an arguably even greater dissatisfaction with Mrs. Thatcher. Such attitudes reinforced existing disenchantment with the United Kingdom and probably contributed to a further tightening of Franco-German links.

Under normal circumstances, it would have been odd for the budget dispute not to have been raised at the Franco-German summit of February 1980. Yet with matters completely overshadowed by the Russian invasion of Afghanistan, this omission was less striking. Instead, discussion was postponed until Schmidt and Giscard met in Hamburg on 16 March, when the two leaders were able to co-ordinate their views on the budgetary dispute. Significantly, the talks again took place just before a European Council session. The meeting was important in a number of respects. The Chancellor had recently had talks

---

[27] On this meeting, see *The Economist*, 6 Dec. 1979.

in London, and he appeared concerned now to solve the argument as speedily as possible. The tense international atmosphere was an important influence in this apparent shift in Schmidt's position. Deeply concerned as ever about international stability, and East–West relations in particular, the Germans were keen to create the impression of a unified Community. The example is instructive; once again, in spite of its economic predominance and the development of its political standing, the Federal Republic felt more exposed than most of its European partners to wider instabilities in international relations.

In spite of German attempts to bring about a solution and a more attractive new proposal put forward by Giscard, which was in turn amended by Schmidt to suit British demands even more closely, no agreement was reached at the European Council meeting in Luxembourg in late April. What is more, matters deteriorated as debate became bogged down in the now linked questions of 1980 farm prices and the establishment of new Common Market organizations for lamb and fisheries. This aspect of the dispute is worthy of note. In the early stages of the 1980 negotiations the British sought to keep the budget isolated from the wider agricultural dispute (an association strongly sought by the French). Yet by 1982, when the budget issue resurfaced, London would be making precisely such a connection between its budgetary position and the level of new farm prices as part of its negotiating strategy.[28] Unfortunately, in neither case were the British entirely successful in their approach. The incidents offer an illustration of a deeper misguidedness that has often marred every British Government's European negotiating strategy since Heath.

Only at the end of May 1980 was a solution finally reached on the budget and the linked agricultural crises.[29] The agreement represented a traditional Community package deal, involving British concessions to France over lamb and farm prices and to Germany on fishing, in return for their accord over the budget. Throughout the crisis, the central role of Bonn and Paris had

---

[28] On this aspect of the 1980 negotiations, see Trevor Parfitt, 'The CAP: reconciling the irreconcilable', *The World Today* (Apr. 1980).

[29] For a very complete analysis, see Trevor Parfitt, 'The Budget and the CAP: A Community crisis averted', *The World Today* (Aug. 1980).

been underlined. This had been most conspicuous following the Luxembourg summit, when both Schmidt and Giscard had made patent their unwillingness to devote a third European Council meeting to the budgetary and farm problems. France and Germany were also the main sources for the additional funds required to finance the budgetary agreement. The Federal Republic in particular accepted a very large increase in its share of Community funding. This was a major concession, especially at a time of great financial stringency at home, and one which involved the Chancellor in considerable internal difficulties.

The budget was only one—albeit the largest—of a number of causes of strain in Britain's relations with its Community partners in the latter half of the Schmidt–Giscard period. The United Kingdom's failure to join the EMS and, more tellingly, its somewhat aloof attitude during the early negotiations, had caused annoyance on the German side.[30] More important, to many observers the country's self-exclusion from the system bore further witness to its ambivalent approach to Community membership. Both Labour and Conservative Governments had placed greater weight on detailed economic drawbacks than on wider political considerations such as a commitment to Community solidarity. Moreover, British non-participation could only serve to highlight and strengthen the central Franco-German role in the system.

Energy policy was a second source of strain. As in the earlier part of the Schmidt–Giscard period, North Sea oil was again the issue. It was not so much the seeming paradox between the United Kingdom's growing status as an oil producer—with obvious benefits to the balance of payments—and its complaints of unjust treatment on the budget that attracted attention.[31] More significant was the question of a (symbolic) political commitment from the British to increase production from the North Sea should any new Community oil shortage arise. This subject was taken up by both Schmidt and Giscard at the European Council meeting of December 1979, where neither leader received any satisfaction. While Britain's desire to retain

[30] See Ludlow, 198.
[31] Though see, for instance, the suggestions of Schmidt's scepticism about Britain's 'poverty' in *The Times*, 5 Feb. 1980.

full control over its oil production was understandable, one may well question the wisdom of not showing at least some passing interest in the energy concerns of European partners. This could perhaps have taken the form of a vague commitment to respond to a crisis if necessary. Such a move would have been particularly advisable at a time when London was seeking substantial budgetary concessions from its partners, notably France and Germany.

Finally, there was the question of fishing policy. This is an extremely complex area, hardly susceptible to brief treatment. Suffice it to say, however, that Britain's interest in maintaining an equitable share of the total Community catch often brought it into conflict with Bonn and Paris. The British refusal in January 1978 to accept a Community compromise formula, for instance, was received with anger and dismay by Schmidt and Giscard at their bilateral summit the following month.[32] Differences re-emerged three years later on the question of increased Community fishing rights off Canada. Though strongly desired by the Germans, the move was persistently blocked by the British as part of a wider disagreement with the French. By the time of the Maastricht summit in March 1981, Schmidt was reportedly very angry with the British. He felt 'cheated' that the expected agreement on a common fisheries policy by the end of 1980, which had formed part of the understanding on reducing Britain's budget contribution, had not come about.[33] In sum, all these disputes, though not necessarily unjustified on Britain's part, soured London's relations with its main Community partners and led to great disenchantment in Bonn and Paris. This in turn contributed to a further improvement in the already well-established *entente* between the two capitals.

Political co-operation

Not every area of Community policy was marked by Franco-German accord. Political co-operation offered a rather more motley picture than most, especially at the outset. Giscard's accession to the presidency certainly opened the way for much greater procedural flexibility, with Paris no longer insisting on

---

[32] See report in *International Herald Tribune*, 8 Feb. 1978.
[33] Reported in *The Economist*, 28 Mar. 1981.

such a rigid distinction between inter-governmentalism and supranationality as in the past. Yet despite the procedural relaxation, as far as policies were concerned some differences of emphasis with the Federal Republic remained.

These were particularly visible in the Community's relations with the Middle East. Accordingly, it is on this area that the present account will concentrate. Two main issues were involved: the question of Palestinian representation in the Euro-Arab dialogue; and later, that of the establishment of an independent Palestinian homeland.[34] While Franco-German disagreement on these topics was generally contained within the Euro-Arab dialogue itself, debate did at times spill over to bilateral level, as, for instance, in February 1975.[35] While the French asserted their willingness to let the Palestinians take part as observers in the Euro-Arab dialogue under certain conditions, the Germans were much more emphatic regarding the PLO's need first to renounce terrorism and accept the state of Israel. This was an established difference of emphasis between the two sides, and it was precisely this dilemma which was in fact holding up the inauguration of the Euro-Arab dialogue itself.

Other aspects of the Palestinian problem were also proving divisive. In February 1974 France had gone against the wishes of the other Community countries by voting for PLO representation at the UN, while in 1975 the PLO was allowed to open an office in Paris, a precedent among Community capitals. Two reasons explain why these advanced French views did not lead to the sort of disputes with the Germans that had been seen in the early 1970s. Foremost was the fact that the reduced tension in the Middle East and decline in the oil threat shifted the entire Arab–Israeli issue some way from centre stage. A common European voice towards the Arabs was desirable, but it was no longer the *sine qua non* that it had been during winter 1973. The fact that the Euro-Arab dialogue specifically excluded contentious topics such as energy and the Arab–Israeli conflict also took

---

[34] On the development of the Euro-Arab dialogue, see Stephen J. Artner, 'The Middle East: A Chance for Europe', *International Affairs* (Summer 1980); Bernard Corbineau, 'Le dialogue euro-arabe, instance du nouvel ordre international (1973–1978)', *RfSP* (June 1980).

[35] See report in *Le Monde*, 4 Feb. 1975, and note also Schmidt's remarks in his interview with *Le Figaro*, 3 Feb. 1975.

much of the heat out of the European debate. Furthermore, the now active American diplomacy in the region contributed to this process by focusing responsibility on Washington.

Secondly, the Federal Republic itself had been moving cautiously towards a more pro-Arab stance under Schmidt. The lessons of the oil crisis and the competition for lucrative contracts in the Middle East were major factors underlining the urgency of better contacts with the Arab world. Furthermore, as time passed, the Federal Republic's own special sense of commitment to Israel had declined. This process appeared to have accelerated following Menachem Begin's accession to power in 1977, when a more extreme Israeli stance reduced moral and historical constraints on the German side and served to give the Federal Republic a little more leeway. Finally, and perhaps most important, Bonn might well have been influenced by the French example. It is quite possible that, just as the French saw advantages in emulating German economic methods, so Schmidt became better aware of the benefits evident in Giscard's Middle Eastern diplomacy.

Hence, by the later 1970s French and German views on the Middle East had drawn closer together. The European Council meeting of July 1977 was a milestone in this process. The European consensus reached on the Palestinian issue was a far cry from the divisions of the early 1970s. Community discussions culminated in the EEC's Middle East initiative of June 1980. With the Russian invasion of Afghanistan adding urgency to the need for a Middle East accord, the Nine now put forward an independent peace plan. The origins of the Venice declaration were instructive; while firmly based on the ideas propounded by Giscard during his March 1980 Gulf tour, the impetus had benefited from bilateral discussions with Schmidt on the President's return.[36] Though there remained differences between the two sides on the emphasis to be placed on Palestinian self-determination, the fact remained that French and German views had become more closely aligned. This *rapprochement* may well have helped the smooth launching of the Community's own

---

[36] On Giscard's tour, see Artner 435–7. For discussions on the Middle East at the bilateral summit, see reports in the *Financial Times*, 17 Mar. 1980 and *Frankfurter Allgemeine Zeitung*, 18 Mar. 1980.

initiative in Venice. It was only to be regretted that wider international circumstances prevented any further development of the European plan. Arab disunity, the long hiatus before the formulation of Reagan's Middle East policy, and Mitterrand's apparent coolness to the Venice ideas at the outset all resulted in the initiative never achieving its expected potential. However, one must also ask how effective an independent European approach might ever be in a region where even the most powerful arbiter—the United States—has difficulty in maintaining an active peace policy between the opposing sides.

International affairs

The last eighteen months of the Schmidt–Giscard period were dominated by international events. First Afghanistan, then Poland, took up the lion's share of bilateral summits and even occasioned unprecedented extensions and a number of additional meetings. While there were some differences of emphasis at the outset, French and German views did eventually converge, at least on the surface. Bilateral contacts began at the start of 1980 against a background of frantic Western diplomacy aimed at achieving a co-ordinated reaction to the Russian invasion of Afghanistan. At the unscheduled meeting between Schmidt and Giscard on 9 January 1980, the two leaders faced the dilemma of wanting to show solidarity with the United States, which had already imposed sanctions on Russia, while at the same time being concerned not to provoke the Soviet Union. Both leaders were anxious not to put the fruits of *détente* at risk. Hence the adoption of a careful compromise formula; while jointly criticizing the Russian action, neither Bonn nor Paris showed any inclination to follow the American lead on trade sanctions, on the ground that such action might only increase international tension. At the same time, however, both capitals made clear their resolve not to allow domestic firms to take advantage of the gap left by the American restrictions. Above all, the two sides stressed the need for a co-ordinated European approach to the crisis.

It was this Community aspect which was the most interesting feature of the talks, particularly in terms of French thinking. Unlike the Polish situation of 1982, when long-standing suspicion of the Soviet Union would result in Mitterrand taking a very resolute line against the Russians, Giscard, surprisingly, had much less room for manœuvre. The President's own inclination and the tradition of Gaullist diplomacy made him keen not to mimic the American stand. Even more important, the rising shadow of the 1981 presidential elections heightened the need to show leadership and an independent approach from France's superpower ally. Hence Giscard's emphasis on establishing a distinctive and unified European stand on the crisis, and the temptation, seized by the President in his fruitless Warsaw meeting with Brezhnev in mid-May, to try to steer some middle course between Moscow and Washington.[37] For all his appreciation of Western interdependence and realism regarding French defence policy, in the Afghanistan crisis a variety of domestic and foreign considerations caused Giscard to revert to a much more traditional Gaullist line.

Forces on the German side were also complex, though less so than they would be in 1982. While not sharing Giscard's need to initiate a policy distinct from that of the United States, Schmidt also had cause to seek a more 'European' approach to the crisis. Most notably, as the prime beneficiary of *détente*, the Germans were anxious not to damage relations with the Soviet Union. As would be the case two years later, Bonn was very wary of taking measures such as economic sanctions which might jeopardize relations with Moscow without necessarily advancing the cause in question. More logical to the Chancellor was the need to indicate displeasure to the Russians while retaining valuable channels of communication in preparation for an eventual negotiated settlement.

Wider problems in relations with the United States also played a part in shaping German views and improving the likelihood of understanding with the French. Earlier differences with Carter over human rights, non-proliferation, and monetary policy had been followed by new causes of strain. The President's mishandling of the neutron bomb affair, and leaks in summer 1977 of official consideration of an option to abandon one-third of Ger-

---

[37] On Giscard's visit, note the comments in Duhamel, *La République de M. Mitterrand*, 74.

many in the wake of a Soviet attack, had exacerbated existing frictions.[38]

Such disagreements were powerful factors pushing Bonn towards Paris. This process would gather pace in the course of 1980 as a result of the strident American criticisms of Schmidt's reservations over economic sanctions and his delayed call for a boycott of the Moscow Olympics.[39] Franco-German co-ordination over Afghanistan, or at least signs of German displeasure with the Americans, might have been even more marked had it not been for the fact that the Chancellor was confronted with Federal elections and a right wing rival in the form of Strauss. The CSU leader made much of the need for a joint strategy with the United States over Afghanistan.[40] Certainly, one can surmise whether the lack of an electoral threat and of so forceful an opponent might, in early 1981 and in early 1982 especially, have had something to do with Schmidt's adoption of a noticeably more flexible stand on the question of Poland.

It was the convergence of such considerations on the French and German sides, almost as much as shared concern about *détente*, which explained the major joint statement on Afghanistan released at the bilateral summit of 3–5 February 1980.[41] Alongside that held in Aachen in September 1978, this meeting ranked as one of the high points of Franco-German co-operation in the Schmidt–Giscard era. It was not just the unprecedented extension of the summit to include a third day of talks, but the actual substance and range of discussions themselves which was striking. Outstanding was the statement on Afghanistan. The two sides, now also concerned about the vehemence of reactions in Washington and London, once again managed to combine their interests and come up with a formula which showed solidarity with the United States—thus appeasing Schmidt's domestic critics—while at the same time indicating

[38] For a good survey of the many different military issues dividing Bonn and Washington, see Alex A. Vardamis, 'German–American Military Fissures', *Foreign Policy* 34 (Spring 1979).

[39] Note the comments by David Watt, 'The Atlantic Alliance needs leaders who face the facts', *The Economist*, 11 Oct. 1980.

[40] See e.g. reports in *The Times* and *Le Monde*, 5 Feb. 1980.

[41] Joint Declaration by France and the Federal Republic of Germany. Franco-German Summit Meeting, Paris, 5 Feb. 1980. French Embassy, New York, Press and Information Division.

the independent European line sought by Giscard. Thus, while emphasizing their countries' loyalty and commitment to the Atlantic Alliance, the French and German leaders also asserted the 'special responsibilities' of Europe to maintain peace and security.

The joint declaration was a significant step, its tone testifying to the growing authority of Bonn and Paris, not just in European, but also in world affairs. It was with a powerful joint voice that the French and German leaders now called for a withdrawal of Russian troops from Afghanistan and warned the Soviet Union that 'détente would not withstand a further shock of the same magnitude'.[42] Yet the benefit of hindsight shows a marked hollowness in the latter threat. The positions that would subsequently be adopted on the Polish crisis, especially in 1982, showed how highly the preservation of *détente* was valued in Bonn and, to a lesser extent, Paris. Quite understandably in view of their special position and the benefits they have derived, the Germans have remained particularly anxious not to damage the status quo. Warnings to the Russians such as that of February 1980 have suffered as a consequence. It is interesting to note that, despite attempts to differentiate itself from the SPD during the 1983 election campaign, once in power the CDU has steered an almost identical course towards the East, indicating the constancy of such concerns in German foreign policy.

Both Schmidt and Giscard made much of the summit of February 1980 as an illustration of their close collaboration. Certainly, the two leaders gained from each other's support. This was particularly true in view of the unexpected vigour of Washington's reaction to the Soviet move in Afghanistan, a response closely matched in London, which had left Bonn and Paris rather isolated as a result. Thus there was more than just normal diplomatic rhetoric to Schmidt's remark that their two capitals had 'quite naturally turned to each other'.[43] In view of their common interests, France and Germany were obvious partners. Seldom had their views on foreign affairs been so closely aligned, and never so confidently expressed. The only jarring note came at the very end of the meeting, when, in

---

[42] Ibid. 1.
[43] Quoted in *The Times*, 6 Feb. 1980.

comments to journalists after Schmidt's departure, Giscard appeared to put a slightly different gloss on the content of the Afghanistan statement. The President now placed a heavier emphasis on the distinctly 'European' and independent aspect of the strategy to be pursued *vis-à-vis* Moscow.[44] It is likely that this change of stress was more a deliberate move to placate his domestic audience than an oversight on the President's part, although there is no firm evidence to confirm this.

With electoral considerations uppermost in Giscard's mind, differences in emphasis towards Moscow were rather more marked by the time of the President's state visit to Germany on 7–11 July 1980. France had not joined the Federal Republic in an Olympic boycott, nor had it provided much information to Bonn prior to Giscard's unexpected trip to see Brezhnev in Warsaw. Instructive comparisons can in fact be drawn between the French and German leaders' separate talks with the Russian First Secretary. Whereas Giscard's meeting had achieved nothing—except, perhaps, to confirm the continuing (albeit less frequent) maverick role of France in the Western alliance—Schmidt's summit with the Soviet leader on 30 June had brought about much more concrete results. The Russians had agreed to withdraw some troops from Afghanistan and to begin talks with the United States on medium-range missile levels. It was a telling acknowledgement of Moscow's differing perceptions of Bonn and Paris that such substantive proposals should have been placed before the German Chancellor. Whereas Giscard's trip had probably been seen by the Russians as a good opportunity to divide and embarrass the West, Schmidt's visit clearly represented a more serious occasion for worthwhile discussions. Even if the Russian initiative had long been planned, its unveiling to coincide with the Chancellor's visit was a valid signal of Moscow's assessment of the Federal Republic's relative importance compared with France.

Yet it was on the broader theme of an independent European voice in world affairs, rather than to any specific foreign policy topic such as Afghanistan, that Giscard dwelt during his visit to Germany in July 1980. Taking up his position from the February Franco-German summit, the President repeatedly referred to the

---

[44] See *Le Monde*, 7 Feb. 1980.

need for France and Germany to work together to restore Europe's power and influence in the world.[45] These entreaties provided one of the very few dissonant notes in an otherwise extremely harmonious visit, and required careful handling by the Germans. Despite its political rise thanks to the *Ostpolitik* and the marked decline in American leadership under Carter, Giscard's calls had to be treated circumspectly by Bonn. It was not just anxiety to avoid the impression of bilateral co-operation with Paris being pursued at the expense of relations with Washington that influenced the Government. Rather, in spite of its political development, the fact remained that West Germany was a country in an exposed position, which was fundamentally dependent on the United States for its security.

Hence, although there were attractions in Giscard's approach, particularly at a time of great German dissatisfaction with American leadership, Schmidt was very careful not to respond directly to the French appeals. In fact, the Chancellor took pains throughout to underline the importance of good relations and of a co-ordinated strategy with the United States.[46] In the diplomatic phrasing of one of Schmidt's aides, 'America is our most important ally, France is our closest ally.'[47] To a much greater extent than for the French, and over and above any transient electoral motives, the Federal Republic was still obliged to shape its foreign policy very much with wider considerations in mind.

Matters had grown rather more complicated by the time of the Franco-German summit on 5–6 February 1981. Certain aspects remained constant: Giscard's call on 27 January for an international conference on Afghanistan was fully in line with his established aim of broadening debate on the crisis—and on international affairs in general—beyond the two superpowers. What had changed was the situation in Poland. This now completely eclipsed Afghanistan and, with many observers expecting an imminent Russian intervention, it formed the dominant topic before the French and German leaders. Yet although the two sides issued another joint statement on foreign

---

[45] See reports in *The Times*, 8–12 July 1980. Giscard's remarks during his review of French troops in Baden–Baden were particularly striking.
[46] See, for instance, Schmidt's comments, reported in *Le Monde*, 13–14 July 1980.
[47] Quoted in *The Times*, 11 July 1980.

policy, there were now signs of a change in attitudes compared with the previous year.[48] While the French appeared to be taking a considerably tougher approach towards the Soviet Union, the Germans seemed to have weakened their stance somewhat. In this respect, the summit of February 1981 represented a transitional point between the positions of early 1980 and those to be adopted by January–February 1982.

Less easy to deduce were the precise reasons behind the change. Thinking on the French side was simpler to evaluate than that in Bonn. A mixture of foreign and domestic influences had caused Giscard to make a more pessimistic appraisal of Russian intentions and of the future of *détente*. First of all, there was genuine fear in Paris of a Russian military intervention in Poland, with a consequent belief that a stronger stand was now necessary.[49] Such a shift was already familiar from traditional Gaullist foreign policy, with France tending to play down its independent approach and instead adopt a much more conformist posture at times of international crisis, as, for instance, over Czechoslovakia in 1968. Furthermore, the fact that Giscard's initiatives for a political solution in Afghanistan had been largely brushed aside by the Russians increased the President's pessimism. Domestic electoral considerations also favoured a tougher approach now. While in 1980 Giscard had opted for a path of independent dialogue with Moscow, Russian intransigence had added weight to existing domestic criticism of a lack of leadership and vigour in relations *vis-à-vis* the Soviet Union, thereby pushing the President towards a more forceful stance.

Although working from similar premises, it was not altogether surprising that Schmidt should have reached slightly different conclusions. If Paris had become more pessimistic about the chances of preserving *détente*, Bonn had become all the more concerned and anxious. The country's geographical location, the future of good relations with the GDR, and the special position of West Berlin all continued to militate against a confrontational approach towards Moscow unless absolutely necessary.

[48] Joint statement reprinted in *Le Monde*, 8–9 Feb. 1981.
[49] On this theme, see reports in *Frankfurter Allgemeine Zeitung*, 5 Feb. 1981, and *International Herald Tribune*, 6 Feb. and 7–8 Feb. 1981.

Two other factors had altered since the previous year, reinforcing such considerations. First of all, the need to maintain harmonious relations with Washington prior to the Federal elections in order to deflect the Opposition had been removed. The Government had won a comfortable majority in October 1980 leaving Schmidt with more room for manœuvre in his external policy *vis-à-vis* both Washington and Moscow. Thus the Chancellor could now afford to take a slightly more distanced line from the Americans if necessary. Secondly, this very factor was compounded by the change of leadership in the White House. Although it was too early to assess Reagan's policies towards the East, the bellicose rhetoric and play on xenophobic tendencies that had characterized much of his election campaign did not augur well for the future. This provided all the more reason, therefore, for the Germans to work actively towards maintaining lines of contact with the Russians and preserving *détente*. It was in this light that Schmidt had already warned the Americans against carrying rearmament too far.[50]

The joint statement on international affairs issued at the bilateral summit of February 1981 should be seen as an attempt to bridge these varying French and German interests. Its diffuse tone, much less forceful than its predecessor twelve months earlier, testified to its origins as a compromise solution. Both sides clearly felt it necessary to speak out on international events, not least so as to scotch rumours of differences between them. However, neither found it quite so easy to reach agreement. The major areas were straightforward. France and Germany declared their readiness to work with the new American Administration and counselled a policy of 'vigilance and dialogue' towards the East. More important, the two countries warned against foreign interference in Poland. Significantly, though, on the Polish question no specific reference was made to the Soviet Union, amid suggestions that the advice was directed as much towards Washington as Moscow.[51] Certainly, both Bonn and Paris were united in not wishing to let the initiative pass entirely to Reagan and his more extreme supporters.

[50] See *Le Monde*, 8–9 Feb. 1981.
[51] Note the reports in the *Financial Times*, 7 Feb. 1981, *Frankfurter Allgemeine Zeitung*, 7 Feb. 1981, and *Le Monde*, 8–9 Feb. 1981.

It was on the topic of *détente* that the joint statement was least satisfactory. The word itself was hardly used, and reference was limited to a repetition of the previous year's warning that East–West *rapprochement* could not stand another shock like Afghanistan. This was hardly adequate, under normal circumstances some more substantial statement would have been required, comprising both a clearer indication of the criteria by which Bonn and Paris intended to judge any future infringements and some better idea of the responses they had in mind. Yet, as has been noted, the joint statement was a compromise, indicative of the differences in perspective that had arisen in French and German views. While the divergence should not be exaggerated, and was more than outweighed by the areas of agreement, it would not be long before the cleft would be much more sharply revealed.

11

Entente Toujours?— Schmidt–Mitterrand–Kohl

1981–1984

Introduction

The largely unexpected result of the 1981 French presidential election, where Mitterrand reversed the close outcome of 1974, gave rise to some dire predictions as to the likely course of bilateral Franco-German relations. Even more important, it called into question the entire pattern of development for the European Community as a whole. Had the Schmidt–Giscard period, which had been so decisive in confirming the paramount nature of co-operation between Paris and Bonn, not also illustrated the key value of close personal relations between the French and German leaders? Shared ministerial backgrounds and like-minded views had greatly assisted in the formation of the Paris–Bonn 'axis'. To many pundits, the prognosis for Franco-German relations under the new President was not good. François Mitterrand stood for a constituency very different from his liberal predecessor's, and his advisers were untried. Moreover, the Government would include four Communist ministers.

Though such facts were undeniable, those who saw the election result as the occasion for an upheaval in intra-European relations concentrated too much on short-term factors and ignored the crucial long-term forces still pushing France and Germany together.[1] Many influences were involved. For symbolic reasons alone, bilateral co-operation would remain an important feature of the foreign policies of both countries. Furthermore, although the French Socialists were keen to dispel

---

[1] For good analyses of Mitterrand's foreign policy, see Duhamel, *La République de M. Mitterrand*, 187–201; Dominique Moïsi, 'Mitterrand's Foreign Policy: The Limits of Continuity', *Foreign Affairs* (Winter 1981–2); Neville Waites, 'France under Mitterrand: external relations', *The World Today* (June 1982); Françoise de la Serre, 'La politique européenne de la France: New Look ou New Deal?', *Politique Étrangère* (Mar. 1982).

the image of too exclusive a relationship with Germany, a factor they had regularly decried under Giscard, it would soon become apparent that no other Community capital, least of all London, as some imagined, could form a viable alternative. Lastly, external factors, chiefly the decline of *détente* and Reagan's accession to power, would lead to a gradual reaffirmation of continuing joint interests for France and Germany.

Certainly, there were sizeable differences of view between them. Above all, the two countries appeared to be on the brink of pursuing radically different economic policies. The fact that French economic thinking has shifted back sharply towards the centre has prevented what might otherwise have been a major rift. The choice of Laurent Fabius as Prime Minister in July 1984 and the Communists' departure from the coalition further indicates the Socialists' more social democratic leanings. Yet one must also bear in mind the possibility of a shift back to the much more left wing options represented by Jean-Pierre Chevènement. This would have a severe effect on Franco-German links. Though bilateral relations since May 1981 have undoubtedly remained strong, and in some cases, notably defence, have visibly improved, the relationship is not immutable. Economic policy in particular, and many of the other topics covered in this chapter in general, bear witness to some of the unresolved options in contemporary relations. Furthermore, in the absence of an adequate historical perspective and without the benefit of hindsight, the areas considered in this chapter will of necessity receive less detailed attention than those in previous pages.

The end of détente?

It was in the realm of external policy, above all, that the gradual alignment of French and German views became apparent after May 1981. Foreign affairs, in the form of Poland and relations with the Eastern bloc, troubles in the Alliance, the Falklands interlude, and the Middle East have dominated the period. Though not always identical at first, French and German responses to these challenges usually drew closer together after joint consultation and reflection. Almost always, the course of American foreign policy was an additional complicating factor.

The obvious change in the climate of East–West relations and the clear signs of Russian territorial opportunism in the 1980s had necessitated careful reconsideration of French and German *détente* policies. The incidents in Poland took this process one stage further. Despite the fact that Poland had been a regular topic of discussion at bilateral level since the rise of social unrest and the Solidarity trade union movement, French and German reactions to the declaration of martial law in December 1981 were strikingly different.

The French response to the Polish crisis was notably robust, a far cry from Giscard's much more flexible opening stance towards the Russian invasion of Afghanistan two years earlier. Mitterrand left no doubt as to his disapproval of what had taken place in Poland, nor of his belief in an almost certain Russian involvement in the turn of events there. In this regard his statements resoundingly echoed the tone of American official comment—a source of both satisfaction and surprise to Washington. The Administration had undoubtedly underestimated Mitterrand's long-standing suspicion of the Soviet Union (nurtured, not least, by his years of difficult relations with the French Communist Party). Moreover, Washington had completely misjudged the effect of Communist participation in the French Government. If anything, Mitterrand was obliged to expound his views still more forcibly in order to highlight his independence from Communist influence. Certainly, there was no temptation to embark on any hurried trips to Warsaw, as had been done by Giscard two years earlier.

Feeling in Bonn was, by contrast, remarkably restrained, at least at the outset. Unlike the French and American Presidents, Schmidt pointedly steered clear of outright criticism of the Soviet Union. Rather, blame was ascribed to Moscow in only the most general of terms, while the sanctions against Poland and Russia demanded by the Americans were greeted with open hostility. It is unlikely that Schmidt was at all convinced by the arguments for strident condemnation and sanctions as a means of easing the situation in Poland. Patience and gentle persuasion seemed to be the Chancellor's favoured methods, in expectation of an eventual understanding between the military authorities and Solidarity. However, as time went by this approach would appear increasingly misjudged and Schmidt more isolated.

In addition, the German Government saw little point in antagonizing the Russians over Poland and thereby putting the fruits of *détente* at risk. The problem was, rather, widely viewed as being best treated as an internal Polish matter. It was even implied in some German circles that martial law might impose some useful social discipline on the Poles and improve the country's chaotic economic performance. In this respect one should not forget the degree of Polish indebtedness to the West and more pointedly, to the Federal Republic in particular. Some 17 per cent of Poland's medium- and long-term debt had in fact been provided by the German commercial banking sector.

Trading reasons were undoubtedly a major additional consideration, certainly as far as Bonn's reluctance to impose economic sanctions was concerned. As has been seen, trade with the Eastern bloc has long meant more to the Federal Republic than to its other Western partners. Unlike the United States, recent German Governments have consistently sought to prevent political differences with the East from spilling over into trading relations. Thus it was felt in Bonn that economic links should as far as possible be kept intact. Not least, contracts from the East were a valuable source of employment at a time of domestic recession.

This apparent German impassivity before the Polish crisis led to some sharp recriminations from Bonn's partners. American criticism was most vehement, French comment little less so. To many observers, the German attitude smacked suspiciously of appeasement. In some quarters at least, it rekindled atavistic feelings of anti-Germanism. French press comment was often bitter, and the situation was obviously viewed sufficiently seriously in Bonn to warrant Schmidt undertaking a special trip to Paris on 13 January 1982 in order to explain his Government's position.

Yet there had already been signs of a shift in German thinking prior to this visit, notably at Schmidt's meeting with Reagan in Washington on 5 January 1982. By the time of the Franco-German summit on 24–5 February, there had been an appreciable convergence of views between Bonn and Paris, chiefly as a result of movement on the German side. Both countries were now in unison in their attitudes towards the military takeover in Warsaw and towards the Soviet Union's role. Furthermore, in a forceful joint declaration the two sides strongly condemned the continuing Russian presence in Afghanistan and the Soviet

Union's excessive level of armaments.[2] But the 'political signal' issued by Bonn and Paris was not directed solely towards the East. Washington too had to take note. Uppermost here was the question of economic sanctions. Although in late December 1981 and January 1982 matters had not gone beyond broad declarations of principle, the issue was now being much more energetically pushed by the Administration, with the result that France and Germany were being driven closer together.

Mitterrand, for all his criticisms of the Soviet Union and the Polish military, had never committed himself to economic sanctions. As discussion of detailed measures against Moscow and Warsaw became increasingly prominent in Atlantic relations in early 1982, so divisions between the United States and its European partners became more evident and exchanges more strained. By mid-January 1982 at the latest, it had become clear that French and German views on sanctions were in fact much closer than their ostensible differences of late 1981 had implied. The French Government was patently unwilling to go beyond verbal criticism of Moscow, while the German position on sanctions had not shifted at all. Thus, while the United States had introduced a series of measures against the Polish and Russian régimes in late December 1981, Bonn and Paris were alike in thinking that the only economic move that would rapidly and directly affect the Soviet Union would be an immediate suspension of American grain sales.

By the Franco-German summit of February 1982, therefore, differences between Europe and America had widened considerably, to embrace the whole question of trade with the Eastern bloc and, most importantly, the proposed Soviet gas pipeline to Europe.[3] Much of the heat would go out of the trade issue by March 1982, when there was a slight increase in European export credit rates. But it was an indication of how far Atlantic relations would deteriorate, that only four months later at least one member of the Administration still chose publicly to posit

---

[2] Joint Franco-German declaration reprinted in *Le Monde*, 27 Feb. 1982.

[3] For differing European and American perspectives on trade with the East see Lawrence Freedman (ed.), *The Troubled Alliance. Atlantic Relations in the 1980s* (London, Heinemann, 1983). See also Stephen Woolcock, 'East–West trade: US policy and European interests', *The World Today* (Feb 1982), and 'US–European Trade Relations', *International Relations* (Autumn 1982).

the existence of a secret Franco-Russian export credit arrangement.[4]

Even more contentious than credit levels was the pipeline issue. Throughout the latter part of 1981, the Administration had expressed strong opposition to the increase in Europe's energy dependence that the Siberian gas supply deal would imply, and to the hard currency it would give to the Soviet Union. As matters grew more complicated following the Polish military takeover, so the pipeline contract, involving sales of American equipment both directly to the Russians and to European firms engaged on the project, became increasingly embroiled in the wider question of economic links with the USSR.

Reagan's decision to suspend export licences for American equipment on the scheme was as damaging to European as to Soviet interests, and was understandably ill received in Paris and Bonn alike. Visiting Bonn on 29 January 1982, Mauroy—echoed by Schmidt—stressed his opposition to the move. The French Prime Minister went so far as to state that breaking off economic relations and going back on the pipeline agreement—steps in the direction of an economic blockade—would be tantamount to 'an act of war'.[5] Similarly, at the following month's Franco-German summit, it was not hard to read implied criticism of the Administration in that section of the joint communiqué emphasizing the need for closer consultations with the Americans in order to achieve a better definition of common objectives and improved co-ordination of interests.[6]

In June 1982, the American Administration further upped the stakes by extending the embargo on crucial pipeline parts to include sales by US subsidiary companies and licence-holders abroad. Apart from the doubtful legality of the move (going far beyond anything Carter had ever attempted), there lay the fundamental question of American interference in the internal affairs of its allies. Bonn and Paris responded very angrily. On his visit to the Netherlands on July 1982, Schmidt made quite clear his country's determination to fulfil its contracts, irrespec-

[4] Reported in *The Times*, 17 July 1982.
[5] Quoted in *Le Monde*, 31 Jan.–1 Feb. 1982.
[6] *Le Monde*, 27 Feb. 1982.

tive of the consequences for Atlantic relations.[7] This was a far cry indeed from the more familiar German reserve of the past.

By late summer 1982, Atlantic relations had reached a nadir. Though his words were received critically in certain quarters, the French Foreign Minister, Cheysson, was not that wide of the mark in speaking of a gradual 'divorce' taking place between the United States and Europe.[8] As far as France and Germany were concerned, the difficulties that arose under Reagan over East–West relations served to highlight similarities in their own perceptions and to reconfirm the closeness of bilateral contacts to a degree familiar from the Schmidt–Giscard period.

Western monetary and trading issues

It is ironic that, whereas it was a weak dollar which was the principal cause of strain in Atlantic relations for much of the Carter presidency, under Reagan it has been high American interest rates and an overvalued currency which have chiefly soured Atlantic discussions over economics. American monetary policies and the Administration's growing budget deficit have forced US interest rates to unprecedented levels and towed European rates in their wake. In Paris and Bonn, these high rates were seen as a severe obstacle to economic recovery. Thus, international economic issues (and US policies in particular) and measures to remedy the situation have been standing topics of discussion at bilateral Franco-German summits throughout the period.

Unfortunately, solutions have not been easy to find, with a number of false starts. Though France and Germany were equally concerned about the course of events at the outset it was the French, particularly keen to stimulate their economy and restore growth, who tended to take the more aggressive line. However, there was undoubtedly a hardening of attitudes in Germany too between the time of Schmidt's first brief meeting with Mitterrand in late May 1981 and their encounter almost exactly one year later. While persuasion was the hallmark of the opening Franco-German approach, as matters remained static, or even deteriorated, by autumn 1981 French and German

---

[7] See the Chancellor's remarks in *The Times*, 10 July 1982.
[8] *The Times*, 23 July 1982.

patience began to ebb, despite American pleas for understanding.

Accordingly, at Mauroy's visit to Bonn in January 1982, the French and Germans issued a strong statement pointing out the direct connection between high American interest rates and Western unemployment, and calling for a cut in American rates to take the pressure off Europe.[9] Then, at the following month's Franco-German summit, frustration with American policy translated itself into a determination to act.[10] The two sides now declared their readiness to take steps, in tandem with Community partners, in order to defend their economies. Though there was some uncertainty as to exactly what form the proposed measures would take, there was no doubt that the decision represented an attempt to create the maximum psychological impact on the White House. Plainly, France and Germany were once again taking the lead.

However, it did not in the end prove necessary for the joint initiative to go any further. By mid-1982, the temperature had (temporarily at least) cooled in the interest rate and monetary disputes. On interest rates, the downward trend in the United States in the summer assisted in a steady decrease in European rates, easing the strain. On the currency front too there had been some progress. At the Versailles economic summit in June 1982, Reagan had come under intense European pressure—led by France and Germany—to amend his policy of benign neglect of the dollar and accept the possibility of occasional interventions to prevent excessive fluctuations in its value. One week later, the American monetary authorities intervened on a substantial scale in order to stem an upsurge in the dollar's value. However, such commitments have tended to be short-lived. Large fluctuations in the value of the dollar remain commonplace, and ill feeling persists. Hence, for example, the calls, chiefly on the French side, for some return to an international system of fixed exchange rates. Though attractive in theory, there is in reality little prospect of such schemes being sustainable against the contemporary background of huge international capital flows and American resistance.

[9] See the *Daily Telegraph*, 30 Jan. 1982.
[10] For the depth of German feeling, note Schmidt's remarks in *The Times*, 20 Feb. 1982. For comment on the Franco-German plans, see the *Financial Times*, 26 and 27 Feb. 1982.

On the trading front, differences between Europe and the United States again served to strengthen Franco-German links. Apart from long-standing differences between the United States and Europe over farm policy (and, more recently, wine), in 1981–2 there arose the crisis over European steel exports. This emerged just as the dispute over interest rates was subsiding. The problem of surplus European capacity in traditional industries such as shipbuilding, textiles, and steel is one which has taxed Community governments and the Commission for some years.[11] Similar problems have faced the Americans too. Hence the Administration (like many European counterparts) has often come under pressure from producers to impose import restrictions. In the case of steel, the allegations investigated by Washington and the subsequent finding against the Europeans led to a lengthy and bitter dispute. This was only settled at the eleventh hour in October 1982, when the Community agreed to some large reductions in its export levels. Yet despite the voluntary restraints agreed, the issue simmers on, for instance in the regular American threats to extend the quotas to include carbon steels, or pipes and tubes.

One cannot speak of a specifically Franco-German role in the 1981–2 steel dispute, as matters were extensively handled by the Commission. Differences in the two countries' economic thinking, more marked at the time, also presented some obstacles. Moreover, long-standing German concern not to damage free international trade and to avoid unnecessarily antagonizing Washington tended to make Bonn more compliant in its approach than Paris. None the less, both capitals were brought closer together by their shared interests in ensuring a system of harmonious, but equitable, Atlantic trade.

Defence policy

In May 1982, many commentators rightly saw the co-ordination of French and German views on defence as likely to be one of the most testing areas of bilateral relations. Contrary to expectations, however, a surprising degree of agreement was in fact rapidly achieved. But the situation was rich in ironies. Whereas

---

[11] On this theme, see Loukas Tsoukalis and Antonio da Silva Ferreira, 'Management of industrial surplus capacity in the European Community', *International Organization* (Summer 1980).

Bonn, traditionally one of the solidest supporters of NATO, had considerable difficulty in implementing controversial Alliance decisions, Paris, that long-established maverick within the Alliance, turned out to be one of its staunchest backers.[12]

The central issue concerned the deployment of new NATO theatre nuclear forces in Europe, and, peripherally, the question of German attitudes to the Alliance. In December 1979 NATO had agreed to deploy new American medium-range nuclear missiles as of late 1983, in response to the build-up of Soviet SS20 rockets targeted on Western Europe.[13] It was the German Chancellor who had been one of the prime movers behind this decision. However, as the issue grew more heated in the Federal Republic (a development not unrelated to wider social changes reflected in the rising support for 'alternative' politics), so a substantial body of German opinion grew increasingly (and sometimes violently) opposed to the idea of a rise in the level of nuclear weapons, particularly on German soil.[14] A number of left-wing SPD deputies also took up the anti-nuclear cause alongside the Greens and others. There resulted major problems for Schmidt, both in the domestic political arena, where he staked his future on the SPD's continued support for NATO policy, and in relations with Bonn's foreign allies.

With continuing distrust in certain NATO capitals of Germany's commitment to the West and of its firmness on defence issues (one only has to recall, for example, the *brouhaha* over German adherence to the agreed 3 per cent real increase in NATO defence spending in the later 1970s), the Chancellor found himself severely handicapped abroad by his domestic difficulties. The Schmidt Government was obliged to play down its feelings of unease about American policy under Reagan, and forced repeatedly to reassert its commitment to a strong Alliance defence policy, notably on Euro-missiles. The Chancellor's summit meeting with Brezhnev in November 1981 well illus-

---

[12] For a good survey of Mitterrand's views, see Samuel F. Well, Jr., 'The Mitterrand Challenge', *Foreign Policy* 44 (Fall 1981). Note also Moïsi, 347–50; Waites, 'France under Mitterrand', 224, 229–30.

[13] On the NATO decision and its background, see Christoph Bertram, 'The Implications of Theatre Nuclear Weapons in Europe', *Foreign Affairs* (Winter 1981–2).

[14] On Community-wide opposition to the deployment of new missiles, see Stanley Hoffmann, 'NATO and Nuclear Weapons: Reason and Unreason', *Foreign Affairs* (Winter 1981–2).

trated the constraints he was facing. Though obviously keen to engage in meaningful discussions with the Russians on arms control—not least so as to undercut some of his domestic critics—Schmidt was also very conscious of the intense attention being focused on his talks, notably in Washington and Paris. The whole question of superpower attitudes to the role of Germany as an actor in the wider context of their own arms limitation talks is one of considerable interest, though beyond the scope of this study. Suffice it to say that Reagan's zero option proposal, made only days before the Soviet leader's arrival in Bonn, was obviously timed with that visit in mind.

What is of primary interest here is the French position on defence matters in 1981–2, and, particularly, reaction in Paris to the contemporary situation in the Federal Republic. Mitterrand's stance on defence policy and on theatre nuclear forces was far less contested than that of Schmidt. Despite his Socialist credentials and Communist participation in government, the French President has followed closely in the tracks of his predecessors, making much of a strong conventional and especially nuclear capability. The Government has, in fact, committed sizeable funds to the latter.[15] Such a course has come as a disappointment to many left-wingers in France and Germany alike, and as a source of considerable surprise and satisfaction to policy-makers in Washington and London.

A large number of reasons explain Mitterrand's preferences. The President is committed to a strong defence posture and has long had a wary attitude towards the Soviet Union. Mitterrand has spoken out against Soviet policies, notably regarding Poland, Afghanistan, and human rights. Sound political judgement, too, has played a part; the Communist presence in the French Government increased its vulnerability to attack from the Right, particularly on an issue as sensitive as defence. If anything, Mitterrand has been obliged to adopt a more determined posture than ever. Hence his strong support for NATO's new missile decision, despite France's continuing self-exclusion from the Alliance's military wing. This contrasts with the position under Giscard, who tended to avoid comment on the Euro-

---

[15] Note, however, that while the budget on the nuclear side is set to rise substantially, the increase for conventional forces, and especially the army, is appreciably smaller.

missiles issue on the pretext of France's non-participation in the Alliance's military activities.

These conflicting backgrounds in Paris and Bonn allowed considerable scope for misunderstanding on defence issues. Differences of emphasis between the two sides were, if anything, highlighted and sometimes even intensified by certain sections of the media, at least at the outset. The impression was occasionally given that there were greater barriers to understanding than in fact existed. Naturally, the Élysée and many sections of the French Government were concerned about the strength of the peace movement in Germany. But, as with French fears of German reunification under Pompidou, concern about the German peace lobby was exaggerated, as were the grave doubts about the Bonn Government's ability to resist the anti-nuclear tide.

Accordingly, it is likely that in 1981 Mitterrand sought specific reassurances from Schmidt on this score. But even at their first brief meeting on 24 May there was a clear indication of the joint position the two leaders would increasingly come to espouse. Both expressed agreement on the need to restore the balance of forces in Europe. At the same time, however, they recognized the necessity for the superpowers to engage in meaningful talks aimed at reducing missile levels. This adherence to NATO's twin-track policy of deployment and negotiation was a hallmark of subsequent bilateral summits.

It is worth considering the major advantage Schmidt derived from this French backing—a boost that was particularly ironic in view of the Chancellor's obvious coolness towards Mitterrand in the presidential election campaign. The fact that such unequivocal endorsement now came from a Socialist French President was a powerful weapon against the arguments of many anti-nuclear left-wingers in West Germany.[16] One can perhaps draw a parallel between the value of French support for Schmidt on the missiles issue and that provided by Pompidou for Brandt—at the beginning at least—over the *Ostpolitik*. The two issues are not, however, strictly comparable: in the latter instance, the German Government was having to deal with the objections of an enraged Opposition, while in the more recent example the main problem was attack from within the SPD itself

[16] Some SPD members, including Brandt, clearly disagreed with Mitterrand's stance towards Moscow. See, for instance, reports in the *Financial Times*, 21 July 1981.

and from extra-Parliamentary forces. None the less, the substantial change of roles that has taken place in Bonn and Paris between the two episodes gives an indication of some of the new ironies in Franco-German relations in the early 1980s.

Most recently, under Mitterrand and Kohl Franco-German discussions on defence have broken new ground. Free, unlike Schmidt, from internal party constraints, the new Chancellor has strongly reaffirmed his predecessor's line on defence, though perhaps at the expense of being too uncritical of Washington. At their first meeting on 4 October 1982, Mitterrand and Kohl decided to initiate a series of regular talks on European security issues. Although the idea of closer consultation on defence had already been broached at the summit between Schmidt and Mitterrand in February 1982, it was a much more ambitious step that was now being taken.[17]

That the new talks would cover a much wider range than anything mooted in the past was confirmed at the Franco-German summit on 20–1 October 1982, where the foreign and defence ministers of the two countries met to establish procedures and guidelines. Taking up a previously under-used clause in the 1963 Franco-German Treaty, it appeared that broad-ranging security and disarmament issues, as well as close co-ordination of joint defence policies, would all be tackled. Although there had been regular talks on joint weapons production and certain other military issues in the past, the summit of October 1982 marked the first time that major strategic questions were being aired in detail. More important, discussions were also believed to have taken place on previously taboo subjects such as the French nuclear deterrent and the modernization of French tactical forces stationed near the border in Alsace. Though talks were still at an early stage, the fact that such matters had been discussed at all marked a new departure. In view of the like-minded assessments of the strategic situation by Mitterrand and Kohl, it was now decided to institutionalize co-operation by way of a permanent committee to co-ordinate the two countries' security policies.

Spurred by Mitterrand's forthright and controversial com-

[17] On Franco-German defence discussions, see Joseph Rovan, 'Le Changement allemand', *Politique Internationale*, 18 (Winter 1982–3), 163; Konrad Seitz, 'Deutsch-französische sicherheitspolitische Zusammenarbeit', *Europa-Archiv* 22 (1982).

ments on Western security in his speech of January 1983 before the Bundestag (which arguably contributed to Kohl's election chances), defence matters again featured at the bilateral summit of May 1983. Discussion on this occasion was limited to the plan to build a new Franco-German anti-tank helicopter and the wider question of the deployment of Cruise and Pershing missiles. The latter issue also dominated the agenda at the Franco-German summit on November 1983, which came soon after the Bundestag's vote in favour of deployment. As with Schmidt, Kohl too had gained considerable comfort from the French President's support for the missile decision (not least via his Bundestag address). At the November summit, Mitterrand in fact went out of his way to congratulate the Chancellor's 'sense of responsibility' and 'courage' in this sphere.[18]

Yet one area of defence policy where France and Germany continue to differ has been on the question of an independent European security role either outside, or, as more recently suggested, within NATO. The issue has featured periodically in Franco-German relations, having been raised by Jobert in November 1973 and, latterly, by Mitterrand himself. Superficially at least, it appears surprising that such an old Gaullist war-horse should have been resurrected by the Socialist President. Yet, as has been seen, Mitterrand's stand on defence matters is little different from his predecessor's—and is in fact rather more explicit than Giscard. The latest tentative initiatives from Paris have taken two forms. In 1981 there was a proposal for an increased role for Western European Union as a forum for discussing matters of common interest on defence. The idea has been further developed more recently, and saw some early results at the meeting of WEU foreign ministers in Paris in mid June 1984. The second French approach came in November 1983, with hints from Mitterrand that closer European co-operation within NATO might follow on from the new Franco-German military dialogue.[19]

As for German reactions, Bonn's prime concern, as ever, has been to prevent any impression of Europe detaching itself from the United States. Thus, German politicians have listened

[18] Mitterrand, quoted in Le Monde, 26 Nov. 1983.
[19] For suggestions, and German reactions, see The Times, 15 Mar. 1981; Le Monde, 26 Nov. 1983; The Economist, 30 Dec. 1983.

politely but cautiously, to the French ideas. Kohl's non-committal reaction to Mitterrand's line of thought in 1983 again illustrated the constraints still active in German foreign and defence policy. While undoubtedly attracted by certain of the French ideas, the CDU-led coalition continues to think (even more than was the case with the SPD under Schmidt) very much with American responses in mind. The question of incorporating France's nuclear deterrent into East–West nuclear arms reduction talks remains a second, potentially divisive, area. While the Kohl Government has consistently backed the French (and British) refusal to participate, there are many in the SPD (and some, Paris suspects, on the right too) who would much prefer to see French and British involvement in an eventual global European arms reduction agreement.

Economic themes

Just as Mitterrand and much of the French Government expressed concern about the growing strength of the German peace movement, so, in 1981–2, the Germans focused on the future course of French economic policy. After the close co-operation with Barre to reduce inflation, economic policies in Paris and Bonn seemed set to diverge dramatically. The Socialists' programme of expansion to boost the economy, their huge campaign of nationalization, and their large increases in social spending all spelled the gravest danger of economic mismanagement and spiralling inflation to the Germans. Bonn also feared the repercussions of these measures on its own economy, potentially pushing up inflation, putting additional strain on the EMS, and further delaying the closer co-ordination of European economic policies already severely hindered by the recession.

It was in the realm of monetary policy that the repercussions of the Socialist victory in France were most immediately felt. The international foreign exchange markets reacted vigorously to the election result, with widespread selling of the franc. It was against this background of heavy monetary pressure that Mitterrand sought reassurance from Schmidt at their first meeting only days after becoming President. The pledges he received on German monetary support were at least as valuable to him (if not more) as those he gave in return to the Chancellor on Euro-missiles and defence policy.

Despite massive French intervention, a weak franc has been an intermittent feature of the EMS, particularly in the first two years of Socialist government. French difficulties stemmed from a variety of factors, especially marked in this early phase. Continuing foreign doubts about the Socialists' economic programme, sizeable balance of payments problems, above-average inflation, and, of course, the strength of the dollar (and Deutschemark) all played a part. As a result, occasional parity realignments were necessary. In October 1981 the franc was devalued by 3.0 per cent and the Deutschemark revalued by 5.5 per cent within the EMS. The smoothness of this operation was rightly hailed as proof of the viability of the system and of the Community's cohesion. But in June 1982, following weeks of speculation, further changes were necessary. The franc was now devalued by 5.75 per cent and the Deutschemark raised by 4.25 per cent. Even this change was insufficient, however, and in March 1983 a further realignment took place, with another small devaluation of the franc and revaluation of the Deutschemark. Although the French Government had negotiated a $4,000 million line of credit with a group of international banks, supplementing this later with a special bilateral credit arrangement with Saudi Arabia, reports in April 1983 showed how the previous month's heavy foreign exchange interventions had already depleted at least part of this pool.[20]

The realignment of March 1983 was highly significant, both in terms of Franco-German relations and as regards developments within the French Government. On the bilateral side, the episode took place against a background of considerable Franco-German acrimony, more reminiscent of the early 1970s than the harmony of later years. Opinion differs as to the depth of the ill feeling aroused, with strong suggestions that much of the hostility and complaining on the French side about German 'arrogance' and 'incomprehension' was designed principally for domestic consumption.[21] In this respect, the bilateral and internal aspects of the realignment overlapped, for the decision to devalue the franc marked a turning-point in French economic policy options. The move represented a major shift towards the

---

[20] On the international line of credit, see reports in *The Times*, 16–18 and 23 Sept. 1982. On the depletion of reserves, see the *Financial Times*, 6 Apr. 1983.

[21] Delors quoted in *The Times*, 21 Mar. 1983.

conservative and pragmatic thinking in the Socialist Party personified by Delors, compared with the left-wing options of leaving the EMS and erecting high protectionist barriers favoured by Chevènement. The latter measures would also have had very damaging consequences for France's relationship with its Community partners. Marking the triumph of Delors's preferences, the devaluation was accompanied by an extremely severe domestic austerity programme. Under the complicated political circumstances, the temptation to present Bonn as at least a partial scapegoat was irresistible. Consistent German reluctance to do anything more than listen politely to French requests for restored economic growth across the Rhine probably only added to the degree of French frustration with their German partners.

Did the troubles of March 1983 mark a nadir in bilateral relations in the monetary sphere and cause irreversible damage owing to the degree of animosity aroused, as some have suggested? More convincing is the view that the March 1983 EMS realignment, though certainly less amicable than those of previous years on account of the particularly difficult economic circumstances, represented no more than a new, rather more passionate, episode in a long-running saga. Ministerial inexperience, especially noticeable in the form alternatively of aloofness or heavy-handedness on the German side, did not help, and contributed to an overall sense of German callousness among the French. Moreover, French annoyance at German reluctance to revalue the Deutschemark was hardly a novel theme in bilateral relations. In the realignment of March 1983 what really mattered was the 8–9 per cent spread required between the two currencies. Bitter arguments over individual movements were secondary. Hardly less familiar was the maladroitly expressed German concern about the pursuit of 'irresponsible' economic policies by the government of another member state.

Details of Franco-German co-ordination of monetary policy in advance of the 1981, 1982, and 1983 EMS realignments remain sketchy. Discussion of European monetary topics between Schmidt and Mitterrand was not as prominent at bilateral summits as had been the case under Giscard. The same can be said of talks between the President and Kohl. This change

probably reflected Mitterrand's considerably weaker background in finance and economics compared with his predecessor.
It did not mean, however, that the bilateral co-operation on
monetary matters so familiar from the period 1974–81 suddenly
came to an end. There were regular contacts at ministerial and
official levels, for example the decision to convene the Community finance ministers' meeting on 4 October 1981 which agreed
to the EMS realignment came of a joint Franco-German
initiative. The strong German support for the franc on the
money markets in 1981–2 gave a further clue as to the co-
ordination of policies. Schmidt himself also played a part. The
Chancellor's statement of May 1981 backing the Socialists'
economic aims, repeated at the bilateral summit in July 1981,
played an important psychological role in buoying up the hard-
pressed French currency at times of great external pressure.

Similar German action was much less evident in March 1983,
yet the conditions were rather different. Some realignment in the
EMS was widely awaited even prior to the German general
election result, owing to the opposing pressures on the French
and German currencies. The return of a CDU-led coalition only
reinforced existing market sentiment, and the franc had already
started to be discounted. Under the circumstances, ministerial
statements denying any German revaluation plans and supporting the franc, irrespective of intentions towards the French, were
of little practical value.

Despite the acrimony of March 1983, on balance the result of
French and German experience in the economic and monetary
fields since May 1981 has been to establish a greater appreciation
in an originally sceptical French Government of the value of
closer collaboration with the Germans. Firm lessons have been
learned in Paris about the external constraints on national
economic policy. Consequently, experience among the Socialists
of economic and monetary management has contributed to a
closer understanding of the many interconnections between the
French and German economies. Personalities have provided
some comfort too. Though the Germans were concerned about
the Socialists' economic plans at the outset, the appointment of
Delors as Minister of Finance provided an important reassurance. His coupling of the revaluations of June 1982 and March
1983 to the introduction of severe austerity packages indicated

recognition of the link between domestic economic policy and the franc's problems abroad. The simultaneous announcement of a temporary wage and price freeze in 1982 demonstrated the Government's determination to combat inflation. Though controversial at home, such measures were welcomed by the Germans, helping to alleviate Bonn's earliest fears about the consequences of French economic policy. That Bonn should have so keenly backed Delors's appointment in July 1984 as the next head of the European Commission came as no shock.

Since 1981 French and German views have also moved closer together on another of Europe's economic problems, unemployment. As jobless totals have risen, both countries have emphasized job creation. Though kept vague to suit the Germans, there was a balanced commitment in the negotiations on the EMS realignment in June 1982. While those devaluing, like the French, accepted the need to deflate, there was an undertaking on the part of those revaluing, like the Germans, to reflate their economies when conditions permitted. (It is doubtful, though, whether the Germans have acted on this commitment.) None the less, methods in the two countries have differed, and the domestic political backgrounds were very dissimilar, but the target of reducing unemployment was one given only a little less priority in Bonn than in Paris.

Certain aspects of trading policy remain potential areas for conflict, however. From the outset, there have been rumblings of protectionism under the Socialists.[22] Nothing concrete has come about, but proposals such as Mauroy's plan of December 1981 for the 'recapture of the internal market' aroused profound unease among the liberal trade-minded Germans.[23] Such fears were intensified by the fact that many of the industrial sectors cited, such as machine tools, were ones where the Germans have captured a substantial share of the French market. French protectionism *vis-à-vis* other Community members has not yet gone beyond the form of words, but France's partners, especially the Germans, remain wary. Particularly striking were the French threats in 1983 to restrict the flow of German exports across the

---

[22] See *The Economist*, 16 Jan. 1982. Note also the earlier plans for restructuring the machine tools industry, reported in *The Economist*, 26 Dec. 1981.

[23] On the recapture of the internal market, see the comments by André Grjebine, 'The Recapture of the Home Market', *JCMS* Special Issue (Sept.–Dec. 1982).

Rhine. This was part of a wider campaign to draw attention to the huge imbalance in trade between the two countries. Some 40 per cent of France's total deficit in 1982 was accounted for by German exports, while the size of the German trade surplus with France increased from DM 12 billion in 1981 to DM 17 billion in 1982.[24] Hence Cresson's suggestion in May 1983 in favour of imposing indirect restrictions on the tide of German products should there be no shift in the German position.[25] Such threats were probably part of wider efforts to persuade Bonn to encourage domestic economic growth, which would stimulate French exports to the Federal Republic and possibly reduce the stream of German goods to France. By 1984 some of the heat has gone out of this issue, due partly to the effect of the French Government's deflationary measures.

A second area of trade policy, and one where the distinction between French and German views has been less clearly defined, concerns Japanese competition. Both Paris and Bonn have expressed anxiety about the level of Japan's imports into their own markets, especially in certain sectors, such as consumer electronics and high technology. However, the two countries have tended to adopt dissimilar approaches to the problem, a reflection of long-standing differences in trading philosophy. The French reaction has been broadly characterized by a mixture of fear and envy: whereas Giscard and his advisers often looked to West Germany as their economic model, it is to Japan that many of Mitterrand's team have turned. At the same time, however, the French Government has taken steps to impose restrictions on certain Japanese exports to France, even if only temporarily or indirectly.[26] Moreover, the Socialists have made strong proposals for independent European solutions in a number of key industries. Though hardly more sanguine about the Japanese challenge, the Germans have taken a less radical line. Traditionally averse to restricting free trade, Bonn has concentrated instead on gaining better access to the Japanese market and on stimulating co-operative ventures and outside investment where

[24] Figures from the *Financial Times*, 10 Mar. 1983, and *The Times*, 17 May 1983.
[25] Reported in the *Financial Times*, 17 May 1983.
[26] See, for instance, the *Financial Times*, 9 Feb. 1982. More recently, the temporary procedure for routeing Japanese video recorder imports through the small customs post at Poitiers springs to mind.

practicable. It remains to be seen, however, whether the German approach will draw closer to that of France if the imbalance in EEC trade with Japan continues to grow.

Community issues

In June 1981 it was made clear by some members of France's new Socialist Government that they would be seeking a loosening in relations with the Germans in favour of a wider network of alliances with other Community partners. It seemed that Britain stood to gain most from this major reassessment of links.[27] At the end of the Schmidt–Mitterrand period, however, and contrary to expectations, co-operation between Paris and Bonn, although a little less exclusive than in the past, continued to play a key role among the Ten. What were the Community factors which helped to maintain this position?

As in the late 1970s, problems relating to Britain's membership dominated the Ten and played an important part. Pre-eminent was the question of Britain's budget contribution. Secondary to that, though little less contentious, was the level of farm prices, particularly in 1982, and the future shape of the CAP. The two issues were closely interwoven as a result of Britain's negotiating strategy, which often argued along the lines that agricultural prices could not be settled prior to a satisfactory resolution of the budgetary dispute. The outcome of this approach has been to cause a great deal of ill feeling among the other member states, not least France and Germany, whose views on both the budget and farm prices have often been closely co-ordinated.

Much of the difficulty over Britain's payments to the budget stemmed from the Community's failure in 1979 to agree to anything beyond a three-year special arrangement for rebates. As the period of this compromise elapsed, so the contentious issue of Britain's contribution resurfaced, souring Community discussions over a long period. Once again, French and German resolve was one of the most conspicuous features of the dispute. Their refusal to bow to British pressure was largely responsible for the gradual erosion of London's expectations on the budget from the original demand at the European Council meeting in

---

[27] See e.g. Cheysson's interview with *The Times*, 17 July 1981.

November 1981 for a permanent arrangement to the situation in
mid-May 1982 when, in the thick of the Falklands conflict, the
British finally accepted a one-year temporary settlement.

Substantial differences on the budget remained, however,
dogging talks through 1983 and up to autumn 1984. While
London refused to give ground on any increase in the Community's 'own resources' in advance of a permanent settlement of the
budgetary dispute, many other member states, and most
importantly France, were antagonized by the inflexible British
negotiating stand. At the Athens summit of December 1983, for
instance, signs of a more conciliatory French approach had
appeared to offer hope of a classic Community package deal. But
a clash of personalities between the British and French leaders,
combined with ineffectual German stewardship, resulted in a
wholly unsuccessful conclusion. The summit of March 1984
suffered a similar fate. Only the broad agreement finally reached
in Fontainebleau in June 1984—subsequently fleshed out in
tense talks at ministerial level culminating in October 1984—
appears to have produced the basis for a lasting settlement.

Results of bilateral Franco-German co-ordination on the
budgetary front under Kohl and Mitterrand were almost as
marked as in the Schmidt–Mitterrand period. Then, shared
views in Bonn and Paris over the budget were undoubtedly
helpful in cementing bilateral relations. Neither country, and
especially not France, was at all willing to make large financial
sacrifices for the British. In the presidential election campaign
Mitterrand had in fact criticized Giscard for having been too
generous with London in the past. From the French point of
view, the budget dispute was a tiresome distraction, diverting
attention away from more important issues such as combating
unemployment and improving social welfare in Europe. The
frustration and resentment aroused in Paris by the British was a
key factor in putting paid to any ideas for a major Anglo-French
rapprochement after May 1981. Thus, despite the Socialists'
disavowals at the outset, it was Bonn which re-emerged as
France's privileged partner. This picture has remained little
changed since Kohl's accession to power.

Under Schmidt, German attitudes to the budget were broadly
similar to those in France, though seldom expressed so forcefully.
Although the Germans went some way to meet Britain's

demands, severe financial pressure prevented Bonn from subsidizing as large a rebate as London would have liked. However, it
was not just internal financial constraints which reduced Bonn's
generosity in 1981–2. Like the French, the Germans too had
become frustrated with the seemingly endless round of British
pleas, claims which, moreover, seldom appeared to be matched
by any lasting demonstrations of Britain's own Europeanism.

Differences over farm prices have, if anything, been even more
acerbic than those over the budget. This was especially true in
1982, a year worth spotlighting, when internal political considerations, coupled with a long-established attachment to the
CAP, went much of the way to explain France's determined
position at the forefront of opposition to London. Britain's
lengthy refusal to agree to an agricultural price package deeply
antagonized a French farm constituency already unhappy with
its Government's performance on agriculture.[28] Hence the
strong wish expressed by both Mitterrand and Cresson (then
Farm Minister) to impose a Community farm price agreement
by majority vote if necessary and to introduce national aids
for French farmers should the British continue to block a
settlement.

The German approach in 1982 was little different from that of
the French. Although Bonn has shared Britain's interest in
reducing the stake of agricultural spending in the Community
budget, its support for the 1982 British stand was limited. A
number of factors were responsible—the weight of the domestic
farm lobby, growing German irritation with Britain and its
tactics, and, perhaps most important, the fact that the Federal
Republic itself has come to benefit substantially from the CAP.
Hence Bonn adopted a much more nuanced line on agricultural
policy and the Germans were certainly not as forthcoming in
their support as the British would have liked. Though 1982
represented an extreme example, it gave an indication of the
effect of (often justified) British demands in agriculture in
driving a wedge between London and other Community
capitals, and in bolstering the role of Franco-German policy co-
ordination.

---

[28] On the wider question of restructuring the CAP, see Joan Pearce, 'The CAP: a guide
to the Commission's new proposals', *The World Today* (Sept. 1981).

Lastly, something must be said about the 1982 Falklands conflict and the light is threw on differences in French and German thinking.[29] While all the member states showed solidarity with the British, at least to begin with, and France and Germany maintained their support throughout, sentiment in the two countries was not identical. Though one should be wary of generalizing (and note that certain sections of opinion in both countries opposed what appeared to be an anachronistic means of solving an international dispute), the different approaches adopted towards the issue in French and German government circles gave an indication of the two countries' dissimilar historical backgrounds.

While France, a former colonial power still possessing a number of small overseas territories, offered extremely resolute backing for the British, the German Government underwent a considerably lengthier period of uncertainty. Some might take this dichotomy to indicate certain fundamental differences in that elusive concept, national character. Others may prefer to suggest that it reflected the Federal Republic's considerably more exposed trading position towards Argentina. Most convincing, however, is the argument that the distinction hinted at deep-seated post-war differences in French and German views on the use of force. Although the Schmidt Government had certainly not turned its back on military options, there is no doubt that the experience and legacy of Nazism have tended to make many Germans adopt a more cautious line—often tinged with heavy moral overtones—towards the use of force as an instrument in resolving conflict than has generally been the case in either France or Britain. Likewise, a similar trend may be discerned in the greater popularity of peace or anti-nuclear movements in Germany than in France.

Some problem areas

Since May 1981, not all foreign policy issues have been marked by the level of Franco-German understanding that was often the hallmark of previous years. Especially at the start of the Mitterrand presidency, certain topics, notably Central America

[29] On Britain, the Community, and the Falkland Islands, see Geoffrey Edwards, 'Europe and the Falklands Crisis 1982', *JCMS* (June 1984).

and North–South questions, were characterized by sharp differences of view, often based on ideological cleavages between the French and German Governments. As regards events in Central America, the Socialists' verbal support for resistance movements, notably in El Salvador, caused concern in the Federal Republic, as they ran counter not only to Bonn's own thinking but also to Washington's.[30] More recently, the slightly lower prominence of Central American problems has tended to ease the situation, a development also assisted by a rather less outspoken French stance than at the outset. Yet Paris has continued to argue for greater social and economic aid for the region rather than the military and political options favoured by Washington.

On North–South relations the position was less clear cut. This stemmed partly from the need to distinguish on the German side between the differing schools of thought represented by Chancellor Schmidt's rather lukewarm interest and Brandt's much more passionate approach. For Schmidt, North–South issues were of limited priority at a time of deep Western economic recession. Mitterrand, on the other hand, came to office with a firm commitment to better relations with the Third World and improve opportunities for it in its dealings with the West.[31] This was reflected in his appointment of Cheysson, formerly EEC Commissioner for relations with the developing countries, as Minister for External Affairs, and in Régis Debray's secondment to the Élysée as a foreign policy adviser.

There is some reason to believe that Mitterrand's concern about Third World issues has diminished slightly since taking office, owing, if nothing else, to the influence of greater priorities. Yet it was clear from his successive summits with Schmidt that the question of North–South relations was not one which struck a special chord between the two men. Perhaps weighed down by the Chancellor's greater concern for the detailed financial aspects (and doubtless also preoccupied by the more pressing world issues that arose), neither party got beyond paying lip-service to the theme in their bilateral discussions. Much the same trend has been evident in relations with Chancellor Kohl.

As to that other major flashpoint of international relations in

---

[30] See, for instance, the report on the Feb. bilateral summit in *The Times*, 26 Feb. 1982.
[31] On this attitude to Third World issues, see Moïsi, 351–5; Waites, 'France under Mitterrand', 228, 231.

the 1980s, the Middle East, Mitterrand came to office determined to shift back the balance of France's relations in the
region more in Israel's favour.[32] The President's courageous visit
to Israel in March 1982 provided ample evidence of this desire.
Notwithstanding its special relationship with Israel, the Federal
Republic has by contrast moved cautiously (and to some effect)
towards better links with the Arab world. Hence, the plaudits
received by Mitterrand stood out against the much sharper
criticisms which Begin at times reserved for Chancellor Schmidt.
Even the replacement of the caustic Begin by the more
restrained Shamir did little to ease the underlying tension in
Israeli–German relations—a pattern again illustrated in Chancellor Kohl's difficult trip to Israel in January 1984.

By contrast, the more friendly tone of Franco-Israeli relations
inaugurated by Mitterrand changed dramatically in summer
1982. In one of the most striking turn-arounds in French foreign
policy under the Socialists, Mitterrand's loud condemnation of
Israel following its invasion of Lebanon and siege of West Beirut
demoted French relations with the Begin Government to much
the same level as that common during the Giscard presidency.
Moreover, it was Mitterrand, of all the European leaders, who
was now singled out for the special ire of many of Begin's
supporters. As for French and German views on the Middle East,
these drew closer together following the Lebanese crisis. Notably,
Paris returned to the opinion, seemingly questioned at one time,
that Europe has an independent role to play in solving the
region's problems.[33] This greater proximity between France and
Germany on the Middle East question has continued into the
Kohl Chancellorship, while France's contribution of troops to
the multinational force in Beirut increased its interest in finding
a Lebanese settlement.

Contemporary themes

In conclusion, something must be said about the French and
German positions on certain of the major contemporary issues
raised in the preceding pages. Without adequate historical
perspective, however, these closing remarks will of necessity be

---

[32] See Moïsi, 352; Duhamel, *La République de M. Mitterrand*, 197–8.
[33] See Duhamel, 197; de la Serre, 'La politique européenne de la France', 132–3.

both brief and cautious. First of all, one should note that bilateral summitry under Mitterrand and Kohl has tended to be preoccupied by defence and strategic matters, followed closely by international economic affairs. A reflection of pressing world issues, perhaps, the new balance is also an indication of the fact that progress within the Community—until mid to late 1984 at least—has been overshadowed by continuing budgetary and agricultural disputes, the former in particular focusing on Britain.

These problems aside, most striking in the Community sphere has been the very positive role adopted by France during its presidency in the first half of 1984. There has been plentiful evidence of a strong desire in Paris to revitalize the Community. Mitterrand's May speech before the European Parliament marked the outstanding example in terms of imagination for the future. Seemingly going back on many established tenets of French Community policy, the President called for a new treaty to expand integration into novel areas, and, most remarkably, for restrictions on the use of the veto. More traditionally, echoing Pompidou and earlier suggestions, Mitterrand also recommended the establishment of a political co-operation secretariat. Though electioneering undoubtedly played a part, it will be interesting to see whether any of Mitterrand's bold initiatives will be translated into action.

Elsewhere, bolstered by its presidency of the Council of Ministers, the more positive French role was witnessed in the three most prominent areas of Community policy—agriculture, the budget, and enlargement. On agriculture, the decision in late March 1984 to impose milk quotas and certain other restrictions marked what may be a major first step towards revising the CAP. Though some of the earlier obstacles removed were of French making, the result owed much to the Socialists' new resolve to breathe fresh life into the Community. It should also be borne in mind, though, that Paris won a long-sought commitment gradually to eliminate MCA's. The latter issue in particular was closely co-ordinated with the Germans. On the budget too, bilateral like-mindedness has been regularly demonstrated. At their extremely cordial summit as Rambouillet in late May 1984, for example, Kohl appeared as determined as Mitterrand to stress that no further monetary concessions would be made to the British beyond those already rejected by Mrs. Thatcher at the Brussels summit in March 1984. There is no doubt that one element in the closeness of the bilateral bond quickly established under Kohl and Mitterrand was an implicit desire to serve notice on the British Government that Bonn and Paris intended to stand firm on its demands. It is worth noting that the budget agreement eventually worked out in June 1984 was on terms which were, if anything, slightly less advantageous to Britain than those previously turned down in Brussels.

A more positive French attitude in 1984 has been almost equally evident towards enlargement. Under the Socialists, Spanish membership in particular, while firmly accepted in principle, was at the outset subjected to well-publicized reservations. Yet keenness to develop the Community (and probably embarrassment at continuing obstruction) have brought about a more favourable French approach. In Germany there has, if anything, been a slightly greater concentration on the financial aspects of new membership. None the less, Bonn remains wholly in favour of Spanish and Portuguese participation. Despite difficult rounds of talks, notably on agriculture (where, significantly, the French have wrested many concessions), the signs are favourable. Even if negotiations are not completed by the end of 1984, prospects for Spanish and Portuguese accession by 1 January 1986 still look fair.

What of progress on the monetary and economic fronts in 1983 and 1984? The U-turn in French economic thinking has brought a slow improvement in the country's external trade position and some decline in inflation. Foreign confidence in French economic policy has risen, and the franc has consequently been under less pressure than in the first two years of Socialist rule. The continuing strength of the dollar in 1984 helped by easing traditional strains between the franc and the Deutschemark in the EMS. However, while the influence of external forces has led to a retrenchment in French economic policy and pushed it closer towards practices familiar in Bonn, frictions within the Government have not been absent. The unpalatable domestic political and economic consequences of the Socialists' deflationary measures, a very poor showing in the June 1984 European elections, and the Cabinet reshuffle in July finally persuaded the Communists to make a break. Despite signs of a shift to the centre, the possibility of a change in the balance of thinking within the Socialist Party itself towards those favouring more radical economic policy options should also not be entirely discounted.

On the monetary side, as during the Schmidt Chancellorship, Paris and Bonn have been united by the continuing high level of American interest rates and the strength of the dollar. However, it should be noted that both countries have also benefited from the surge in exports to the United States which the dollar's high value has permitted. The need for measures to reduce the huge US budget deficit has been another shared theme. At the London economic summit in June 1984, for example, both Kohl and Mitterrand emphasized the need for American action. The degree of German determination on interest rates has been particularly striking. One reason has certainly been a stronger perception of the implications of high American rates for the international debtor countries and the possible danger of a world banking crisis. In their recent meetings both the French and German Governments have emphasized not just the European but also the world dimensions of American monetary policy. One monetary theme that has subsided, however, is revising the international monetary system and obtaining greater stability in exchange rates. It is recognized that little progress can be made unless the American Administration is willing to discuss the link between its own monetary and fiscal policies and the dollar's value, and until it alters its view that market forces are the key determinant. However, in response to Mitterrand's continuing insistence, one outcome of the June 1984 London conference was to offer a reluctant commitment to continue studying this theme.

As far as international trade is concerned, certain differences remain between French and German views in 1984. Notably, the French have shown greater reservations than the German concerning a possible new round of GATT talks later this decade. Paris continues to favour more insular intra-Community solutions to some of the trading challenges of the 1980s, particularly regarding Japanese competition. However, with bilateral trading 'arrangements' on the increase and with many Third World countries already deflating severely owing to their debt problems, one must question more than ever the timeliness of this French approach. As far as Atlantic trade is concerned,

French and German views have been more closely aligned. Differences between the United States and the Community have persisted, for example on special steels. Above all, the Administration's emphasis on gaining better access for American agricultural products into protected markets like the EEC is bound to lead to renewed friction and will most likely foster closer co-ordination of French and German positions.

It is defence co-operation between France and Germany which has improved most strikingly. The worsening state of East–West relations has concentrated thinking on defence in both Bonn and Paris. Both countries are also acutely conscious of the need for a stronger European role within NATO, not least for domestic reasons, so as to prevent the Alliance appearing wholly under the influence of the United States. The French initiative for a revival of WEU is one aspect of this thinking, intended to contribute to a more coherent European voice in NATO. Mitterrand's spectacular suggestion in February 1984 of an orbiting European space station was another case in point. Yet it should be noted that the idea was not just put forward as a way of improving security. It also illustrated Mitterrand's belief that European integration needs to break away from contentious and stale areas like farming and the budget into ambitious new projects, especially in classical fields of 'high' politics like defence.

In a similar vein, both the President and Kohl have pushed ahead with their own bilateral defence co-ordination. (Though it should be noted that Franco-German talks on specific military projects have often been presented as precursors to wider European partnerships.) At the bilateral summit in May 1984, firm agreement was reached on going ahead with an anti-tank helicopter, while a wide variety of other schemes such as a new generation of anti-tank and anti-aircraft missiles have also been put up for consideration. Even an idea for military observation satellites is to be put before a bilateral study group. In sum, Franco-German co-operation under Mitterrand and Kohl has proceeded well on almost every front, but the bilateral summit of May 1984 confirmed that it is in the defence sector that relations have reached their closest.

12

Conclusion

Developments in French and German foreign policy since 1969

The period from 1969 to 1984 represents probably the most important era in French and German post-war history. The years can, in fact, be divided into three distinct phases. The first, spanning the Brandt–Pompidou era, was a decisive period of transition, while the second, comprising the Schmidt–Giscard years, was chiefly one of consolidation, in which many of the developments inaugurated earlier (and a number of new initiatives) came to fruition. With the elections of March 1983 returning a stable CDU-led Government in Bonn, the intermediate Schmidt–Mitterrand years have merged into the beginning of the Kohl Chancellorship to form a third, not yet fully characterized, phase in Franco-German relations.

The celebrations of January 1983 marking the twentieth anniversary of the signing of the Franco-German Treaty represented the culmination of a continuous process which, irrespective of periodization, can now safely be said to have reached full bloom. The festivities of 1983, with Mitterrand addressing a specially convened session of the Bundestag, and Kohl effusively praising the results of bilateral co-operation, represented the culmination of a long-running process. Critics may taunt that ministerial eulogies and publicity-minded gestures (such as performances by the newly formed Franco-German Symphony Orchestra and Chorus) merely illustrated once again the superficial, sometimes rather contrived, public façade of bilateral co-operation. Yet the fact that Franco-German links have survived, flourished, and had so much influence over European affairs since 1963 is not an event that should go entirely unsung.

In its own way, this book, too, has tried to document some of the influential occurences in bilateral and Community relations since the late 1960s, and to analyse them in terms of their bearing both for France and German individually and for the European Community as a whole. That so much attention has been paid to the period between 1969 and 1974 is a testament to that era's significance as one of crucial transition, in which many barriers were removed and the framework established for the much closer co-operation of the Schmidt–Giscard years and thereafter. In fact, 1974 marks a pivotal point in bilateral relations. Consequently, one of the aims of this conclusion will be to draw comparisons between the earlier and later periods, making certain revaluations where necessary.

In the Federal Republic, it was the *Ostpolitik* above all which contributed to the greater assurance and enhanced German role in international affairs of the 1970s. This situation was reinforced by the country's steadily growing economic strength, a process spotlighted by the elevation of international monetary affairs into the major preoccupation of Atlantic relations in the earlier part of the decade. By the autumn of 1973, West Germany's new weight had made itself felt in the country's relations with all its major partners. Not only were certain German politicians, notably Schmidt and Ertl, speaking with a confidence that belied the defensiveness of many of their predecessors; the Federal Republic had now also become more predisposed to bringing its considerable economic strength to bear on its external policy. As has been seen, this characteristic became commonplace after 1974.

In addition, an overtly didactic streak, especially on the economic side, became increasingly evident in German foreign policy in the early 1970s, growing even more familiar under Schmidt.[1] One notable aspect of this trend was the tendency to regard national economic doctrine as a model for others to copy. By the 1980s, this approach has become very regular. This emphasis on *Modell Deutschland* can, arguably, be interpreted as an outlet and part compensation for the continuing constraints on other aspects of German foreign policy. Since the mid-1970s, the tendency has also become apparent in the political field. German support for new democracies such as Spain and Portugal, and trouble-spots like Turkey and Poland, can be seen not only as a reflection of Bonn's greater readiness to use

---

[1] On this theme, see the leader, 'In Sachen Europa müssen wir kämpfen', in the *Frankfurter Allgemeine Zeitung*, 9 June 1979. Note also Emminger's comments in 'Die Stellung der Deutschen Mark in der Welt', 75. For French views, note Gergorin in DFI, *Deutschland, Frankreich und die europäische Krise*, 64.

economic prowess as an instrument in its foreign policy, but also as a means of publicly demonstrating its own embrace of democratic qualities (while coincidentally helping to safeguard German economic interests abroad). The approach can additionally be presented as one which assists in sharing the burden of defending Western interests.

While Germany's role in the world undoubtedly gained weight throughout the 1970s, between 1969 and 1974 certain factors made for the creation of a distorted image. First of all, the very process of transition under Brandt in itself created a confusing picture. This complicates precise analysis of Bonn's position *vis-à-vis* its partners, and is possibly one reason behind the greater attention that has been focused on the more stable Schmidt years. More important, the differences of personality within the Brandt Government and the problems of co-ordination that often occurred in German European policy inhibit the identification of any exact or wholly consistent line in German foreign policy during the period. The Chancellor's own attitude towards collegiate decision-making exacerbates matters. Only under Schmidt, a tough manager of government with a clear understanding of the complex economic and financial issues that have become increasingly important in international relations, could one speak of a more cogent German posture in world affairs, and especially in Europe. Hence the identification of a coherent German external line is greatly facilitated after 1974. Under Kohl, the situation remains uncertain, though some early signs suggest a move some way back towards the Brandt model.

Between 1969 and 1974, what emerged was a highly volatile pattern in German European policy, in which there was almost as much evidence of independent ministerial action as of carefully co-ordinated governmental planning on European issues. The forceful personalities of ministers like Schiller, Schmidt, and Ertl, the tradition of ministerial independence, and the powerful pressure group backing they enjoyed, all allowed them a considerable say over policy-making. This at times gave rise to an erratic representation of Germany's external opportunities. On occasion, ministerial positions themselves came into conflict, causing strife within the Cabinet and confusion abroad. One obvious example of this tendency was the clash between Schmidt's desire to combat inflation in 1972–3, partly by way of a farm price freeze, and Ertl's pursuit of real agricultural price rises. Much tighter management of the Cabinet under Schmidt after 1974 greatly reduced the frequency of such disputes, to the obvious benefit of German foreign policy. The indications are that Chancellor Kohl does not enjoy—nor necessarily seek—such a grip.

Such disagreements over foreign policy in the early 1970s were symptomatic of failings in the decision-making system in Bonn and of imperfections in the policy co-ordinating network during the period. Again, matters improved after 1974. Though not yet equalling that of Paris, Bonn's foreign policy gained consistency and came to bear a more marked political stamp. However, certain long-term problems persist. Certainly, the long-standing dichotomy between European federation and German reunification has become much less conspicuous. Yet an underlying conflict remains in the agricultural sector, where the short-run expedient of appeasing the farmers by offering real price rises stands out against the long-run objective of modifying the CAP. This problem was not resolved under Schmidt. Despite first steps towards resolution by all the member states at Community level in March 1984, it appears to be proving only a little less taxing under Kohl.

As to wider questions of German foreign policy in the 1970s, it should at all times be borne in mind that although the *Ostpolitik* greatly increased Bonn's room for manœuvre, major constraints remained. These if anything became more conspicuous after 1974 as a result of the seeming paradox between the Federal Republic's economic and political strength, and the general reluctance of German politicians to exploit their position to the full. Most obviously, the psychological effect of the Second World War and the suspicion with which the Federal Republic was, and still is, regarded in many quarters restricted the country's range of external opportunities. The upshot has been a desire in Bonn to avoid controversial unilateral actions as far as possible and instead to seek the widest possible participation in new initiatives. Such tendencies were particularly apparent in the Brandt period (as seen for example, in Bonn's policy towards a joint Community float from 1971 to 1973) and also under Schmidt. Most notably, the Germans took care to emphasize the joint French role in creating the EMS. Similarly, Bonn consistently sought the widest possible participation in the scheme, to the extent of offering substantial financial inducements to countries like Italy and Ireland to join in.

Of all the member states, including even the Benelux countries, the Federal Republic retains the greatest interest in the EEC's economic and especially its political survival. Bonn has nothing to gain from a Community that is weak or divided. This is particularly true in a period of considerable East–West tension like the 1980s. Similarly, unlike obvious counterparts in France or Britain, no political party in the Federal Republic can make electoral capital out of a predominantly anti-Market policy. Furthermore, the Community also provides a bonus from the security angle, its contribution to regional stability greatly valued in a country that remains particularly susceptible to international tension, and in which all parties consequently place *détente* high on their list of priorities.

In sum, one can identify a highly issue-oriented German approach to Community affairs throughout the 1970s and 1980s. West Germany's singular position has meant that its leaders were—and are—reluctant or unable to bring their country's full economic weight to bear on the course of Community policy. Rather, in order to avoid friction and advance its aims, the Federal Republic has sought as far as possible to maintain a policy of consensus, pioneering or developing initiatives in harness with other member states. Those instances when the Germans have acted alone or showed particular assertiveness have almost invariably been linked with the protection of key economic interests—notably regarding inflation—and also, to a much lesser extent, agriculture.

During the Brandt Chancellorship, for example, greater German self-assurance, combined with the detrimental effect of the dollar crisis on the money supply, resulted in Bonn's cautious participation in the Community's call in September 1971 for an American devaluation. By mid-1973, this tougher German attitude towards American monetary policy had become much more evident. In the EEC, German concern with inflation (and expenditure) were key elements in the friction that developed with France over the establishment of the first stage of EMU and the creation of the European Monetary Reserve Fund. Similarly,

in 1972–3 domestic political considerations were partly responsible for shaping Schmidt's restrictive approach to German
Community spending and for his characterization of the Federal
Republic as the 'paymaster' of Europe, but internal economic
factors—above all the control of inflation—were the prime
determinants.

A similar emphasis was wholly characteristic of the period
after 1974. The credit to Italy in August 1974, with its tight
conditions in terms of domestic economic management, forms
the prime example. The growing frustration with the uncertainties of American monetary policy later in the decade, which
greatly contributed to Schmidt's interest in a new Community
monetary initiative, came closely behind. Finally, the constant
German stress on controlling the Community budget, which was
most forcefully asserted in 1974–5, provided yet another
illustration of the same tendency.[2]

Such special emphasis on the domestic economic side in shaping German European policy was heightened during the Brandt
years by the appointment of powerful figures to key ministries like
finance, economics, and agriculture. Schiller was Minister of
Economics between 1969 and 1972 and 'Superminister' of Finance as well as Economics from 1971 to 1972. Schmidt took over
the Finance Ministry in 1972 and remained at the helm until
1974. In agriculture, Ertl continued to preside until March 1983, a
very impressive thirteen-and-a-half-year reign.

The presence of such forceful ministers gave an added edge to
the existing level of German determination in these key areas.
The effect of such personality factors is best seen in terms of a
comparison with events after 1974. While a very marked issue-
based approach remained a hallmark of German foreign policy
under Schmidt, there were far fewer instances of those distortions
caused by personality factors that were so evident during the
Brandt years. In consequence, German European policy gained
consistency and was marked by a clearer appreciation of the
bounds within which the country could operate as well as a more
balanced understanding of how best to proceed on that basis in
order to maximize the benefits of Community membership.

---

[2] On this topic, see Michael Leigh, 'Germany's changing role in the EEC', *The World Today* (Dec. 1975).

The 1970s, or at least the earlier half of the decade, are in many ways easier to analyse in the case of France than Germany. Certainly, the efficiency of the French policy co-ordination system—the early reversal over the Werner Report apart—was such that misleading shifts typical of the Federal Republic were successfully veiled. Yet problems of analysis remain. Though to a lesser extent than with Brandt, the Pompidou presidency was also one of transition, marking the post-de Gaulle adjustment of French foreign policy to a more pragmatic and interdependent footing. In the Community sphere, there was no longer any question after 1969 about the certainty of France's commitment to the EEC. His approach was marked by a considerable degree of caution, but Pompidou's belief in the future of Europe was never in doubt. The President also appeared to place greater weight on the specifically European aspect of French foreign policy compared to de Gaulle. This approach was perhaps partly motivated by the desire to gain a European dimension to his presidency. Above all—at least until 1972–3—there was a patent change of style under Pompidou, with an increased realism and reduced stress on doctrine.[3]

The impression of opening and relaxation in French Community policy was visible in many areas. Pre-eminent was the decision to sanction enlargement (though the General himself had been moving in this direction). Little less important was the impetus for a *relance* of the Community's activities and its progress into new areas of integration. The rise of political co-operation and steps towards closer economic and monetary links most clearly exemplified these developments. On a longer term basis, Pompidou also showed a readiness to entertain new ideas for Europe, an approach seen in his interest in the creation of Ministers for Europe and in steps towards some vague form of European Confederation.

Yet the force of continuity often matched such progressive tendencies. This was witnessed most strikingly in relation to the Community's institutional development, where there was no diminution in presidential opposition to supranationality and stress on an inter-governmental future for Europe. Unanimity

---

[3] On this question, note the comments made by M. Merle, 'Politique extérieure entre l'immobilisme et l'ouverture', *Projet* 48 (Sept.–Oct. 1970), 955.

remained the watchword in decision-making. Nor was there any change in French hostility to increased powers for the Commission or the European Parliament. This cautious, inter-governmental approach emerged most clearly in those two new areas of policy, EMU and political co-operation, where the new President himself had been a chief instigator. The rigid distinction that France maintained between meetings of the Council of EEC Foreign Ministers and sessions of the same group of men gathered to discuss political co-operation was most conspicuous. The differentiation was taken to an extreme in November 1973, and only under Giscard were such distinctions eased.

Continuity was as evident in Pompidou's emphasis on the CAP. The new President appeared to place a weight on this sector which transcended its mere economic interest to France, and which suggested, rather, that agriculture held some greater social and almost philosophical significance in Pompidou's view of the structure of society.[4] The appointment of Chirac, a trusted protégé, as farm minister can be seen as a more tangible sign of Pompidou's interest. In the wider realm of French foreign policy too, the continued emphasis after 1969 on France's prestige and position in the world remained a prime element, tempered only now by the greater sense of realism in international affairs that Pompidou imparted.

There exists, however, a serious complicating factor in this transitional picture of French foreign policy between 1969 and 1974, namely the apparent change of direction that took place between 1972 and 1974, which resulted in a considerably more cautious and often abrupt approach to European and international affairs. The entire question of whether such a shift actually did take place, and, if so, to what extent the result could be seen as a return to a more orthodox type of Gaullist stance, has taxed many observers and sparked off lively debate in the literature. This book has tried to show that such a shift did indeed occur, although it was one which, in line with Pompidou's character, was more a pragmatic response to circumstances rather than a premeditated and ideologically based reaction typical of de Gaulle. A number of factors can be adduced as

---

[4] Note Rials, *Les Idéees politiques du Président*, 37–40, 82–5. See also Jobert's comments in *L'Autre Regard*, 165.

causes for the change of tack. Internally, the referendum of April 1972 was highly significant, signalling (to the President at least) popular disenchantment with his European policy, and seriously weakening Pompidou *vis-à-vis* his party's old guard. The President's illness must also be identified as a part cause, demoralizing him and contributing to the pessimistic view he increasingly adopted towards international developments in 1973–4.

Most important, however, were external circumstances. Uppermost amongst these was American foreign policy. The incidents during Pompidou's 1970 visit to the United States, and, more tellingly, the frictions caused by the American trade and monetary measures of 1971, left their mark. Pre-eminent, however, was the Nixon Administration's increasing emphasis on bloc diplomacy, embodied in the superpower negotiations on nuclear weapons of 1973, and the American President's explicit evocation of a future pentagonal world power bloc structure. It should be noted that this was a system which, while apparently granting Western Europe and Japan an autonomous role, was designed very much to submerge their interests beneath an American-ordained overall approach. In conjunction with the heavy pressure being exerted on the Europeans as part of Kissinger's vigorous efforts to restore American preponderance in the Alliance, there resulted a much more abrupt French stance towards Washington and a renewed emphasis on multipolarity on the part of the French Government. Even before the problems of 1973, the question of an independent European identity in world affairs was one which had exercised Pompidou's mind.[5] By 1973 itself, with Washington for the first time in many years exerting not just economic, but extremely strong political leverage on the Nine, this European independence required much more forceful expression. Hence France's adoption of a leading role in guiding the Community towards a more autonomous and, from the American point of view, confrontational line in international affairs. In this context, the elevation of Jobert, a close confidant, to the post of Foreign Minister was wholly appropriate. Not only did the opionions held by

---

[5] See, for instance, Pompidou's television speech of 21 Apr. 1972, reported in *Le Monde*, 23–4 Apr. 1972, and his remarks quoted in *Le Monde*, 10 Feb. 1972.

Jobert—describable alternatively as an 'advanced Gaullist' or a 'Gaullist aberration', depending on one's point of view—chime fully with Pompidou's own appraisals by this stage; his promotion also served internal purposes, giving the ailing President an important ally within the Government against Giscard.[6]

The change of tack in 1972–4 illustrates the difficulties of giving a clear portrayal of French foreign policy under Pompidou. As with Brandt in the Federal Republic, so with Pompidou in France, the period defies simple explanation. Although some commentators have inferred a lack of knowledge on Pompidou's part regarding foreign affairs as a means of interpreting the shift that took place in the latter part of his presidency, the evidence is by no means conclusive. Certainly, there is a danger of misreading the caution and consequent lack of brio in Pompidou's approach to foreign affairs as a sign of uncertainty and insufficient understanding. Yet perhaps the best explanation is also one of the simplest; namely that the very task of following a figure like de Gaulle in itself imposed a severely constraining influence. As one French commentator has observed, 'Pompidou cannot allow himself to differ from the General. Even less can he permit himself to resemble him.'[7]

While the Pompidou presidency emerges as one of both continuity and opening in terms of its foreign policy, the Giscard years represent an acceleration of the latter trend, marking a further move away from the rigidities and doctrinaire considerations of the 1960s. Thus the post-1974 period should be seen as a culminaton of the transitory forces partly set in motion by Pompidou, rather than as a complete break with the past.

Such evolutionary change was visible in most areas of French Community policy after 1974. Even the most momentous institutional development, direct elections, was balanced by a much more traditional approach towards both Parliamentary powers and the role of the Commission. Thus Giscard was firmly opposed to the institutional recommendations contained in the

---

[6] A number of authoritative sources interviewed by the author referred to Pompidou's mixed admiration and distrust for his Minister of Finance. See also Roussel, *Pompidou*, 331; *L'Express*, No. 1159 (24–30 Sept. 1973), 58–9.

[7] Alain-Gérard Slama, 'La République et ses rois', *Contrepoint* 14 (1974), 173. Note also Roussel, op. cit. 388, 417.

Tindemans Report. What is more, it was Pompidou's emphasis on inter-governmentalism and desire for regular summit meetings which was taken up and finally enacted in Giscard's initiative for the creation of the European Council.

Other areas of French European policy showed similar signs of continuity. Giscard's motives for closer monetary links between the Nine were little different from Pompidou's own, while in the agricultural sector, there was no diminution in French emphasis on safeguarding the CAP. Admittedly, Giscard did not show the same emotional commitment towards the role of agriculture as Pompidou. He adopted, rather, a narrower approach based chiefly on the financial advantages involved and on the political need to woo the farmers for domestic purposes. The latter requirement was demonstrated most strikingly in Giscard's obstruction of the EMS on account of the dispute over MCAs.

Even on enlargement, that other major change of the Giscard era, traditional forces remained strongly in evidence. Although Paris firmly backed Greek membership, Giscard's early enthusiasm for Spanish participation was soon transformed into a rearguard action, aimed at blocking or at least delaying matters as long as possible. In sum, while loaded more towards change, the balance between traditional and novel forces in French European policy under Giscard was by no means one-sided. Both the President's own inclination and, more important, domestic political constraints, tempered the speed of new developments.

It was principally in terms of style that the greatest change was visible in French European policy after 1974. Despite the restrictions imposed by the nationalist leanings of Gaullists and Communists alike, the French approach to Community affairs —and foreign policy in general—became markedly more pragmatic. There was a less obvious stress on national independence and a move away from the strict demarcations of the past. This development was most evident in the field of political co-operation. It was also witnessed in Giscard's considerably more co-operative approach to the question of joint Western energy consultations.

In the wider realm of foreign policy, Giscard's more relaxed stance bore greatest fruit in terms of relations with the United States. This transition was already under way early in the Pompidou years, though, as has been seen, it was sharply deflected in the President's last year of office. (Giscard's more favourable attitude to Washington, which stemmed from a better appreciation of economic and political interdependence and a less strict observance of the Gaullist doctrine of multipolarity improved the climate of understanding between France and the United States. Less evidence in the Carter presidency of the type of bloc diplomacy practised by the Nixon Administration greatly facilitated this process. Furthermore, although independence and a stronger European role in world affairs remained a primary element of Giscard's presidential platform, these were no longer presented with the same competitive edge that had characterized them under de Gaulle—or, for that matter, Pompidou in his closing year. As has been seen, this more accommodating line contributed significantly to the French *entente* with the Federal Republic after 1974.)

As for French Community policy under Mitterrand, there has been marked progress, notably in the first half of 1984. The President's interest in new social and industrial measures, which was quickly translated into action at domestic level, has also been reflected in French European policy. Thus, the Socialists have put forward ambitious proposals for the creation of an 'espace social européen' and 'espace industriel européen'. However, despite French efforts to the contrary, until autumn 1984 at least, the pressure of circumstances forced a shift of attention away from such novel areas back towards more familiar Community ground such as the budget, Britain's EEC contribution, and enlargement.

It is here that French policy has been very active. Significantly, Paris has been prepared to accept new budgetary mechanisms for the British, though only as part of an overall increase in the Community's own resources, due to rise from 1 per cent to 1.4 per cent of national VAT contributions as of 1986. On the CAP too the French have taken a leading role. Surprisingly for some, Paris has accepted a system of milk production quotas, as well as a variety of other cost-saving measures. France's presidency of the Council of Ministers in 1984 was instrumental in this readiness to take steps which would have been almost inconceivable in the past. On enlargement too, strong French reservations have finally been put aside and the talks have progressed. Yet French policy under Mitterrand has shown a consistently pragmatic streak. The watershed agricultural price agreement of March 1984 also contained a commitment gradually to eliminate MCAs. Similarly, Paris has adopted a tough line throughout the detailed negotiations on Spanish membership of the Community.

As to relations with the United States, there has been an interesting shift under Mitterrand. In the economic and trading sectors, the President has often adopted a hostile line towards Washington, generally much less restrained than under his predecessor. In monetary policy too, Mitterrand's call for a return to an international system of fixed parities was a direct response to the strength of the dollar and the damage caused by monetary uncertainty. Yet in the military and strategic fields, by contrast, Paris and Washington have seen eye to eye. Though many Americans were unhappy about Communist participation in the French Government, Mitterrand's resolute stand on defence, his reserved stance towards the Soviet Union, and his support for the deployment of new American missiles, have struck a harmonious chord in Washington. Although French suggestions for tighter European co-operation on defence have met with mixed feelings in the American capital, elsewhere on the defence front French and American views have undoubtedly drawn closer together.

Developments at European level

The 1970s in particular were as important a period for the European Community as a whole as for France and German individually. The Hague summit of 1969 marked a watershed in post-war European history comparable to the Messina conference of 1955. As a result of the decisions reached in December 1969, the member states were set to bring the Community's transitional period to a close and to embark on a number of ambitious new initiatives. Not least, they were also finally able to agree on the enlargement of the EEC. Only the Paris summit of December 1974 can be said to have rivalled the Hague conference in terms of importance for the Community's future. Even then, however, the scope of the meeting was narrower than that of its predecessor five years earlier. In a very difficult economic climate, much greater emphasis was placed on safeguarding existing policies and on maintaining the

Community as it stood than on breaking new ground in integration.

In the early 1970s, it was EMU which was the major initiative and certainly the most contentious issue. In retrospect, the much-discussed plans for an economic and monetary union by 1980 appear delusory. Yet it was changes in the external environment which were primarily responsible for the downfall of the scheme. The vicissitudes of the dollar, combined with the dissimilar appeals of Community currencies as havens for speculative funds, resulted in severe economic and political variations between the member states. Differing national inflation rates added to these problems. By late 1973 and early 1974, with the Community's plans for EMU racked by successive relative parity changes and floats, the marked dilution of the policy's second stage well illustrated the degree to which former targets had been downgraded.

It is interesting to compare EMU with the much less ambitious EMS of the later 1970s. Certainly, the arrival of the new scheme was greatly eased by the more stable international monetary climate into which it was born. Though dollar instability was an important factor behind Schmidt's backing for the venture, international monetary unrest was by no means of the same order as that which had finally sunk EMU. The fact that the Snake was already in place and most central banks had gained experience of operating their currencies within it was also a bonus. Moreover, a learning process had taken place. No longer was there any question of grand, long-term strategies for tightly-bound European monetary links, but rather a much more pragmatic and gradualist approach, with limited, but feasible, shorter-term aims. As a result, the benefits of the EMS have largely lived up to its founders' expectations, and even the occasional realignments—albeit more frequent than was originally envisaged—have confirmed faith in the system rather than cast doubt on it.

A similar evolution is visible over the wider span of European monetary policy. With the benefit of hindsight, the repetitive and seemingly very important discussions that were typical of the early 1970s on the question of relative parity levels and competitiveness now appear out of place (although it must be admitted that the Franco-German monetary clashes of March

1983 called to mind earlier days). Since 1974, not only have there been much larger parity changes than in the early 1970s, but these have also been seen to have had surprisingly little effect. With the experience of protracted floating, government attitudes shifted markedly, and a greater readiness to sanction currency appreciations evolved. This lesson has extended to the agricultural side, where the repercussions of parity changes and the resulting need for MCAs came to be accepted as a matter of course, and were generally tackled with far less friction than in the past. The agreement in 1984 to eliminate MCAs may result in the complete disappearance of this issue over the next few years.

As for the second major Community initiative of the Brandt–Pompidou era, political co-operation, matters were more successful from the outset than for EMU. It is true that the policy was held back in its early years by procedural difficulties, which stemmed chiefly from France. Yet despite such obstacles, considerable progress was made even in this period. The results were most visible in the Community's joint preparations and common stand at the Helsinki conference and also in the member states' voting patterns at the UN.

Yet it is since 1974 that political co-operation really came into its own. This was partly a consequence of the procedural relaxation sanctioned by Giscard. Impressive achievements were made, notably in terms of relations with the Middle East. Yet despite the improvements, certain flaws remained. These were most evident in the Community's tardy or even non-existent responses to major international crises, such as the Russian invasion of Afghanistan. The fault can partly be ascribed to the consequence of circumstances in the Brandt–Pompidou era; even under Giscard, however, no progress was made on the touchy subject of creating a permanent political co-operation secretariat, whose existence might well have helped to overcome some of the delays and inadequacies that were exposed. This gap has not been filled even by 1984.

Concerning institutional developments as a whole in the Community, there was again only limited progress between 1969 and 1974. Once more, this was chiefly on account of the French. Differences were manifested not only regarding the political secretariat, but also concerning the ambitious developments envisaged in the Werner Report. Similarly, no advance was made on direct elections—despite Brandt's considerable enthusiasm. It is interesting to bear in mind the diminution that took place in the Chancellor's calls for direct elections during his period of office. The shift can be partly ascribed to a growing appreciation of the obstacles on the French side. As has been seen, only under Giscard were barriers finally lifted, though in the teeth of fierce domestic opposition. Yet despite this change, it should be recalled that the President retained a highly cautious approach towards other institutional developments.

What institutional progress there was between 1969 and 1974 was firmly of an inter-governmental order. Foremost was the rise of Community summit meetings. While not new, such gatherings of the EEC's Heads of State or Government took on a novel and highly important role—one to be consolidated and extended after 1974. The Hague summit in particular represented a decisive turning-point. Yet a number of other, less favourable, observations must also be made regarding the Community's summits of the early 1970s. First of all, the 1972 Paris summit stands out for the tendency, evident throughout the period, to adopt grand but often empty gestures of 'high' politics. Notably, this occurred with the proposal to establish a 'European Union' by 1980. The target was never adequately defined, and it appears in retrospect to have been almost totally devoid of substance. Mitterrand's speech before the European Parliament in May 1984, voicing strong support for a new treaty between the member states to take integration into new areas, may mark a more solidly grounded boost for the concept. But it remains to be seen whether the President's remarks will be followed by worthwhile action. Possibly they should be placed more in the context of Socialist Party electioneering in the prelude to the European elections of June 1984.

Secondly, as regards Community summits, in the wake of the 1973 Copenhagen summit in particular there was evident a distinct contrast between the grand statements and declarations made by the national leaders concerning matters of 'high' politics, and the severe differences that erupted between their technical ministers once negotiations of detailed issues of 'low' politics began in earnest. Both these characteristics threw light on the particular importance of the public relations side in

Community summitry during the period. This role of public relations was accentuated by the relative novelty of summit meetings and their image as special 'events'. The fact that the two main participants, Brandt and Pompidou, were newcomers to the forefront of the international political stage also played a part.

Many of these considerations remained active after 1974. Marked differences of emphasis persisted between discussions at summit and ministerial levels. Yet there were a number of important changes too. These originated principally from the institutionalization of summit meetings. The greater frequency of contacts, combined with the linked fact that the European Council became increasingly obliged to handle more mundane issues passed up from technical Councils, meant that the triennial Community summits lost some of their lustre compared to their pre-1975 counterparts. Yet this development was also partly attributable to a deliberate—though not entirely success-ful—attempt by the Heads of State and Government to improve decision-making by removing some of the pomp and parapher-nelia from their meetings. While Pompidou's aim of regular, slimmed-down 'fireside chats' did not entirely materialize, there was some movement in this direction.

The trend towards greater efficiency in decision-making at European Council level has to some extent been compromised by the fact that meetings have often been dominated by down-to-earth matters such as fishing quotas or methods of calculating budget contributions. Thus, meetings have not always provided Community leaders with the opportunity for surveying the broad lines of policy from above as was originally intended. This process has not, however, gone unopposed. Hostility was witnessed most noticeably in Schmidt and Giscard's joint refusal to devote a third European Council meeting to the British budgetary dispute following the failure to reach agreement at the December 1979 and May 1980 summits. For both leaders, discussion at the Community's most senior level had been blocked long enough.

The rise of summits must be viewed as a major factor in the trend towards greater inter-governmentalism in the Community that was evident in the early 1970s, and which accelerated following the creation of the European Council. Although the

Commission has managed to retain a role at summit meetings, the initiative has conclusively passed to the national governments. However, as much as the development of summitry, it can be argued that it was the influence of monetary unrest in the Brandt–Pompidou period which contributed to the drift towards inter-governmentalism. The discussions that took place on monetary issues and on questions of relative parity levels tended to leave the Commission on the sidelines. The exclusion of the Commission was often further accentuated by the fact that monetary matters regularly involved negotiations at Atlantic level and took place in organizations such as the IMF or Group of Ten. Finally, the French policy of systematically barring the Commission from political co-operation meetings wherever possible intensified the inter-governmental drift.

All these factors remained in evidence after 1974, and have persisted since 1981. Above all, under both Giscard and Mitterrand, the French have continued to seek the Commission's exclusion from non-EEC gatherings. Thus it was only after a lengthy wrangle that in May 1977 Paris finally gave way and sanctioned Commission participation at the Western economic summits which had been inaugurated at Rambouillet in November 1975. The move had been avidly sought by the smaller member states, both as a means of emphasizing the Commission's role and a Community presence in world affairs and, probably more important, as a way of providing them with a proxy in a group from which they were otherwise excluded.

What can be said of Europe's international role in the 1970s and early 1980s? During the Brandt–Pompidou years, the most striking indication of the Community's effect on others as a major economic force was witnessed in the American commercial restrictions of August 1971. In Washington, the EEC had already come to be recognized as a very significant actor in international trade. The Community's common external tariff, particularly in agriculture, and its preferential trading arrangements with other areas, were deeply resented by the Americans. Such feelings contributed to the brutality of Nixon's measures.[8] Elsewhere, Europe's combined influence in international com-

---

[8] Schaetzel suggests that the aggressive American tactics were also partly a response and a consequence of the precedent set by de Gaulle. See *The Unhinged Alliance*, 106–7.

merce was manifested by its preparations and subsequent joint stand in the Nixon round of GATT.

This picture hardly altered in the second half of the 1970s. While the Community gained in stature as a major trading bloc, American resentment at European commercial practices, particularly in agriculture, continued to fester. Matters were exacerbated now by the world economic recession, which intensified existing competition in foreign trade. Yet despite these increased competitive pressures, there was no repetition of the protectionist moves of 1971. It can well be argued that, paradoxically, the very difficulty of the economic circumstances and the shared appreciation of the need to avoid beggar-thy-neighbour policies actually contributed to this restraint. Certainly, there was a widespread reluctance to be the first to trigger a chain protectionist reaction. The rise of Western economic summitry in the period, allowing regular top-level contacts, assisted in the process. It is interesting to note that meetings of the mid-1970s were dominated by the topic of avoiding protectionism.

Only in the early 1980s have differences come closer to a head in Atlantic trade. Although the long-running dispute over European steel exports to the United States was brought to an amicable conclusion (at least in the short term) the years ahead signal difficulties for US–EEC relations in the international trading arena both over manufactured and agricultural products. The issue of further American restrictions on European special steels continues to simmer, while friction over a whole range of agricultural goods has become commonplace.

Politically the early 1970s were considerably more complex than economically. Although political co-operation often contributed to the formation of a more coherent European posture, this was not always the case. More important, European actions cannot be viewed in isolation. The events of 1973, in particular, brought to the fore the importance of the external environment in shaping integration. American policy has consistently been the most significant determinant here. Yet there has been a dynamic process at work. Although Washington's encouragement was a major factor in the development of Europe in the 1950s and 1960s, by the early 1970s this mood had altered, largely as a result of economic competition and the EEC's image in the United States as a protectionist bloc. The upshot was a much more hostile American approach to the Community between 1969 and 1974.

Yet, that the Community should, after an initial divisive phase, have united in opposition to the American monetary policy of 'unbenign neglect' and to Nixon's trade moves bore witness to the role of the American tactics as an external integrator. Similarly, in 1973, until the outbreak of the Middle East war at least, one could once again discern a perhaps surprising degree of European cohesion towards Kissinger's plans. In both cases the evidence suggests that, by the 1970s, the coherence of the Community and the importance of maintaining solidarity had come to be perceived by all the member states as being sufficiently valuable to outweigh the more threatening American tactics of the period. This picture contrasts sharply with that of the 1950s and early 1960s, when American encouragement was often a crucial factor in promoting fragile integration. Apart from the obvious solidification of links between the member states and appreciation of the benefits derived from their economic co-operation, one of the decisive causes behind this greater European cohesion was the increased German confidence of the period and Bonn's diminished susceptibility to American pressure.

This trend of greater German assurance was intensified as the 1970s progressed. Combined with Bonn's *rapprochement* with Paris after 1974, it was one factor behind the improved European political unity of the period. Freed from many of the divisions of the Brandt–Pompidou era—some of which, at least, were based on differing French and German levels of vulnerability towards the United States—the Community was able to deal more effectively with Washington. The Carter Administration's shift away from bloc diplomacy, and the much reduced American pressure on the Europeans both in the strategic and commercial fields also assisted. Giscard's own more pragmatic approach towards the United States played an additional part. As a result, US–EEC relations were placed on a much more businesslike footing than had been the case at the close of the Brandt–Pompidou era.

Under Reagan, the position has altered once again, with the Americans putting new pressures on the Europeans. Notably, the United States has embarked on an aggressive line on trading matters. In the military field the picture has shifted even more sharply. Reagan's tough, some might say, bellicose, approach, not only towards East–West relations, but also to Central America, the Caribbean, and the Middle East, has caused great anxiety in European capitals. But although certain contemporary questions have been discussed amongst the Ten themselves as part of their political co-operation process, what dialogue there has been with Washington has tended to take place either on a strictly bilateral basis or in non-Community institutions such as NATO or the annual Western economic summit meetings.

Hence Europe's input into American foreign policy-making has been severely restricted, and many Community leaders have felt that their views have been taken for granted. The change of power from Schmidt to Kohl has also played some part in this process. The new German Chancellor is less authoritative a figure in the American capital than his predecessor. Whereas Schmidt was often able to act as an effective spokesman for European interests in Washington, it is questionable whether Kohl will ever be able to adopt this mantle. Finally, though, one should also note that the Reagan Administration, for its part, regularly continues to bemoan a lack of European co-operation in conducting its foreign policy.

As to other areas of the Community's external relations, there was some evidence in the later 1970s and early 1980s of a more unified European voice in world affairs. This evolved principally from the improvement and increased scope of political co-operation. The Community's Middle East peace initiative of June 1980 represented a zenith. Furthermore, the very extension of the Community's size first to ten, and possibly to twelve, members, has granted it additional weight in world affairs. Yet Europe has still not developed its full international potential. Shortcomings have been most evident at times of crisis in East–West relations, such as over Afghanistan and Poland. The EEC has often failed to respond with the speed or unity necessary to grant its voice the authoritative international hearing it deserves.

In considering European policy, something must be said of the energy sector, so crucial in the 1970s, and of the Community's reaction to the two oil crises of the period. These episodes severely tested the EEC's political and economic unity. Yet one is aware of a marked evolution between Europe's responses of the earlier and later parts of the decade. In the 1973–4 crisis, the shortage of oil, combined with American pressure to adopt a unified Western approach, precipitated severe divisions within European ranks. The member states did manage to retain some, albeit strained, measure of unity regarding the Middle East—witnessed in their calls for a ceasefire. But once the consequences of the oil shortage were clearly appreciated and, perhaps more important, the disparities between the member states made themselves increasingly evident, sharp divisions arose. Although the situation was viewed in primarily political terms by the French, for the other member states the split that took place at the Washington conference was one which, though most certainly not devoid of political significance was principally economic in origin. In the earlier trade and monetary crises of the 1970s, American policy had eventually resulted in a *rapprochement* and strengthening of European bonds, but in the energy crisis, which struck forcefully at the economies of the Community countries, the centrifugal tendencies unleashed were much greater than in the past. These would most likely have remained highly active had it not been for the internal changes that took place in Britain, Germany, and France within three months of the Washington meeting. Combined with internal difficulties in the White House, these European developments allowed for a period of reassessment and conciliation.

As has been seen, it was the change of power in France, above all, which opened the way to a gradual accommodation on energy matters. Giscard's better appreciation of Western economic interdependence prepared the ground for the closer Atlantic co-operation in the energy field of the mid- and later 1970s. No longer did the French allow political rivalry with the United States to obstruct Western co-ordination. This development, in conjunction with the reduced severity of the 1979 oil crisis compared to its predecessor, permitted the rise of a more unified Western approach. The new stance was less clouded by political factors than in 1973–4 and freer from the scramble for privileged access and bilateral deals that had so marred Atlantic and Community relations earlier in the decade. Yet it is an illustration of the complexity and divisiveness of the energy issue that even in the early 1980s, with the oil market slacker than for many years, the Community has remained unable to unite on a common energy policy of its own.

Finally, mention must be made of the part played by the individual member states in European integration since 1969. The role of France and Germany will be examined in detail in the next section, and comment will be reserved here for Britain and the other Community countries. Perhaps one of the greatest ironies in West European affairs in the post-war period has been the deception of the smaller member states regarding British membership of the EEC. First of all, London has proved far from the fount of new ideas that was at one time imagined. During the Heath Government the British approach to Community affairs often seemed motivated chiefly by the desire to maximize short-term benefits from membership rather than emphasizing a longer-term political commitment. This attitude stemmed principally from the need to demonstrate the material advantages of participation in the EEC to the domestic electorate and to offset national expenditure on Community policies. Such a strategy was most conspicuous in the British approach towards the regional fund.

This approach was intensified after 1974, when the influence of short-term domestic considerations was magnified as a result of party political factors. Wrangles within the Labour Party over its attitude to Community membership, combined with the need for Labour pro-Marketeers to differentiate themselves from their Conservative counterparts, led to the renegotiation episode. Difficulties persisted throughout the decade as British politicians failed to strike the right balance between airing genuine grievances, especially over the budget, and finding the correct note of Europeanism to create a suitable climate for agreement. Not even the return of a Conservative Government in 1979, nominally committed to the European Community, eased this situation. In fact, Mrs. Thatcher's determined and at times abrasive style occasionally exacerbated matters. The Conservatives' re-election in 1983 did not change this practice in the least, with the Prime Minister as combative as ever. Thus, in many European circles Britain's membership of the EEC has often come to be regarded more as a thorn in the flesh of a smooth-running Community than a source of inspiration for the future of integration.

British participation in the EEC has embodied even less the alternative to Franco–German bilateralism and barrier to an inter-governmental future that had once been envisaged by the Benelux countries in particular. One can in fact point to a nascent trilateralism in the Community between the run-up to Britain's accession in January 1973 and Heath's fall from power in February 1974. Within this tripartite grouping there was manifest in turn a growing Anglo-French *rapprochement* built around a limited convergence of interests: notably, similar pragmatic approaches to the development of the Community and its institutions, and also towards its political relations with the rest of the world.

That this triangular relationship between Bonn, Paris, and London did not last after Heath's downfall can largely be attributed to the subsequent vacillation and political manœuvring in Britain on the European issue. To a lesser extent, the country's relative economic weakness compared to its major European partners was also responsible. More recently, difficulties with Mrs. Thatcher have played a part, while former anti-Market tendencies in the Labour Party also helped to cast the United Kingdom's European convictions into doubt. Labour's reassessment of Community links in 1983–4 still lacks sufficient conviction to remedy earlier negative foreign impressions. As a result of all these factors, former notions of a triumvirate guiding the Community have finally been laid to rest, and are highly unlikely to be resurrected.

As for the smaller member states, continuity was the most evident characteristic of the 1970s. Something must first of all be said of the special position of Italy among Community countries. It can plausibly be argued that the degree and, to some extent, exclusivity, of Franco-German bilateralism that was apparent early in the decade and which was later intensified under Schmidt and Giscard, highlighted the isolation of Rome (and, after 1974, London) in a category somewhat to one side of Bonn and Paris among the member states. At the same time, however, their status was definitely above that of the Benelux capitals. Italy's role since 1969 cannot be described as decisive. Although a determined Italian approach was consistently evident over regional policy, where Rome acted with vigour to ensure that programmes would be established, elsewhere the Italian voice tended to be more muted. The Rome Government emerged more as an effective go-between behind the scenes than a major actor. The preoccupation of domestic political instability, and Italy's relative economic weakness compared to its Community partners can be taken as the major causes for this situation. In the monetary field, the instability of the lira was an extra debilitating factor. Yet despite these restrictions, it is worth bearing in mind Colombo's observation of 1980 along the lines that the close friendship between Paris and Bonn would be exceedingly short-lived were it not for the active agreement of the other member states.[9] Such remarks indicated a simultaneous acceptance of the status quo and assertion of the rights of those left out.

As for the Benelux countries, there is no doubt that these smaller states have shown a readiness to block or instigate progress in the Community incommensurate with their size. Though never so forcefully expressed during the 1970s as during the Fouchet negotiations of the early 1960s, the Benelux countries have always been prepared vociferously to expound their views and policy preferences. They have been particularly voluble regarding institutional matters. The three countries, Holland and Belgium in particular, have consistently upheld the importance of supranationality and the role of the Commission. Such an approach has stemmed partly from their firm European convictions, and also from their long-standing fears of domination by their larger partners. Certainly, they have often enjoyed a disproportionately large say, particularly regarding institutional issues. But in the major areas of policy, although the agreement of all the member states was a necessity, it was the Franco-German role that was paramount.

The Franco-German role in European integration

The importance of the dialogue between Paris and Bonn at the heart of the European Community and the indispensability of agreement between them for wider progress in the EEC have spanned over three decades since the inception of European integration. These themes have formed the leitmotivs of this book. The exchange of interests at the Hague summit and the

[9] Reported in *The Times*, 13 Aug. 1980.

subsequent negotiations on enlargement, Economic and Monetary Union, political co-operation, the role of France and Germany in preparing the path towards international monetary reform—all testified to the importance of accord between the two countries. After 1974, this process was extended. It was no longer out of place to speak of a developing Franco-German 'axis' in Europe, one unaffected by the first enlargement of the EEC. The establishment of the European Monetary System, settlement of Britain's renegotiation and long-running subsequent budgetary disputes (temporarily at least), and steps towards the Community's second enlargement, all owed in large measure to Franco-German understanding.

Central to this pattern were the biannual summits between Bonn and Paris. These meetings fulfilled a number of functions.[10] First and foremost, they prepared the way for new initiatives. This occured most visibly in 1972 with the *relance* of EMU following the February bilateral summit. It recurred just as conspicuously in 1978 in the contacts between Schmidt and Giscard regarding closer Community monetary links prior to the July European Council meeting. Secondly, bilateral summits unblocked disagreements—frequently turning on France and Germany—at lower levels. This was seen, for instance, in the breakthrough on EMU in January 1971 and in the progress made on the EMS in September 1978. It should be recognized, however, that it is not always possible to distinguish between these two aspects. Furthermore, even on those occasions when no progress was made at Franco-German level, it can be argued that the papering over of differences that often took place was not always wholly negative. Indeed, at certain times a useful breathing-space was gained.

There was undoubtedly a reanimation of bilateral summit meetings after 1969. Various factors were responsible. Above all, the reinvigoration of the Community after the Hague summit injected new life into the bilateral talks following a fallow period. In addition, the onset of a less doctrinaire and more realistic French foreign policy under Pompidou also contributed. Paris

[10] On the organization of bilateral summits and official Franco-German meetings generally, see Paul Noack, 'L'Information franco-allemande au niveau gouvernemental', in *Documents* (Dec. 1979), Special Number on 'Information et Communication', 70–3.

was ready to look much more favourably at new Community developments, and, at least until the difficulties in Atlantic relations of winter 1973–4, the French no longer appeared to demand impossible choices from Bonn in its external relations. Finally, developments in German foreign policy also share some responsibility. There is little doubt that talks on the *Ostpolitik*, a major and frequent theme at bilateral summits, added weight to the meetings and contributed to their greater impact after 1969.

As has been seen, many of these factors were intensified after 1974. Better personal relations between the French and German leaders and strongly shared views on many pressing political and economic issues brought about a marked *rapprochement*. This was greatly facilitated both by Giscard's highly pragmatic approach to international affairs and by the greater distance gradually introduced by Schmidt into German relations with the United States, a consequence of the various differences of perception that arose in the period.

Yet some qualifications must be made to this model of Franco-German pre-eminence in the Community. Without doubt there existed (and, in many cases, there remain) certain limiting factors to the scope of bilateral Franco-German influence. Principally, one must underline the divergences in French and German economic structures and philosophies which have often impeded progress. Many issues, whether agricultural or trade-related, exposed the differing, often structurally based, priorities in French and German policy. Even in the 1980s, despite the evolution of French trading patterns, differences in history, resource allocations, and trading ideology have meant that the Federal Republic's approach to international trade remains in many ways closer to that of, say, Holland than France. Structurally based policy differences have likewise hindered bilateral economic co-operation.

Between 1969 and 1974, such divisions were also highly apparent in the political sphere. Despite the greater freedom of action afforded to the Federal Republic by the *Ostpolitik* and economic strength, Bonn remained more vulnerable than Paris to American pressure. Although this apsect became less important in the latter half of the Brandt Chancellorship (and declined markedly under Schmidt) the severe friction that emerged in bilateral Franco-German relations in May 1971 bore witness to the former divisive potential of American actions.

Above all, though, it was the 1973–4 oil crisis which spotlighted the highly dissimilar range of political options open to France and Germany. By late 1973, Paris and London were pushing Bonn towards an Arab-orientated Middle East policy faster than its special relationship with Israel could bear. The situation highlighted the particular psychological constraints on German foreign policy imposed by the Second World War. Though by no means restricted to the Middle East, it is in this area that the problem is brought into the sharpest relief and the contrast with France seen at its most marked. However, there has been a gradual evolution at work: certainly, the cautiously pro-Arab stance adopted by Schmidt in his trip to Saudi Arabia in May 1981, although calling forth a very hostile reaction in Israel, indicated the—albeit very gradual—'normalization' of German foreign policy into a mould closer to that of Bonn's main European partners. A similar path is currently being pursued by Chancellor Kohl, though his 1984 visit to Israel illustrated anew the major problems facing West German foreign policy in this region.

Another important, though less definable, restriction on bilateral Franco-German co-operation has been the existence of certain especially sensitive areas in French and German European policy. The CAP in France and the control of inflation in Germany can be identified as fields where, for reasons of history, psychology, or simple electoral expediency, governmental room for manœuvre has been significantly constrained, thereby impeding compromise. In the Brandt—Pompidou period, one commentator goes too far in describing the preservation of the CAP as the 'alpha and omega' of the French President's European policy.[11] But the result was to make worthwhile discussion on changes in agriculture taboo at bilateral summits. To a lesser extent, the sensitivity in Germany to its position as 'paymaster' of Europe in 1972–3 (repeated in 1974–5) can also be included in this special category. Yet here the consequence was to provoke rather than stifle debate.

Such tendencies became slightly less marked under Schmidt

---

[11] Berger, *M. Pompidou*, 106.

and Giscard. The causes were not difficult to identify. On the one hand, inflation came to be almost universally regarded as among the gravest of economic ills, greatly narrowing the gap between French and German views. On the other hand, the increasing pressure of the CAP on the Community budget, to which France became a small net contributor, required recognition, in Paris and not just elsewhere, of the need for some measure of reform. Thus there was progress towards bridging the ground between the French and German capitals. Most recently of all, despite marked differences at the outset, there has developed a closer alignment between the views of Chancellor Kohl and President Mitterrand.

It is in the defence sector, however, that the gap was (at least until recently) at its widest. In the Brandt–Pompidou years there was certainly a decline in the French chauvinism that had led to the collapse of the EDC in the 1950s. However, the continuing position of national security as one of the key areas of 'high' politics, combined with a persistent underlying sense of unease in France *vis-à-vis* West Germany, prevented any more active collaboration over defence than that stimulated by economic considerations (and, to a lesser extent, the desire to demonstrate political reconciliation), in the joint production of military equipment. Most notably, the highly conspicuous difference of opinion between Leber and Jobert over the future of European security at the WEU meeting in November 1973 drew attention to the cleft between Bonn and Paris on defence, which, throughout the 1970s, prevented bilateral discussion on the subject extending beyond a mere exchange of views. However, new ground has been broken under Kohl and Mitterrand, and it remains to be seen just how far discussions on defence and joint strategy will eventually go.

One continuing important external restraint on Franco-German co-operation, which has remained valid throughout the entire span of European integration, especially since the signing of the 1963 Franco–German Treaty, has been the sensitivity of the smaller member states to any impression of an over-exclusive dialogue between Paris and Bonn. The upshot has been an implicit constraint, partly on the range, and certainly on the manner of presentation, of bilateral Franco-German co-operation. As a consequence, the latter's role has sometimes been left

deliberately vague. This consideration regarding outside opinions gained weight following the intensification of bilateral
collaboration under Giscard and Schmidt. The Germans, in
particular, were quick to point out their awareness of feelings in
the other member states towards any impression of too exclusive
a bilateral dialogue. It is, however, worth recalling in this context
the change that has come about in French Government thinking
since May 1981. While a shift towards a less exclusive
relationship with Bonn seemed likely at the outset, the experience of office and lack of suitable alternatives convinced many
Socialists that close bilateral collaboration remained as necessary
as ever.

Finally, something must be said of the role of personal factors
in bilateral relations. Between 1969 and 1974, difficulties in
Franco–German understanding at governmental level were
certainly not relieved by the poor rapport between Brandt and
Pompidou. There was at the outset a sincere desire for good
relations on both sides. Brandt in particular, partly for internal
reasons—to demonstrate that *entente* with Paris was not exclusive
to the CDU—wished to pursue the tradition of close Franco-
German ties. More practically, the Chancellor took steps to
improve his French. However, personal relations between the
two leaders remained strictly businesslike, never developing the
warmth that had existed between de Gaulle and Adenauer, or,
for that matter, which arose between Pompidou and Heath.
Brandt and the President, extremely different in background
and temperament, had very little in common. Pompidou's
academic and business training contrasted sharply with the
Chancellor's path to power. Politically, the two leaders represented very different schools. This heterogeneity was no less
marked in their characters. Pompidou, precise and assertive—
'homme des réalités et des chiffres', in Jobert's words[12]—differed
greatly from the reflective and often distant Chancellor. Thus,
for instance, it is interesting to note that Brandt's slow way of
talking, sometimes incorporating wide vistas, used to irritate the
much more matter of fact President. Pompidou in fact perhaps
never managed to fathom his German counterpart. Jobert points
out some of the perplexities that arose. Writing of the Hague

---

[12] Jobert, *Mémoires*, 180.

summit, he observes, 'and the Chancellor was not the virtuoso or slave of every dossier. He was often remote, without it being possible to tell very easily whether this distancing was deliberate or not'.[13] By the time of Brandt's visit to Paris in January 1973, Jobert comments: 'Never did the Chancellor appear more distant, more vague, floating above the issues. Georges Pompidou asked himself about his interlocutor's health.'[14] The not infrequent lapses in German policy co-ordination added to this confusion on the French side.

Personal relations were further complicated by Brandt's rising stature on the international stage, which kindled a mixture of disapproval and envy in Paris. The award of the Nobel Prize to the Chancellor was treated mockingly by Pompidou, who, in addition, frowned on what he felt to be Brandt's excessive courting of publicity and his 'spectacular' gestures. The Chancellor's kneeling before the monument to the inhabitants of the Warsaw ghetto was particularly deprecated. (This was very controversial in Germany too.) Jobert describes Pompidou's opinion:

publicity did not merit every sacrifice, and the emotional steps which could be undertaken to this end became intolerable to him. Brandt's public kneelings shocked him.[15]

In sum, there is little doubt that difficulties on the personal level were an inhibiting, although certainly not wholly obstructive, influence on bilateral relations between 1969 and 1974.

This picture changed radically in the Schmidt–Giscard period, when the very warm personal relationship between the two leaders was one of the most striking features of both bilateral and Community relations. Though hardly less disparate in background than their predecessors, Schmidt and Giscard were swiftly able to establish a confident mutual rapport based on their like-minded views and shared experience as ministers of finance. This technocratic training was to stand them in good stead for the economically dominated discussions of the years after 1974.

More important, the two leaders were obviously aware of the

---

[13] Ibid., 185.
[14] Jobert, *L'Autre Regard*, 256. See also 16.
[15] Jobert, *Mémoires*, 185–6. See also de Saint Robert, 152.

advantages in public relations terms of their very good working relationship. This they exploited to the full. Such maximization of public relations benefits served domestic electoral ends by adding lustre to each incumbent and emphasized the importance both sides placed on one another's friendship. Certainly, the close bond between Schmidt and Giscard was demonstrated, even spotlighted, with a panache unimaginable in the past, barring heavy-handed attempts such as Pompidou's birthday trip down the Rhine. Whether it was Giscard's astonishing walk down the Rue du Faubourg St Honoré to accompany the Chancellor back to his hotel following their first Élysée dinner of May 1974, the televised conversation between the two leaders in Bonn and Paris of January 1975 (which also provided a chance to demonstrate the capabilities of the newly launched Franco-German communications satellite 'Symphonie'; or just their regular strolls through the gardens of the Schaumburg or Élysée palaces after bilateral summits to explain their discussions to attendant newsmen, each occasion testified to the vitality of bilateral relations and, by implication, to the importance of the two leaders and their countries in both European and world affairs.

Such incidents were but the most showmanly examples of a more widespread relaxation in the style of bilateral summitry under Schmidt and Giscard. On a less publicity-minded note, it was only after 1974, for example, that the custom of paying private visits to each other's houses became commonplace (such calls had been reciprocated between de Gaulle and Adenauer in the past). Giscard travelled to Hamburg on three separate occasions to see the Schmidts *chez eux*, and the Chancellor paid numerous informal visits to Giscard—though only at the Élysée. The former ritual of regular Bonn–Paris summits was also broken. Meetings were now held in locations as widely spaced as the outskirts of Nice, Hamburg, and Aachen. Furthermore, the custom of the unscheduled flying visit was introduced. Thus the two leaders occasionally met for quiet working dinners in Bonn, Paris, and even on 'neutral' ground such as a choice restaurant in Alsace. On an even less formal note, Schmidt and Giscard instigated the pattern of regular telephone conversations to discuss topical issues. Again, this was a precedent. It would be interesting to know, in fact, just how frequently such calls were made. The rise of telephone conversations also highlighted a more important, though less tangible, bonus to Franco-German relations under Schmidt and Giscard, namely the fact that the two men were both fluent in English, which became their lingua franca. Never before had such ease of communication been possible between French and German leaders.

All these developments were indicative of the much improved climate of personal relations after 1974. Outstanding was the speed and frequency with which meetings could be arranged, and the more relaxed style in which they were conducted.[16] The upshot of these changes was to convey the impression that Schmidt and Giscard actually enjoyed meeting to discuss international and Community issues rather than just doing so out of a sense of duty, as had often appeared the case in the past. Yet one should not suppose that the relaxed format of bilateral contacts after 1974 meant that the two leaders neglected the ceremonial side of their duties. In July 1980, Giscard paid the first state visit of a French leader to the Federal Republic since de Gaulle's trip of September 1962 (having previously made a formal journey to Berlin in October 1979); President Scheel had already gone to France on a state visit in April 1975. All these occasions were used as opportunities to underline the closeness and cordiality of bilateral bonds.

One should, however, be wary of painting too rosy a picture. Naturally, there were occasional lapses in bilateral relations under Schmidt and Giscard—although never of their former magnitude. In September and October 1974, differences arose over agricultural policy, spilling over into the bilateral summit of February 1975.[17] German slowness that year in enacting special war crimes legislation desired by the French also caused a certain amount of friction.[18] More damaging was a series of incautious remarks made by the Chancellor on French domestic politics. These were keenly seized on by Giscard's political

---

[16] Note, for instance, Giscard's own comments on this theme, reported in the *Guardian*, 7 July 1980.

[17] See Trevor Parfitt, 'CAP—beginning to take stock'. Note also the reports in *Observer Foreign News Service*, 14 Jan. 1975; *The Times*, 5 Feb. 1975; *Die Zeit*, 25 Apr. 1975.

[18] See reports in *Le Monde*, 3, 5, and 10 July 1974; *Frankfurter Allgemeine Zeitung*, 9 and 10 July 1974.

opponents in order to embarrass the President.[19] Probably the
worst episode in bilateral relations, however, was the bitterness
that arose, in the media more than at governmental level,
regarding the anti-terrorist drive in Germany, which reached its
peak in 1976–7. Many French critics reacted angrily to the
Federal Republic's heavy-handed tactics at the time. Yet it is
interesting to note that feelings were raised on the German side
too, notably with regard to the extradition from France of the
lawyer Klaus Croissant.[20] There were strong German suggestions
of too lenient a French attitude on the issue, and annoyance at
the excessive publicity it was felt the defendant's views had been
given.

However, on balance, such episodes were minor compared to
the achievements of the Schmidt–Giscard era, when the long-
standing policy of Franco-German reconciliation can safely be
said to have reached maturity. Building on the achievements of
their predecessors, Schmidt and Giscard cemented a pattern
which has remained the yardstick for co-operation between
successive French and German leaders and is likely to continue
so for many years to come.

In some ways it can be said that the speed with which a good
working relationship was established between Schmidt and
Mitterrand in the face of certain obvious impediments was a
testament to the achievements of the previous period. There
were certainly grounds for mutual suspicion at the outset. In the
late 1970s, Schmidt had spoken imprudently about the possible
outcome of a Socialist electoral victory, while Mitterrand had
been a vocal critic of West Germany's record on civil liberties.
The Socialist leader had even headed a French committee to
monitor the subject. Matters had been exacerbated in May 1981
by the rather too public German expressions of doubt about the
likely repercussions of Socialist economic policy and the possibility of Communist participation in the Government.

Yet a number of factors worked to create a steady improve-

---

[19] There were a number of different incidents. See e.g. the reports in *The Economist*, 7
Dec. 1974; *Observer Foreign News Service*, 14 Jan. 1975; *Frankfurter Allgemeine Zeitung*, 7 July
1976; *Le Monde*, 7 July 1976; Pickles, *Contemporary French Politics*, 87–8.
[20] On this theme, see especially ch. 2 n. 74. See also the subsequent discussions on anti-
terrorist measures at both bilateral and Community levels, reported in *Le Monde*, 8 July
1976; *The Times*, 23 Sept. 1977; *The Economist*, 10 Dec. 1977.

ment in relations. Notably, Schmidt's visit to Paris in May 1981 and the July bilateral summit established a better climate for understanding. The former meeting was of particular interest, as it helped to confirm a trend in bilateral relations. Thus, French and German leaders since 1974 have visited each other within days of coming to office: Schmidt saw Giscard very shortly after the latter's inauguration; Mitterrand received the Chancellor speedily in May 1981; and most recently of all, Kohl's first foreign trip as Chancellor was to see the French President. Such swift diplomatic exchanges have served to underline the continuity in thinking on both sides of the Rhine at times of domestic political change and have helped to emphasize the priority placed on bilateral relations by new incumbents.

An improvement in personal relations was an important step towards eliminating mutual suspicion between Schmidt and Mitterrand. Hence the Chancellor's trip to the President's country house in October 1981 was valuable especially in marking a return to the friendly pattern that had been established with Giscard. Yet it was the summit of February 1982 which provided the most striking demonstration of the new bilateral relationship that had come about. The closeness of the new bond, whose principal strength lay in its foundation on a practical convergence of interests rather than any inflated expectations, was demonstrated in the frequency of high-level Franco-German contacts in early 1982. Furthermore, one of the most obvious handicaps on relations between the two leaders —that of language—had already begun to be overcome. Although still some way from the frequent phone contacts of the Schmidt–Giscard years, the Chancellor and the new French President in March 1982 had their first direct telephone conversation with the aid of interpreters. In sum, although not allowed the full opportunity to develop, it can fairly be said that Franco-German relations in the Schmidt–Mitterrand period changed more in style than substance.

Most recently, the Mitterrand–Kohl partnership appears at first glance even more unlikely than that which it replaced. Certainly, the lofty and occasionally disdainful French President, whose manner at times almost recalls de Gaulle, seems an incongruous interlocutor for the genial and sometimes too relaxed German Chancellor. Kohl's *bonhomie* and Mitterrand's

Olympian streak undoubtedly sit oddly side by side. Yet, as with Chancellor Schmidt, an effective dialogue has quickly been established. Not least, both the French and German leaders remain fully aware of the value of good relations and the continuing necessity of co-operation between their two capitals.

Hence, only hours after being sworn in as Chancellor in October 1982, Kohl visited Mitterrand in Paris in order to emphasize the 'special status' his government would continue to give to bilateral relations. Since then, the two men have moved gradually towards the sort of cordial relationship that has come to be expected between leaders in Bonn and Paris. There have been working breakfasts—in December 1982 and at the Athens summit in December 1983—as well as private meetings away from either capital. In February 1984 Mitterrand and Kohl met in the Rhineland village of Edenkoben (the meeting was originally intended to be held in Kohl's home village in the region). This was followed by another private meeting in May in Saarbrücken, a prelude to the full bilateral summit at the end of the month.

The contemporary issues themselves have helped. Just as the dialogue between Schmidt and Giscard was reinforced by the prominence of international economic questions, so too the rapport that has been established between Mitterrand and Kohl has undoubtedly been assisted by the two leaders' like-minded views on European security and the deployment of Cruise and Pershing missiles. Thus, for example, at their informal meeting in Alsace in November 1983 these subjects were well to the fore. Yet it should also be noted that in five hours of talks the two leaders not only covered such pressing international topics, they also found time to underline the friendliness of their relations. As if to demonstrate that such conviviality was not exclusive to Schmidt and Giscard alone, the Kohl–Mitterrand meeting, entirely casual in tone and dress, was capped by a short village stroll. Similarly, at the Franco-German summit in Paris in May 1983 the President made a point of relaxing the formality of certain set functions, the standard official dinner, for example, being replaced by a working meal with fewer guests present. It is also worth noting that Mitterrand deliberately chose to start his second day of talks with the Chancellor over a working breakfast at his private residence, a move designed to emphasize both the personal and cordial nature of bilateral relations. Such steps have continued at more recent bilateral gatherings. Most striking of all in illustrating the strength of the contemporary bond was the moving ceremony attended by Kohl and Mitterrand in September 1984 at Verdun to commemorate the war dead of both countries.

Though not directly connected to the personal side, one should also bear in mind the closer—government inspired—economic and technical co-operation that has come about under Mitterrand and Kohl. The reasons are complex, a mixture of outside economic factors and the pressure to liberalize and foster closer European industrial collaboration. France and Germany agreed in November 1983 to establish a joint mobile telephone system (tenders were put out in Spring 1984). The two countries have also decided to open part of their domestic telephone handset market to each other's firms. Both moves are in line with French wishes to stimulate wider European industrial co-operation in key technological areas. A further sign of closer bilateral collaboration came in the German decision of December 1983 to order French satellite ground station equipment. Most ambitiously of all, renewed co-operation has been authorized on the latest A320 Airbus project. Last, but certainly not least, it was agreed at the bilateral summit in May 1984 to abolish customs formalities for private citizens travelling between the two countries as of July. At a more mundane level, it should also be borne in mind that, since spring 1984, German visitors to France have been able to withdraw money from their savings bank accounts at a large number of post offices. Though differing widely in scope, all these schemes have served to underline the impetus of greater bilateral co-operation between France and Germany, which, since 1974, have consistently been personified at Head of State or Government level.

Bilateral Franco-German relations, the Ostpolitik, *and its repercussions*

While the key role of Franco-German accord for progress in the EEC has formed one of the central themes in this book, the effect of the two countries' changing status on their bilateral relations—and consequently on the Community as a whole—has represented another. In the later 1960s, the gradual transition of the Federal Republic's economic strength into a more assertive political stance had a profound influence on France. This was seen notably in the increased attractiveness for Paris of British membership of the Community. Above all, in the early 1970s Brandt's *Ostpolitik* compounded these feelings of unease on the French side. The shared anxieties that were provoked in Paris and, to a lesser extent, London were a significant additional factor in the developing rapport between the two capitals. Enlargement and Franco-British *rapprochement* apart, the consequences of the new balance between Bonn and Paris were primarily evident in the greater German confidence and say in European affairs in the period.

The role of the *Ostpolitik*, affecting as it did both the bilateral and Community sectors, requires special attention. Brandt's opening to the East brought to light a number of problems in contacts between Paris and Bonn. In particular, the uncertainty that was apparent on the French side in summer 1973 regarding the future of the Federal Republic and the possibility of a German drift towards neutrality testified to the extent of French misunderstanding of West Germany and the options open to it. While limitations in Pompidou's knowledge of Germany possibly contributed to his misjudgement of the country's objectives, such views, it should be noted, were not restricted to the Élysée. They were also prevalent at the Quai d'Orsay, where, according to one French ex-diplomat, they represented deep-seated feeling. Furthermore, two French ex-ambassadors to Bonn both spoke to the author of the general lack of knowledge or interest at the Quai d'Orsay in the Federal Republic, and the ubiquity rather of 'backward ideas' and stereotypes. There was, in the words of one, 'une méconnaissance des problèmes'. One can well suppose that the contemporary belief in reunification as Bonn's ultimate aim indicated an insufficient understanding of German history and society, while the *Ostpolitik*'s political consequences were overrated and the continuing constraints on German foreign policy seriously undervalued.

However, even in the Schmidt–Giscard period, such misconceptions remained alive for the French, albeit in attenuated form. A less active American role in Europe or German disillusionment with Washington, enticements from the Russians, hinting perhaps at improved relations with the GDR, or internal pressures within the Federal Republic itself, were all still treated in Paris as potential causes for a German drift to the East. Such misconceptions were facilitated by the continuing shortcomings in French knowledge and information about the Federal Republic. Thus it is interesting to note that, even in 1980, one serving French diplomat confirmed the persistence of doubts about Germany's future intentions within the French Foreign Ministry.

Most recently of all, it is worth bearing in mind the anxiety that has arisen in Paris regarding the strength of the German anti-nuclear movement and Bonn's ability to resist this and neutralist tendencies. Certainly, it is ironic that the Socialists were greatly reassured by the return of a right-wing government in the Federal Republic following the elections of March 1983. The French were deeply concerned about the possibility of an indecisive result, which might have brought an unstable and vulnerable government to power. Though exaggerated French anxieties remain about both German neutralism and, more diffusely, reunification, the orthodox line on defence pursued by Kohl has appreciably eased the situation.

Two additional factors should be borne in mind when considering French attitudes towards the *Ostpolitik* in the early 1970s. Principally, it should be recalled that France was by no means alone in nursing doubts about Brandt's intentions. Behind a façade of approbation, Kissinger in particular, as well as other leaders in Washington and London, were uncertain and anxious about the implications of the *Ostpolitik*. Secondly, traditional French methods of thinking played a part in accentuating existing anxieties. This aspect is well captured by Kissinger, whose comment, although primarily aimed at French attitudes towards the United States, is no less apt *vis-à-vis* feeling towards Bonn:

To be sure, French history and a Cartesian educational system occasionally produced convoluted theories of the motivations of others, especially Americans, that at times caused French policy to seek reassurance against mirages.[21]

Yet it would be wrong to view the changes in bilateral Franco-German relations initiated by the *Ostpolitik* as entirely one-sided. At the outset especially there was very much a two-way process

---

[21] Kissinger, *White House Years*, 421.

involved. The German Government's desire for the *Ostpolitik* undoubtedly left it more willing to make concessions and more susceptible to French leverage. This vulnerability was implicit in almost all the bilateral Franco-German summits in the early negotiating phase of the *Ostpolitik*, and it emerged most clearly in the exchange of interests over EMU and German Eastern policy at the meeting in January 1971. Brandt's relative weakness *vis-à-vis* Paris at this stage was compounded by his government's slim Parliamentary majority and by the Opposition's fierce attacks on his Eastern policy. Hence French endorsement for the *Ostpolitik* was all the more important—in turn increasing France's power of leverage. Thus, talk at the Hague summit of the emergence of the Federal Republic as the new leader of Europe was premature. Only after the ratification of the *Ostpolitik* treaties and the elections of November 1972 could one begin to speak of a convincing shift in the balance of power between Bonn and Paris.

It is worth noting here the German Opposition's persistent use of reports of French discontent with the *Ostpolitik* as a weapon in its own domestic campaign. The result was to weaken the Government in its dealings with foreign counterparts. Certainly, in illustration of the unique nature of West German politics, it is hard to imagine any French (or British) opposition party being able to make such electoral capital out of a rift in bilateral relations with a European partner. The distinction is noteworthy, demonstrating the Federal Republic's relative external vulnerability and the particular significance of foreign affairs in the country's domestic political process.

Something must also be said of the interaction between Community and non-Community topics in bilateral Franco-German relations in the early 1970s. Again, this link was most evident regarding the *Ostpolitik*. In particular, the bilateral differences of summer 1973 had marked ramifications for the Community as a whole. This was seen most clearly in the close connection between the French Government's pessimistic appraisals of the *Ostpolitik* and its interpretation of (and reaction to) German attitudes towards the CAP in 1973. The evidence suggests that the critical stance adopted by Ertl and others towards the Community's farm policy lent credence to French fears of a possible German drift to the East.

Post-war Franco-German reconciliation

It is fitting that this book should conclude by appraising the role of European integration on post-war Franco-German relations, and by assessing the value of bilateral links between Bonn and Paris as an instrument in establishing closer relations between them. Certainly, the co-operation that has taken place between the two countries in the framework of the European Communities has played a major part in cementing, and even accelerating, their reconciliation. Originally in the economic domain, then increasingly in the political sphere, co-operation under the aegis of the Communities has obliged French and German policy-makers to think in collaborative terms, and, at personal level, has often brought them into closer contact. It is hard to imagine interaction of such a degree, and so soon after the war, had it not been for the economic and political inducement offered by integration.

As for the bilateral Franco-German element in the reconciliation process, the evidence from opinion polls and surveys, the only quantifiable data available, testifies to the strength of the bond that has been established. Particularly as a result of the 1963 bilateral treaty, co-operation at governmental and bureaucratic levels has developed to the extent that close contacts have been formed. Thanks to the institutionalization of co-operation in regular meetings at a variety of levels—quarterly between foreign ministers and monthly between high officials—and reinforced by the primary role of France and Germany in the Community, politicians and civil servants in Bonn and Paris have tended to be in more frequent contact, and to know one another better, than has been the case with colleagues abroad. The direct exchange of government officials, though still organized on a limited basis, is a small token of the wider co-operation that has taken place, and has in itself improved the climate of confidence by reinforcing existing bureaucratic contacts and creating new ones.[22]

That two countries whose relations had once been so clouded by conflict embarked on such an unprecedented and generally successful exercise in reconciliation begs the question of whether

---

[22] Thus some young French administrators take a *stage* in the Federal Republic, while a number of German counterparts attend the École Nationale d'Administration each year.

their experience is applicable to others. For instance, the possibility of a similar, though more limited, arrangement between Britain and the Federal Republic has been mooted. Perhaps more valuable, however, would be an Anglo-Irish initiative along similar lines. Certainly, the lesson of Franco-German bilateral co-operation is one which makes the subject worth closer attention. Furthermore, although the position of London and Dublin in the European Community is by no means as central as that of Paris and Bonn, the very fact of their joint membership likens their case to the Franco-German model and offers a potential, and so far under-exploited, forum for contact and bridge-building.

However, two important reservations must be made to the optimistic picture of Franco-German co-operation that has been presented in the pages above. First of all, that underlying strains and misunderstandings do still exist in bilateral relations testifies to the difficulty—even impossibility—of wholly eradicating deep-rooted historical enmity based on the carnage and destruction of three major wars in under a century. In addition, although there have been great improvements, shortcomings in mutual information and misconceptions in the media have to some extent fostered misunderstandings and perpetuated anachronistic images, obstructing reconciliation. Secondly, especially at the level of summit meetings, one can at times identify a divergence between the grand statements voiced by national leaders and the actual fruits of collaboration. As has been seen, this stricture applied as much to the Community as to the bilateral level. The divergence appertained particularly to French attitudes to the *Ostpolitik* in the early 1970, when an increasingly keen distinction became evident between the Government's public support and its private misgivings.

Finally, linked to this theme and central to the whole question of post-war Franco-German relations is the role of personalities in establishing and furthering the two countries' bilateral co-operation. The course of relations between Bonn and Paris since the Second World War has fully borne out Jean Monnet's dictum that 'Rien n'est possible sans les hommes, rien n'est durable sans les institutions.'[23] The rapport between successive

---

[23] Jean Monnet, *Mémoires* (Paris, Fayard, 1976), 360

leaders in France and Germany has undoubtedly had a valuable effect on relations between their two countries and consequently for Europe as a whole. Genuine friendship and mutual respect between de Gaulle and Adenauer gave the impetus to bilateral co-operation. The same qualities between Giscard and Schmidt injected new life into Europe after 1974. Yet what this book has tried to show is that a convergence of interests between the two countries is more important than any personal element. The warmth between Adenauer and de Gaulle could not prevent the considerable tension that arose between Bonn and Paris within a very short time of their treaty being signed. Divergent national interests *and* a lack of mutual sympathy between the General and Erhard produced a nadir in Franco-German relations between 1964 and 1966. Similarly, the policy differences and, at best, tepid bond between Pompidou and Brandt at times made for difficulties in the early 1970s. However, in all these cases, Monnet's aphorism was correct in so far as the accumulated momentum of institutionalized co-operation kept up contacts between the two sides. As the Schmidt–Mitterrand period showed, and the Mitterrand–Kohl partnership appears to confirm, the symbolic value of Franco-German friendship and the established institutional links between them, combined with the two countries' political and economic pre-eminence among the member states meant that bilateral co-operation remained the most conspicuous feature of the Community landscape. This factor is unlikely to change in the foreseeable future.

Bibliography

PRIMARY SOURCES

Official Documents and Government Publications

Bulletin of the European Communities (various years).

Bundesrat Verfassungsorgen, *Der Bundesrat als Verfassungs- und politische Kraft — Beiträge zum 25 jährigen Bestehen des Bundesrates der Bundesrepublik Deutschland* (Bad Honnef, Darmstadt, Neue Darmstädter Verlagsamt, 1974).

Deutsche Bundesbank, *Währung und Wirtschaft in Deutschland 1876–1975* (Frankfurt, Deutsche Bundesbank, 1976).

Deutscher Bundestag, *Stenographische Berichte* (various years).

ECSC–EEC–EAEC Commission, *General Annual Reports on the Activities of the Community.*

EEC Commission, *General Annual Reports on the Activities of the Community.*

European Communities Commission, *Report of the Study Group 'Economic and Monetary Union 1980'* (Mar. 1975).

European Communities, Statistical Office, *General Statistical Bulletin* 3 (Mar. 1973).

French Embassy, London, Press and Information Service, Final press conference given by President Georges Pompidou and Chancellor Willy Brandt, 11 Feb. 1972.

—— Opening speech by President Georges Pompidou at the Paris summit, 19 Oct. 1972.

—— President Pompidou's interview with *Epoca*, Feb. 1972.

—— Press conference given by President Georges Pompidou, 21 Jan. 1971.

—— Press conference given by President Georges Pompidou, 23 Sept. 1971.

French Embassy, New York, Press and Information Division, Joint Declaration by France and the Federal Republic of Germany. Franco-German summit meeting, Paris, 5 Feb. 1980.

Gesetz zu der gemeinsamen Erklärung und zu dem Vertrag vom 22. Januar 1963 zwischen der Bundesrepublik Deutschland und der Französischen Republik über die deutsch-französische Zusammenarbeit (Bonn, Presse- und Informationsamt der Bundesregierung).

Journal officiel de la République Française, Débats Parlementaires: Assemblée Nationale, 5 Nov. 1970.

Lapie, Pierre-Olivier, and Schmid, Carlo, *La Coopération franco-allemande* (Paris, La Documentation Française, 1977).

Latest from Germany (various years).

Notes et Études Documentaires, 26 May 1970, No. 5693.

OECD, *France* (Paris, OECD) (various years).

—— *Germany* (Paris, OECD) (various years).

—— Series C. *Commodity Trade: Exports* (various years).

—— Series C. *Commodity Trade: Imports* (various years).

—— *Statistics on Energy* (various years).

OEEC *Commodity Trade Figures*, Series IV (Jan.–Dec. 1958).

Office Franco-Allemand pour la Jeunesse [OFAJ] — Deutsch-Französische Jugendwerk [DFJW], 'Les 15–24 ans et les échanges franco-allemands', *Rapports et Documents* 9 and 10 (1976) (Bad Honnef, OFAJ/DFJW).

—— *15 ans Office franco-allemand pour la jeunesse 1963–78*. Service de Presse et d'information de l'OFAJ (Bad Honnef, OFAJ/DFJW, 1978).

—— 'Ce que je sais sur l'Allemagne', *Rapports et Documents* 1 (1979) (Bad Honnef, OFAJ/DFJW).

—— 'Les Problèmes d'information dans les relations franco-allemands', *Bulletin de Liaison* (June 1974).

—— *Rapport d'activité/Tätigkeitsbericht 1963–73* (Bad Honnef, OFAJ/DFJW, 1973).

Schmid, Prof. Dr Carlo, *Die deutsch-französische Zusammenarbeit*. Report of the Co-ordinator for Franco-German Co-operation for the year 1976 (Bonn, Apr. 1977).

US Information Service, Secretary of State Kissinger's press conference, 10 Jan. 1974.

Memoirs and speeches

Brandt, Willy, *People and Politics. The Years 1960–1975*, trans. J. H. Brownjohn (London, Collins, 1978).

Chaban-Delmas, Jacques, *L'Ardeur* (Paris, Stock, 1975.

Frank, Paul, *Entschlüsselte Botschaft. Ein Diplomat macht Inventur* (Stuttgart, Deutsche Verlags-Anstalt, 1981).

Giroud, Françoise, *La Comédie du pouvoir* (Paris, Le Livre de Poche, 1979).

Jobert, Michel, *L'Autre Regard* (Paris, Grasset, 1976).

—— *Mémoires d'avenir* (Paris, Le Livre de Poche, 1976).

Kissinger, Henry, *The White House Years* (London, Weidenfeld and Nicholson/Michael Joseph, 1979).
—— *Years of Upheaval* (London, Weidenfeld and Nicholson/Michael Joseph, 1982).
Mitterrand, François, *L'Abeille et l'architecte* (Paris, Flammarion, 1978).
—— *Le Paille et le grain* (Paris, Flammarion, 1975).
Moersch, Karl, *Kurs-Revision. Deutsche Politik nach Adenauer* (Frankfurt, Societäts-Verlag, 1978).
Monnet, Jean, *Mémoires* (Paris, Fayard, 1976).
Pompidou, Georges, *Entretiens et discours*, ed. E. Balladur, 2 vols. (Paris, Plon, 1975).
—— *Pour rétablir une vérité* (Paris, Flammarion, 1982).
Schmid, Carlo, *Erinnerungen* (Bern, Scherz Verlag, 1979).
Seydoux, François, *Dans l'Intimité franco-allemande* (Paris, Albatros, 1977).

SECONDARY SOURCES

Books

Abelein, Manfred, and Bondy, François, *Deutschland und Frankreich. Geschichte einer wechselvollen Beziehung* (Düsseldorf, Econ Verlag, 1973).
Averyt, William F., Jr., *Agropolitics in the European Community. Interest Groups and the Common Agricultural Policy* (New York, Praeger, 1977).
Baring, Arnulf, *Aussenpolitik in Adenauers Kanzlerdemokratie*, Schriftenreihe des Forschungsinstituts der DGAP, 28 (Munich, Oldenbourg, 1969).
—— *Machtwechsel. Die Ära Brandt–Scheel* (Stuttgart, Deutsche Verlags-Anstalt, 1982).
Berger, Vincent, *Monsieur Pompidou et la construction de l'Europe*, Mémoire pour le diplôme d'études supérieures de Science Politique (Paris, Université de Droit, d'Économie et de Sciences Sociales, 1973).
Besson, Waldemar, *Die Aussenpolitik der Bundesrepublik. Erfahrungen und Massstäbe* (Munich, Piper, 1970).
Boyer, B. M., *L'Étude scientifique des stéréotypes nationaux dans les rapports franco-allemands* (Paris, Université de Paris 1, Département de Science Politique, 1972).
Brandon, Henry, *The Retreat of American Policy* (London, The Bodley Head, 1973).
Braunthal, Gerard, *The Federation of German Industry in Politics* (New York, Cornell University Press, 1965).
Bredin, J.-D., *La République de Monsieur Pompidou* (Paris, Fayard, 1974).

Calleo, David, F., and Rowland, Benjamin N., *America and the World Political Economy* (Bloomington, Indiana University Press, 1973).

Carr, Jonathan, *Helmut Schmidt–Helmsman of Germany* (London, Weidenfeld and Nicholson, 1985).

Cousté, Pierre-Bernard, and Visine, François, *Pompidou et l'Europe* (Paris, Librairies Techniques, 1974).

Debbasch, Charles, *La France de Pompidou* (Paris, Presses Universitaires de France, 1974).

Dettke, Dieter, *Allianz im Wandel,* Schriften des Forschungsinstituts der DGAP (Frankfurt, Metzler Verlag, 1976).

Deutsch-Französisches Institut, *Deutschland, Frankreich und die europäische Krise,* (II. Deutsch-Französischen Kolloquium, 10–13 October 1974, Ludwigsburg), Schriftenreihe des Deutsch-Französischen Instituts Ludwigsburg, 2 (Ludwigsburg, Deutsch-Französisches Institut, 1975).

—— *Strukturprobleme der deutsch-französischen Wirtschaftsbeziehungen* (III. Deutsch-Französischen Kolloquium, 13–19 October 1975, Ludwigsburg), Schriftenreihe des Deutsch-Französischen Instituts Ludwigsburg, 3 (Ludwigsburg, Deutsch-Französischen Institut, 1976).

Deutscher Rat der Europäischer Bewegung, *Deutschland und Frankreich in den siebziger Jahren* (X. Deutsch-Französische Konferenz Paris 1970), Schriftenreihe des Deutschen Rates der Europäischen Bewegung, 20 (Bonn, 1971).

—— *Frankreich, Deutschland und die Zukunft Europas* (XI. Deutsch-Französische Konferenz, Bad Godesberg 1973), Schriftenreihe des Deutschen Rates der Europäischen Bewegung, 21 (Bonn, 1974).

Duhamel, Alain, *La République de M. Mitterrand* (Paris, Grasset, 1982).

—— *Le République giscardienne* (Paris, Grasset, 1980).

Edinger, L. J., *Politics in Germany* (Boston, Little Brown, 1977).

Ehrmann, H. W., *Organized Business in France* (Princeton, Princeton University Press, 1957).

—— *Politics in France* (3rd edn.) (Boston, Little Brown, 1976).

Ellwein, Thomas, *Das Regierungssystem der Bundesrepublik Deutschland* (4th edn.)(Opladen, Westdeutscher Verlag, 1972).

Emminger, Otmar, *The D-Mark in the Conflict between internal and External Equilibrium 1948–1975,* Essays in International Finance, 122 (International Finance Section, Dept. of Economics, Princeton University, Princeton, New Jersey, June 1977).

Farquharson, John E., and Holt, Stephen C., *Europe from Below. An Assessment of Franco-German Popular Contacts* (London, George Allen and Unwin, 1975).

Forschungsinstitut der Deutschen Gesellschaft für Auswärtige Politik, *Aussenpolitik nach der Wahl des 6. Bundestages* (Opladen, Leske, 1969).

Forschungsinstitut der Deutschen Gesellschaft für Auswärtige Politik, *Aussenpolitische Perspektiven des westdeutschen Staates* (Munich, Oldenbourg, 1971), 3 vols.

Frears, J. F., *France in the Giscard Presidency* (London, George Allen and Unwin, 1981).

Freedman, Lawrence (ed.), *The Troubled Alliance. Atlantic Relations in the 1980s* (London, Heinemann, 1983).

Giscard d'Estaing, Valéry, *Démocratie française* (Paris, Fayard, 1976).

Grosser, Alfred, *Die Bundesrepublik Deutschland. Bilanz einer Entwicklung* (Tübingen, 1967).

—— *Les Occidentaux* (Paris, Fayard, 1978).

—— (ed.), *Les Politiques extérieures Européennes dans la crise*, Fondation Nationale des Sciences Politiques, Travaux et recherches de Science Politique, 43 (Paris, Presses de la FNSP, 1976).

Haftendorn, Helga, *et al.* (edd.), *Verwaltete Aussenpolitik—Sicherheits- und entspannungspolitische Entscheidungsprozesse in Bonn* (Cologne, Verlag Wissenschaft und Politik/Nottbeck, 1978).

Hanrieder, Wolfram F., *The United States and Western Europe* (Cambridge, Mass., Winthrop, 1974).

—— and Auton, Graeme P., *The Foreign Policies of West Germany, France, and Britain* (Englewood Cliffs, New Jersey, Prentice Hall, 1980).

Heisler, Martin O. (ed.), *Politics in Europe* (New York, McKay, 1974).

Hoffmann, Stanley, *Primacy or World Order. American Foreign Policy since the Cold War* (New York, McGraw-Hill, 1978).

Ionescu, Ghita (ed.), *The New Politics of European Integration* (London, Macmillan, 1972).

Jahn, Egbert, and Rittberger, Volker (edd.), *Die Ostpolitik der Bundesrepublik—Triebkräfte, Widerstände, Konsequenzen* (Opladen, Westdeutscher Verlag, 1974).

Johnson, Nevil, *Government in the Federal Republic of Germany—the Executive at Work* (Oxford, Pergamon Press, 1973).

Kaht, Hilmar, *Die Wirkungen der europäischen Integration auf die Einführen der Bundesrepublik Deutschland* HWWA, Institut für Wirtschaftsforschung (Hamburg, Verlag Weltarchiv, 1975).

Kaiser, Karl, and Morgan, Roger (ed.), *Britain and West Germany* (London, OUP/RIIA, 1971).

Kaiser, Rolf, *Die Interdependenz politischer und ökonomischer Interessen in der Weltwährungskrise 1971*, Doctoral Dissertation (Eberhard Karls Universität, Tübingen, 1976).

Kirchner, Emil J., *Trade Unions as a Pressure Group in the European Community* (Farnborough, Saxon House, 1977).

Kitzinger, Uwe, *Diplomacy and Persuasion* (London, Thames and Hudson, 1973).

Kohl, Wilfrid L. (ed.), *Economic Foreign Policies of Industrial States* (Lexington, Mass., Lexington Books, 1977).

——, and Bassevi, Giorgio (edd.), *West Germany. A European Global Power* (Lexington, Mass., Lexington Books, 1980).

Kolodziej, Edward J., *French International Policy under de Gaulle and Pompidou. The Politics of Grandeur* (Ithaca, Cornell University Press, 1974).

Kripendorff, Ekkehart, and Rittberger, Volker (edd.), *The Foreign Policy of West Germany. Formation and Contents* (London, Sage, 1980).

Lasserre, René, Neumann, Wolfgang and Picht, Robert (edd.), *Deutschland—Frankreich: Bausteine zum Systemvergleich*, 2 vols. (Gerlingen, Bleicher, 1980–1).

Ludlow, Peter, *The Making of the European Monetary System* (London, Butterworths, 1982).

Marsh, John S., and Swanney, Pamela J., *Agriculture and the European Community* (London, UACES/George Allen and Unwin, 1980).

Martinet, Gilles, *Le Système Pompidou* (Paris, Seuil, 1973).

Mayntz, Renate, and Scharpf, Fritz W., *Policy-Making in the German Federal Republic* (Amsterdam, Elsevier, 1975).

Ménudier, Henri, *L'Allemagne après 1945*, Fondation Nationale des Sciences Politiques—Bibliographies françaises de sciences sociales, Guide de recherches, 4 (Paris, Colin, 1972).

—— *L'Allemagne selon Willy Brandt* (Paris, Stock, 1976).

Merkl, Peter H., *German Foreign Policies West and East* (Santa Barbara, ABC-Clio, 1974).

Meyer, Michel, *Le Mal franco-allemand* (Paris, Denoël, 1979).

Meynaud, Jean, and Sidjanski, Dusan, *Les Groupes de pression dans la Communauté Européenne* (Brussels, Institut d'Études Européennes, 1971).

Morgan, Annette, *From Summit to Council: Evolution in the EEC* (London, Chatham House/PEP, 1976).

Morgan, Roger, *The United States and West Germany 1945–1972. A Study in Alliance Politics* (London, RIIA/OUP, 1974).

—— *West Germany's Foreign Policy Agenda*, The Washington Papers, VI/54 (Beverly Hills, Sage Publications, 1978).

Morse, Edward L., *Foreign policy and interdependence in Gaullist France* (Princeton, Princeton University Press, 1978).

Nass, Klaus Otto, *Gefährdete Freundschaft* (Bonn, Europa Union Verlag, 1971).

Nay, Catherine, *Le Noir et le rouge, ou l'histoire d'une ambition* (Paris, Grasset, 1984).

Newhouse, John, *et al.*, *U.S. Troops in Europe. Issues, Costs, and Choices* (Washington, The Brookings Institution, 1971).

Niblock, Michael, *The EEC: National Parliaments in Community Decision-Making* (London, Chatham House/PEP, 1971).

Panek, Hans-Thomas, *Die Währungskrisen vom November 1968 bis Mai 1971 im politischen Prozess der Bundesrepublik Deutschland*, Institut für Wirtschaftspolitik an der Universität zu Köln. Untersuchungen, 41 (Cologne, 1977).

Paterson, William E., *The SPD and European Integration* (Farnborough, Saxon House/Lexington Books, 1974).

—— and Thomas, A. H., *Social Democratic Parties in Europe* (London, Croom Helm, 1977).

—— and Wallace, William (edd.), *Foreign Policy-making in Western Europe* (Farnborough, Saxon House, 1978).

Pelassy, Dominique, *Helmut Schmid ou le réalisme* (Paris, Albatros, 1982).

Peyrefitte, Alain, *Le Mal français* (Paris, Plon, 1976).

Picht, Robert (ed.), *Das Bündnis im Bündnis. Deutsch-französische Beziehungen im internationalen Spannungsfeld* (Berlin, Severin and Siedler, 1982).

—— *Deutschland–Frankreich–Europa. Bilanz einer schwierigen Partnerschaft* (Munich, Piper, 1978).

Pickles, Dorothy, *Problems of Contemporary French Politics* (London, Methuen, 1982).

Poidevin, Raymond and Bariéty, Jacques, *Les Relations franco-allemandes 1815–1975* (Paris, Colin, 1977).

Pridham, Geoffrey, *Christian Democracy in West Germany. The CDU–CSU in Government and Opposition 1945–76* (London, Croom Helm, 1977).

Prittie, Terence, *Willy Brandt. Portrait of a Statesman* (London, Weidenfeld and Nicholson, 1974).

Rials, Stéphane, *Les Idées politiques du Président Georges Pompidou* (Paris, Presses Universitaires de France, 1977).

Rideau, Joël, *et al.*, (edd.), *La France et les communautés européennes* (Paris, LGDJ, 1975).

Roussel, Eric, *Georges Pompidou* (Paris, Lattès, 1984).

Rovan, Joseph, *Histoire de la social-démocratie allemande* (Paris, Seuil, 1978).

—— *L'Allemagne du changement* (Paris, Calmann-Lévy, 1983).

Saint Robert, Philippe de, *Les Septennats interrompus* (Paris, Laffont, 1977).

Sandoz, Gérard (ed.) *Les Allemands sans miracle* (Paris, Colin, 1983).

Sasse, Christoph, *et al.* (edd.), *Decision-making in the European Community*

(New York, Praeger, for European Community Institution for University Studies, 1977).

Schaetzel, Robert J., *The Unhinged Alliance. America and the European Community* (New York, Harper and Row, 1975).

Schmid, Gunther, *Entscheidung in Bonn. Die Entstehung der Ost- und Deutschlandpolitik 1969/70* (Cologne, Verlag Wissenschaft und Politik, 1979).

Schwarz, Hans-Peter (ed.), *Handbuch der deutschen Aussenpolitik* (Munich, Piper, 1976).

Schwarz, Jürgen, *Die Europapolitik Frankreichs unter Georges Pompidou als Problem der westeuropäischen Gemeinschaftsbildung* (Ebenhausen/Isar, Stiftung Wissenschaft und Politik, 1973).

Shepherd, Robert James, *Public Opinion and European Integration* (Farnborough, Saxon House, 1975).

Shonfield, Andrew (ed.), *International Economic Relations of the Western World 1959–71* 2 vols. (London, RIIA/OUP, 1976).

Sontheimer, Kurt, and Röhring, Hans H., *Handbuch des politischen Systems der Bundesrepublik Deutschland* (Munich, Piper, 1978).

Stillman, Edmond, *et al.*, *L'Envol de la France dans les années 80* (Paris, Hudson Institute, 1973).

Szokoloczy-Syllara, J., *Les Organisations professionelles françaises et le Marché Commun* (Paris, Colin, 1965).

Thomson, David, *Democracy in France since 1870* (5th edn.) (London, OUP/RIIA, 1969).

Tilford, Roger (ed.), *The Ostpolitik and political change in Germany* (Farnborough and Lexington, Mass., Saxon House/Lexington Books, 1975).

Tsoukalis, Loukas, *The European Community and its Mediterranean Enlargement* (London, George Allen and Unwin, 1981).

—— *The Politics and Economics of European Monetary Integration* (London, George Allen and Unwin, 1977).

Wadbrook, William P., *West German Balance of Payments Policy* (New York, Praeger, 1972).

Wallace, Helen, *Budgetary Politics: The Finances of the European Communities* (London, UACES/George Allen and Unwin, 1980).

—— *National Governments and the European Communities* (London, Chatham House/PEP, 1973).

——, Wallace, William, and Webb, Carole (edd.), *Policy-making in the European Communities* (London, Wiley, 1977).

Whetten, Lawrence L., *Germany's Ostpolitik* (London, RIIA/OUP, 1971).

Willis, F. Roy, *France, Germany and the New Europe* (2nd edn.) (London, Stanford/OUP, 1968).

Wright, Vincent, *The Government and Politics of France* (London, Hutchinson, 1978).

Ziebura, Gilbert, *Die deutsch-französischen Beziehungen seit 1945. Mythen und Realitäten* (Pfullingen, Neske, 1970).

Articles

Abelein, Manfred, 'Frankreichs Vertrag mit der Bundesrepublik. Vorgeschichte und Bedeutung', *Europa-Archiv* 18 (1963).

Adenauer, Konrad, 'The German Problem—a world problem', *Foreign Affairs* (Oct. 1962).

—— 'Germany and Europe', *Foreign Affairs* (Apr. 1953).

Adrien, Bernard, 'La France et les interrogations allemandes', *Politique Étrangère* 4 (Dec. 1982).

Allemann, Fritz-René, 'Mille Jours de Coalition', *Documents* (Sept.–Oct. 1972).

Allen, David, 'The Euro-Arab Dialogue', *Journal of Common Market Studies* 4 (1977–8).

Altmayer, F., 'Das deutsch-französische Jugendwerk', *Aussenpolitik* 5 (1964).

Artner, Stephen J., 'The Middle East: A Chance for Europe?', *International Affairs* (Summer 1980).

Aszkenazy, Henry, 'La RFA et le flottement du franc', *Documents* (Jan.–Feb. 1974).

Barzel, Rainer, 'L'Intégration européenne et l'Ostpolitik', *Chronique du Politique Étrangère* (July 1971).

Bergsten, C. Fred, 'The New Economics and US Foreign Policy' *Foreign Affairs* (Jan. 1972).

Bertram, Christoph, 'The Implications of Theater Nuclear Weapons in Europe', *Foreign Affairs* (Winter 1981–2).

Besser, Joachim, 'Die Angst vor den Deutschen', *Dokumente* 4 (1971).

Besson, Waldemar, 'Prinzipienfragen der westdeutschen Aussenpolitik', *Politische Vierteljahresschrift* 9 (1968).

Bibes, Geneviève, *et al.*, 'L'Élection européenne en France, en Grande Bretagne, en Italie et en République fédérale d'Allemagne', *Revue française de Science Politique* (Dec. 1979).

Bilger, François, 'Les Relations économiques franco-allemandes de 1945 à 1971. Bilan et perspectives', *La Revue d'Allemagne* (July–Sept. 1972).

Brandt, Willy, 'Aktuelle Fragen der deutschen Aussenpolitik', *Europa-Archiv* 13 (1971).

Braun, Nicole Céline, 'Le Patronat français et l'intégration Européenne', *Revue du Marché Commun* (Mar. 1969).

Bulmer, Simon, 'Domestic Politics and EC Decision-Making', *Journal of Common Market Studies* (June 1983).

Burkett, Tony, 'Germany divided: the 1976 Bundestag elections', *The World Tody* (Nov. 1976).

Butler, Nicholas, 'The Ploughshares War between Europe and America', *Foreign Affairs* (Fall 1983).

Campbell, Alan, 'Anglo-French Relations a Decade Ago: A New Assessment', *International Affairs* (Spring, Summer 1982).

Carl-Sime, Carol, and Hall, Jane, 'The predictable Germans: 1980 election retrospect', *The World Today* (Dec. 1980).

Carmoy, Guy de, 'La Politique de la France à l'épreuve des faits: de Charles de Gaulle à Georges Pompidou', *France-Forum* 98–9 (Oct.–Nov. 1969).

—— 'Industrie française et industrie allemande: Performances et stratégies', *Politique internationale* 6 (Winter 1979/80).

'Le Chancelier fédéral à Paris', *Documents* (Jan.–Feb. 1971).

Clément, J. C., 'L'Univers de Georges Pompidou', *Réalités* (June 1970).

Collard, Daniel, 'Convergences et Divergences Politiques', *Documents* (Mar.–Apr. 1974).

Corbineau, Bernard, 'Le dialogue euro-arabe, instance du nouvel ordre international (1973–1978)', *Revue française de Science Politique* (June 1980).

Cornides, Wilhelm, 'Die Bundesrepublik vor der Ratifizierung des deutsch-französischen Vertrages', *Europa-Archiv* 18 (1963).

Criddle, Byron, 'The French presidential election', *The World Today* (June 1974).

—— and Bell, David S., 'The 1981 French elections: the victory of the left', *The World Today* (July–Aug. 1981).

Delcourt, Roland, 'Ein Fall von Schizophrenie. Deutsche Ostpolitik aus Pariser Sicht', *Der Monat* (Aug. 1970).

Denton, Geoffrey, 'European monetary co-operation: the Bremen proposals', *The World Today* (Nov. 1978).

Deubner, Christian, 'The expansion of West German capital and the founding of Euratom', *International Organization* (Spring 1979).

—— 'The southern enlargement of the European Community: opportunities and dilemmas from a West German point of view', *Journal of Common Market Studies* (Mar. 1980).

Documents, 'Information et communication. Les Media et les relations franco-allemandes', Special Number (Dec. 1979).

Dokumente, 'Die deutsch-französischen Beziehungen seit 1963', Special Number (Dec. 1978).

Edwards, Geoffrey, 'Europe and the Falklands Crisis 1982', *Journal of Common Market Studies* (June 1984).

Edwards, Geoffrey, and Wallace, Helen, 'EEC: the British Presidency in retrospect', *The World Today* (Aug. 1977).

—— —— 'Germany in the chair', *The World Today* (Jan. 1979).

Emminger, Otmar, 'Europe and America: economic and monetary relations', *The World Today* (Feb. 1983).

Esambert, Bernand, 'La Politique industrielle de Georges Pompidou', *Revue des Deux Mondes* (Jan. 1984).

Étienne, Henri, 'Community integration: The external environment', *Journal of Common Market Studies* 4 (1979-80).

Everling, Ulrich, 'Die Europäische Gemeinschaft auf dem Wege zur Europäischen Union—Zu den Ergebnissen der Parisen Gipfelkonferenz', *Europa-Archiv* 23 (1972).

—— 'Die europapolitischen Strategien der Bundesregierung in den Siebziger Jahren—Historischer Rückblick und Bestandsaufnahme', unpublished paper, 26 Sept. 1978.

'J.F.', 'Bonn face à la crise monétaire', *Documents* (Sept.–Oct. 1971).

Firsch, Alfred, '1978: L'Année franco-allemande', *Documents* 4 (1978).

—— 'La France, l'Allemagne fédérale et la défense européenne' *Documents* 4 (1979).

Focke, Katherina, 'Europa-Politik nach Den Haag', *Europa-Archiv* 8 (1970).

Fontaine, Pascal, 'V. Giscard d'Estaing et la construction de l'Europe', *Projet* (Jan. 1980).

Frank, Paul, 'La Co-opération franco-allemande: une nécessité politique', *Politique Étrangère* 4 (Dec. 1981).

Frears, J. F., 'France after the elections', *The World Today* (June 1978).

—— 'The French Parliament and the European Community' *Journal of Common Market Studies* 2 (1975-6).

Friedrich, Paul, 'The SPD and the Politics of Europe: From Willy Brandt to Helmut Schmidt', *Journal of Common Market Studies* 4 (1974-5).

Frisch, Alfred, 'Face à la crise monétaire', *Documents* (Nov.–Dec. 1971).

—— 'Les relations franco-allemandes, une amitié solide et fragile à la fois', *Documents* (Sept. 1976).

—— 'Une symphonie inachevée, *Documents* (Mar.–Apr. 1974).

Goldsborough, James O., 'France, the European crisis and the Alliance', *Foreign Affairs* (Apr. 1974).

—— 'The Franco-German Entente', *Foreign Affairs* (Apr. 1976).

Gorce, Paul-Marie de la, 'Bilan d'un septennat: la politique extérieure de la France', *Politique Étrangère* 1 (Mar. 1981).

Grjebine, André, 'The Recapture of the Home Market', *Journal of Common Market Studies*, Special Issue (Sept.–Dec. 1982).

Grosser, Alfred, 'Après le referendum. Quelle politique extérieure' *Études* (June 1972).

—— 'Europe: Community of Malaise', *Foreign Policy* 15 (Summer 1975).

—— 'Le gouvernement Brandt à mi-parcours', *La Revue d'Allemagne* (Jan.–Mar. 1972).

Grosser, Alfred, 'La France et la RFA à l'heure du Chancelier Kohl', *Politique Internationale* 18 (Winter 1982–3).

—— 'La Politique extérieure française. Continuités et discontinuités, *L'Univers politique* (1969).

—— *Wann wird die Bundesrepublik ein normaler Staat?*, Bergsdorfer Gesprächskreis pamphlet.

Hahn, Walter H., 'West Germany's Ostpolitik. The Grand Design of Egon Bahr', *Orbis* (Winter 1973).

Hanrieder, Wolfgang F., 'Germany as Number Two?', *International Studies Quarterly* (Mar. 1982).

Hansen, Niels, 'Politische Zusammenarbeit in Westeuropa', *Europa-Archiv* 13 (1971).

Herterich, K. W., 'Les Investissements allemands en France', *Documents* (Mar.–Apr. 1972).

Hill, Christopher, and Wallace, William, 'Diplomatic trends in the European Community', *International Affairs* (Jan. 1979).

Hirsch, Mario, 'Influence without power: small states in European politics', *The World Today* (Mar. 1976).

Hoffmann, Stanley, 'NATO and Nuclear Weapons: Reason and Unreason', *Foreign Affairs* (Winter 1981–2).

Hollick, Julian Crandall, 'Direct elections to the European Parliament: the French debate', *The World Today* (Dec. 1977).

—— 'France under Giscard d'Estaing—a retrospect', *The World Today* (June 1981).

—— 'French intervention in Africa in 1978', *The World Today* (Feb. 1979).

Hu, Yao-Su, 'German agricultural power: the impact on France and Britain', *The World Today* (Nov. 1979).

Hurd, Douglas, 'Political Co-operation', *International Affairs* (Summer 1981).

Irving, R. E. M., 'The European Policy of the French and Italian Communists', *International Affairs* (July 1977).

—— and Paterson, W. E., 'The West German Parliamentary Elections of November 1972', *Parliamentary Affairs* (1973–4).

Jobert, Michel, 'De l'Allemagne', *Politique Étrangère* n.s. 1 (1979).

Johnson, Paul M., 'Washington and Bonn: dimensions of change in bilateral relations', *International Organization* (Autumn 1979).

Journal of Common Market Studies, 'The Policy Implications of Direct Elections', Special Number (June 1979).

Kahler, Miles, 'America's Foreign Economic Policy: Is the Old-Time Religion Good Enough', *International Affairs* (Summer 1980).

Kaiser, Karl, 'Europe and America; a critical phase', *Foreign Affairs* (July 1974).

Kaiser, Karl, 'The Great Nuclear Debate: German American Disagreements', *Foreign Policy* 30 (Spring 1978).

Katzenstein, Peter J. (ed.), 'Between Power and Plenty—Foreign Economic Policies of advanced industrial States', *International Organization*, Special Number (Autumn 1977).

—— 'International relations and domestic structures: Foreign Economic Policies of Advanced Industrial States', *International Organization* (Winter 1976).

Kaufmann, Herbert, 'Réflexions sur une diplomatie française', *Documents* (Mar.–Apr. 1974).

Klasen, Karl, 'Die Verwirklichung der Wirtschafts- und Währungs union in der EWG aus der Sicht der Deutschen Bundesbank', *Europa-Archiv* 13 (1970).

Koch, Susan J., 'The Local Impact of the European Economic Community: The Economic and Social Ties of Alsace with West Germany', *International Organization* (Spring 1974).

Koenig, Pierre, 'La Réforme de la chancellerie fédérale et du travail gouvernemental en Allemagne de l'ouest', *La Revue d'Allemagne* (Oct.–Dec. 1971).

Kolodziej, Edward J., 'France and the Arms Trade', *International Affairs* (Jan. 1980).

Kress, Kurt, 'La Politique agricole européenne. Avantage ou inconvénient pour l'Allemagne?', *Documents* (Jan.–Mar. 1975).

Lacharrière, René de, 'Gaullism Mark II: the elections of 1973', *Government and Opposition* (1973).

Laloy, Jean, 'Les Relations franco-allemandes: mythes et réalités', *Documents* 4 (1977).

Lancelot, A., 'Il ne faut pas jurer de rien. Le referendum du 23 Avril 1972', *Projet* 67 (July–Aug. 1972).

Le Gloannec, Anne-Marie, 'La Montée en puissance de la République fédérale d'Allemagne', *Revue française de Science Politique* (Apr. 1980).

Leigh, Michael, 'Germany's changing role in the EEC', *The World Today* (Dec. 1975).

—— 'Giscard and the European Community', *The World Today* (Feb. 1977).

—— 'Linkage Politics—the French Referendum and the Paris Summit of 1972', *Journal of Common Market Studies* 2 (1975–6).

Leigh, Michael, 'Mediterranean agriculture and the enlargement of the EEC', *The World Today* (June 1977).

Leroy, Jacques-Guillaume, 'Le petit homme, la France, et l'Europe', *Contrepoint* 15 (1974).

Levi, Mario, 'Réflexions sur l'avenir de la co-opération européenne', *Politique Étrangère* 5 (1959).

Lewis, Flora, 'Alarm Bells in the West', *Foreign Affairs* 3 (1981–2).

Lieber, Robert, J., 'Europe and America in the world energy crisis', *International Affairs* (Oct. 1979).

Linden, Marcel, 'Face au défi japonais, pas de protectionnisme', *Documents* 4 (1980).

Loch, Theo, 'Ausgangspositionen für die europäische Gipfelkonferenz in Den Haag', *Europa-Archiv* 20 (1969).

Lodge, Juliet 'The Organization and Control of European Integration in the Federal Republic of Germany', *Parliamentary Affairs* 4 (1974–5).

—— 'The Rôle of the EEC Summit Conference', *Journal of Common Market Studies* 3 (1973–4).

Losser, Alphonse, 'Bilan économique de la R.F.A. 1948–68, *La Revue d'Allemagne* (Jan.–Mar. 1969).

—— 'La Politique monétaire de la R.F.A.', *Documents* (Sept.–Oct. 1973).

McGeehan, Robert, 'The Atlantic Alliance and the Reagan Administration', *The World Today* (July–Aug. 1981).

Mackintosh, John, 'Britain in Europe. Historical perspective and contemporary reality', *International Affairs* (Apr. 1969).

Marquand, David, 'Parliamentary accountability and the European Community', *Journal of Common Market Studies* (Mar. 1981).

Mellah, F., 'L'Attitude de l'Europe face à la crise pétrolière', *Chronique de Politique Étrangère* (May 1974).

Mendl, Wolf, 'After de Gaulle: Continuity and change in French foreign policy', *The World Today* (Jan. 1971).

Ménil, Georges de, 'De Rambouillet à Versailles: Un bilan des sommets économiques', *Politique Étrangère* 2 (June 1982).

Ménudier, Henri, 'L'Allemagne à la télévision française—ou le bastion du passéisme', *Études* (Apr. 1975).

—— 'De quelle Allemagne parlez-vous?', *Documents* (Dec. 1977).

—— 'Divergences franco-allemandes et construction européenne', *Études* (May 1974).

—— 'L'Europe et les élections françaises', *Études* (May 1973).

—— 'L'Image de l'Allemagne à la télévision française', *Études* (Oct. 1972).

—— 'L'information en France sur la RFA', *Documents* (Jan.–Feb. 1974).

Ménudier, Henri, 'Die Information—Quelle für Konflikte oder für Kooperation?', *Dokumente* Special Number (Dec. 1978).

—— 'La "Ostpolitik" du Chancelier Willy Brandt', *L'Univers politique* (1970).

Menyesch, Dieter, and Uterwedde, Henrik, 'Der deutsch-französische Vertrag und seine Verwirklichung', *Dokumente* Special Number (Dec. 1978).

Merle, M., 'Politique extérieure entre l'immobilisme et l'ouverture', *Projet* 48 (Sept.–Oct. 1970).

Moïsi, Dominique, 'Mitterrand's Foreign Policy: The Limits of Continuity', *Foreign Affairs* (Winter 1981–2).

Morgan, Roger, 'Can Europe have a foreign policy?', *The World Today* (Feb. 1974).

—— 'A new phase in European summitry', *The World Today* (Jan. 1975).

—— 'New tasks for the European Parliament', *The World Today* (Oct. 1979).

—— 'Political Prospects in Bonn', *The World Today* (Aug. 1972).

—— 'Washington and Bonn. A Case study in Alliance Politics', *International Affairs* (July 1971).

—— and Bray, Caroline, 'Berlin in the post-détente era', *The World Today* (Mar. 1982).

Moxon Browne, E., 'The EEC after Tindemans: the institutional balance', *The World Today* (Dec. 1976).

Nagel, Günter, 'Mark flottant et unification monétaire', *Documents* (May–June 1971).

Nass, Klaus Otto, 'Incertitudes Allemandes', *Dokumente* 5–6 (1970).

Nerlich, Uwe, 'West European defence identity: the French paradox', *The World Today* (May 1974).

Noack, Paul, 'Information franco-allemande au niveau gouvernemental', *Documents* Special Number (Dec. 1979).

Odell, John S., 'The US and the emergence of floating exchange rates: an analysis of foreign policy change', *International Organization* (Winter 1979).

Parfitt, Trevor, 'Bad blood in Brussels' *The World Today* (June 1977).

—— 'The Budget and the CAP: A Community crisis averted', *The World Today* (Aug. 1980).

—— 'CAP—beginning to take stock', *The World Today* (Nov. 1974).

—— 'The Cap: reconciling the irreconcilable', *The World Today* (Apr. 1980).

—— 'Keeping the CAP on', *The World Today* (Mar. 1975).

Paterson, William E., 'The SPD after Brandt's fall—Change or Continuity?' *Government and Opposition* 10 (1975).

Paterson, William E., 'The West German Elections', *The World Today* (Dec. 1972).

Pearce, Joan, 'The CAP: a guide to the Commission's new proposals' *The World Today* (Sept. 1981).

Picaper, Jean-Paul, 'Les Constantes de la politique éxtérieure de la République Fédérale', *Politique Étrangère* 1 (1975).

Picht, Robert, 'La Réception de l'information par l'opinion publique', *Documents* (Jan.–Mar. 1974).

Picht, Robert, 'La RFA, un allié pas comme les autres', *Politique Étrangère* 2 (June 1981).

Pick, Otto, 'Theme and variations: the foreign policy of France', *The World Today* (Oct. 1980).

Pickles, Dorothy, 'The Decline of Gaullist Foreign Policy', *International Affairs* (Apr. 1975).

Pierre, Andrew J., 'What Happened to the Year of Europe?', *The World Today* (Mar. 1974).

Pinder, John, 'Renegotiation: Britain's costly lesson?', *International Affairs* (Apr. 1975).

Pridham, Geoffrey, 'A "Nationalisation" Process? Federal Politics and State Elections in West Germany', *Government and Opposition* 8 (1973).

Rabier, Jacques-René, 'Préjugés français et préjugés allemands', *Documents* (Jan.–Feb. 1969).

Rademacher, Hans, 'Une nouvelle industrie', *Documents* 1 (1976).

Revue D'Allemagne, 1a 'Cent Ans de Rapports franco-allemands' Special Number (July–Sept. 1972).

Rovan, Joseph, 'Le Changement allemand', *Politique Internationale* 18 (Winter 1982–3).

—— 'Les Relations franco-allemandes dans le domaine de la jeunesse et de la culture populaire de 1945 à 1971', *La Revue d'Allemagne* 3 (1972).

Rudnick, David, 'Spain's long road to Europe', *The World Today* (Apr. 1976).

Ruehl, Lothar, 'Von Charles de Gaulle zu Georges Pompidou — Kontinuität und Öffnung', *Europa-Archiv* 14 (1969).

Samuelson, Alain, 'L'Expérience du mark flottant, ses incidences jusqu'au réalignement des monnaies', *La Revue d'Allemagne* (Jan.–Mar. 1972).

Scheel, Walter, 'Aktuelle Probleme der Aussenpolitik der Bundesrepublik Deutschland', *Europa-Archiv* 13 (1973).

Scheinman, Lawrence, 'Some preliminary notes on bureaucratic relations in the EEC', *International Organization* (Autumn 1966).

Schiller, K., 'Die internationale Währungslage nach der Bonner Konferenz der Zehnergruppe', *Europa-Archiv* 1 (1969).

Schmid, Klaus-Peter, 'Idées et controverses', *Documents* (Jan.–Mar. 1975).

—— 'Le Monde und die Bundesrepublik Deutschland', *Aus Politik und Zeitgeschichte* 2 (Dec. 1979).

Schmiegelow, Henrik and Schmiegelow, Michèle, 'The new mercantilism in international relations. The case of France's external monetary policy', *International Organization* (Spring 1975).

Schumacher, Hanns H., 'Europe's Airbus programme and the impact of British participation', *The World Today* (Aug. 1979).

Schütze, Walter, 'Frankreichs Aussenpolitik im Wandel von de Gaulle zu Pompidou', *Europa-Archiv* 11 (1972).

—— 'La République fédérale d'Allemagne et le marché international des armements', *Documents* 1 (1976).

—— 'Frankreichs Aussen- und Sicherheitspolitik unter François Mitterrand', *Europa-Archiv* 20 (1982).

Schweigler, Gebhard, 'A new political giant? West German foreign policy in the 1970s', *The World Today* (Apr. 1975).

Seitz, Konrad, 'Deutsch-französische sicherheitspolitische Zusammenarbeit', *Europa-Archiv* 22 (1982).

Serfati, Simon, 'The Fifth Republic under Giscard d'Estaing: steadfast or changing?', *The World Today* (Mar. 1976).

Serre, Françoise de la, 'L'Europe des Neuf et le conflit israélo-arabe', *Revue française de Science Politique* (Aug. 1974).

—— 'La politique européenne de la France: New Look ou New Deal?', *Politique Étrangère* 1 (Mar. 1982).

Seydoux, François, 'Le Traité franco-allemand', *Politique Étrangère* 6 (1963).

Shlaim, Avi, 'The Paris summit', *The World Today* (Dec. 1972).

Simonet, Henri, 'Energy and the Future of Europe', *Foreign Affairs* (Apr. 1975).

Simonet, Philippe, 'Pompidous europäische Gleichgewicht', *Dokumente* 2 (1971).

Simonian, Haig, 'France, Germany and Europe', *Journal of Common Market Studies* (Mar. 1981).

Slama, Alain-Gérard, 'La République et ses rois', *Contrepoint* 14 (1974).

Smart, Ian, 'The new Atlantic Charter', *The World Today* (June 1973).

Smouts, Marie-Claude, 'French Foreign Policy: The Domestic Debate', *International Affairs* (Jan. 1977).

Staden, Berndt von, 'Politische Zusammenarbeit der EG Staaten', *Aussenpolitik* (Apr. 1972).

Statler, Jocelyn, 'The European Monetary System: From conception to birth', *International Affairs* (Apr. 1979).

Steinbrink, Christoph, 'Bilan critique des relations franco-allemandes dix ans après le traité entre la France et la RFA', *L'Allemagne d'aujourd'hui* (Sept.–Oct. 1973).

Stern, Fritz, 'Germany in a Semi-Gaullist Europe', *Foreign Affairs* (Spring 1980).

Story, Jonathan, 'The Franco-German Alliance within the Community', *The World Today* (June 1980).

Strange, Susan, 'The Dollar Crisis 1971', *International Affairs* (Apr. 1972).

Tavernier, Yves, 'Le Syndicalisme paysan et la Ve République', *Revue française de Science Politique* (Oct. 1966).

Taylor, Paul, 'Interdependence and autonomy in the European Communities: the case of the European Monetary System', *Journal of Common Market Studies* (June 1980).

Teyssier, Jean-Pierre, 'L'Année 1973 dans la politique étrangère du Président Pompidou', *Politique Étrangère* 4–5 (1974).

Tsoukalis, Loukas, 'Is the Relaunching of Economic and Monetary Union a Feasible Proposal?', *Journal of Common Market Studies* (June 1977).

—— and Silva Ferreira, Antonio da, 'Management of industrial surplus capacity in the European Community', *International Organization* (Summer 1980).

Turner, Louis, 'The Politics of the Energy Crisis', *International Affairs* (July 1974).

—— 'The Washington Energy Conference', *The World Today* (Mar. 1974).

Ullmann, Marc, 'Security Aspects in French Foreign Policy', *Survival* (Nov.–Dec. 1973).

Vaillant, Jérôme, 'La Crise gouvernementale en RFA', *L'Allemagne d'aujourd'hui* (May–June 1972).

—— 'La Grève des services publics en RFA', *L'Allemagne d'aujourd'hui* (Mar.–Apr. 1974).

Van Well, Günther, 'Die Entwicklung einer gemeinsamen Nahost-Politik der Neun', *Europa-Archiv* 4 (1976).

Vardamis, Alex A., 'German–American Military Fissures', *Foreign Policy* 34 (Spring 1979).

Volle, Angelika and Wallace, William, 'How common a fisheries policy?', *The World Today* (Feb. 1977).

Vries, T. de, 'Saving the dollar', *The World Today* (Jan. 1979).

Wagner, Wolfgang, 'Kanzlerwechsel in Bonn. Der Rücktritt Willy Brandts und das neue Kabinett Schmidt–Genscher', *Europa-Archiv* 11 (1974).

Waites, Neville, 'Britain and France: towards a stable relationship', *The World Today* (Dec. 1976).
—— 'France under Mitterrand: external relations', *The World Today* (June 1982).
Walton, Ann-Margaret, 'Atlantic bargaining over energy', *International Affairs* (Apr. 1976).
Weisenfeld, Ernst, 'Geprägt von Monnet und de Gaulle. Frankreichs Aussenpolitik im Wandel', unpublished paper (July 1979).
Well, Samuel F. Jr., 'The Mitterrand Challenge', *Foreign Policy* 44 (Fall 1981).
West European Politics, 'Trade Unions and Politics in Western Europe', Special Number (Jan. 1980).
Whetten, Lawrence L., 'Scope, Nature and Change in Inner German Relations', *International Affairs* (Jan. 1981).
Wiss-Verdier, A., 'La Crise d'avril-mai 1972', *Documents* (May-June 1972).
—— 'La Conjoncture politique', *Documents* (Mar.-Apr. 1974).
—— 'La Fin de l'ère Brandt', *Documents* (May-June 1974).
—— 'La Guerre israélo-arabe et les suites', *Documents* (Nov.-Dec. 1973).
—— 'La Perturbation entre Bonn et Paris', *Documents* (Sept.-Oct. 1973).
—— 'La Rencontre Brandt-Pompidou, ou l'Europe des incertitudes', *Documents* (July-Aug. 1973).
Woolcock, Stephen, 'East-West trade: US policy and European interests', *The World Today* (Feb 1982).
—— 'US-European Trade Relations', *International Affairs* (Autumn 1982).
Yannopoulos, G. N., 'Mediterranean labour in an era of slow Community growth', *The World Today* (Dec. 1979).
Yondorf, Walter, 'Monnet and the Action Committee: the formative period of the European Communities', *International Organization* (Autumn 1965).
Young, Simon Z., 'Britain and the Community: the meaning of renegotiation', *The World Today* (Sept. 1974).
'Z.', 'The Year of Europe', *Foreign Affairs* (Jan. 1974).
Ziebura, Gilbert, 'Frankreichs oder Deutschlands Ostpolitik — Konvergenz oder Divergenz?', *Dokumente* 1 (1971).
——'Neue deutsche Ostpolitik in Pariser Sicht', *Dokumente* 5-6 (1969).
Zorgbibe, Charles, 'La France: les initiatives d'une "puissance moyenne"', *Revue française de Science Politique* (Aug. 1976).

OTHER PUBLISHED SOURCES

L'Aurore	*Neue Zürcher Zeitung*
Combat	*Newsweek*
Daily Telegraph	*New York Times*
The Economist	*Le Nouvel Observateur*
L'Express	*Observer*
Le Figaro	*Le Point*
Financial Times	*Der Spiegel*
Frankfurter Allgemeine Zeitung	*Sunday Telegraph*
Guardian	*Sunday Times*
L'Humanité	*Süddeutsche Zeitung*
International Herald Tribune	*The Times*
Keesing's Contemporary Archives	*Die Zeit*
Le Monde	

INTERVIEWS (DATES IN PARENTHESES)

Biographical details of those interviewed generally relate to the date of the interview, not to the present. Those marked with an obelus (†) have since died.

Bariéty, Jacques, Director of the Institute of Contemporary History, University of Strasbourg (5 December 1979).

Boegner, Dr Jean-Marc, French Permanent Representative to the European Communities 1961–72; French Representative to OECD 1975–8 (25 October 1979).

Braun, Sigismund von, German Ambassador to Paris 1968–70; State Secretary in the Auswärtigues Amt 1970–2; German Ambassador to Paris 1972–6 (15 June 1979).

Bredow, Prof. Dr Wilfried von, Professor of Political Science, University of Marburg (5 March 1978).

Corterier, Dr Peter, SPD Member of the Bundestag since 1969. Member of the Bundestag Foreign Affairs Committee. Member of the European Parliament since 1973 (28 June 1979).

Dettke, Dr Dieter, Party official, SPD Parliamentary Party, Bonn (1 June 1979).

Dreyfus, Prof, François-Georges, Professor at the University of Strasbourg. Director of the Institut d'Études Politiques, Strasbourg (29 November 1979).

Everling, Prof. Dr Ulrich, Ministerialdirektor in the German Ministry of Economics. 1970–80, Head of the Europaabteilung. Since 1980 German judge at the European Court of Justice, Luxembourg (30 May 1979).

400   *Bibliography*

Feit, Dr Christian, Desk Officer with responsibility for the European Community, Auswärtiges Amt. Formerly official at the German Embassy, Paris (28 June 1979).

Focke, Dr Katharina, SPD Member of the Bundestag 1969–80. 1969–72, Parliamentary State Secretary in the Kanzleramt. 1972–6, Minister of Youth, Family and Health. Member of the European Parliament (27 June 1979).

Fontaine, André, Editor in Chief, *Le Monde* (30 November 1979).

Frank, Dr Paul, 1970–4, State Secretary in the Auswärtiges Amt. 1974–9, State Secretary to the Presidency (27 June 1979).

Gablenz, Otto von der, Official in the Kanzleramt. Formerly Desk Officer in the Auswärtiges Amt. Now Ambassador to the Netherlands (8 June 1979).

Grosser, Prof. Alfred, Professor and Director of Research at the Institut d'Études Politiques, Paris (21 November 1979).

Hager, Wolfgang, Researcher, Deutsche Gesellschaft für Auswärtige Politik, Bonn (5 July 1979).

Hansen, Dr Niels, Formerly Desk Officer with responsibility for the European Communities, France, and the Benelux countries in the Auswärtiges Amt. Head of the Planning Division, Auswärtiges Amt. Since 1981 Ambassador to Israel. (20 June 1979).

Harkort, Dr Gunther, German Permanent Representative to the European Communities 1961–5. Ministerialdirektor in the Auswärtiges Amt 1965–9. State Secretary in the Auswärtiges Amt 1969–70 (8 June 1979).

Hoffman, Prof. Stanley, Professor of Government, Harvard University (14 December 1979).

Jacobsen, Prof. Dr Hans-Adolf, Professor of Political Science, University of Bonn (22 May 1979).

Jaspert, Gunther, Official Foreign Affairs Committee, Deutscher Bundesrat, Bonn (3 July 1979).

Jobert, Michel, Directeur adjoint (1963–6) and Directeur (1966–8) de Cabinet of Georges Pompidou. Secretary-General at the Élysée, 1969–73. Foreign Minister April 1973 to May 1974. Minister for Foreign Trade, May 1981–March 1983. (9 November 1979).

Kaiser, Prof. Dr Karl, Professor of Political Science, University of Cologne. Director of the Research Institute, Deutsche Gesellschaft für Auswärtige Politik, Bonn (5 July 1979).

Krause, Albrecht, Assistant Secretary-General (1963–8) and Secretary-General (1968–74) of the Franco-German Youth Office (7 June 1979).

Kyau, Dr von, Desk Officer in the Auswärtiges Amt with responsibility for the European Communities (4 July 1979).

Laloy, Jean, Professor at the Institut d'Études Politiques, Paris

Professor at the École Nationale d'Administration 1952–72. Since 1978 President of the Commission Interministérielle pour les questions de coopération entre la France et la RFA (18 December 1979).

Ménudier, Henri, Lecturer at the Institut d'Études Politiques, Paris. Researcher at the Fondation Nationale des Sciences Politiques (18 December 1979).

Moersch, Karl, FDP Member of the Bundestag 1964–76. Parliamentary State Secretary (1970–4), then Minister of State (1974–6) for the Auswärtiges Amt (26 June 1979; 10 July 1979).

Morawitz, Rudolf, Official in the Ministry of Economics, Bonn (28 May 1979).

Paterson, Dr William, Reader, Department of Politics, University of Warwick (13 December 1978).

Picht, Dr Robert, Head of the Deutsch-Französisches Institut, Ludwigsburg (22 June 1979; 9 July 1979).

Rovan, Prof. Joseph, Professor of German Civilization at the University of Paris-Vincennes (10 December 1979).

†Schmid, Prof. Dr Carlo, SPD Member of the Bundestag 1949–72. Member of the European Parliament. Co-ordinator for Franco-German Co-operation 1969–80 (26 June 1979).

Schmid, Klaus-Peter, Paris Correspondent, *Die Zeit* (31 October 1979).

Schmidt, Dr Martin, SPD Member of the Bundestag. Chairman of the Bundestag Food and Agriculture Committee (26 June 1979).

Schütze, Walter, Researcher, Institut Français des Relations Internationales, Paris (29 October 1979).

Schwarz, Prof. Dr Hans-Peter, Professor of Political Science, University of Cologne (11 July 1979).

Schweizer, Prof. Dr C. C., Professor of Political Science, University of Bonn. SPD Member of the Bundestag 1972–4 (23 May 1979).

†Seydoux, François, French Ambassador to Bonn 1958–62 and 1965–70 (19 November 1979).

Speks, Dr Franz-Josef, Official at the Ministry of Food and Agriculture, Bonn (2 July 1979).

Ullmann, Marc, Journalist, *L'Express* (11 December 1979).

Volle, Angelika, Researcher, Deutsche Gesellschaft für Auswärtige Politik, Bonn (2 May 1979).

Weisenfeld, Ernst, Paris Correspondent, Zweites Deutsches Fernsehen (3 December 1979; 8 December 1979).

Wormser, Olivier, French Ambassador to Moscow 1966–8. Governor of the Bank of France 1969–74. Ambassador to Bonn 1974–7 (26 October 1979).

Ziebura, Prof. Dr Gilbert, Professor of Political Science, Technical University of Braunschweig (13 June 1979).

Index

Index